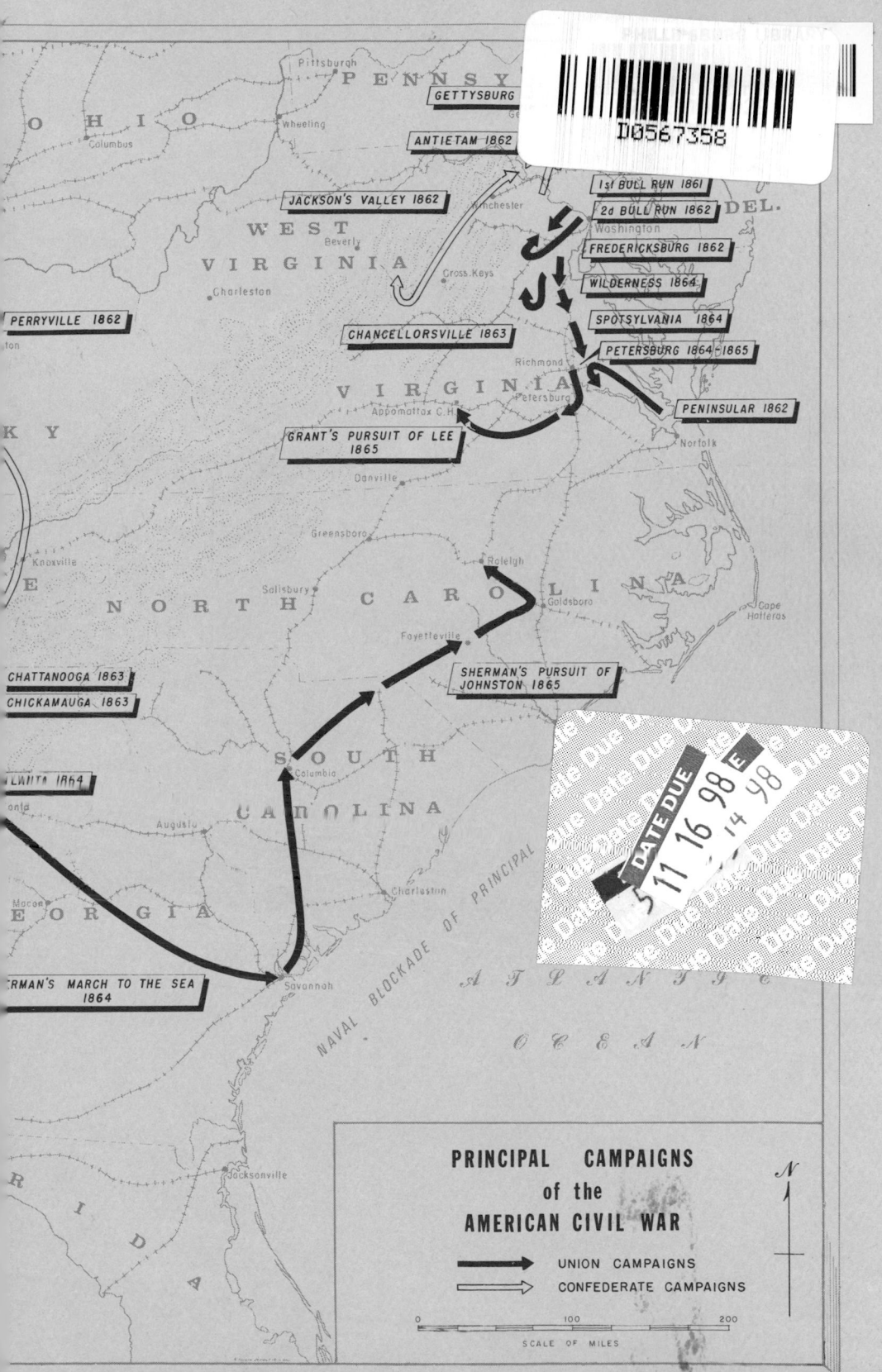

PRINCIPAL CAMPAIGNS
of the
AMERICAN CIVIL WAR

➡ UNION CAMPAIGNS
⇨ CONFEDERATE CAMPAIGNS

0   100   200
SCALE OF MILES

N

GETTYSBURG

ANTIETAM 1862

1st BULL RUN 1861

2d BULL RUN 1862

FREDERICKSBURG 1862

WILDERNESS 1864

SPOTSYLVANIA 1864

PETERSBURG 1864-1865

PENINSULAR 1862

JACKSON'S VALLEY 1862

CHANCELLORSVILLE 1863

PERRYVILLE 1862

GRANT'S PURSUIT OF LEE 1865

SHERMAN'S PURSUIT OF JOHNSTON 1865

CHATTANOOGA 1863

CHICKAMAUGA 1863

ATLANTA 1864

SHERMAN'S MARCH TO THE SEA 1864

NAVAL BLOCKADE OF PRINCIPAL

ATLANTIC OCEAN

JOHN BROWN'S BODY

Stephen Vincent Benét

JOHN BROWN'S BODY

with an introduction and notes by
Jack L. Capps and C. Robert Kemble
Department of English
United States Military Academy

HOLT, RINEHART and WINSTON, INC.
New York   Chicago   San Francisco   Atlanta
Dallas   Montreal   Toronto

811

TO MY MOTHER
AND TO THE MEMORY
OF MY FATHER

❧ CONTENTS ❧

⚜ LIST OF MAPS ⚜

❧ PREFACE ❧

Stephen Vincent Benét begins his prefatory note to *John Brown's Body* by declaring that his work is "a poem, not a history." Yet his remaining remarks, like the poem itself, confirm the factual foundation of his work. Without violating the historian's discipline Benét performs the poet's functions freely; his unerring faculty for providing the sensitive relation of historical event to human experience releases *John Brown's Body* from the strictures of historical narrative and gives it the insight required of enduring literature.

Benét comes without political thesis, regional or racial, to confront us with a clear-eyed view of our heritage, displayed in the lives and beings of the principals of his poem. Our annotation, therefore, is intended only to enhance the reader's visualization of the broad milieu that Benét's poetry brings to incisive focus. We have avoided interpretive notes that might encumber the poem, but have identified the author's major sources and marked recurring motifs that contribute significantly to the poetic structure.

In *John Brown's Body*, Benét offers the "cup of silver air" that is vitalized history; and we, in this edition, have attempted to accentuate his perceptive articulation of the past.

JACK L. CAPPS

C. ROBERT KEMBLE

West Point, New York
August 1968

✤ NOTE ✤

As this is a poem, not a history, it has seemed unnecessary to me to encumber it with notes, bibliography, and other historical apparatus. Nevertheless—besides such original sources as the Official Records, the series of articles in *Battles and Leaders of the Civil War*, and the letters, memoirs, and autobiographies of the various leaders involved—I should like to acknowledge my indebtedness to Channing's *The War for Southern Independence** and McMaster's *The United States Under Lincoln's Administration*, to Oswald Garrison Villard's *John Brown: A Biography Fifty Years After*, to the various Lives of Lincoln by Lord Charnwood, Carl Sandburg, and Ida Tarbell and the monumental work of Nicolay and Hay, to Nathaniel Wright Stephenson's *Abraham Lincoln: An Autobiography*, and, finally, my very particular debt to that remarkable first-hand account of life in the Army of the Potomac, *Four Brothers in Blue*, by Captain Robert Goldthwaite Carter, from which the stories of Fletcher the sharpshooter and the two brothers at Fredericksburg are taken.

In dealing with known events I have tried to cleave to historical fact where such fact was ascertainable. On the other hand, for certain thoughts and feelings attributed to historical characters, and for the interpretation of those characters in the poem, I alone must be held responsible.

The account of the defeated Union army pouring into Washington after the first Bull Run is founded on a passage in Whitman's *Specimen Days and Collect*.

The Black Horse Troop is an entirely imaginary organization and not to be confused with the so-called Black Horse Cavalry. In general, no fictional character in the poem is founded upon a real person, living or dead.

On page 57, in the inscription written by John Brown for his own monument, the dates of the deaths of his two sons are incorrectly given. They are so given in the original manuscript, now in the possession of the Genealogical Society of Pennsylvania, and I have not felt at liberty to alter the original wording.

STEPHEN VINCENT BENÉT

Neuilly-sur-Seine, April, 1928

---

* Volume VI of Edward Channing's *A History of the United States*. [Editors' note].

❧ FOREWORD ❧

John Brown's Body is a long poem dealing with some of the things that happened in our Civil War and how they affected various kinds of Americans, North and South, East and West. A good many of the people described in it are real people who played their part in history —Lincoln, Lee, Judah P. Benjamin, John Brown. A good many others —Jack Ellyat, Clay Wingate, Melora Vilas—are imaginary people, fictional characters. All I can claim is that nothing happens to any one of the fictional characters that did not happen or could not have happened to real people who lived in that time. It was a remarkable time—one of the great and crucial periods of our history—and it summoned forth great men and small, strong figures and weak ones. It decided how we were going to live as a nation—whether we were going to live as two nations or as one—and all the America we know today is built upon that decision. If we had decided to live as two nations instead of as one, our own daily lives would be very different. Moreover, the Civil War produced, on both sides, men and deeds of the heroic kind. And such things are worth writing about so that they can be remembered.

Nevertheless, I do not think of the poem as being primarily a poem about war itself. What I was trying to do was to show certain realities, legends, ideas, landscapes, ways of living, faces of men that were ours, that did not belong to any other country. Our history is not just a list of names and dates, declarations and proclamations. It is made up of the lives of millions upon millions of ordinary men and women who lived through war and peace, strove, struggled, succeeded, failed, built something together. It is made of the look of mountains and the flow of rivers, heat and cold, wind and rain, the stones in the old burying-grounds and the casual ballads of the people. It is not tucked away in the past, to be learned by rote and forgotten. Those who came before us in this country were living people, they faced problems very like our own, they made decisions that affect us still. Because I felt this, and feel it, I tried to write a poem that could deal with all sorts of Americans, from Jack Ellyat, the Connecticut Yankee, to Luke Breckinridge, the Southern mountaineer.

The scheme of the poem is a fairly simple one. It begins shortly before John Brown's raid upon Harper's Ferry—it ends just after the close of the war and Lincoln's assassination. There are two main fictional characters, Jack Ellyat, the Northerner, and Clay Wingate, the Southerner, and the poem follows their various adventures, shifting from side to side. The Border States and the growing West are represented by Melora Vilas and her father, John Vilas. Other fictional characters, a runaway slave, a Pennsylvania farmer, a Southern belle, appear and disappear during the course of the narrative, and we hear something of their various stories and different points of view. To Clay Wingate the war means one thing, to Luke Breckinridge another, to Bailey, the sergeant in Sherman's army, a third. Not all were particularly heroic, not every thread is wound up. But there were people like each of them, though not with those names.

The poem is written in a variety of meters and that is deliberate. When I planned it first, I had rather an elaborate scheme for it— historical characters were always to be dressed in blank verse, and so forth. Such a scheme proved too complicated to follow rigidly. But, as it stands, three meters do most of the work: blank verse itself, as in the soliloquies of Benjamin and Lincoln; the light, swift meter, suggesting dancing and riding, which is used for most of the Wingate episodes; and the longer and rougher line, "They reached the Maryland Bridge of Harper's Ferry," which is particularly evident in Book Three. You can think of them, if you want, as musical themes, particularly the Wingate meter which, to me, suggests something of the courtesy and dash of the prewar South. The long rough line is used for a purpose. I wanted a meter in which I could talk about a lot of different American things, such as johnnycake and Harper's Ferry, and still have it sound as if I were talking, not orating. Also, it gives a change from the rhythm of blank verse.

In closing this brief foreword, I should like to say one thing more. Poetry is meant to be read, it is meant to be heard. It is meant for everybody, not only for the scholars. It is not a highly complicated puzzle box which you can open only with a special set of keys. It tells its story in a different way from prose—it uses rhyme and meter and the words go to a beat. You cannot read it precisely as you read prose, any more than you can sing the words of a song without knowing the tune. With poetry, the tune is in the words themselves—and once you begin to hear it, it will stay with you. Nor is it so difficult to hear. Most of the basic rhythms of poetry are very old ones—rhythms hammered out by men who wanted to tell a story or convey an idea more intensely, more swiftly and memorably than they could in prose. Sometimes they succeeded in this, sometimes they did not. You will be able to judge for yourself whether an individual poem succeeds in making you see more clearly or feel more deeply—whether it enters your stock of memories and remains there. But poetry itself is not restricted to any special class, to any special section of life. It is open to any reader who likes the sound and the swing of rhythm, the color and fire of words.

STEPHEN VINCENT BENÉT

New York
November, 1941

JOHN BROWN'S BODY

❧ INVOCATION ❧

American muse, whose strong and diverse heart
So many men have tried to understand
But only made it smaller with their art,
Because you are as various as your land,

As mountainous-deep, as flowered with blue rivers,   5
Thirsty with deserts, buried under snows,
As native as the shape of Navajo quivers,
And native, too, as the sea-voyaged rose.°

Swift runner, never captured or subdued,
Seven-branched elk beside the mountain stream,   10
That half a hundred hunters have pursued
But never matched their bullets with the dream,

Where the great huntsmen failed, I set my sorry
And mortal snare for your immortal quarry.°

You are the buffalo-ghost, the broncho-ghost   15
With dollar-silver in your saddle-horn,
The cowboys riding in from Painted Post,
The Indian arrow in the Indian corn,

And you are the clipped velvet of the lawns
Where Shropshire grows from Massachusetts sods,   20
The grey Maine rocks—and the war-painted dawns
That break above the Garden of the Gods.

The prairie-schooners crawling toward the ore
And the cheap car, parked by the station-door.

Where the skyscrapers lift their foggy plumes   25
Of stranded smoke out of a stony mouth
You are that high stone and its arrogant fumes,
And you are ruined gardens in the South

8 *sea-voyaged* rose: the figure formed by a compass face or card.   1–14 The Invocation opens and closes with the English sonnet form.

And bleak New England farms, so winter-white
Even their roofs look lonely, and the deep 30
The middle grainland where the wind of night
Is like all blind earth sighing in her sleep.

A friend, an enemy, a sacred hag
With two tied oceans in her medicine-bag.

They tried to fit you with an English song 35
And clip your speech into the English tale.
But, even from the first, the words went wrong,°
The catbird ° pecked away the nightingale.°

The homesick men begot high-cheekboned things
Whose wit was whittled with a different sound 40
And Thames and all the rivers of the kings
Ran into Mississippi and were drowned.

They planted England with a stubborn trust.
But the cleft° dust was never English dust.

Stepchild of every exile from content 45
And all the disavouched, hard-bitten pack
Shipped overseas to steal a continent
With neither shirts nor honor to their back.

Pimping grandee and rump-faced regicide,
Apple-cheeked younkers from a windmill-square, 50
Puritans stubborn as the nails of Pride,
Rakes from Versailles and thieves from County Clare,

The black-robed priests who broke their hearts in vain
To make you God and France or God and Spain.

35–37 *fit you with an English song . . . the words went wrong*: literally, "America"
to the tune of "God Save the King." 38 *catbird*: American mimic. *nightingale*:
European, here English, songbird. 44 *cleft*: as an incision made for the cleft-grafting
of plants.

These were your lovers in your buckskin-youth.   55
And each one married with a dream so proud
He never knew it could not be the truth
And that he coupled with a girl of cloud.°

And now to see you is more difficult yet
Except as an immensity of wheel   60
Made up of wheels, oiled with inhuman sweat
And glittering with the heat of ladled steel.

All these you are, and each is partly you,
And none is false, and none is wholly true.

So how to see you as you really are,   65
So how to suck the pure, distillate, stored
Essence of essence from the hidden star
And make it pierce like a riposting sword.

For, as we hunt you down, you must escape
And we pursue a shadow of our own   70
That can be caught in a magician's cape
But has the flatness of a painted stone.

Never the running stag, the gull at wing,
The pure elixir, the American thing.

And yet, at moments when the mind was hot   75
With something fierier than joy or grief,
When each known spot was an eternal spot
And every leaf was an immortal leaf,

I think that I have seen you, not as one,
But clad in diverse semblances and powers,   80
Always the same, as light falls from the sun,
And always different, as the differing hours.

Yet, through each altered garment that you wore
The naked body, shaking the heart's core.

58 *coupled with a girl of cloud:* Compare Ixion's union with the cloud image of **Hera**.

All day the snow fell on that Eastern town   85
With its soft, pelting, little, endless sigh
Of infinite flakes that brought the tall sky down
Till I could put my hands in the white sky

And taste cold scraps of heaven on my tongue
And walk in such a changed and luminous light   90
As gods inhabit when the gods are young.
All day it fell. And when the gathered night

Was a blue shadow cast by a pale glow
I saw you then, snow-image, bird of the snow.

And I have seen and heard you in the dry   95
Close-huddled furnace of the city street
When the parched moon was planted in the sky
And the limp air hung dead against the heat.

I saw you rise, red as that rusty plant,
Dizzied with lights, half-mad with senseless sound,   100
Enormous metal, shaking to the chant
Of a triphammer striking iron ground.

Enormous power, ugly to the fool,
And beautiful as a well-handled tool.

These, and the memory of that windy day   105
On the bare hills, beyond the last barbed wire,
When all the orange poppies bloomed one way
As if a breath would blow them into fire,

I keep forever, like the sea-lion's tusk
The broken sailor brings away to land,   110
But when he touches it, he smells the musk,
And the whole sea lies hollow in his hand.

So, from a hundred visions, I make one,
And out of darkness build my mocking° sun.

114 *mocking*: imitating.

And should that task seem fruitless in the eyes   115
Of those a different magic sets apart
To see through the ice-crystal of the wise
No nation but the nation that is Art,

Their words are just. But when the birchbark-call
Is shaken with the sound that hunters make   120
The moose comes plunging through the forest-wall
Although the rifle waits beside the lake.

Art has no nations—but the mortal sky
Lingers like gold in immortality.

This flesh was seeded from no foreign grain   125
But Pennsylvania and Kentucky wheat,
And it has soaked in California rain
And five years tempered in New England sleet°

To strive at last, against an alien proof
And by the changes of an alien moon,°   130
To build again that blue, American roof
Over a half-forgotten battle-tune°

And call unsurely, from a haunted ground,
Armies of shadows and the shadow-sound.

In your Long House° there is an attic-place   135
Full of dead epics and machines that rust,
And there, occasionally, with casual face,
You come awhile to stir the sleepy dust;

125–128 *This flesh was seeded . . . :* Benét was born in Pennsylvania; his mother was from Philadelphia; his father was born in Kentucky. As son of an Army officer, he lived at various posts in the United States, including Benicia Arsenal, California (1907–1911); he spent five years at Yale (B.A., 1919; M.A., 1920).   129–130 *alien proof . . . alien moon:* John Brown's Body was written in Paris, 1926–1927. 132 *half-forgotten battle-tune:* "John Brown's Body Lies a-Mouldering in the Grave," sung to a melody set down in 1852 by John W. Steffe. Having heard the song repeatedly sung by soldiers during a tour of Union camps, Julia Ward Howe was moved to write "The Battle Hymn of the Republic" to the same tune in 1862.   135 *Long House:* Iroquois community dwelling.

Neither in pride nor mercy, but in vast
Indifference at so many gifts unsought,   140
The yellowed satins, smelling of the past,
And all the loot the lucky pirates brought.

I only bring a cup of silver air,
Yet, in your casualness, receive it there.

Receive the dream too haughty for the breast,   145
Receive the words that should have walked as bold
As the storm walks along the mountain-crest
And are like beggars whining in the cold.

The maimed presumption, the unskilful skill,
The patchwork colors, fading from the first,   150
And all the fire that fretted at the will
With such a barren ecstasy of thirst.

Receive them all—and should you choose to touch them
With one slant ray of quick, American light,
Even the dust will have no power to smutch them,   155
Even the worst will glitter in the night.

If not—the dry bones littered by the way
May still point giants toward their golden prey.

❧ PRELUDE—THE SLAVER ❧

He closed the Bible carefully, putting it down
As if his fingers loved it.   ·
                         Then he turned.
"Mr. Mate."
          "Yes, sir."
                    The captain's eyes held a shadow.
"I think, while this weather lasts," he said, after a pause,
"We'd better get them on deck as much as we can.   5
They keep better that way. Besides," he added, unsmiling,
"She's begun to stink already. You've noticed it?"

The mate nodded, a boyish nod of half-apology,
"And only a week out, too, sir."
                    "Yes," said the skipper.
His eyes looked into themselves. "Well. The trade," he said,   10
"The trade's no damn perfume-shop." He drummed with his fingers.
"Seem to be quiet tonight," he murmured, at last.
"Oh yes sir, quiet enough." The mate flushed. "Not
What you'd call quiet at home but—quiet enough."

"Um," said the skipper. "What about the big fellow?"   15

"Tarbarrel, sir? The man who says he's a king?
He was praying to something—it made the others restless.
Mr. Olsen stopped it."
                    "I don't like that," said the skipper.
"It was only an idol, sir."
                    "Oh."
                         "A stone or something."
"Oh."
          "But he's a bad one, sir—a regular sullen one—   20
He—eyes in the dark—like a cat's—enough to give you—"
The mate was young. He shivered. "The creeps," he said.

"We've had that kind," said the skipper. His mouth was hard
Then it relaxed. "Damn cheating Arabe!" ° he said,

24 *Arabe:* Muslim slave traders of the coastal regions bought captives from the
stronger African tribes and, in turn, sold them to seagoing slavers.

9

"I told them I'd take no more of their pennyweight kings,   25
Worth pounds to look at, and then when you get them aboard
Go crazy so they have to be knocked on the head
Or else just eat up their hearts and die in a week
Taking up room for nothing."

The mate hardly heard him, thinking of something else.   30
"I'm afraid we'll lose some more of the women," he said.
"Well, they're a scratch lot," said the skipper, "Any sickness?"

"Just the usual, sir."
                "But nothing like plague or—"
                                  "No sir."
"The Lord is merciful," said the skipper.
His voice was wholly sincere—an old ship's bell   35
Hung in the steeple of a meeting-house
With all New England and the sea's noise in it.
"Well, you'd better take another look-see, Mr. Mate."
The mate felt his lips go dry. "Aye aye, sir," he said,
Wetting his lips with his tongue. As he left the cabin   40
He heard the Bible being opened again.

Lantern in hand, he went down to the hold.
Each time he went he had a trick of trying
To shut the pores of his body against the stench
By force of will, by thinking of salt and flowers,   45
But it was always useless.
                      He kept thinking:
When I get home, when I get a bath and clean food,
When I've gone swimming out beyond the Point
In that cold green, so cold it must be pure
Beyond the purity of a dissolved star,   50
When I get my shore-clothes on, and one of those shirts
Out of the linen-closet that smells of lavender,
Will my skin smell black even then, will my skin smell black?

The lantern shook in his hand.
                          This was black, here,
This was black to see and feel and smell and taste,   55
The blackness of black, with one weak lamp to light it
As ineffectually as a firefly in Hell,
And, being so, should be silent.

But the hold
Was never silent.
      There was always that breathing.
Always that thick breathing, always those shivering cries.   60

A few of the slaves
Knew English—at least the English for water and Jesus.
"I'm dying." "Sick." "My name Caesar."
      Those who knew
These things, said these things now when they saw the lantern
Mechanically, as tamed beasts answer the whipcrack.   65
Their voices beat at the light like heavy moths.
But most made merely liquid or guttural sounds
Meaningless to the mate, but horribly like
The sounds of palateless men or animals trying
To talk through a human throat.
      The mate was used   70
To the confusion of limbs and bodies by now.
At first it had made him think of the perturbed
Blind coil of blacksnakes thawing on a rock
In the bleak sun of Spring, or Judgment Day
Just after the first sounding of the trump   75
When all earth seethes and crumbles with the slow
Vast, mouldy resurrection of the dead.
But he had passed such fancies.
      He must see
As much as he could. He couldn't see very much.
They were too tightly packed but—no plague yet,   80
And all the chains were fast. Then he saw something.
The woman was asleep but her baby was dead.
He wondered whether to take it from her now.
No, it would only rouse the others. Tomorrow.
He turned away with a shiver.
      His glance fell   85
On the man who said he had been a king, the man
Called Tarbarrel, the image of black stone
Whose eyes were savage gods.
      The huge suave muscles
Rippled like stretching cats as he changed posture,
Magnificence in chains that yet was ease.   90
The smolder in those eyes. The steady hate.

The mate made himself stare till the eyes dropped.
Then he turned back to the companionway.
His forehead was hot and sweaty. He wiped it off,
But then the rough cloth of his sleeve smelt black.

The captain shut the Bible as he came in.
"Well, Mister Mate?"
                                        "All quiet, sir."
                                                    The captain
Looked at him sharply. "Sit down," he said in a bark.
The mate's knees gave as he sat. "It's—hot down there,"
He said, a little weakly, wanting to wipe
His face again, but knowing he'd smell that blackness
Again, if he did.
                    "Takes you that way, sometimes,"
Said the captain, not unkindly, "I remember
Back in the twenties." °
                            Something hot and strong
Bit the mate's throat. He coughed.
                                        "There," said the captain,
Putting the cup down. "You'll feel better now.
You're young for this trade, Mister, and that's a fact."

The mate coughed and didn't answer, much too glad
To see the captain change back to himself
From something made of steam, to want to talk.
But, after a while, he heard the captain talking,
Half to himself.
                    "It's a fact, that," he was saying,
"They've even made a song of me—ever heard it?"
The mate shook his head, quickly, "Oh yes you have.
You know how it goes." He cleared his throat and hummed:

> *"Captain Ball was a Yankee slaver,*
> *Blow, blow, blow the man down!*
> *He traded in niggers and loved his Saviour,*
> *Give me some time to blow the man down."*

104 *the twenties:* the 1720s, when the slave trade was approaching its height. The
first Negro slaves arrived in 1619; slave trade was prohibited after 1808.

The droning chanty filled the narrow cabin   120
An instant with grey Massachusetts sea,
Wave of the North, wave of the melted ice,
The hard salt-sparkles on the harder rock.
The stony islands.
                Then it died away.
"Well," said the captain, "if that's how it strikes them—   125
They mean it bad but I don't take it bad.
I get my sailing-orders from the Lord."
He touched the Bible. "And it's down there, Mister,
Down there in black and white—the sons of Ham°—
Bondservants—sweat of their brows." His voice trailed off   130
Into texts. "I tell you, Mister," he said fiercely,
"The pay's good pay, but it's the Lord's work, too.
We're spreading the Lord's seed—spreading his seed—"

His hand made the outflung motion of a sower
And the mate, staring, seemed to hear the slight   135
Patter of fallen seeds on fertile ground,
Black, shining seeds, robbed from a black king's storehouse,
Falling and falling on American earth
With light, inexorable patter and fall,
To strike, lie silent, quicken.
                Till the Spring   140
Came with its weeping rains, and the ground bore
A blade, a shadow-sapling, a tree of shadow,
A black-leaved tree whose trunk and roots were shadow,
A tree shaped like a yoke, growing and growing
Until it blotted all the seamen's stars.   145

Horses of anger° trampling, horses of anger,
Trampling behind the sky in ominous cadence,
Beat of the heavy hooves like metal on metal,
Trampling something down. . . .
                Was it they, was it they?
Or was it cold wind in the leaves of the shadow-tree   150
That made such grievous music?

---

129 *sons of Ham:* See Genesis 9:22–25.   146 *Horses of anger:* Initially, Benét's
working title for *John Brown's Body* was *Horses of Anger.* The image recurs throughout the poem.

Oh Lordy Je-sus
Won't you come and find me?
They put me in jail, Lord,
Way down in the jail.   155
Won't you send me a pro-phet
Just one of your prophets
Like Moses and Aaron
To get me some bail?

I'm feeling poorly   160
Yes, mighty poorly,
I ain't got no strength, Lord,
I'm all trampled down.
So send me an angel
Just any old angel   165
To give me a robe, Lord,
And give me a crown.

Oh Lordy Je-sus
It's a long time comin'
It's a long time co-o-min'   170
That Jubilee time.
We'll wait and we'll pray, Lord,
We'll wait and we'll pray, Lord,
But it's a long time, Lord,
Yes, it's a long time.   175

The dark sobbing ebbed away.
The captain was still talking. "Yes," he said,
"And yet we treat 'em well enough. There's no one
From Salem to the Guinea Coast can say
They lose as few as I do." He stopped.
                              "Well, Mister?"   180
The mate arose. "Good night sir and—"
                                    "Good night."

The mate went up on deck. The breeze was fresh.
There were the stars, steady. He shook himself
Like a dog coming out of water and felt better.
Six weeks, with luck, and they'd be back in port   185
And he could draw his pay and see his girl.
Meanwhile, it wasn't his watch, so he could sleep.

The captain still below, reading that Bible. . . .
Forget it—and the noises, still half-heard—
He'd have to go below to sleep, this time,   190
But after, if the weather held like this,
He'd have them sling a hammock up on deck.
You couldn't smell the black so much on deck
And so you didn't dream it when you slept.

BOOK ONE

Jack Ellyat had been out all day alone,
Except for his new gun and Ned, the setter,
The old wise dog with Autumn in his eyes,
Who stepped the fallen leaves so delicately
They barely rustled. Ellyat trampled them down   5
Crackling, like cast-off skins of fairy snakes.
He'd meant to hunt, but he had let the gun
Rest on his shoulder.

               It was enough to feel
The cool air of the last of Indian summer
Blowing continually across his cheek   10
And watch the light distill its water of gold
As the sun dropped.

               Here was October,° here
Was ruddy October, the old harvester,
Wrapped like a beggared sachem° in a coat
Of tattered tanager° and partridge feathers,   15
Scattering jack-o-lanterns everywhere
To give the field-mice pumpkin-colored moons.
His red clay pipe had trailed across the land
Staining the trees with colors of the sumach:
East, West, South, North, the ceremonial fume   20
Blue and enchanted as the soul of air
Drifted its incense.

               Incense of the wild,
Incense of earth fulfilled, ready to sleep
The stupefied dark slumber of the bear
All winter, underneath a frozen star.   25

Jack Ellyat felt that turning of the year
Stir in his blood like drowsy fiddle-music
And knew he was glad to be Connecticut-born
And young enough to find Connecticut winter
Was a black pond to cut with silver skates   30
And not a scalping-knife against the throat.
He thought the thoughts of youth, idle and proud.

12 *October:* October 1859. 14 *sachem:* Algonquin Indian chief. 15 *tanager:*
American songbird. The males of all species are more or less red and subject to sea-
sonal change.

Since I was begotten
My father's grown wise
But he has forgotten   35
The wind in the skies.
I shall not grow wise.

Since I have been growing
My uncle's got rich.
He spends his time sowing   40
A bottomless ditch.
I will not grow rich.

For money is sullen
And wisdom is sly,
But youth is the pollen   4
That blows through the sky
And does not ask why.

O wisdom and money
How can you requite
The honey of honey   5
That flies in that flight?
The useless delight?

So, with his back against a tree, he stared
At the pure, golden feathers in the West
Until the sunset flowed into his heart   5
Like a slow wave of honey-dropping dew
Murmuring from the other side of Sleep.
There was a fairy hush
Everywhere. Even the setter at his feet
Lay there as if the twilight had bewitched   6
His russet paws into two russet leaves,
A dog of russet leaves who did not stir a hair.

Then something broke the peace.
Like wind it was, the flutter of rising wind,
But then it grew until it was the rushing   6
Of winged stallions,° distant and terrible,
Trampling beyond the sky.
                          The hissing charge

66 *Of winged stallions* . . .: Compare Prelude, lines 146–149.

Of lightless armies of angelic horse
Galloping down the stars.
     There were no words
In that implacable and feathery thunder,   70
And yet there must have been, or Ellyat's mind
Caught them like broken arrows out of the air.

 Thirteen sisters beside the sea,
 (Have a care, my son.)
 Builded a house called Liberty   75
 And locked the doors with a stately key.
 None should enter it but the free.
 (Have a care, my son.)

 The walls are solid as Plymouth Rock.
 (Rock can crumble, my son.)   80
 The door of seasoned New England stock.
 Before it a Yankee fighting-cock
 Pecks redcoat kings away from the lock.
 (Fighters can die, my son.)

 The hearth is a corner where sages sit.   85
 (Sages pass, my son.)
 Washington's heart lies under it.
 And the long roof-beams are chiseled and split
 From hickory tough as Jackson's wit.
 (Bones in the dust, my son.)   90

 The trees in the garden are fair and fine.
 (Trees blow down, my son.)
 Connecticut elm and Georgia pine.
 The warehouse groans with cotton and swine.
 The cellar is full of scuppernong-wine.°   95
 (Wine turns sour, my son.)

 Surely a house so strong and bold,
 (The wind is rising, my son,)
 Will last till Time is a pinch of mould!
 There is a ghost, when the night is old.   100
 There is a ghost who walks in the cold.
 (The trees are shaking, my son.)

---

95 *scuppernong-wine:* wine from the scuppernong (muscadine) grapes native to the
southeastern United States.

The sisters sleep on Liberty's breast,
(The thunder thunders, my son,)
Like thirteen swans in a single nest.
But the ghost is naked and will not rest
Until the sun rise out of the West.
(The lightning lightens, my son.)

All night long like a moving stain,
(The trees are breaking, my son,)
The black ghost wanders his house of pain.
There is blood where his hand has lain.
It is wrong he should wear a chain.
(The sky is falling, my son.)

The warning beat at his mind like a bird and passed.
Ellyat roused. He thought: they are going South.
He stared at the sky, confused. It was empty and bleak.
But still he felt the shock of the hooves on his heart.
—The riderless horses never bridled or tamed—
He heard them screaming like eagles loosed from a cloud
As they drove South to trample the indolent sun,
And darkness sat in his mind like a shadow enthroned.
He could not read the riddle their flight had set
But he felt wretched, and glad for the dog's cold nose
That now came nuzzling his hand.
                                    Who has set you free?
Who has driven you out in the sky with an iron whip
Like blind, old thunders stubbornly marching abreast
To carry a portent high on shoulders of stone
The length and breadth of the Union?
The North and South are at peace and the East and West,
The tomahawk is buried in prairie-sod.
The great frontier rolls westward with the sun,
And the new States are crowding at the door,
The buckskin-States, the buffalo-horned, the wild
Mustangs with coats the color of crude gold.°

130–135 *The North and South are at peace . . . The tomahawk is buried in prai-rie-sod . . .* : During this period when there was comparatively little Indian warfare, the Kansas-Nebraska Act of 1854 sustained an uneasy balance between free and slave factions as new states, formed from the Louisiana Purchase, were accepted into the nation.

Their bodies, naked as the hunter's moon,
Smell of new grass and the sweet milk of the corn.
Defiant virgins, fiercely unpossessed
As the bird-stars that walk the night untrodden.
They drag their skies and sunsets after them   140
Like calico ponies on a rawhide rope,
And who would ride them must have iron thighs
And a lean heart, bright as a bowie-knife.°
Were they not foaled with treasure in their eyes
Between the rattlesnake and the painted rock?   145
Are they not matches for vaquero° gods?
Are they not occupation for the strength
Of a whole ruffian world of pioneers?
And must they wait like spayed ° mares in the rain,
While Carolina and Connecticut   150
Fight an old quarrel out before a ghost? °

So Ellyat talked to his young indignation,
Walking back home with the October moon.
But, even as he mused, he tried to picture
The South, that languorous land where Uncle Toms   155
Groaned Biblically underneath the lash,
And grinning Topsies mopped and mowed behind
Each honeysuckle vine.
           They called them niggers
And cut their ears off when they ran away,
But then they loved their mammies— there was that—   160
Although they sometimes sold them down the river—
And when the niggers were not getting licked
Or quoting Scripture, they sang funny songs,
By the Swanee river,° on the old plantation.

The girls were always beautiful. The men   165
Wore varnished boots, raced horses and played cards
And drank mint-juleps till the time came round
For fighting duels with their second cousins

143 *bowie-knife:* single-edged sheath knife associated with the West and named for Colonel James Bowie (killed at the Battle of the Alamo, 1836). 146 *vaquero:* cowboy. 149 *spayed:* sterilized. 151 *ghost:* See lines 100–111, above. 155–164 *Uncle Toms . . . Topsies . . . funny songs/By the Swanee river:* For a decade preceding the war, such works as Harriet Beecher Stowe's *Uncle Tom's Cabin,* 1852, and Stephen Foster's early songs (here, "Old Folks at Home," 1851) influenced the northern image of the South.

Or tar-and-feathering some God-damn Yankee. . . .
The South . . . the honeysuckle . . . the hot sun . . .   170
The taste of ripe persimmons and sugar-cane . . .
The cloyed and waxy sweetness of magnolias . . .
White cotton, blowing like a fallen cloud,
And foxhounds belling the Virginia hills . . .

And then the fugitive slave he'd seen in Boston,   175
The black man with the eyes of a tortured horse. . . .

He whistled Ned. What do you think of it, Ned?
We're abolitionists, I suppose, and Father
Talks about Wendell Phillips and John Brown°
But, even so, that doesn't have to mean   180
We'll break the Union up for abolition,
And they can't want to break it up for slavery—
It won't come to real fighting, will it, Ned?
But Ned was busy with a rabbit-track.
There was the town—the yellow window of home.   185

Meanwhile, in Concord, Emerson and Thoreau
Talked of an ideal state,° so purely framed
It never could exist.
                    Meanwhile, in Boston
Minister Higginson and Dr. Howe°
Waited for news about a certain project   190
That had to do with pikes and Harper's Ferry.

Meanwhile, in Georgia, Clay Wingate dreamed.

Settled more than a hundred year
By the river and county of St. Savier,°
The Wingates held their ancestry   19

179 *Wendell Phillips and John Brown*: By 1859 both were recognized leaders in the abolitionist movement; Phillips as an orator, Brown as an activist.   187 *Talked of an ideal state*: See, for example, Emerson's journal entry (October 17, 1840) regarding the Brook Farm experiment and Thoreau's concluding paragraphs to "Civil Disobedience" (1847).   189 *Minister Higginson and Dr. Howe*: Thomas Wentworth Higginson (Harvard, 1841), author, Unitarian minister, and Civil War army officer; Samuel Gridley Howe, Boston physician and editor, husband of Julia Ward Howe. Both men gave active, though secret, support to the Harper's Ferry raid. 194 *St. Savier:* The region apparently is Benét's creation.

As high as Taliaferro or Huger,
Maryland Carroll, Virginia Lee.°
They had ill-spelt letters of Albemarle's
And their first grant ran from the second Charles,°
Clerkly inscribed upon parchmentries   200
"To our well-beloved John Wingate, these,"
Though envy hinted the royal mood
Held more of humor than gratitude
And the well-beloved had less applied
To honest John than his tall young bride,   205
At least their eldest to John's surprise,
Was very like Monmouth° about the eyes,
Till his father wondered if every loyalty
Was always so richly repaid by royalty,
But, having long found that the principal question   210
In a happy life is a good digestion
And the worst stomachic of all is jealousy
He gave up the riddle, and settled zealously
To farming his acres, begetting daughters,
And making a study of cordial waters   215
Till he died at ninety of pure senility
And was greatly mourned by the local gentility.

John the Second was different cloth.
He had wings—but the wings of the moth.
Courtly, unlucky, clever and wise,   220
There was a Stuart in his eyes,°
A gambler that played against loaded dice.
He could harrow the water and plough the sand,
But he could not do the thing at hand.
A fencing-foil too supple for use,   225
A racing colt that must run at loose.
And the Wingate acres had slipped away
If it had not been for Elspeth Mackay.

196–197 *Taliaferro or Huger,/Maryland Carroll, Virginia Lee*: established southern families; Taliaferro, pronounced "tolliver," and Huger, pronounced "you-jee." 198–199 *Albermarle's . . . the second Charles*: Duke of Albemarle, George Monk (Monck), was a major power, military and political, in both Commonwealth and Restoration England. Monk's efforts were a significant factor in restoring Charles II of the House of Stuart to the English throne (1660). 206–207 *their eldest . . . like Monmouth*: Charles II fathered a number of illegitimate children, including James Scott, Duke of Monmouth, and, as this narrative suggests, the fictional John Wingate II. 220–221 *Courtly, unlucky . . . Stuart in his eyes*: See line 207, above.

She was his wife, and her heart was bold
As a broad, bright guinea of Border gold.   230
Her wit was a tartan of colored weather.
Her walk was gallant as Highland heather.
And whatever she had, she held together.

It was she who established on Georgia soil
Wingate honor and Wingate toil   235
When John and his father's neighbors stood
At swords' points over a county feud
And only ill-fortune and he were friends.
—They prophesied her a dozen ends,
Seeking new ground for a broken man   240
Where only the deer and the rabbit ran
And the Indian arrow harried both,
But she held her word and she kept her troth,
Cleared the forest and tamed the wild
And gave the breast to the new-born child   245
While the painted Death° went whooping by
—To die at last as she wished to die
In the fief ° built out of her blood and bone
With her heart for the Hall's° foundation-stone.

Deep in her sons, and the Wingate blood,   250
She stamped her sigil ° of fortitude.
Thrift and love for the house and the chief
And a scone on the hob° for the son of grief.
But a knife in the ribs for the pleasant thief.
And deep in her sons, when she was gone,   255
Her words took root, and her ghost lived on.
The slow voice haunting the ocean-shell
To counsel the sons of her sons as well.
And it was well for the Wingate line
To have that stiffening set in its spine.   260
For once in each breeding of Wingate kin
There came a child with an olive skin
And the mouth of Charles, the merry and sad,
And the bright, spoilt charm that Monmouth had.
Luckily seldom the oldest born   265

246 *painted Death:* hostile Indians.   248 *fief:* feudal estate; here, plantation.   249
Hall's: Wingate Hall; see line 297, below.   251 *sigil:* seal.   253 *scone on the hob:*
bread on the hearth.

To sow the nettle in Wingate corn
And let the cotton blight on its stalk
While he wasted his time in witty talk,
Or worse, in love with no minister handy,
Or feeding a spaniel on nuts and brandy   270
And taking a melancholy pride
In never choosing the winning side.

Clay Wingate was the last to feel
The prick of that spur of tarnished steel,
Gilt, but crossed with the dubious bar°   275
Of arms won under the bastard's star,
Rowel his mind, at that time or this,
With thoughts and visions that were not his.
A sorrow of laughter, a mournful glamor
And the ghostly stroke of an airy hammer   280
Shaking his heart with pity and pride
That had nothing to do with the things he eyed.
He was happy and young, he was strong and stout,
His body was hard to weary out.
When he thought of life, he thought of a shout.   285
But—there was a sword in a blackened sheath,
There was a shape with a mourning wreath:
And a place in his mind was a wrestling-ring
Where the crownless form of an outlawed king°
Fought with a shadow too like his own,   290
And, late or early, was overthrown.

It is not lucky to dream such stuff—
Dreaming men are haunted men.
Though Wingate's face looked lucky enough
To any eye that had seen him then,   295
Riding back through the Georgia Fall
To the white-pillared porch of Wingate Hall.
Fall of the possum, fall of the 'coon,
And the lop-eared hound-dog baying the moon.
Fall that is neither bitter nor swift   300

275 *dubious bar:* The bar sinister (more correctly, *bend* sinister) indicates bastardy
in the family line. See line 207, above.   289 *crownless form of an outlawed king:*
Upon the accession of James II in 1685, the Protestant Pretender (Duke of Monmouth) raised an army to seize the throne, but was finally defeated at Sedgemoor,
captured, and beheaded. See line 207, above.

But a brown girl bearing an idle gift,
A brown seed-kernel that splits apart
And shows the Summer yet in its heart,
A smokiness so vague in the air
You feel it rather than see it there,   30
A brief, white rime° on the red clay road
And slow mules creaking a lazy load
Through endless acres of afternoon,
A pine-cone fire and a banjo-tune,
And a julep mixed with a silver spoon.   31

Your noons are hot, your nights deep-starred,
There is honeysuckle still in the yard,
Fall of the quail and the firefly-glows
And the pot-pourri° of the rambler-rose,
Fall that brings no promise of snows . . .   31

Wingate checked on his horse's rein
With a hand as light as a butterfly
And drank content in body and brain
As he gazed for a moment at the sky.
This was his Georgia, this his share   32
Of pine and river and sleepy air,
Of summer thunder and winter rain
That spills bright tears on the window-pane
With the slight, fierce passion of young men's grief,
Of the mockingbird and the mulberry-leaf.   32
For, wherever the winds of Georgia run,
It smells of peaches long in the sun,
And the white wolf-winter, hungry and frore,°
Can prowl the North by a frozen door
But here we have fed him on bacon-fat   33
And he sleeps by the stove like a lazy cat.
Here Christmas stops at everyone's house
With a jug of molasses and green, young boughs,
And the little New Year, the weakling one,
Can lie outdoors in the noonday sun,   3
Blowing the fluff from a turkey-wing
At skies already haunted with Spring—

306 *brief, white rime*: morning frost.   314 *pot-pourri*: a scent jar of spice and dried
rose petals.   328 *frore*: cold.

Oh, Georgia . . . Georgia . . . the careless yield!
The watermelons ripe in the field!
The mist in the bottoms that tastes of fever   340
And the yellow river rolling forever . . . !

So Wingate saw it, vision or truth,
Through the colored window of his own youth,
Building an image out of his mind
To live or die for, as Fate inclined.   345

He drank his fill of the air, and then,
Was just about to ride on again
When—what was that noise beyond the sky,
That harry of unseen cavalry°
Riding the wind?
        His own horse stirred,   350
Neighing. He listened. There was a word.
He could not hear it—and yet he heard.
It was an arrow from ambush flung,
It was a bell with a leaden tongue
Striking an hour.
        He was young   355
No longer. He and his horse were old,
And both were bound with an iron band.
He slipped from the saddle and tried to stand.
He struck one hand with the other hand.
But both were cold.   360

The horses, burning-hooved, drove on toward the sea,
But, where they had passed, the air was troubled and sick
Like earth that the shoulder of earthquake heavily stirs.
There was a whisper moving that air all night,
A whisper that cried and whimpered about the house   365
Where John Brown prayed to his God, by his narrow bed.

JOHN BROWN'S PRAYER

Omnipotent and steadfast God,
Who, in Thy mercy, hath

349 *unseen cavalry*: Compare Prelude, lines 146–149.

Upheaved in me Jehovah's rod
And his chastising wrath,   37

For fifty-nine unsparing years
Thy Grace hath worked apart
To mould a man of iron tears
With a bullet for a heart.

Yet, since this body may be weak   37
With all it has to bear,
Once more, before Thy thunders speak,
Almighty, hear my prayer.

I saw Thee when Thou did display
The black man and his lord   38
To bid me free the one, and slay
The other with the sword.

I heard Thee when Thou bade me spurn
Destruction from my hand
And, though all Kansas bleed and burn,°   38
It was at Thy command.

I hear the rolling of the wheels,
The chariots of war!
I hear the breaking of the seals
And the opening of the door!   3

The glorious beasts with many eyes
Exult before the Crowned.°
The buried saints arise, arise
Like incense from the ground!

Before them march the martyr-kings,   3
In bloody sunsets drest,
O, *Kansas, bleeding Kansas,*
You will not let me rest!

385 *Kansas bleed and burn:* During the 1850s, "Bloody Kansas" was the scene of
bitter guerrilla fighting between free-staters and proslavery advocates.   391–392 *The
glorious beasts . . . before the Crowned:* "And before the throne there . . . were
four beasts full of eyes. . . ." See Revelation 4:6.

I hear your sighing corn again,
I smell your prairie-sky,   400
And I remember five dead men
By Pottawattomie.°

Lord God it was a work of Thine,
And how might I refrain?
But Kansas, bleeding Kansas,   405
I hear her in her pain.

Her corn is rustling in the ground,
An arrow in my flesh.
And all night long I staunch a wound   410
That ever bleeds afresh.

Get up, get up, my hardy sons,°
From this time forth we are
No longer men, but pikes and guns
In God's advancing war.

And if we live, we free the slave,   415
And if we die, we die.
But God has digged His saints a grave
Beyond the western sky.

Oh, fairer than the bugle-call
Its walls of jasper° shine!   420
And Joshua's sword° is on the wall
With space beside for mine.

And should the Philistine° defend
His strength against our blows,
The God who doth not spare His friend,   425
Will not forget His foes.

---

402 *Pottawattomie* [*sic*]: a massacre of five proslavery men near Pottawatomie Creek
(May 24, 1856) planned and executed by John Brown and his followers.   411 *my*
hardy sons: John Brown was twice married, the father of twenty children. Six of
Brown's sons accompanied him to Kansas; only two, Oliver and Watson, participated
in the Harper's Ferry raid.   420 *walls of jasper*: ". . . the wall of [the heavenly
Jerusalem] was of jasper." Revelation 21:18.   421 *Joshua's sword*: Joshua led the
Israelites in the conquest of the promised land after forty years' wandering from
Egyptian bondage.   423 *the Philistine*: traditional enemy of the Israelite, though not
of Joshua.

They reached the Maryland bridge of Harper's Ferry
That Sunday night. There were twenty-two in all,°
Nineteen were under thirty, three not twenty-one,
Kagi, the self-taught scholar, quiet and cool,   430
Stevens, the cashiered soldier, Puritan-fathered,
A singing giant, gunpowder-tempered and rash.
Dauphin Thompson, the pippin-cheeked country-boy,
More like a girl than a warrior; Oliver Brown,
Married last year when he was barely nineteen;   435
Dangerfield Newby, colored and born a slave,
Freeman now, but married to one not free
Who, with their seven children, waited him South,
The youngest baby just beginning to crawl;
Watson Brown, the steady lieutenant, who wrote   440
Back to his wife,°
                "Oh, Bell, I want to see you
And the little fellow very much but must wait.
There was a slave near here whose wife was sold South.
They found him hanging in Kennedy's orchard next morning.   445
I cannot come home as long as such things are done here.
I sometimes think that we shall not meet again."

These were some of the band. For better or worse
They were all strong men.
                The bearded faces look strange

428–455 *There were twenty-two in all* . . . : Of the twenty-two besides John Brown,
Benét mentions nine by name: Aaron Dwight Stevens, born 1831, convicted of
"engaging in a drunken riot" during Mexican War service, escaped confinement and
became a colonel in the Kansas militia under an alias; John Henry Kagi, born in
Bristolville, Ohio, 1835, longtime lieutenant of Brown's, taught school in Virginia,
admitted to the bar in Nebraska, served under Stevens in Kansas; Dangerfield Newby,
born in Fauquier County, Virginia, son of a slave mother and her Scotch master;
Dauphin Osgood Thompson, twenty-one-year-old neighbor of the Brown family in
North Elba, New York, and his older brother William (line 681), whose sister was
married to Watson Brown; Oliver and Watson Brown, two of John Brown's sons
by his second wife, Mary Day; Stewart Taylor (line 698), a wagonmaker, born in
Canada in 1836 of American parents, the only raider who was not an American citi-
zen; and William H. Leeman (lines 648 ff.), who joined Brown's forces in 1856 at
the age of seventeen. For biographical details, see Oswald Garrison Villard, *John
Brown, 1800–1859: A Biography Fifty Years After,** pp. 678–687. Benét acknowl-
edges his principal sources in his "Note," p. xiii. First references to these sources have
been marked in footnotes by an asterisk(*). Thereafter, shortened forms are cited.
440–441 *Watson Brown* . . . *wrote/Back to his wife:* September 1859, from the
Kennedy Farm, about five miles from Harper's Ferry, where John Brown gathered
his forces for the raid. See Villard, pp. 415–417.

In the old daguerreotypes:° they should be the faces
Of prosperous, small-town people, good sons and fathers,   450
Good horse-shoe pitchers, good at plowing a field,
Good at swapping stories and good at praying,
American wheat, firm-rooted, good in the ear.
There is only one whose air seems out of the common,
Oliver Brown. That face has a masculine beauty   455
Somewhat like the face of Keats.
                                They were all strong men.

They tied up the watchmen and took the rifleworks.
Then John Brown sent a raiding party away
To fetch in Colonel Washington from his farm.
The Colonel was George Washington's great-grand-nephew,   460
Slave-owner, gentleman-farmer, but, more than these,
Possessor of a certain fabulous sword
Given to Washington by Frederick the Great.°
They captured him and his sword and brought them along
Processionally.
                The act has a touch of drama,   465
Half costume-romance, half unmerited farce.
On the way, they told the Washington slaves they were free,
Or free to fight for their freedom.
                                The slaves heard the news
With the dazed, scared eyes of cattle before a storm.
A few came back with the band and were given pikes,   470
And, when John Brown was watching, pretended to mount
A slipshod guard over the prisoners.
But, when he had walked away, they put down their pikes
And huddled together, talking in mourning voices.
It didn't seem right to play at guarding the Colonel   475
But they were afraid of the bearded patriarch
With the Old Testament eyes.
                        A little later
It was Patrick Higgins' turn. He was the night-watchman
Of the Maryland bridge, a tough little Irishman
With a canny, humorous face, and a twist in his speech.   480

449 *daguerreotypes:* early photographs on treated glass or metal.   462–463 *fabulous sword/given . . . by Frederick the Great:* Brown hoped to possess this sword as well as a pistol given George Washington by Lafayette, which Colonel Lewis Washington (1812–1871) also owned, as the "new American revolution" began. See Villard, pp. 431–432.

He came humming his way to his job.
                              "Halt!" ordered a voice.
He stopped a minute, perplexed. As he told men later,
"Now I didn't know what 'Halt!' mint, any more
Than a hog knows about a holiday."
                              There was a scuffle.
He got away with a bullet-crease in his scalp   515
And warned the incoming train. It was half-past-one.
A moment later, a man named Shepherd Heyward,
Free negro, baggage-master of the small station,
Well-known in the town, hardworking, thrifty and fated,
Came looking for Higgins.
                    "Halt!" called the voice again,   490
But he kept on, not hearing or understanding,
Whichever it may have been.
                        A rifle cracked.
He fell by the station-platform, gripping his belly,
And lay for twelve hours of torment, asking for water
Until he was able to die.
                      There is no stone,   495
No image of bronze or marble green with the rain
To Shepherd Heyward, free negro of Harper's Ferry,
And even the books, the careful, ponderous histories,
That turn live men into dummies with smiles of wax
Thoughtfully posed against a photographer's background   500
In the act of signing a treaty or drawing a sword,
Tell little of what he was.
                        And yet his face
Grey with pain and puzzled at sudden death
Stares out at us through the bookworm-dust of the years
With an uncomprehending wonder, a blind surprise.   505
"I was getting along," it says, "I was doing well.
I had six thousand dollars saved in the bank.
It was a good town, a nice town, I liked the folks
And they liked me. I had a good job there, too.
On Sundays I used to dress myself up slick enough   510
To pass the plate in church, but I wasn't proud
Not even when trashy niggers called me Mister,
Though I could hear the old grannies over their snuff
Mumbling along, 'Look, chile, there goes Shepherd Heyward.
Ain't him fine in he Sunday clo'es—ain't him sassy and fine? 515
You grow up decent and don't play ball in the street,

And maybe you'll get like him, with a gold watch and chain.'
And then, suddenly—and what was it all about?
Why should anyone want to kill me? Why was it done?"

So the grey lips. And so the hurt in the eyes.   520
A hurt like a child's, at punishment unexplained
That makes the whole child-universe fall to pieces.
At the time of death, most men turn back toward the child.

Brown did not know at first that the first man dead
By the sword he thought of so often as Gideon's sword °   525
Was one of the race he had drawn that sword to free.
It had been dark on the bridge. A man had come
And had not halted when ordered. Then the shot
And the scrape of the hurt man dragging himself away.
That was all. The next man ordered to halt would halt.   530
His mind was too full of the burning judgments of God
To wonder who it had been. He was cool and at peace.
He dreamt of a lamb, lying down by a rushing stream.

So the night wore away, indecisive and strange.
The raiders stuck by the arsenal, waiting perhaps   535
For a great bell of jubilation to toll in the sky,
And the slaves to rush from the hills with pikes in their hands,
A host redeemed, black rescue-armies of God.
It did not happen.
                    Meanwhile, there was casual firing.
A townsman named Boerley was killed. Meanwhile, the train   540
Passed over the bridge to carry its wild news
Of abolition-devils sprung from the ground
A hundred and fifty, three hundred, a thousand strong°
To pillage Harper's Ferry, with fire and sword.
Meanwhile the whole countryside was springing to arms.   545
The alarm-bell in Charlestown clanged "Nat Turner° has come.

---

525 *Gideon's sword:* See Judges 7:14–18.   543 *A hundred and fifty . . . a thou-sand strong:* The initial dispatch in *The National Intelligencer* in Washington re-ported "about two hundred and fifty whites, followed by a band of negroes." There were warnings of exaggerations from the first, but one report put "500 to 700 whites and blacks in the outbreak."   546 *Nat Turner:* a visionary slave leader who hoped to establish an empire of fugitive slaves in Virginia's Dismal Swamp. In an abortive three-day revolt in August 1831, Turner and his followers killed some fifty-five white persons. He was subsequently captured and hanged, along with sixteen of the other slaves involved.

Nat Turner has come again, all smoky from Hell,
Setting the slave to murder and massacre!"
The Jefferson Guards° fell in. There were boys and men.
They had no uniforms but they had weapons.   55
Old squirrel-rifles, taken down from the wall,
Shot guns loaded with spikes and scraps of iron.
A boy dragged a blunderbuss as big as himself.
They started for the Ferry.
                          In a dozen
A score of other sleepy, neighboring towns   55
The same bell clanged, the same militia assembled.

The Ferry itself was roused and stirring with dawn.
And the firing began again.
                          A queer, harsh sound
In the ordinary streets of that clean, small town,
A desultory, vapid, meaningless sound.   56

God knows why John Brown lingered! Kagi, the scholar,
Who, with two others, held the rifle-works,
All morning sent him messages urging retreat.
They had the inexorable weight of common sense
Behind them, but John Brown neither replied   56
Nor heeded, brooding in the patriarch-calm
Of a lean, solitary pine that hangs
On the cliff's edge, and sees the world below
A tiny pattern of toy fields and trees,
And only feels its roots gripping the rock   57
And the almighty wind that shakes its boughs,
Blowing from eagle-heaven to eagle-heaven.

Of course they were cut off. The whole attempt
Was fated from the first.
                          Just about noon
The Jefferson Guards took the Potomac Bridge   57
And drove away the men Brown posted there.

There were three doors of possible escape
Open to Brown. With this the first slammed shut.
The second followed it a little later
With the recapture of the other bridge   58

549 *Jefferson Guards:* the Charlestown [Virginia] militia.

That cut Brown off from Kagi and the arsenal
And penned the larger body of the raiders
In the armory.
            Again the firing rolled,
And now the first of the raiders fell and died,
Dangerfield Newby, the freed Scotch-mulatto   585
Whose wife and seven children, slaves in Virginia,
Waited for him to bring them incredible freedom.
They were sold South instead, after the raid.
His body lay where the townspeople could reach it.
They cut off his ears for trophies.
                If there are souls,   590
As many think that there are or wish that there might be,
Crystalline things that rise on light wings exulting
Out of the spoilt and broken cocoon of the body,
Knowing no sorrow or pain but only deliverance,
And yet with the flame of speech, the patterns of memory,   595
One wonders what the soul of Dangerfield Newby
Said, in what terms, to the soul of Shepherd Heyward,
Both born slave, both freed, both dead the same day.
What do the souls that bleed from the corpse of battle
Say to the tattered night?
             Perhaps it is better   600
We have no power to visage what they might say.

The firing now was constant, like the heavy
And drumming rains of summer. Twice Brown sent
Asking a truce. The second time there went
Stevens and Watson Brown with a white flag.   605
But things had gone beyond the symbol of flags.
Stevens, shot from a window, fell in the gutter
Horribly wounded. Watson Brown crawled back
To the engine house that was the final fort
Of Brown's last stand, torn through and through with slugs.   610

A Mr. Brua, one of Brown's prisoners,
Strolled out from the unguarded prison-room
Into the bullets, lifted Stevens up,
Carried him over to the old hotel
They called the Wager House, got a doctor for him,   615
And then strolled back to take his prisoner's place
With Colonel Washington and the scared rest.

I know no more than this of Mr. Brua
But he seems curiously American,
And I imagine him a tall, stooped man   62
A little yellow with the Southern sun,
With slow, brown eyes and a slow way of talking,
Shifting the quid of tobacco in his cheek
Mechanically, as he lifted up
The dirty, bloody body of the man   62
Who stood for everything he most detested
And slowly carrying him through casual wasps
Of death to the flyspecked but sunny room
In the old hotel, wiping the blood and grime
Mechanically from his Sunday coat,   63
Settling his black string-tie with big, tanned hands,
And, then, incredibly, going back to jail.
He did not think much about what he'd done
But sat himself as comfortably as might be
On the cold bricks of that dejected guard-room   63
And slowly started cutting another quid
With a worn knife that had a brown bone-handle.

He lived all through the war and died long after,
This Mr. Brua I see. His last advice
To numerous nephews was "Keep out of trouble,   6
But if you're in it, chew and don't be hasty,
Just do whatever's likeliest at hand."

I like your way of talking, Mr. Brua,
And if there still are people interested
In cutting literary clothes for heroes   6
They might do worse than mention your string-tie.

There were other killings that day. On the one side, this,
Leeman, a boy of eighteen° and the youngest raider,
Trying to flee from the death-trap of the engine-house
And caught and killed on an islet in the Potomac.   6
The body lay on a tiny shelf of rock
For hours, a sack of clothes still stung by bullets.

648 *Leeman, a boy of eighteen:* See note, line 428, above. According to Villard,
Leeman was born March 20, 1839, and was therefore twenty at the time of the
Harper's Ferry raid.

On the other side—Fontaine Beckham, mayor of the town,
Went to look at Heyward's body with Patrick Higgins.
The slow tears crept to his eyes. He was getting old.   655
He had thought a lot of Heyward. He had no gun
But he had been mayor of the town for a dozen years,
A peaceful, orderly place full of decent people,
And now they were killing people, here in his town,
He had to do something to stop it, somehow or other.   660
He wandered out on the railroad, half-distraught
And peeped from behind a water-tank at the raiders.
"Squire, don't go any farther," said Higgins, "It ain't safe."
He hardly heard him, he had to look out again.
Who were these devils with horns who were shooting his people?   665
They didn't look like devils. One was a boy
Smooth-cheeked, with a bright half-dreamy face, a little
Like Sally's eldest.
                    Suddenly, the air struck him
A stiff, breath-taking blow. "Oh," he said, astonished.
Took a step and fell on his face, shot through the heart.   670
Higgins watched him for twenty minutes, wanting to lift him
But not quite daring. Then he turned away
And went back to the town.
                    The bars had been open all day,
Never to better business.
When the news of Beckham's death spread from bar to bar,   675
It was like putting loco-weed in the whiskey,
The mob came together at once, the American mob,
They mightn't be able to take Brown's last little fort
But there were two prisoners penned in the Wager House.
One was hurt already, Stevens, no fun killing him.   680
But the other was William Thompson, whole and unwounded,
Caught when Brown tried to send his first flag of truce.

They stormed the hotel and dragged him out to the bridge,
Where two men shot him, unarmed, then threw the body
Over the trestle. It splashed in the shallow water,   685
But the slayers kept on firing at the dead face.
The carcass was there for days, a riven target,
Barbarously misused.
                    Meanwhile the armory yard
Was taken by a new band of Beckham's avengers,
The most of Brown's prisoners freed and his last escape cut off.   690

What need to tell of the killing of Kagi the scholar,
The wounding of Oliver Brown and the other deaths?
Only this remains to be told. When the drunken day
Reeled into night, there were left in the engine-house
Five men, alive and unwounded, of all the raiders.   695
Watson and Oliver Brown
Both of them hurt to the death, were stretched on the floor
Beside the corpse of Taylor, the young Canadian.
There was no light, there. It was bitterly cold.
A cold chain of lightless hours that slowly fell   700
In leaden beads between two fingers of stone.
Outside, the fools and the drunkards yelled in the streets,
And, now and then, there were shots. The prisoners talked
And tried to sleep.
          John Brown did not try to sleep,
The live coals of his eyes severed the darkness;   705
Now and then he heard his young son Oliver calling
In the thirsty agony of his wounds, "Oh, kill me!
Kill me and put me out of this suffering!"
John Brown's jaw tightened. "If you must die," he said,
"Die like a man." Toward morning the crying ceased.   710
John Brown called out to the boy but he did not answer.
"I guess he's dead," said John Brown.
                    If his soul wept
They were the incredible tears of the squeezed stone.
He had not slept for two days, but he would not sleep.
The night was a chained, black leopard that he stared 'down,   715
Erect, on his feet. One wonders what sights he saw
In the cloudy mirror of his most cloudy heart,
Perhaps God clothed in a glory, perhaps himself
The little boy who had stolen three brass pins
And been well whipped for it.
              When he was six years old   720
An Indian boy had given him a great wonder,
A yellow marble,° the first he had ever seen.
He treasured it for months but lost it at last,
Boylike. The hurt of the loss took years to heal.
He never quite forgot.
           He could see it now,   725
Smooth, hard and lovely, a yellow, glistening ball,

719–722 *three brass pins* . . . *A yellow marble* . . . : details from Brown's own
account of his youth. See Villard, p. 2.

But it kept rolling away through cracks of darkness
Whenever he tried to catch it and hold it fast.
If he could only touch it, he would be safe,
But it trickled away and away, just out of reach,   730
There by the wall . . .
           Outside the blackened East
Began to tarnish with a faint, grey stain
That caught on the fixed bayonets of the marines.
Lee of Virginia,° Light Horse Harry's son,
Observed it broaden, thinking of many things,   735
But chiefly wanting to get his business done,
A curious, wry, distasteful piece of work
For regular soldiers.
           Therefore to be finished
As swiftly and summarily as possible
Before this yelling mob of drunk civilians   740
And green militia once got out of hand.
His mouth set. Once already he had offered
The honor of the attack to the militia,
Such honor as it was.
           Their Colonel had
Declined with a bright nervousness of haste.   745
"Your men are paid for doing this kind of work.
Mine have their wives and children." Lee smiled briefly,
Remembering that. The smile had a sharp edge.
Well, it was time.
           The whooping crowd fell silent
And scattered, as a single man walked out   750
Toward the engine-house, a letter in his hand.
Lee watched him musingly. A good man, Stuart.°
Now he was by the door and calling out.
The door opened a crack.
           Brown's eyes were there
Over the cold muzzle of a cocked carbine.   755
The parleying began, went on and on,
While the crowd shivered and Lee watched it all
With the strict commonsense of a Greek sword °

---

734 *Lee of Virginia*: Robert Edward Lee (USMA, 1829), then a Brevet-Colonel,
was the son of Henry ("Light Horse Harry") Lee, who had served as a general
officer under Washington. By direction of President Buchanan, Lee took command
of the marine force that had been ordered to Harper's Ferry.   752 *Stuart*: James
Ewell Brown Stuart (USMA, 1854), later Major General "Jeb" Stuart, the most
famous of Confederate cavalry leaders.   758 *a Greek sword*: two-edged, short,
efficient.

And with the same sure readiness.
                              Unperceived,
The dawn ran down the valleys of the wind,   760
Coral-footed dove, tracking the sky with coral . . .
Then, sudden as powder flashing in a pan,
The parleying was done.
                        The door slammed shut.
The little figure of Stuart jumped aside
Waving its cap.
                And the marines came on.   765

Brown watched them come. One hand was on his carbine.
The other felt the pulse of his dying son.
"Sell your lives dear," he said. The rifle-shots
Rattled within the bricked-in engine-room
Like firecrackers set off in a stone jug,   770
And there was a harsh stink of sweat and powder.
There was a moment when the door held firm.
Then it was cracked with sun.
                              Brown fired and missed.
A shadow with a sword ° leaped through the sun.
"That's Ossawattomie,°" said the tired voice   775
Of Colonel Washington.
                        The shadow lunged
And Brown fell to his knees.
                            The sword bent double,
A light sword, better for parades than fighting,
The shadow had to take it in both hands
And fairly rain his blows with it on Brown   780
Before he sank.
                Now two marines were down,
The rest rushed in over their comrades' bodies,
Pinning one man of Brown's against the wall
With bayonets, another to the floor.

Lee, on his rise of ground, shut up his watch.   785
It had been just a quarter of an hour

774 A *shadow with a sword*: Lieutenant Israel Green of Lee's troops, who volun-
teered to lead the twelve-man assault on the engine-house. See Villard, pp. 452–453.
775 *Ossawattomie* [*sic*]: "Old Osawatomie Brown" was the full epithet generally
applied to John Brown after his stand against organized proslavery forces at Osawatomie, Kansas Territory, on August 30, 1856.

Since Stuart gave the signal for the storm,
And now it was over.
                    All but the long dying.°

Cudjo, the negro, watched from the pantry
The smooth glissades° of the dancing gentry,   790
His splay-feet tapping in time to the tune
While his broad face beamed like a drunken moon
At candles weeping in crystal sconces,
Waxed floors glowing like polished bronzes,
Sparkles glinting on Royal Worcester°   795
And all the stir and color and luster
Where Miss Louisa and Miss Amanda,
Proud dolls scissored from silver paper,
With hoopskirts wide as the front veranda
And the gypsy eyes of a caged frivolity,   800
Pointed their toes in a satin caper
To the nonchalant glory of the Quality.

And there were the gentlemen, one and all,
Friends and neighbors of Wingate Hall—
Old Judge Brooke from Little Vermilion   805
With the rusty voice of a cracked horse-pistol
And manners as stiff as a French cotillion.
Huger Shepley and Wainscott Bristol,
Hawky arrogant sons of anger
Who rode like devils and fought like cocks   810
And watched, with an ineffable languor
Their spoilt youth tarnish a dicing-box.
The Cazenove boys and the Cotter brothers,
Pepperalls from Pepperall Ride.
Cummings and Crowls and a dozen others,   815
Every one with a name and a pride.
Sallow young dandies in shirts with ruffles,
Each could dance like a blowing feather,
And each had the voice that Georgia muffles
In the lazy honey of her May weather.   820

---

788 *the long dying*: Brown was captured on October 18, 1859. The month between
the pronouncement of his sentence and his execution on December 2 of that year
was filled with bitter public controversy regarding his conviction.   790 *glissades*:
gliding steps as in ballet.   795 *Royal Worcester*: porcelain made in Worcester, England, since 1751.

Cudjo watched and measured and knew them,
Seeing behind and around and through them
With the shrewd, dispassionate, smiling eye
Of the old-time servant in days gone by.
He couldn't read and he couldn't write,   825
But he knew Quality, black or white,
And even his master could not find
The secret place in the back of his mind
Where witch-bones talked to a scarlet rag
And a child's voice spoke from a conjur-bag.   830
For he belonged to the hidden nation,
The mute, enormous confederation
Of the planted earth and the burden borne
And the horse that is ridden and given corn.
The wind from the brier-patch brought him news   835
That never went walking in white men's shoes
And the grapevine whispered its message faster
Than a horse could gallop across a grave,
Till, long ere the letter could tell the master,
The doomsday rabbits° had told the slave.   840

He was faithful as bread or salt,
A flawless servant without a fault,
Major-domo of Wingate Hall,
Proud of his white folks, proud of it all.
They might scold him, they might let him scold them,   845
And he might know things that he never told them,
But there was a bond, and the bond would hold,
On either side until both were cold.

So he didn't judge, though he knew, he knew,
How the yellow babies down by the Slough,°   850
Had a fourth of their blood from old Judge Brooke,
And where Sue Crowl got her Wingate look,
And the whole, mad business of Shepley's Wager,
And why Miss Harriet married the Major.
And he could trace with unerring ease   855
A hundred devious pedigrees

840 *doomsday rabbits:* a superstition from English tradition. The sight of a white rabbit at dusk foretold a death in the family.   850 *Slough:* a backwater in bottom land, pronounced "sloo."

Of man and horse, from the Squire's Rapscallion
Back to the stock of the Arab stallion,
And the Bristol line through its baffling dozens
Of doubly-removed half-second-cousins,   860
And found a creed and a whole theology
On the accidents of human geology.

He looked for Clay in the dancing whirl,
There he was, coming down the line,
Hand in hand with a dark, slim girl   865
Whose dress was the color of light in wine
Sally Dupré from Appleton
Where the blackshawled ladies rock in the sun
And young things labor and old things rule,
A proud girl, taught in a humbling school   870
That the only daughters of misalliance°
Must harden their hearts against defiance
Of all the uncles and all the aunts
Who succor such offspring of mischance
And wash them clean from each sinful intention   875
With the kindliest sort of incomprehension.

She had the Appleton mouth, it seemed,
And the Appleton way of riding,
But when she sorrowed and if she dreamed,
Something came out from hiding.   880
She could sew all day on an Appleton hem
And look like a saint in plaster,
But when the fiddles began to play
And her feet beat fast but her heart beat faster
An alien grace inhabited them   885
And she looked like her father, the dancing-master,
The scapegrace elegant, "French" Dupré,
Come to the South on a luckless day,
With bright paste buckles sewn on his pumps.
A habit of holding the ace of trumps,   890
And a manner of kissing a lady's hand
Which the county failed to understand.
He stole Sue Appleton's heart away
With eyes that were neither black nor grey,

871 *daughters of misalliance:* girls whose parents are not social equals.

And broke the heart of the Brookes' best mare   8⁹
To marry her safely with time to spare
While the horsewhip uncles toiled behind—
He knew his need and she knew her mind.
And the love they had was as bright and brief
As the dance of the gilded maple-leaf,   9(
Till she died in Charleston of childbed fever
Before her looks or his heart could leave her.
It took the flavor out of his drinking
And left him thoughts he didn't like thinking,
So he wrapped his child in the dead girl's shawl   9
And sent her politely to Uncle Paul
With a black-edged note full of grief and scruples
And half the money he owed his pupils,
Saw that Sue had the finest hearse
That I. O. U.'s could possibly drape her   9
And elegized her in vile French verse
While his hot tears spotted the borrowed paper.

He still had manners, he tried to recover,
But something went when he buried his lover.
No women with eyes could ever scold him   9
But he would make places too hot to hold him,
He shrugged his shoulders and kept descending—
Life was a farce, but it needed ending.
The tag-line° found him too tired to dread it
And he died as he lived, with an air, on credit,   9
In his host's best shirt and a Richmond garret,
Talking to shadows and drinking claret.

He passed when Sally was barely four
And the Appleton kindred breathed once more
And, with some fervor, began to try
To bury the bone of his memory
And strictly expunge from his daughter's semblance
All possible traces of a resemblance.
Which system succeeded, to outward view,
As well as most of such systems do
And resulted in mixing a martyr's potions
For "French" Dupré in his daughter's notions.

919 *tag-line:* the final line of a play.

And slander is sinful and gossip wrong,
But country memories are long,
The Appleton clan is a worthy clan   935
But we remember the dancing-man.
The girl is pretty, the girl seems wise,
The girl was born with her father's eyes.
She will play with our daughters and know our sons,
We cannot offend the Appletons.   940
Bristols and Wingates, Shepleys and Crowls,
We wouldn't hurt her to save our souls.
But after all—and nevertheless—
For one has to think—and one must confess—
And one should admit—but one never knows—   945
So it has gone, and so it goes,
Through the sun and the wind and the rainy weather
Whenever ladies are gathered together,
Till, little by little and stitch by stitch,
The girl is put in her proper niche   950
With all the virtues that we can draw
For someone else's daughter-in-law,
A girl to be kind to, a girl we're lucky in,
A girl to marry some nice Kentuckian,
Some Alabaman, some Carolinian—   955
In fact, if you ask me for my opinion,
There are lots of boys in the Northern sections
And some of them have quite good connections—
She looks charming this evening, doesn't she?
If she danced just a little less *dashingly!*   960

Cudjo watched her as she went by,
"She's got a light foot," thought Cudjo, "Hi!
A light, swif' foot and a talkin' eye!
But you'll need more'n dat, Miss Sally Dupré
Before you proposals with young Marse Clay.   965
And soon as de fiddles finish slewin'
Dey's sixteen things I ought to be doin'.
The Major's sure to be wantin' his dram,
We'll have to be cuttin' a second ham,
And dat trashy high-yaller,° Parker's Guinea,   970
Was sayin' some Yankee name Old John Brown

---

970 *high-yaller:* mulatto.

Has raised de Debil back in Virginny
And freed de niggers all over town,
He's friends with de ha'nts° and steel won't touch him
But the paterollers° is sure to cotch him.   97
How come he want to kick up such a dizziness!
Nigger-business ain't white-folks' business."

There was no real moon in all the soft, clouded night,
The rats of night had eaten the silver cheese,
Though here and there a forgotten crumb of old brightness   98
Gleamed and was blotted.
              But there was no real moon,
No bowl of nacre,° dripping an old delusive
Stain on the changed, strange grass, making faces strange;
There was only a taste of warm rain not yet fallen,
A wine-colored dress, turned black because of no moon,   98
—It would have been spangled in moon—and a broadcloth coat,
And two voices talking together, quite softly, quite calmly.
The dance. Such a lovely dance. But you dance so lightly.
Amanda dances so well. But you dance so lightly.
Louisa looks so pretty in pink, don't you think?   99
Are you fond of Scott? ° Yes, I'm very fond of Scott.
Elegant extracts from gilt-edged volumes called Keepsakes°
And Godey's Lady's Book° words.
              If I were a girl,
A girl in a Godey's Lady's Book steel-engraving,
I would have no body or legs, no aches or delusions.   9
I would know what to do. I would marry a man called Mister.
We would live in a steel-engraving, in various costumes
Designed in the more respectable Paris modes,
With two little boys in little plush hats like muffins,
And two little girls with pantalettes to their chins.   10
I must do that, I think.
              But now my light feet know
That they will be tired and burning with all my dancing

974 *ha'nts:* ghosts.   975 *paterollers:* patrols used to capture runaway slaves.   982
nacre: mother of pearl.   991 *Scott:* Sir Walter Scott's novels of romantic chivalry
were particularly popular in the South. Mark Twain went so far as to declare that
"the Scott disease" was "in great measure responsible for the [Civil] War"; see *Life
on the Mississippi,* Chapter XLVI.   992 *Keepsakes:* any of a number of nineteenth-
century American literary annuals and gift books.   993 *Godey's Lady's Book:* a
Philadelphia monthly miscellany (1830–1892) featuring illustrated ladies fashions.

Before I cool them in the exquisite coolness
Of water or the cool virginal sheets of virgins,
And a face comes swimming toward me out of black broadcloth   1005
And my heart knocks.

                Who are you, why are you here?
Why should you trouble my eyes?

                        No, Mr. Wingate,
I cannot agree with you on the beauties of Byron.°
But why should something melt in the stuff of my hand,
And my voice sound thin in my ears?

                      This face is a face   1010
Like any other face. Did my mother once
Hear thin blood sing in her ears at a voice called Mister?
And wish for—and not wish for—and when the strange thing
Was consummate, then, and she lay in a coil of darkness,
Did she feel so much changed? What is it to be   1015
A woman?

            No, I must live in a steel-engraving.

His voice said. But there was other than his voice.
Something that heard warm rain on unopened flowers
And spoke or tried to speak across swimming blackness
To the slight profile and the wine-colored dress.   1020
Her hair was black. Her eyes might be black or grey.
He could not remember, it irked him not to remember.
But she was just Sally Dupré from Appleton
Only she was not. Only she was a shadow
And a white face—a terrible, white shut face   1025
That looked through windows of inflexible glass
Disdainfully upon the beauties of Byron
And every puppy that ever howled for the moon
To brush warm raindrops across the unopened flower
And so quiet the heart with—what?

                    But you speak to her aunts.   1030
You are Wingate of Wingate Hall. You are not caught
Like a bee drunk with the smell of honey, the smell of sleep,
In a slight flower of glass whose every petal
Shows eyes one cannot remember as black or grey.
You converse easily on elegant subjects   1035

1008 *the beauties of Byron:* Byron's narrative poetry was in vogue, but "controver-
sially daring" in comparison to the works of Scott and others.

Suitable for young ladies.
                    You do not feel
The inexorable stairs of the flesh ascended
By an armed enemy with a naked torch.
This has been felt before, this has been quenched
With fitting casualness in flesh that has   104
A secret stain° of the sun.
                    It is not a subject
Suitable for the converse of young ladies.

"My God, My God, why will she not answer the aching?
My God, My God, to lie at her side through the darkness!"

And yet—is it real—do I really—
                    The wine-colored dress   10
Rose. Broadcloth rose and took her back to the dance.

The nickeled lamp threw a wide yellow disk
On the red tablecloth with the tasseled fringes.
Jack Ellyat put his book down with a slight
Impatient gesture.
                    There was mother, knitting   10
The same grey end of scarf while Father read
The same unaltered paper through the same
Old-fashioned spectacles with the worn bows.

Jane with one apple-cheek and one enshadowed,
Soundlessly conjugated Latin verbs,   10
"Amo, amas, amat," ° through sober lips,
"Amamus, amatis, amant," and still no sound.
He glanced at the clock. On top of it was Phaëton°
Driving bronze, snarling horses down the sharp,
Quicksilver, void, careening gulfs of air.   10
Until they smashed upon a black-marble sea.
The round spiked trophy of the brazen sun
Weighed down his chariot with its heavy load
Of ponderous fire.
                    To be like Phaëton

1040–1041 *flesh that has/A secret stain:* Negro.   1056 *Amo, amas, amat:* from *amare,* to love.   1058 *Phaëton:* son of Helios, the sun god. Having borrowed his father's chariot, the sun, Phaeton (Phaëthon) drove it so recklessly that Zeus struck him down with a thunderbolt to prevent his setting fire to the world.

And drive the trophy-sun!
       But he and his horses   1065
Were frozen in their attitude of snarling,
Frozen forever to the tick of a clock.
Not all the broomstick witches of New England
Could break that congealed motion and cast down
The huge sun thundering on the black marble   1070
Of the mantelpiece, streaked with white veins of foam.

If once such things could happen, all could happen,
The snug, safe world crack up like broken candy
And the young rivers, roaring, rush to the sea;
White bulls that caught the morning on their horns   1075
And shook the secure earth until they found
Some better recompense for life than life,
The untamed ghost, the undiminished star.

But it would not happen. Nothing would ever happen.
He had been here, like this, ten thousand times,   1080
He would be here, like this, ten thousand more,
Until at last the little ticks of the clock
Had cooled what had been hot, and changed the thin,
Blue, forking veins across the back of his hand
Into the big, soft veins on Father's hand.   1085
And the world would be snug.
        And he would sit
Reading the same newspaper, after dinner,
Through spectacles whose bows were getting worn
While a wife knitted on an endless scarf
And a child slowly formed with quiet lips   1090
"Amo, amas, amat," and still no sound.
And it would be over. Over without having been.

His father turned a creaking page of paper
And cleared his throat. "The *Tribune*° calls," he said,
"Brown's raid the work of a madman. Well, they're right, 1095
But—"
    Mrs. Ellyat put her knitting down.
"Are they going to hang him, Will?"
         "It looks that way."

1094 *Tribune: The New York Tribune*, October 19, 1859.

"But, Father, when—"

                  "They have the right, my son,
He broke the law."

               "But, Will! You don't believe—"
A little spark lit Mr. Ellyat's eyes.
"I didn't say I thought that he was wrong.
I said they had the right to hang the man,
But they'll hang slavery with him."

                 A quick pulse
Beat in Jack Ellyat's wrist. Behind his eyes
A bearded puppet creaked upon a rope
And the sky darkened because he was there.
Now it was Mother talking in a strange
Iron-bound voice he'd never heard before.
"I prayed for him in church last Sunday, Will.
I pray for him at home here every night.
I don't know—I don't care—what laws he broke.
I know that he was right. I pray to God
To show the world somehow that he was right
And break these Southern people into knowing!
And I know this— in every house and church,
All through the North—women are praying for him,
Praying for him. And God will hear those prayers."

"He will, my dear," said Mr. Ellyat gently,
"But what will be His answer?"

                 He took her hand,
Smoothing it for a moment. Then she sighed
And turned back to the interminable scarf.
Jack Ellyat's pulse beat faster.

                Women praying,
Praying at night, in every house in the North,
Praying for old John Brown until their knees
Ached with stiff cold.

              Innumerable prayers
Inexorably rising, till the dark
Vault of the midnight was so thronged and packed
The wild geese could not arrow through the storm
Of terrible, ascendant, women's prayers. . . .

The clock struck nine, and Phaëton still stood
Frozenly urging on his frozen horses,

But, for a moment, to Jack Ellyat's eyes,
The congealed hoofs had seemed to paw the air
And the bronze car roll forward.

On Saturday, in Southern market towns,   1135
When I was a boy with twenty cents to spend,
The carts began to drift in with the morning,
And, by the afternoon, the slipshod Square
And all broad Center Street were lined with them;
Moth-eaten mules that whickered at each other   1140
Between the mended shafts of rattletrap wagons,
Mud-spattered buggies, mouldy phaetons,
And, here and there, an ox-cart from the hills
Whose solemn team had shoulders of rough, white rock,
Innocent noses, black and wet as snailshells,   1145
And that inordinate patience in their eyes.

There always was a Courthouse in the Square,
A cupolaed Courthouse, drowsing Time away
Behind the grey-white pillars of its porch
Like an old sleepy judge in a spotted gown;   1150
And, down the Square, always a languid jail
Of worn, uneven brick with moss in the cracks
Or stone weathered the grey of weathered pine.
The plump jail-master wore a linen duster
In summer, and you used to see him sit   1155
Tilted against the wall in a pine-chair,
Spitting reflectively in the warm dust
While endless afternoons slowly dissolved
Into the longer shadow, the dust-blue twilight.
Higgledy-piggledy days—days that are gone—   1160
The trotters are dead, all the yellow-painted sulkies
Broken for firewood—the old Courthouse grins
Through new false-teeth of Alabama limestone—
The haircloth lap-robe weeps on a Ford radiator—

But I have seen the old Courthouse. I have seen   1165
The flyspecked windows and the faded flag
Over the judge's chair, touched the scuffed walls,
Spat in the monumental brass spittoons
And smelt the smell that never could be aired,
Although one opened windows for a year,   1170

The unforgettable, intangible
Mixture of cheap cigars, worm-eaten books,
Sweat, poverty, negro hair-oil, grief and law.
I have seen the long room packed with quiet men,
Fit to turn mob, if need were, in a flash—
Cocked-pistol men, so lazily attentive
Their easy languor knocked against your ribs
As, hour by hour, the lawyers droned along,
And minute on creeping minute, your cold necknape
Waited the bursting of the firecracker,
The flare of fury.
          And yet, that composed fury
Burnt itself out, unflaring—was held down
By a dry, droning voice, a faded flag.
The kettle never boiled, the pistol stayed
At cock but the snake-head hammer never fell. . . .
The little boys climbed down beyond the windows. . . .

So, in the cupolaed Courthouse there in Charlestown,
When the jail-guards had carried in the cot
Where Brown lay like a hawk with a broken back,
I hear the rustle of the moving crowd,
The buzz outside, taste the dull, heavy air,
Smell the stale smell and see the country carts
Hitched in the streets.
          For a long, dragging week
Of market-Saturdays the trial went on.
The droning voices rise and fall and rise.
Stevens lies quiet on his mattress, breathing
The harsh and difficult breath of a dying man,
Although not dying then.
          Beyond the Square
The trees are dry, but all the dry leaves not fallen—
Yellow leaves falling through a grey-blue dusk,
The first winds of November whirl and scatter them. . . .

Read as you will in any of the books,
The details of the thing, the questions and answers,
How sometimes Brown would walk, sometimes was carried,
At first would hardly plead, half-refused counsel,
Accepted later, made up witness-lists,
Grew fitfully absorbed in his defense,

Only to flare in temper at his first lawyers
And drive them from the case.
                         Questions and answers,
Wheels creaking in a void.
                              Sometimes he lay   1210
Quiet upon his cot, the hawk-eyes staring.
Sometimes his fingers moved mechanically
As if at their old task of sorting wool,
Fingertips that could tell him in the dark
Whether the wool they touched was from Ohio   1215
Or from Vermont. They had the shepherd's gift.
It was his one sure talent.
                              Questions creaking
Uselessly back and forth.
                              No one can say
That the trial was not fair. The trial was fair,
Painfully fair by every rule of law,   1220
And that it was made not the slightest difference.
The law's our yardstick, and it measures well
Or well enough when there are yards to measure.
Measure a wave with it, measure a fire,
Cut sorrow up in inches, weigh content.   1225
You can weigh John Brown's body well enough,
But how and in what balance weigh John Brown?

He had the shepherd's gift, but that was all.
He had no other single gift for life.
Some men are pasture. Death turns back to pasture,   1230
Some are fire-opals on that iron wrist,
Some the deep roots of wisdoms not yet born.
John Brown was none of these,
He was a stone,
A stone eroded to a cutting edge   1235
By obstinacy, failure and cold prayers.
Discredited farmer, dubiously involved
In lawsuit after lawsuit, Shubel Morgan°
Fantastic bandit of the Kansas border,
Red-handed murderer at Pottawattomie,   1240
Cloudy apostle, whooped along to death
By those who do no violence themselves

1238 *Shubel Morgan:* an alias used by John Brown in Kansas.

But only buy the guns to have it done,
Sincere of course, as all fanatics are,
And with a certain minor-prophet air,   124
That fooled the world to thinking him half-great
When all he did consistently was fail.

So far one advocate.
                    But there is this.

Sometimes there comes a crack in Time itself.
Sometimes the earth is torn by something blind.   12?
Sometimes an image that has stood so long
It seems implanted as the polar star
Is moved against an unfathomed force
That suddenly will not have it any more.
Call it the *mores,* call it God or Fate,   12
Call it Mansoul° or economic law,
That force exists and moves.
                    And when it moves
It will employ a hard and actual stone
To batter into bits an actual wall
And change the actual scheme of things.
                    John Brown   12
Was such a stone—unreasoning as the stone,
Destructive as the stone, and, if you like,
Heroic and devoted as such a stone.
He had no gift for life, no gift to bring
Life but his body and a cutting edge,   12
But he knew how to die.
                    And yardstick law
Gave him six weeks to burn that hoarded knowledge
In one swift fire whose sparks fell like live coals
On every State in the Union.
                    Listen now,
Listen, the bearded lips are speaking now,   12
There are no more guerilla-raids to plan,
There are no more hard questions to be solved
Of right and wrong, no need to beg for peace,
Here is the peace unbegged, here is the end,
Here is the insolence of the sun cast off,   12
Here is the voice already fixed with night.

1256 *Mansoul:* the allegorical city of the soul in John Bunyan's *The Holy War.*

JOHN BROWN'S SPEECH

I have, may it please the Court, a few words to say.°

In the first place I deny everything but what I have all along admitted: of a design on my part to free slaves. . . .   1280

Had I interfered in the matter which I admit, and which I admit has been fairly proved . . . had I so interfered in behalf of the rich, the powerful, the intelligent, or the so-called great . . . and suffered and sacrificed, what I have in this interference, it would have been all right. Every man in this Court would have deemed it an act worthy   1285 of reward rather than punishment.

I see a book kissed which I suppose to be the Bible, or at least the New Testament, which teaches me that all things whatsoever I would that men should do unto me, I should do even so to them. It teaches me further to remember them that are in bonds as bound   1290 with them. I endeavored to act up to that instruction. I say I am yet too young to understand that God is any respecter of persons. I believe that to have interfered as I have done, as I have always freely admitted I have done in behalf of His despised poor, I did no wrong, but right. Now, if it is deemed necessary that I should   1295 forfeit my life for the furtherance of the ends of justice and mingle my blood further with the blood of my children and with the blood of millions in this slave country whose rights are disregarded by wicked, cruel and unjust enactments, I say, let it be done.

Let me say one word further. I feel entirely satisfied with the   1300 treatment I have received on my trial. Considering all the circumstances, it has been more generous than I expected. But I feel no consciousness of guilt. I have stated from the first what was my intention and what was not. I never had any design against the liberty of any person, nor any disposition to commit treason or incite slaves   1305 to rebel or make any general insurrection. I never encouraged any man to do so but always discouraged any idea of that kind.

Let me say also, in regard to the statements made by some of those connected with me, I hear it has been stated by some of them that I have induced them to join with me. But the contrary is true.   1310 I do not say this to injure them, but as regretting their weakness. Not one but joined me of his own accord, and the greater part at their own expense. A number of them I never saw, and never had a word

1277–1315 Benét has here quoted from a declaration made by Brown in Charlestown on November 2, 1859.

of conversation with, till the day they came to me, and that was for
the purpose I have stated.

    Now I have done.   1̇

The voice ceased. There was a deep, brief pause.
The judge pronounced the formal words of death.
One man, a stranger, tried to clap his hands.
The foolish sound was stopped.
There was nothing but silence then.

                                   No cries in the court,   1
No roar, no slightest murmur from the thronged street,
As Brown went back to jail between his guards.
The heavy door shut behind them.
There was a noise of chairs scraped back in the court-room
And that huge sigh of a crowd turning back into men.   1

A month between the sentence and the hanging.
A month of endless visitors, endless letters.
A Mrs. Russell ° came to clean his coat.
A sculptor° sketched him.

                        In the anxious North,
The anxious Dr. Howe most anxiously   1
Denied all godly connection with the raid,
And Gerrit Smith° conveniently went mad
For long enough to sponge his mind of all
Memory of such an unsuccessful deed.
Only the tough, swart-minded Higginson   1
Kept a grim decency, would not deny.
Pity the portly men, pity the pious,
Pity the fool who lights the powder-mine,
They need your counterfeit penny, they will live long.

In Charlestown meanwhile, there were whispers of rescue.   1
Brown told them,
"I am worth now infinitely more to die than to live."

1328 *Mrs. Russell:* Mrs. Thomas Russell, wife of a Boston judge in whose home
Brown stayed in April 1857, while attempting to arrange support for his antislavery
operations in Kansas.   1329 *A sculptor:* Edward Augustus Brackett of Boston.
1332 *Gerrit Smith:* New York philanthropist, Congressman, and abolitionist. Smith
was a close friend of Brown's, who "went insane" and after recovery denied any
recollection of preparations for the Harper's Ferry raid.

And lived his month so, busily.
A month of trifles building up a legend
And letters in a pinched, firm handwriting   1345
Courageous, scriptural, misspelt and terse,
Sowing a fable everywhere they fell
While the town filled with troops.
                          The Governor came,
Enemies, friends, militia-cavaliers,
Old Border Foes.
                          The month ebbed into days,   1350
The wife and husband met for the last time,
The last letter was written:

"To be inscribed ° on the old family Monument at North Elba,°
Oliver Brown born 1839 was killed at Harpers Ferry, Va. Nov. 17th 1859
Watson Brown born 1835 was wounded at Harpers Ferry Nov. 17th and 1355
     died Nov. 19th 1859
(My Wife can) supply *blank* dates to above
John Brown born May 9th 1800 was executed at Charlestown Va.
     December 2nd 1859."

At last the clear warm day, so slow to come.   1360

          The North that had already now begun
          To mold his body into crucified Christ's,
          Hung fables about those hours—saw him move
          Symbolically, kiss a negro child,°
          Do this and that, say things he never said,   1365
          To swell the sparse, hard outlines of the event
          With sentimental omen.
                          It was not so.
          He stood on the jail-porch in carpet-slippers,
          Clad in a loose ill-fitting suit of black,
          Tired farmer waiting for his team to come.   1370
          He left one last written message:

1353–1357 *To be inscribed . . . :* Both Oliver and Watson Brown died at Harper's Ferry on October 18, 1859, not on the November dates shown. See Benét's "Note," p. xiii. 1353 *North Elba:* North Elba, New York, a Negro settlement on the lands of Gerrit Smith in the Adirondacks; see line 1332, above. John Brown moved his family there in the spring of 1849. See Villard, pp. 70–77. 1364 *kiss a negro child:* This detail of the Brown legend was widely accepted as fact.

"I, John Brown, am now quite *certain* that the crimes of this *guilty land: will* never be purged *away:* but with Blood. I had *as I now think: vainly* flattered myself that without *very much* bloodshed; it might be done." °   13°

They did not hang him in the jail or the Square.
The two white horses dragged the rattling cart
Out of the town. Brown sat upon his coffin.
Beyond the soldiers lay the open fields
Earth-colored, sleepy with unfallen frost.   13
The farmer's eye took in the bountiful land.
"This *is* a beautiful country," said John Brown.

The gallows-stairs were climbed, the death-cap fitted.
Behind the gallows,
Before a line of red-and-grey cadets,   13
A certain odd Professor T. J. Jackson°
Watched disapprovingly the ragged militia
Deploy for twelve long minutes ere they reached
Their destined places.
The Presbyterian sabre of his soul   13
Was moved by a fey° breath.
                            He saw John Brown,
A tiny blackened scrap of paper-soul
Fluttering above the Pit that Calvin° barred
With bolts of iron on the unelect;
He heard the just, implacable Voice speak out   1°
"Depart ye wicked to eternal fire."
And sternly prayed that God might yet be moved
To save the predestined cinder from the flame.

Brown did not hear the prayer. The rough black cloth
Of the death-cap hid his eyes now. He had seen   1
The Blue Ridge Mountains couched in their blue haze.
Perhaps he saw them still, behind his eyes—

1372–1375 In this case, Benét's quotation is exact. 1386 *Professor T. J. Jackson:* Professor of Natural and Experimental Philosophy at Virginia Military Institute (1851–1861), later Lieutenant General "Stonewall" Jackson, CSA. 1391 *fey:* fated; here, predestined. 1393 *Calvin:* John Calvin (1509–1564), Protestant reformer, one of the founders of Presbyterianism.

Perhaps just cloth, perhaps nothing any more.
"I shall look unto the hills from whence cometh my help." °

The hatchet cut the cord. The greased trap fell.   1405

Colonel Preston:

"So perish all such enemies of Virginia,
All such enemies of the Union,
All such foes of the human race." °

———————

John Brown's body lies a-mouldering in the grave.
He will not come again with foolish pikes   1410
And a pack of desperate boys to shadow the sun.
He has gone back North. The slaves have forgotten his eyes.
John Brown's body lies a-mouldering in the grave.
John Brown's body lies a-mouldering in the grave.
Already the corpse is changed, under the stone,   1415
The strong flesh rotten, the bones dropping away.
Cotton will grow next year, in spite of the skull.
Slaves will be slaves next year, in spite of the bones.
Nothing is changed, John Brown, nothing is changed.

"There is a song in my bones. There is a song   1420
In my white bones."

I hear no song. I hear
Only the blunt seeds growing secretly
In the dark entrails of the preparate earth,
The rustle of the cricket under the leaf,   1425
The creaking of the cold wheel of the stars.

"Bind my white bones together—hollow them
To skeleton pipes of music. When the wind
Blows from the budded Spring, the song will blow."

I hear no song. I only hear the roar   1430
Of the Spring freshets, and the gushing voice
Of mountain-brooks that overflow their banks,
Swollen with melting ice and crumbled earth.

1404 *"I shall look unto the hills . . . "*: Psalm 121. 1406–1408 The quotation
is from Colonel J. T. L. Preston, witness to the execution. See Villard, pp. 556–557.

"That is my song.
It is made of water and wind. It marches on."   1430

No, John Brown's body lies a-mouldering,
A-mouldering.

"My bones have been washed clean
And God blows through them with a hollow sound,
And God has shut his wildfire in my dead heart."   1440

I hear it now,
Faint, faint as the first droning flies of March,
Faint as the multitudinous, tiny sigh
Of grasses underneath a windy scythe.

"It will grow stronger."   1444

It has grown stronger. It is marching on.
It is a throbbing pulse, a pouring surf,
It is the rainy gong of the Spring sky
Echoing,
John Brown's body,   1450
John Brown's body.
But still it is not fierce. I find it still
More sorrowful than fierce.

"You have not heard it yet. You have not heard
The ghosts that walk in it, the shaking sound."   1455

Strong medicine,
Bitter medicine of the dead,
I drink you now. I hear the unloosed thing,
The anger of the ripe wheat—the ripened earth
Sullenly quaking like a beaten drum   1460
From Kansas to Vermont. I hear the stamp
Of the ghost-feet. I hear the ascending sea.

>   "Glory, Glory, Hallelujah,
>   Glory, Glory, Hallelujah,
>   Glory, Glory, Hallelujah!" °   1465

1465 *Glory, Glory, Hallelujah!*: See note, Invocation, line 132.

What is this agony of the marching dust?
What are these years ground into hatchet blades?

"Ask the tide why it rises with the moon,
My bones and I have risen like that tide
And an immortal anguish plucks us up   1470
And will not hide us till our song is done."

The phantom drum diminishes—the year
Rolls back. It is only winter still, not spring,
The snow still flings its white on the new grave,
Nothing is changed, John Brown, nothing is changed   1475
John . . . Brown . . .

⚜ BOOK TWO ⚜

A smoke-stained Stars-and-Stripes droops from a broken tooth-pick and ninety tired men march out of fallen Sumter to their ships,° drums rattling and colors flying.

Their faces are worn and angry, their bellies empty and cold, but the stubborn salute° of a gun, fifty times repeated, keeps their backs   5 straight as they march out, and answers something stubborn and mute in their flesh.

Beauregard, ° *beau sabreur,*° hussar-sword ° with the gilded hilt, the gilded metal of the guard twisted into lovelocks and roses, vain as Murat,° dashing as Murat, Pierre Gustave Toutant Beauregard is a pose   10 of conquering courtesy under a palmetto-banner.° The lugubrious little march goes grimly by his courtesy, he watches it unsmiling, a light half-real, half that of invisible footlights on his French, dark, handsome face.

The stone falls in the pool, the ripples spread.   15
The colt in the Long Meadow kicked up his heels.
"That was a fly," he thought, "It's early for flies."
But being alive, in April,° was too fine
For flies or anything else to bother a colt.
He kicked up his heels again, this time in pure joy,   20
And started to run a race with the wind and his shadow.
After the stable stuffiness, the sun.
After the straw-littered boards, the squelch of the turf.
His little hoofs felt lighter than dancing-shoes,
He scared himself with a blue-jay, his heart was a leaf.   25
He was pure joy in action, he was the unvexed
Delight of all moving lightness and swift-footed pace,

2 *march out . . . to their ships:* On April 4, 1861, Federal troops surrendered Fort Sumter in Charleston (South Carolina) harbor. Under terms of the agreement, they were evacuated to the United States fleet. 5 *stubborn salute:* before departing, the Union forces fired a final fifty-gun salute to their flag. 8 *Beauregard:* Brigadier General P. G. T. Beauregard of the Confederate Army; Louisiana-bred West Point officer, Class of 1848; when Louisiana seceded, he resigned his commission in the United States Army and with it his newly appointed position as Superintendent of the U.S. Military Academy. *beau sabreur:* dashing soldier, especially a cavalryman. *hussar-sword:* of the type used by European light cavalry; hussar units were noted for their brilliant, elaborately decorated uniforms. 10 *Murat:* Joachim Murat (1767–1815), French cavalry officer, Napoleon's brother-in-law and one of his marshals. 11 *palmetto-banner:* flag of South Carolina. 18 *April:* April 1861.

The pride of the flesh, the young Spring neighing and rearing.
Sally Dupré called to him from the fence.
He came like a charge in a spatter of clean-cut clods,   30
Ears back, eyes wide and wild with folly and youth.
He drew up snorting.

             She laughed and brushed at her skirt
Where the mud had splashed it.

                    "There, Star—there, silly boy!
Why won't you ever learn sense?"

                But her eyes were hot,
Her hands were shaking as she offered the sugar   35
—Long-fingered, appleblossom-shadow hands—
Star blew at the sugar once, then mumbled it up.
She patted the pink nose. "There, silly Star!
That's for Fort Sumter, Star!" How hot her eyes were!
"Star, do you know you're a Confederate horse?   40
Do you know I'm going to call you Beauregard?"

Star whinnied, and asked for more sugar. She put her hand
On his neck for a moment that matched the new green leaves
And sticky buds of April.

                You would have said
They were grace in quietness, seen so, woman and horse. . . .   45

The widened ripple breaks against a stone
The heavy noon walks over Chancellorsville
On brazen shoes, but where the squadron rode
Into the ambush, the blue flies are coming
To blow on the dead meat.°   50

Carter, the telegraph-operator, sighed
And propped his eyes awake again.

                  He was tired.
Dog-tired, stone-tired, body and mind burnt up
With too much poker last night and too little sleep.
He hated the Sunday° trick. It was Riley's turn   55
To take it, but Riley's wife was having a child.

47–50 *Chancellorsville . . . the ambush . . . dead meat:* The Battle of Chancellorsville is generally considered the high noon of Confederate fortunes. While the foreshadowing indicated by the squadron in ambush is difficult to relate to any specific event, it nonetheless suggests the eventual fate of the southern cavalry, the decline of which parallels that of the Old South. 55 *Sunday:* April 14, 1861, the day Fort Sumter was evacuated.

He cursed the child and the wife and Sunday and Riley.
Nothing ever happened at Stroudsburg Siding°
And yet he had to be here and keep awake
With the flat, stale taste of too little sleep in his mouth   60
And wait for nothing to happen.
                     His bulky body
Lusted for sleep with every muscle and nerve.
He'd rather have sleep than a woman or whiskey or money.
He'd give up the next three women that might occur
For ten minutes' sleep, he'd never play poker again,   65
He'd—battered face beginning to droop on his hands—
Sleep—women—whiskey—eyelids too heavy to lift—
"Yes, Ma, I said, 'Now I lay me.' "—
                   The sounder chattered
And his head snapped back with a sharp, neck-breaking jerk.
By God, he'd nearly— *chat—chitter-chatter-chat-chat—*   70
For a moment he took it in without understanding
And then the vein in his forehead began to swell
And his eyes bulged wide awake.
                "By Jesus!" he said,
And stared at the sounder as if it had turned to a snake.
"By Jesus!" he said, "By Jesus, they've done it!" he said.   75

The cruelty of cold trumpets wounds the air.
The ponderous princes draw their gauntlets on.
The captains fit their coal-black armor on.

Judah P. Benjamin,° the dapper Jew,
Seal-sleek, black-eyed, lawyer and epicure,   80
Able, well-hated, face alive with life,
Looked round the council-chamber with the slight
Perpetual smile he held before himself
Continually like a silk-ribbed fan.
Behind the fan, his quick, shrewd, fluid mind   85
Weighed Gentiles in an old balance.
                There they were.
Toombs, the tall, laughing, restless Georgian,
As fine to look at as a yearling bull,

51–58 *Carter . . . Riley . . . Stroudsburg Siding:* all apparently fictitious.   79 *Judah P. Benjamin* Benjamin was a leading barrister and U.S. Senator from Louisiana before the war, the first Attorney General (later Secretary of War and Secretary of State) of the Confederacy, and reputedly Davis' closest adviser.

As hard to manage.
                    Stephens, sickly and pale,   9(
Sweet-voiced, weak-bodied, ailingly austere,
The mind's thin steel wearing the body out,
The racked intelligence, the crippled charm.
Mallory—Reagan—Walker—at the head
Davis.°
            The mind behind the silk-ribbed fan
Was a dark prince, clothed in an Eastern stuff,   9
Whose brown hands cupped about a crystal egg
That filmed with colored cloud. The eyes stared, searching.

"I am the Jew.° What am I doing here?
The Jew is in my blood and in my hands,
The lonely, bitter and quicksilver drop,   10(
The stain of myrrh that dyes no Gentile mind
With tinctures out of the East and the sad blare
Of the curled ramshorn on Atonement Day.°
A river runs between these men and me,
A river of blood and time and liquid gold,   10!
—Oh white rivers of Canaan,° running the night!—
And we are colleagues. And we speak to each other
Across the roar of that river, but no more.
I hide myself behind a smiling fan.
They hide themselves behind a Gentile mask   11
And, if they fall, they will be lifted up,
Being the people, but if I once fall
I fall forever, like the rejected stone.°
That is the Jew of it, my Gentile friends,
To see too far ahead and yet go on   11
And I can smile at it behind my fan
With a drowned mirth that you would find uncouth
For here we are, the makeshift Cabinet
Of a new nation, gravely setting down

86–94 *There they were. . . . :* General Robert Toombs, Secretary of State; Alexander Stephens, Vice-President; Stephen R. Mallory, Secretary of Navy; John H. Reagan, Postmaster-General; General Leroy P. Walker, Secretary of War; Jefferson Davis, President.   98–124 *I am the Jew. . . . :* Benjamin was the son of an English tradesman of Jewish descent and a West Indian Jewess of Spanish and Portuguese blood. His life was a series of great achievements and profound personal tragedies. 103 *ramshorn on Atonement Day:* deriving from Exodus 30:10 and Leviticus 16. 106 *Canaan:* the promised land.   113 *like the rejected stone:* See Psalms 118:22, Mark 12:11.

Rules, precedents and cautions, never once   120
Admitting aloud the cold, plain Franklin sense
That if we do not hang together now
We shall undoubtedly hang separately.°
It is the Jew, to see too far ahead—

I wonder what they're doing in the North,   125
And how their Cabinet shapes, and how they take
Their railsplitter, and if they waste their time
As we waste ours and Mr. Davis's.

Jefferson Davis, pride of Mississippi,
First President of the Confederate States,   130
What are you thinking now?
                        Your eyes look tired.
Your face looks more and more like John Calhoun.°
And that is just, because you are his son
In everything but blood, the austere child
Of his ideas, the flower of states-rights.   135
I will not gird against you, Jefferson Davis.
I sent you a challenge once,° but that's forgotten,
And though your blood runs differently from mine,
The Jew salutes you from behind his fan,
Because you are the South he fell in love with   140
When that young black-haired girl with the Gentile-eyes,
Proud, and a Catholic, and with honey-lips,
First dinted her French heels upon his heart. . . .
We have changed since, but the remembered Spring
Can change no more, even in the Autumn smokes.   145
We cannot help that havoc of the heart°
But my changed mind remembers half the spring
And shall till winter falls.
                        No, Jefferson Davis,

121–123 *hang together . . . hang separately:* a paraphrase of Franklin's remark at
the signing of the Declaration of Independence.   132 *John Calhoun:* Senator from
South Carolina and former Vice-President, recognized intellectual leader of the South.
137 *I sent you a challenge once:* Benjamin, offended by Davis during a debate in
the Senate June 8, 1858, delivered a challenge; Davis apologized at the next day's
session and the incident was closed.   141–146 *young black-haired girl . . . that
havoc of the heart:* Benjamin's wife, a French-Creole beauty, was sixteen when they
married in 1833. A devout Catholic more interested in society than domesticity, and
having limited education, she was a poor match for him. In 1845 she left her husband and moved to Paris, where he visited her almost annually.

You are not she—you are not the warm night
On the bayou, or the New Orleans lamps,   150
The white-wine bubbles in the crystal cup,
The almond blossoms, sleepy with the sun:
But, nevertheless, you are the South in word,
Deed, thought and temper, the cut cameo
Brittle but durable, refined but fine,   155
The hands well-shaped, not subtle, but not weak,
The mind set in tradition but not unjust,
The generous slaveholder, the gentleman
Who neither forces his gentility
Nor lets it be held lightly—
                              and yet, and yet   160
I think you look too much like John Calhoun,
I think your temper is too brittly-poised,
I think your hands too scholar-sensitive,
And though they say you mingle in your voice
The trumpet and the harp, I think it lacks   165
That gift of warming men which coarser voices
Draw from the common dirt you tread upon
But do not take in your hands. I think you are
All things except success, all honesty
Except the ultimate honesty of the earth,   170
All talents but the genius of the sun.
And yet I would not have you otherwise,
Although I see too clearly what you are.

Except—except—oh honeydropping Spring,
Oh black-haired woman with the Gentile eyes!   175
Tell me, you Gentiles, when your Gentile wives
Pray in the church for you and for the South,
How do they pray?—not in that lulling voice
Where some drowned bell of France makes undertones
To the warm river washing the levee.   180
You do not have so good a prayer as mine.
You cannot have so good a prayer as mine."

———————

Lincoln, six feet one in his stocking feet,
The lank man, knotty and tough as a hickory rail,
Whose hands were always too big for white-kid gloves,   185
Whose wit was a coonskin sack of dry, tall tales,
Whose weathered face was homely as a plowed field—

Abraham Lincoln, who padded up and down
The sacred White House in nightshirt and carpet-slippers,
And yet could strike young hero-worshipping Hay°   190
As dignified past any neat, balanced, fine
Plutarchan sentences carved in a Latin bronze;
The low clown out of the prairies, the ape-buffoon,
The small-town lawyer, the crude small-time politician,
State-character but comparative failure at forty   195
In spite of ambition enough for twenty Caesars,
Honesty rare as a man without self-pity,
Kindness as large and plain as a prairie wind,
And a self-confidence like an iron bar:
This Lincoln, President now by the grace of luck,   200
Disunion, politics, Douglas and a few speeches°
Which make the monumental booming of Webster
Sound empty as the belly of a burst drum,
Lincoln shambled in to the Cabinet meeting
And sat, ungainly and awkward. Seated so   205
He did not seem so tall nor quite so strange
Though he was strange enough. His new broadcloth suit
Felt tight and formal across his big shoulders still
And his new shiny top-hat was not yet battered
To the bulging shape of the old familiar hat   210
He'd worn at Springfield,° stuffed with its hoard of papers.
He was pretty tired. All week the office-seekers
Had plagued him as the flies in fly-time plague
A gaunt-headed, patient horse. The children weren't well
And Mollie° was worried about them so sharp with her tongue.   215
But he knew Mollie and tried to let it go by.
Men tracked dirt in the house and women liked carpets.
Each had a piece of the right, that was all most people could stand.

Look at his Cabinet here. There were Seward and Chase,°
Both of them good men, couldn't afford to lose them,   220
But Chase hates Seward like poison and Seward hates Chase
And both of 'em think they ought to be President

190 *hero-worshipping Hay:* John Hay was a private secretary to Lincoln; his "diary rings with admiration. . . ." See Nathaniel W. Stephenson, *Lincoln,** pp. 324–325.
201 *Douglas and a few speeches:* The famous debates with Stephen Douglas, Lincoln's Democratic opponent for the Senate in 1856, did much to gain for Lincoln the national attention necessary to win the presidency in 1860. 211 *Springfield:* Springfield, Illinois. 215 *Mollie:* Mary Todd Lincoln. 219 *Seward and Chase:* William H. Seward, Secretary of State; Salmon P. Chase, Secretary of Treasury.

Instead of me. When Seward wrote me that letter°
The other day, he practically told me so.
I suppose a man who was touchy about his pride   225
Would send them both to the dickens when he found out,
But I can't do that as long as they do their work.
The Union's too big a horse to keep changing the saddle
Each time it pinches you. As long as you're sure
The saddle fits, you're bound to put up with the pinches   230
And not keep fussing the horse.
                          When I was a boy
I remember figuring out when I went to town
That if I had just one pumpkin to bump in a sack
It was hard to carry, but once you could get two pumpkins,
One in each end of the sack, it balanced things up.   235
Seward and Chase'll do for my pair of pumpkins.
And as for me—if anyone else comes by
Who shows me that he can manage this job of mine
Better than I can—well, he can have the job.
It's harder sweating than driving six cross mules,   240
But I haven't run into that other fellow yet
And till or supposing I meet him, the job's my job
And nobody else's.
                    Seward and Chase don't know that.
They'll learn it, in time.
                    Wonder how Jefferson Davis
Feels, down there in Montgomery,° about Sumter.   245
He must be thinking pretty hard and fast,
For he's an able man, no doubt of that.
We were born less than forty miles apart,°
Less than a year apart—he got the start
Of me in age, and raising too, I guess,   250
In fact, from all you hear about the man,
If you set out to pick one of us two
For President, by birth and folks and schooling,
General raising, training up in office,

---

223 *that letter:* a private paper, entitled "Thoughts for the President's Con-
sideration," which expressed the view that there should be a single mind leading
governments in crisis and that Lincoln, if he was not able to handle it himself,
should pass the responsibility to a member of the Cabinet. See Ida M. Tarbell,
*The Life of Abraham Lincoln,** II, 28–30.   245. *Montgomery:* Montgomery, Alabama, capital of the Confederacy.   248 *born less than forty miles apart:* in central
Kentucky.

I guess you'd pick him, nine times out of ten   255
And yet, somehow, I've got to last him out.

These thoughts passed through the mind in a moment's flash.
Then that mind turned to business.
                                        It was the calling
Of seventy-five thousand volunteers.°

Shake out the long line of verse like a lanyard of woven steel   260
And let us praise while we can what things no praise can deface,
The corn that hurried so fast to be ground in an iron wheel
The obdurate, bloody dream that slept before it grew base.

Not the silk flag and the shouts, the catchword patrioteers,
The screaming noise of the press, the preachers who howled for blood,   265
But a certain and stubborn pith in the hearts of the cannoneers
Who hardly knew their guns before they died in the mud.

They came like a run of salmon where the ice-fed Kennebec° flings
Its death at the arrow-silver of the packed and mounting host,
They came like the young deer trooping to the ford by Eutaw Springs,°   270
Their new horns fuzzy with velvet, their coats still rough with the frost.

North and South they assembled, one cry and the other cry,
And both are ghosts to us now, old drums hung up on a wall,
But they were the first hot wave of youth too-ready to die,
And they went to war with an air, as if they went to a ball.   275

Dress-uniform boys who rubbed their buttons brighter than gold,
And gave them to girls for flowers and raspberry-lemonade,
Unused to the sick fatigue, the route-march made in the cold,
The stink of the fever camps, the tarnish rotting the blade.

We in our time have seen that impulse going to war°   280
And how that impulse is dealt with. We have seen the circle complete.
The ripe wheat wasted like trash between the fool and the whore.
We cannot praise again that anger of the ripe wheat.

259 *seventy-five thousand volunteers:* Lincoln's first decisive act to meet the crisis
was to call for 75,000 men for a three-month period, the maximum allowable under
existing laws, which limited the period of service to one month beyond the next meeting of Congress.   268 *Kennebec:* Kennebec River, Maine; Arnold's route to Quebec,
October 1775.   270 *Eutaw Springs:* Eutaw Springs, South Carolina, site of Nathaniel Greene's victory, September 1781.   280 *We in our time . . . going to war:*
World War I.

This we have seen as well, distorted and half-forgotten
In what came before and after, where the blind went leading the blind,   28
The first swift rising of youth before the symbols were rotten,
The price too much to pay, the payment haughty in kind.

So with these men and then. They were much like the men you know,
Under the beards and the strangeness of clothes with a different fit.
They wrote mush-notes to their girls and wondered how it would go,   29
Half-scared, half-fierce at the thought, but none yet ready to quit.

Georgia, New York, Virginia, Rhode Island, Florida, Maine,
Piney-woods squirrel-hunter and clerk with the brand-new gun,
Thus they were marshalled and drilled, while Spring turned Summer
      again,
Until they could stumble toward death at gartersnake-crooked Bull Run.°   29

Wingate sat in his room at night
Between the moon and the candle-light,
Reading his Byron with knitted brows,
While his mind drank in the peace of his house,
It was long past twelve, and the night was deep   3(
With moonlight and silence and wind and sleep,
And the small, dim noises, thousand-fold,
That all old houses and forests hold.
The boards that creak for nothing at all,
The leaf that rustles, the bough that sighs,   3
The nibble of mice in the wainscot-wall,
And the slow clock ticking the time that dies
All distilled in a single sound
Like a giant breathing underground,
A sound more sleepy than sleep itself.   3
Wingate put his book on the shelf
And went to the window. It was good
To walk in the ghost through a silver wood
And set one's mettle against the far
Bayonet-point of the fixed North Star.   3
He stood there a moment, wondering.
North Star, wasp with the silver sting
Blue-nosed star on the Yankee banners,

295 *stumble toward death at . . . Bull Run:* scene of the first major battle of the
war, July 21, 1861.

We are coming against you to teach you manners!
With crumbs of thunder and wreaths of myrtle   320
And cannon that dance to a Dixie chorus,
With a song that bites like a snapping-turtle
And the tiger-lily of Summer before us,
To pull you down like a torn bandanna,
And drown you deeper than the Savannah!   325

And still, while his arrogance made its cry,
He shivered a little, wondering why.

There was his uniform, grey as ash,
The boots that shone like a well-rubbed table,
The tassels of silk on the colored sash   330
And sleek Black Whistle down in the stable,
The housewife,° stitched from a beauty's fan,
The pocket-Bible with Mother's writing,
The sabre never yet fleshed in man,
And all the crisp new toys of fighting.   335
He gloated at them with a boyish pride,
But still he wondered, Monmouth-eyed.°
The Black Horse Troop was a cavalier
And gallant name for a lady's ear.
He liked the sound and the ringing brag   340
And the girls who stitched on the county flag,
The smell of horses and saddle-leather
And the feel of the squadron riding together,
From the loose-reined canter of colts at large,
To the crammed, tense second before the charge: 345
He liked it all with the young, keen zest
Of a hound unleashed and a hawk unjessed.

And yet—what happened to men in war?
Why were they all going out to war?

He brooded a moment. It wasn't slavery,   350
That stale red-herring of Yankee knavery
Nor even states-rights, at least not solely,
But something so dim that it must be holy.
A voice, a fragrance, a taste of wine,

---

332 *housewife*: a soldier's pocket-sized sewing kit.   337 *Monmouth-eyed*: See note,
Book I, lines 206–207.

A face half-seen in old candleshine,   35
A yellow river, a blowing dust,
Something beyond you that you must trust,
Something so shrouded it must be great,
The dead men building the living State
From 'simmon-seed on a sandy bottom,   36
The woman South in her rivers laving
That body whiter than new-blown cotton
And savage and sweet as wild-orange-blossom,
The dark hair streams on the barbarous bosom,
If there ever has been a land worth saving—   36
In Dixie land, I'll take my stand,
And live and die for Dixie! . . .

And yet—and yet—in some cold Northern room,
Does anyone else stare out the obdurate moon
With doubtful passion, seeing his toys of fighting   37
Scribbled all over with such silver writing
From such a heart of peace, they seem the stale
Cast properties of a dead and childish tale?
And does he see, too soon,
Over the horse, over the horse and rider,   37
The grey, soft swathing shadowness of the spider,
Spinning his quiet loom?
No—no other man is cursed
With such doubleness of eye,
They can hunger, they can thirst,   38
But they know for what and why.

I can drink the midnight out,
And rise empty, having dined.
For my courage and my doubt
Are a double strand of mind,   3
And too subtly intertwined.
They are my flesh, they are my bone,
My shame and my foundation-stone.
I was born alone, to live alone.

Sally Dupré, Sally Dupré,   3
Eyes that are neither black nor grey,
Why do you haunt me, night and day?

Sea-changing eyes, with the deep, drowned glimmer
Of bar-gold crumbling from sunken ships,
Where the sea-dwarfs creep through the streaked, green shimmer   395
To press the gold to their glass-cold lips.
They sculpture the gold for a precious ring,
In the caverns under the under-skies,
They would marry the sea to a sailor-king!
You have taken my heart from me, sea-born eyes.   400
You have taken it, yes, but I do not know.
There are too many roads where I must go.
There are too many beds where I have slept
For a night unweeping, to quit unwept,
And it needs a king to marry the sea.   405

Why have you taken my heart from me?
I am not justice nor loyalty.
I am the shape of the weathercock,
That all winds come to and all winds mock.
You are the image of sea-carved stone,   410
The silent thing that can suffer alone,
The little women are easier,
The easy women make lighter love,
I will not take your face to the war,
I will not carry your cast-off glove.   415

Sally Dupré, Sally Dupré,
Heart and body like sea-blown spray,
I cannot forget you, night or day.

So Wingate pondered in Wingate Hall,
And hated and loved in a single breath,   420
As he tried to unriddle the doubtful scrawl
Of war and courage and love and death,
And then was suddenly nothing but sleep—
And tomorrow they marched—to a two-months chasing
Of Yankees running away like sheep   425
And peace in time for the Macon racing.°

---

426 *peace in time for the Macon racing:* The Macon (Georgia) racing began in
April.

He got in his bed. Where the moonlight poured,
It lay like frost on a sleeping sword.

It was stuffy at night in the cabins, stuffy but warm.
And smells are a matter of habit. So, if the air   43
Was thick as black butter with the commingled smells
Of greens and fried fat and field-sweat and heavy sleep,
The walls were well-chinked, the low roof kept out the rain.
Not like the tumble-down cabins at Zachary's place
Where the field-hands lived all year on hominy-grits   43
And a piece of spoiled pork at Christmas.
                                        But Zachary
Was a mean man out of the Bottoms, no quality to him.
Wingate was quality. Wingate cared for its own.
A Wingate cabin was better than most such cabins,
You might have called it a sty, had they set you there;   44
A Middle Age serf might have envied the well-chinked walls.
While as for its tenants then, being folk unversed
In any law but the law of the Wingate name,
They were glad to have it, glad for fire on the hearth,
A roof from the dark-veined wind.
                                Their bellies were warm   4
And full of food. They were heavy in love with each other.
They liked their cabin and lying next to each other,
Long nights of winter when the slow-burning pine-knots
Danced ghosts and witches over the low, near ceiling,
Short nights of summer, after the work of the fields,   4
When the hot body aches with the ripened sweetness
And the children and the new tunes are begotten together.

"What you so wakeful for, black boy?"
                            "Thinkin', woman."
"You got no call to be thinkin', little black boy,
Thinkin's a trouble, a h'ant lookin' over de shoulder,   4
Set yo' head on my breas' and forget about thinkin'."

"I got my head on yo' breas', and it's sof' dere, woman,
Sof' and sweet as a mournin' out of de Scriptures,
Sof' as two Solomon doves.° But I can't help thinkin'."

459 *Solomon doves:* In Song of Solomon 1:5, the woman is described as "black but comely," and the speakers repeatedly liken their lovers to doves.

"Ain't I good enough for you no more, black boy?   460
Don' you love me no more dat you mus' keep thinkin'?"

"You's better'n good to me and I loves you, woman,
Till I feels like Meshuck° down in de fiery furnace,
Till I feels like God's own chile. But I keeps on thinkin',
Wonderin' what I'd feel like if I was free."   465

"Hush, black boy, hush for de Lord's sake!"
                                "But listen, woman—"

"Hush yo'self, black boy, lean yo'self on my breas',
Talk like that and paterollers'll git you,
Swinge you all to bits with a blacksnake whip,
Squinch-owl carry yo' talk to de paterollers,   470
It ain't safe to talk like that."
                        "I got to, woman,
I got a feelin' in my heart."
                        "Den you sot on dat feelin'!
Never heard you talk so in all my born days!
Ain't we got a good cabin here?"
                                "Sho', we got a good cabin."
"Ain't we got good vittles, ain't old Mistis kind to us?"   475

"Sho' we got good vittles, and ole Mistis she's kind.
I'se mighty fond of ole Mistis."
                        "Den what you talkin',
You brash fool-nigger?"
                        "I just got a feelin', woman.
Ole Marse Billy, he's goin' away tomorrow,
Marse Clay, he's goin' with him to fight de Yankees,   480
All of 'em goin', yes suh."
                        "And what if dey is?"

"Well, sposin' de Yankees beats?"
                                "Ain't you got *no* sense, nigger?
Like to see any old Yankees lick old Marse Billy
And young Marse Clay!"

463 *Meshuck:* Meshach, Shadrach, and Abed-nego were three Israelite captives of
the Babylonians who were thrown into the fiery furnace by King Nebuchadnezzar
but emerged unharmed. Daniel 3.

      "Hi, woman, ain't dat de trufe!"
"Well, den——"
      "But I sees 'em all, jus' goin' and goin',   4
Goin' to war like Joshua, goin' like David,
And it makes me want to be free. Ain't you never thought
At all about bein' free?"
      "Sho', co'se I thought of it.
I always reckoned when ole Marse Billy died,
Old Mistis mebbe gwine to set some of us free,   4
Mebbe she will."
      "But we-uns gwine to be old den,
We won't be young and have the use of our hands,
We won't see our young 'uns growin' up free around us,
We won't have the strength to hoe our own co'n ourselves,
I want to be free, like me, while I got my strength."

"You might be a lot worse off and not be free,
What'd you do if ole man Zachary owned us?"

"Kill him, I reckon."
      "Hush, black boy, for God's sake hush!"

"I can't help it, woman. Dey ain't so many like him
But what dey is is too pizen-mean to live.
Can't you hear dat feelin' I got, woman? I ain't scared
Of talk and de paterollers, and I ain't mean.
I'se mighty fond of ole Mistis and ole Marse Billy,
I'se mighty fond of 'em all at de Big House,
I wouldn't be nobody else's nigger for nothin'.
But I hears 'em goin' away, all goin' away,
With horses and guns and things, all stompin' and wavin',
And I hears de chariot-wheels and de Jordan River,
Rollin' and rollin' and rollin' thu' my sleep,
And I wants to be free. I wants to see my chillun
Growin' up free, and all bust out of Egypt!
I wants to be free like an eagle in de air,
Like an eagle in de air."

———

Iron-filings scattered over a dusty
Map of crook-cornered States in yellow and blue.
Little, grouped male and female iron-filings,
Scattered over a patchwork-quilt whose patches

Are the red-earth stuff of Georgia, the pine-bough green of Vermont.
Here you are clustered as thick as a clump of bees
In swarming time. The clumps make cities and towns.   520
Here you are strewn at random, like single seeds
Lost out of the wind's pocket.
                      But now, but now,
The thunderstone has fallen on your map
And all the iron-filings shiver and move
Under the grippings of that blinded force,   525
The cold pull of the ash-and-cinder star.°

The map is vexed with the long battle-worms
Of filings, clustered and moving.
                    If it is
An enemy of the sun who has so stolen
Power from a burnt star to do this work,   530
Let the bleak essence of the utter cold
Beyond the last gleam of the most outpost light
Freeze in his veins forever.
                 But if it is
A fault in the very metal of the heart,
We and our children must acquit that fault   535
With the old bloody wastage, or give up
Playing the father to it.
                 O vexed and strange,
Salt-bitter, apple-sweet, strong-handed life!
Your million lovers cast themselves like sea
Against your mountainy breast, with a clashing noise   540
And a proud clamor—and like sea recoil,
Sucked down beneath the forefoot of the new
Advancing surf. They feed the battle-worms,
Not only War's, but in the second's pause
Between the assaulting and the broken wave,   545
The voices of the lovers can be heard,
The sea-gull cry.

Jake Diefer, the barrel-chested Pennsylvanian,
Hand like a ham and arms that could wrestle a bull,
A roast of a man, all solid meat and good fat,   550

523–526 *thunderstone . . . ash-and-cinder star*: magnetite, a natural lodestone frequently found in meteorite.

A slow-thought-chewing Clydesdale horse° of a man,
Roused out of his wife's arms. The dawn outside
Was ruddy as his big cheeks. He yawned and stretched
Gigantically, hawking and clearing his throat.
His wife, hair tousled around her like tousled corn,
Stared at him with sleep-blind eyes.

                                      "Jake, it ain't come morning,
Already yet?"

                         He nodded and started to dress.
She burrowed deeper into the bed for a minute
And then threw off the covers.

                              They didn't say much
Then, or at breakfast. Eating was something serious.
But he looked around the big kitchen once or twice
In a puzzled way, as if trying hard to remember it.
She too, when she was busy with the first batch
Of pancakes, burnt one or two, because she was staring
At the "SALT" on the salt-box, for no particular reason.
The boy ate with them and didn't say a word,
Being too sleepy.

                    Afterwards, when the team
Was hitched up and waiting, with the boy on the seat,
Holding the reins till Jake was ready to take them,
Jake didn't take them at once.

                           The sun was up now,
The spilt-milk-mist of first morning lay on the farm,
Jake looked at it all with those same mildly-puzzled eyes,
The red barn, the fat rich fields just done with the winter,
Just beginning the work of another year.
The boy would have to do the rest of the planting.

He blew on his hands and stared at his wife dumbly.
He cleared his throat.

                    "Well, good-by, Minnie," he said,
"Don't you hire any feller for harvest without you write me,
And if any more of those lightning-rodders come around,
We don't want no more dum lightning-rods."

                                He tried
To think if there was anything else, but there wasn't.
She suddenly threw her big, red arms around his neck,

551 *Clydesdale horse*: heavy-boned draft horse.

He kissed her with clumsy force.
                    Then he got on the wagon
And clucked to the horses as she started to cry.

Up in the mountains where the hogs are thin   585
And razorbacked, wild Indians of hogs,
The laurel's green in April—and if the nights
Are cold as the cold cloud of watersmoke
Above a mountain-spring, the midday sun
Has heat enough in it to make you sweat.   590

They are a curious and most native stock,
The lanky men, the lost, forgotten seeds
Spilled from the first great wave-march toward the West
And set to sprout by chance in the deep cracks
Of that hill-billy world of laurel-hells.°   595
They keep the beechwood-fiddle and the salt
Old-fashioned ballad-English of our first
Rowdy, corn-liquor-drinking, ignorant youth;
Also the rifle and the frying-pan,
The old feud-temper and the old feud-way   600
Of thinking strangers better shot on sight
But treating strangers that one leaves unshot
With border-hospitality.
                    The girls
Have the brief-blooming, rhododendron-youth
Of pioneer women, and the black-toothed age.   605
And if you yearn to meet your pioneers,
You'll find them there, the same men, inbred sons
Of inbred sires perhaps, but still the same;
A pioneer-island in a world that has
No use for pioneers—the unsplit rock   610
Of Fundamentalism, calomel,°
Clan-virtues, clannish vices, fiddle-tunes
And a hard God.
                    They are our last frontier.
They shot the railway-train when it first came,
And when the Fords first came, they shot the Fords.   615
It could not save them. They are dying now

595 *laurel-hells:* impenetrable tangles of rhododendron or mountain laurel. 611
calomel: a natural salt used as a home remedy.

Or being educated, which is the same.
One need not weep romantic tears for them,
But when the last moonshiner buys his radio,
And the last, lost, wild-rabbit of a girl
Is civilized with a mail-order dress,
Something will pass that was American
And all the movies will not bring it back.

They are misfit and strange in our new day,
In Sixty-One they were not quite so strange,
Before the Fords, before the day of the Fords . . .

Luke Breckinridge, his rifle on his shoulder,
Slipped through green forest alleys toward the town,
A gawky boy with smoldering eyes, whose feet
Whispered the crooked paths like moccasins.
He wasn't looking for trouble, going down,
But he was on guard, as always. When he stopped
To scoop some water in the palm of his hand
From a sweet trickle between moss-grown rocks,
You might have thought him careless for a minute,
But when the snapped stick cracked six feet behind him
He was all sudden rifle and hard eyes.
The pause endured a long death-quiet instant,
Then he knew who it was.
                    "Hi, Jim," he said,
Lowering his rifle. The green laurel-screen
Hardly had moved, but Jim was there beside him.
The cousins looked at each other. Their rifles seemed
To look as well, with much the same taut silentness.

"Goin' to town, Luke?"
                    "Uh-huh, goin' to town,
You goin'?"
          "Looks as if I was goin'."
                              "Looks
As if you was after squirrels."
                         "I might be.
You goin' after squirrels?" "I might be, too."
"Not so many squirrels near town."
                         "No, reckon there's not."

Jim hesitated. His gaunt hands caressed
The smooth guard of his rifle. His eyes were sharp.   650
"Might go along a piece together," he said.
Luke didn't move. Their eyes clashed for a moment,
Then Luke spoke, casually.
               "I hear the Kelceys
Air goin' to fight in this here war," he said.
Jim nodded slowly, "Yuh, I heerd that too."   655
He watched Luke's trigger-hand.
               "I might be goin'
Myself sometime," he said reflectively
Sliding his own hand down. Luke saw the movement.
"We-uns don't like the Kelceys much," he said
With his eyes down to pinpoints.
             Then Jim smiled.   660
"We-uns neither," he said.
             His hand slid back.

They went along together after that
But neither of them spoke for half-a-mile,
Then finally, Jim said, half-diffidently,
"You know who we air goin' to fight outside?   665
I heard it was the British. Air that so?"
"Hell, no," said Luke, with scorn. He puckered his brows.
"Dunno's I rightly know just who they air."
He admitted finally, "But 'tain't the British.
It's some trash-lot of furriners, that's shore.   670
They call 'em Yankees near as I kin make it,
But they ain't Injuns neither."
            "Well," said Jim
Soothingly, "Reckon it don't rightly matter
Long as the Kelceys take the other side."

It was noon when the company marched to the railroad-station.   675
The town was ready for them. The streets were packed.
There were flags and streamers and pictures of Lincoln and Hamlin.°
The bad little boys climbed up on the trees and yelled,
The good little boys had clean paper-collars on,
And swung big-eyed on white-painted wicket-gates,   680

677 *Hamlin:* Hannibal Hamlin, Lincoln's Vice-President.

Wanting to yell, and feeling like Fourth of July.
Somebody fastened a tin can full of firecrackers
To a yellow dog's tail and sent him howling and racketing
The length of the street.

        "There goes Jeff Davis!" said somebody,
And everybody laughed, and the little boys   65
Punched each other and squealed between fits of laughing
"There goes Jeff Davis—lookit ole yellow Jeff Davis!"
And then the laugh died and rose again in a strange
Half-shrill, half-strangled unexpected shout
As they heard the Hillsboro' Silver Cornet Band   66
Swinging "John Brown's Body" ahead of the soldiers.
I have heard that soul of crowd go out in the queer
Groan between laughter and tears that baffles the wise.
I have heard that whanging band.

"We'll hang Jeff Davis on a sour-apple tree." °   6
Double-roll on the snare-drums, double squeal of the fife,
"We'll hang Jeff Davis on a sour-apple tree!"
Clash of the cymbals zinging, throaty blare of cornets,
"We'll hang Jeff Davis on a sour-apple tree!"
"On to Richmond! On to Richmond! On to Richmond!"   7
"Yeah! There they come! *Yeah! Yeah!"*
And they came, the bearskin drum-major leading the band,
Twirling his silver-balled baton with turkey-cock pomp,
The cornet-blowers, the ranks. The drum-major was fine,
But the little boys thought the captain was even finer,   7
He looked just like a captain out of a book
With his sword and his shoulder-straps and his discipline-face.
He wasn't just Henry Fairfield, he was a captain,
—Henry Fairfield worried about his sword,
Hoping to God that he wouldn't drop his sword,   7
And wondering hotly whether his discipline-face
Really looked disciplined or only peevish—
"Yeah! There they come! There's Jack! There's Charlie! Yeah! Yeah!"
The color-guard with the stiff, new flapping flag,
And the ranks and the ranks and the ranks, the amateur   7
Blue, wavering ranks, in their ill-fitting tight coats,
Shoulders galled already by their new guns,

695 *"We'll hang Jeff Davis on a sour-apple tree"*: another popular Union war song
to the tune of "John Brown's Body Lies a-Mouldering in the Grave."

—They were three-months' men,° they had drilled in civilian clothes
Till a week ago—"There's Charlie! There's Hank, yeah, yeah!"
"On to Richmond, boys! Three cheers for Abe Lincoln!   720
Three cheers for the boys! Three groans for old Jeff Davis
And the dirty Rebs!"
"We'll hang Jeff Davis on a sour-apple tree!"

Jack Ellyat, marching, saw between blue shoulders
A blur of faces. They all were faces he knew,   725
Old Mrs. Cobb with her wart and her Paisley shawl,
Little George Freeman, the slim Tucker girls,
All of them cheering and shouting—and all of them strange
Suddenly, different, faces he'd never seen.
Faces somehow turned into one crowd-face.   730
His legs went marching along all right but they felt
Like somebody else's legs, his mind was sucked dry.
It was real, they were going away, the town was cheering them.
Henry Fairfield was marching ahead with his sword.
Just as he'd thought about it a thousand times,   735
These months—but it wasn't the way that he'd thought about it.
"On to Richmond! On to Richmond! On to Richmond!"
There were Mother and Father and Jane and the house.
Jane was waving a flag. He laughed and called to them.
But his voice was stiff in his throat, not like his real voice.   740
This, everything, it was too quick, too crowded, not Phaëton°
Charging his snarling horses at a black sea,
But a numb, hurried minute with legs that marched
Mechanically, feeling nothing at all.
The white crowd-face—the sweat on the red seamed neck   745
Of the man ahead—"On to Richmond!"—blue shoulders bobbing—
Flags—cheering—somebody kissed him—Ellen Baker—
She was crying—wet mouth of tears—didn't want her to kiss him—
Why did she want to—the station—*halt*—Mother and Jane.
The engineer wore a flag in his coat-lapel.   750
The engine had "On to Richmond!" chalked all over it.
Nothing to say now—Mother looks tired to death—
I wish I weren't going—no, I'm glad that I am—
The damn band's playing "John Brown's Body" again,
I wish they'd stop it!—I wish to God we could start—   755
There—*close up, men!*—oh my God, they've let Ned out!

718 *three-months' men:* See note, line 259, above.   741 *not Phaëton* . . . : See
note, Book I, line 1058.

I told them for God's sake to lock him up in the cellar,
But they've let him out—maybe he got out by himself—
He's got too much sense—"No, down, Ned! Down, good dog!
Down, I tell you!—"
            "Good-by, boys! Good-by! We'll hang Jeff Davis!"   76

The engine squealed, the packed train started to move.
Ned wanted to come, but they wouldn't let him come.
They had to kick him away, he couldn't see why.

————————

In another column, footsore Curly Hatton
Groaned at the thought of marching any more.   76
His legs weren't built for marching and they knew it,
Butterball-legs under a butterball-body.
The plump good-tempered face with its round eyes
Blue and astonished as a china-doll's,
Stared at the road ahead and hated it   77
Because there was so much of it ahead
And all of it so dry.
                He didn't mind
The rest so much. He didn't even mind
Being the one sure necessary joke
Of the whole regiment. He'd always been   7
A necessary joke—fat people were.
Fat babies always were supposed to laugh.
Fat little boys had fingers poked at them.
And, even with the road, and being fat,
You had a good time in this funny war,   7
Considering everything, and one thing most.

His mind slipped back two months. He saw himself
In the cool room at Weatherby's Retreat
Where all the girls were sewing the new star
In the new flag for the first volunteers.   7
He hadn't thought of fighting much before,
He was too easy-going. If Virginia
Wanted secession, that was her affair.
It seemed too bad to break the Union up
After some seventy years of housekeeping.   7
But he could understand the way you'd feel
If you were thin and angry at the Yanks.

He knew a lot of Yankees that he liked,
But then he liked most people, on the whole
Although most girls and women made him shy.   795
He loved the look of them and the way they walked,
He loved their voices and their little sweet mouths,
But something always seemed to hold him back,
When he was near them.
                          He was too fat, too friendly,
Too comfortable for dreams, too easy-shy.   800
The porcelain dolls stood on the mantelpiece,
Waiting such slim and arrant cavaliers
As porcelain dolls must have to make them proud,
They had no mercy for fat Cupidons,
Not even Lucy, all the years before,   805
And Lucy was the porcelain belle of the world!
And so when she said.
                          And he couldn't believe
At first.
                But she was silver and fire and steel
That day of the new stars and the new flag,
Fire and bright steel for the invading horde   810
And silver for the men who drove them off,
And so she sewed him in her flag and heart:
Though even now, he couldn't believe she had
In spite of all the letters and the socks
And kissing him before he went away.   815
But it was so—the necessary joke
Made into a man at last, a man in love
And loved by the most porcelain belle of the world.
And he was ready to march to the world's end
And fight ten million Yanks to keep it so.   820

"Oh God, after we're married—the cool night
Over the garden—and Lucy sitting there
In her blue dress while the big stars come out."

His face was funny with love and footsore pride,
The man beside him saw it, gave a laugh,   825
"Curly's thinking it's time for a julep, boys!
Hot work for fat men, Curly!"

The crows fly over the Henry House,° through the red sky of evening,
     cawing,
Judith Henry, bedridden,° watches them through the clouded glass of
     old sight.
(July is hot in Virginia—a parched, sun-leathered farmer sawing   8
Dry sticks with a cicada-saw that creaks° all the lukewarm night.)

But Judith Henry's hands are cool in spite of all midsummer's burning,
Cool, muted and frail with age like the smoothness of old yellow linen,
     the cool touch of old, dulled rings.
Her years go past her in bed like falling waters and the waters of a
     millwheel turning,
And she is not ill content to lie there, dozing and calm, remembering
     youth, to the gushing of those watersprings.   8

She has known Time like the cock of red dawn and Time like a tired
     clock slowing;
She has seen so many faces and bodies, young and then old, so much
     life, so many patterns of death and birth.
She knows that she must leave them soon. She is not afraid to flow
     with that river's flowing.
But the wrinkled earth still hangs at her sufficed breast like a weary
     child, she is unwilling to go while she still has milk for the
     earth.

She will go in her sleep, most likely, she has the sunk death-sleep
     of the old already,   8
(War-bugles by the Potomac, you cannot reach her ears with your
     brass lyric, piercing the crowded dark.)
It does not matter, the farm will go on, the farm and the children
     bury her in her best dress, the plow cut its furrow, steady,
(War-horses of the Shenandoah, why should you hurry so fast to tramp
     the last ashy fire from so feeble and retired a spark?)

There is nothing here but a creek and a house called the Henry House,
     a farm and a bedridden woman and people with country faces.
There is nothing for you here. And La Haye Sainte° was a quiet farm
     and the mile by it a quiet mile.

828 *the Henry House:* See map. p. 92.   829–841 *Judith Henry, bedridden . . . :* "Mrs. Henry was in her eighty-fifth year and bedridden. . . . She was
the widow of Dr. Isaac Henry, a surgeon of the U. S. Navy," Robert G. Carter, *Four
Brothers in Blue,** p. 18.   831 *cicada-saw that creaks:* The reference is to the sound
of the locust (cicada) that in midsummer begins to call at dusk.   845 *La Haye
Sainte:* in Belgium, the site of the Battle of Waterloo, June 18, 1814.

And Lexington° was a place to work in like any one of a dozen dull,
    little places.
And they raised good crops at Blenheim° till the soldiers came and
    spoiled the crops for a while.

The red evening fades into twilight, the crows have gone to their trees,
    the slow, hot stars are emerging.
It is cooler now on the hill—and in the camps it is cooler, where the
    untried soldiers find their bivouac hard.
Where, from North and South, the blind wrestlers of armies converge
    on the forgotten house like the double pincers of an iron claw
    converging.   850
And Johnston hurries his tired brigades from the Valley,° to bring them
    up in time before McDowell ° can fall on Beauregard.

    The congressmen came out to see Bull Run,°
    The congressmen who like free shows and spectacles.
    They brought their wives and carriages along,
    They brought their speeches and their picnic-lunch,   855
    Their black constituent-hats and their devotion:
    Some even brought a little whiskey, too,
    (A little whiskey is a comforting thing
    For congressmen in the sun, in the heat of the sun.)
    The bearded congressmen with orator's mouths,   860
    The fine, clean-shaved, Websterian congressmen,
    Come out to see the gladiator's show
    Like Iliad gods, wrapped in the sacred cloud
    Of Florida-water,° wisdom and bay-rum,
    Of free cigars, democracy and votes,   865
    That lends such portliness to congressmen.

846 *Lexington:* Lexington, Massachusetts, where the minutemen engaged the British regulars in the American Revolution, April 1775. 847 *Blenheim:* where Marlborough defeated Louis IV during the War of the Spanish Succession, August 1704. 851 *Johnston . . . from the Valley:* General Joseph E. Johnston (USMA, 1829), commanding the Confederate Army of the Shenandoah [Valley]. *McDowell:* Brigadier General Irvin McDowell, commanding the Union Army. 852 *congressmen came out to see Bull Run:* "The bivouacs . . . were thronged by visitors, official and unofficial . . . giving the scene the appearance of a monster military picnic," James B. Fry in *Battles and Leaders of the Civil War,* I, 183. The initial edition (1887) of *Battles and Leaders* was based on "The Century War Series," which appeared in *Century Magazine* beginning in 1884. Whatever edition Benét used, this appears to have been his primary source for military events. 864 *Florida-water:* a kind of toilet water.

(The gates fly wide, the bronze troop marches out
Into the stripped and deadly circus-ring,
"*Ave, Caesar!*" the cry goes up, and shakes
The purple awning over Caesar's seat.)   8⁷
"*Ave, Caesar! Ave*, O congressmen,
We who are about to die,
Salute you, congressmen!"
Eleven States,
New York, Rhode Island, Maine,   8⁷
Connecticut, Michigan and the gathered West,
Salute you, congressmen! °
The red-fezzed Fire-Zouaves,° flamingo-bright,
Salute you, congressmen!
The raw boys still in their civilian clothes,   8⁸
Salute you, congressmen!
The second Wisconsin in its homespun grey,
Salutes you, congressmen!
The Garibaldi Guards in cocksfeather hats,
Salute you, congressmen!   8
The Second Ohio with their Bedouin-caps,
Salutes you, congressmen!
Sherman's brigade,° grey-headed Heintzelman,°
Ricketts' and Griffin's doomed and valiant guns,°
The tough, hard-bitten regulars of Sykes°   8
Who covered the retreat with the Marines,
Burnside and Porter, Willcox° and McDowell,
All the vast, unprepared, militia-mass

874–877 *Eleven States . . . Salute you, congressmen!*: The Northern order-of-battle included troops from the states named plus New Hampshire, New Jersey, Massachusetts, Vermont, Pennsylvania, Ohio, Minnesota, and Wisconsin—thirteen in all. 878–884 *red-fezzed Fire-Zouaves . . .* : The bizarre uniforms described are pictured in *Battles and Leaders*. The Fire Zouaves were the 11th New York Militia; the Garibaldi guards (line 884), the 39th New York. 888 *Sherman's brigade:* the Third Brigade of the First Division, commanded by Colonel (later General) William Tecumseh Sherman. *Heintzelman:* Colonel Samuel P. Heintzelman, commanding the Third Division. 889 *Ricketts' and Griffin's doomed and valiant guns:* "The men [of Captains James B. Ricketts' and Charles Griffin's 1st and 5th Artillery Batteries] were mostly shot down where they bravely stood by their guns," Beauregard in *Battles and Leaders*, I, 213. 890 *Sykes:* Major (later Major General) George Sykes, commanding a battalion of infantry regulars. 892 *Burnside and Porter, Willcox:* Colonel (later Major General) Ambrose E. Burnside, commanding the Second Brigade, Second Division; Colonel Andrew Porter, commanding the Second Division; Colonel Orlando B. Willcox, commanding the Second Brigade, Third Division.

Of boys in red and yellow Zouave pants,
Who carried peach-preserves inside their kits   895
And dreamt of being generals overnight;
The straggling companies where every man
Was a sovereign and a voter—the slack regiments
Where every company marched a different step;
The clumsy and unwieldy-new brigades   900
Not yet distempered into battle-worms;
The whole, huge, innocent army, ready to fight
But only half-taught in the tricks of fighting,
Ready to die like picture-postcard boys
While fighting still had banners and a sword   905
And just as ready to run in blind mob-panic,
Salutes you with a vast and thunderous cry,
Ave, Caesar, ave, O congressmen,
Ave, O Iliad gods who forced the fight!
You bring your carriages and your picnic-lunch   910
To cheer us in our need.
                You come with speeches,
Your togas smell of heroism and bay-rum.
You are the people and the voice of the people
And, when the fight is done, your carriages
Will bear you safely, through the streaming rout   915
Of broken troops, throwing their guns away.
You come to see the gladiator's show,
But from a high place, as befits the wise:
You will not see the long windrows of men
Strewn like dead pears before the Henry House   920
Or the stone-wall of Jackson° breathe its parched
Devouring breath upon the failing charge,
Ave, Caesar, ave, O congressmen,
Cigar-smoke wraps you in a godlike cloud,
And if you are not to depart from us   925
As easily and divinely as you came,
It hardly matters.
              Fighting Joe Hooker° once
Said with that tart, unbridled tongue of his
That made so many needless enemies,

921 *the stone-wall of Jackson* . . . : See lines 1158–1182, below. 927 *Fighting Joe Hooker*: Major General Joseph Hooker, a veteran of Indian and Mexican campaigns; like Burnside (line 892, above), one of several generals who later commanded the Army of the Potomac.

"Who ever saw a dead cavalryman?"

     The phrase   930
Stings with a needle sharpness, just or not,
But even he was never heard to say,
"Who ever saw a dead congressman?"
And yet, he was a man with a sharp tongue.

The day broke,° hot and calm. In the little farm-houses 935
That are scattered here and there in that rolling country
Of oak and rail-fence, crooked creeks and second-growth pine,
The early-risers stand looking out of the door
At the long dawn-shadows for a minute or two
—Shadows are always cool—but the blue-glass sky 940
Is fusing with heat even now, heat that prickles the hairs
On the back of your hand.

    They sigh and turn back to the house.
"Looks like a scorcher today, boys!"

     They think already
Of the cool jug of vinegar-water down by the hedge.

Judith Henry wakened with the first light, 945
She had the short sleep of age, and the long patience.
She waited for breakfast in vague, half-drowsy wonderment
At various things. Yesterday some men had gone by
And stopped for a drink of water. She'd heard they were soldiers.
She couldn't be sure. It had seemed to worry the folks 950
But it took more than soldiers and such to worry her now.
Young people always worried a lot too much.
No soldiers that had any sense would fight around here.
She'd had a good night. Today would be a good day.

A mile and a half away, before the Stone Bridge, 955
A Union gun opened fire.

Six miles away, McDowell had planned his battle
And planned it well, as far as such things can be planned—
A feint° at one point, a flanking march at another
To circle Beauregard's left and crumple it up. 960

---

935 *The day broke:* July 21, 1861. 955–959 *before the Stone Bridge . . . A feint . . .* :See map, facing. "Tyler's First Division . . . was to move at 2:30 A.M., threaten the Stone Bridge and . . . divert attention from the movements of the turning column," Fry in *Battles and Leaders,* I, 184.

There were Johnston's eight thousand men to be reckoned with
But Patterson should be holding them, miles away,
And even if they slipped loose from Patterson's fingers°
The thing might still be done.
                              If you take a flat map
And move wooden blocks upon it strategically,   965
The thing looks well, the blocks behave as they should.
The science of war is moving live men like blocks.
And getting the blocks into place at a fixed moment.
But it takes time to mold your men into blocks
And flat maps turn into country where creeks and gullies   970
Hamper your wooden squares. They stick in the brush,
They are tired and rest, they straggle after ripe blackberries,
And you cannot lift them up in your hand and move them.
—A string of blocks curling smoothly around the left
Of another string of blocks and crunching it up—   975
It is all so clear in the maps, so clear in the mind,
But the orders are slow, the men in the blocks are slow
To move, when they start they take too long on the way—
The General loses his stars° and the block-men die
In unstrategic defiance of martial law   980
Because still used to just being men, not block-parts.
McDowell was neither a fool nor a fighting fool;
He knew his dice, he knew both armies unready,
But congressmen and nation wanted a battle
And he felt their hands on his shoulders, forcing his play.   985
He knew well enough when he played that he played for his head
As Beauregard and Johnston were playing for theirs,
So he played with the skill he had—and does not lie
Under a cupolaed gloom on Riverside Drive.°
Put Grant in his place that day and with those same dice,   990
Grant might have done little better.
                              Wherefore, now,
Irvin McDowell, half-forgotten general,

---

963 *slipped loose from Patterson's fingers:* At 1 P.M. on the 18th, Major General Robert Patterson wired Winfield Scott in Washington, "I have succeeded . . . in keeping General Johnston's force at Winchester." At that moment Johnston's advanced guard was in fact leaving for Manassas Junction. See *Battles and Leaders,* I, pp. 182–183.   979 *The General loses his stars:* In this case, McDowell was not reduced in rank, but within the week General McClellan had taken his place as the Union commander in the field.   989 *a cupolaed gloom on Riverside Drive:* Grant's Tomb in New York City.

Who tried the game and found no luck in the game
And never got the chance to try it again
But did not backbite the gamblers who found more luck in it   995
Then or later in double-edged reminiscences;
If any laurel can grow in the sad-colored fields
Between Bull Run and Cub Run and Cat Hairpin Bend °
You should have a share of it for your hardworking ghost
Because you played as you could with your cold, forced dice   1000
And neither wasted your men like the fighting fools
Nor posed as an injured Napoleon twenty years later.°
Meanwhile, McDowell watched his long flanking column
File by, on the Warrentown pike, in the first dawn-freshness.
"Gentlemen, that's a big force," he said to his staff.   1005

A full rifled battery begins to talk spitefully to Evans' Carolinians.°
The grey skirmish-line, thrown forward on the other side of Bull
Run, ducks its head involuntarily as a locomotive noise goes by in
the air above it, and waits for a flicker of blue in the scrub-oaks
ahead.°   1010

Beauregard, eager *sabreur*, whose heart was a French
Print of a sabretasche-War° with "La Gloire" ° written under it,
Lovable, fiery, bizarre, picturesque as his name,
Galloped toward Mitchell's Ford ° with bald, quiet Joe Johnston,
The little precise Scotch dominie° of a general,   1015
Stubborn as flint, in advance not always so lucky,
In retreat more dangerous than a running wolf—
Slant shadow, sniffing the traps and the poisoned meat,
And going on to pause and slash at the first
Unwary dogs before the hunters came up.   1020
Grant said of him once,

998 *Cub Run and Cat Hairpin Bend*: For Cub Run and Catharpin (Cat Hairpin)
Creek, see map, p. 92.   1002 *an injured Napoleon twenty years later*: Retro-
spective apologias, written long after Appomattox, were not unusual. Several appear
in "The Century War Series" (1887), see note, line 852, above. The description
here certainly fits George McClellan, who was known as "The Little Napoleon,"
was relieved of command by Lincoln, and protested the "injustice" for years to come.
1006 *Evans' Carolinians*: Colonel N. G. Evans led a makeshift command of as-
sorted South Carolina troops.   1009–1010 *in the scrub-oaks ahead*: near the Stone
Bridge, see map, p. 92.   1012 a *sabretasche-War . . . :* a romanticized con-
ception of cavalry action. The sabretasche was a flat leather case worn by European
cavalry units.   "*La Gloire*": glory; fame.   1014 *Mitchell's Ford*: See map, p. 92.
1015 *dominie*: schoolmaster.

"I was always anxious with Joe Johnston in front of me,
I was never half so anxious in front of Lee." °
He kissed his friends in the Nelson-way° we've forgotten,
He could make men cheer him after six-weeks retreating.°   1⦁
Another man said of him, after the war was done,
Still with that puzzled comparison we find
When Lee, the reticent sword, comes into the question,
"Yes, Lee was a great general, a good man;
But I never wanted to put my arms round his neck   1⦁
As I used to want to with Johnston."
                              The two sayings
Make a good epitaph for so Scotch a ghost,
Or would if they were all.
                       They are not quite all,
He had to write his reminiscences, too,
And tell what he would have done if it had not been   1
For Davis and chance and a dozen turns of the wheel.
That was the thistle in him—the other strain—
But he was older then.
                       I'd like to have seen him
That day as he galloped along beside Beauregard,
Sabreur and dominie planning the battle-lines.   1
They'd ordered Jackson up to the threatened left
But Beauregard was sure that the main assault
Would come on the right. He'd planned it so—a good plan—
But once the blocks start moving, they keep on moving.

The hands of the scuffed brown clock in the kitchen of the Henry
    House point to nine-forty-five.   1
Judith Henry does not hear the clock, she hears in the sky a vast dim
    roar like piles of heavy lumber crashingly falling.
They are carrying her in her bed to a ravine below the Sudley Road,
    maybe she will be safe there, maybe the battle will go by and
    leave her alive.

1022–1023 *I was always anxious* . . . : "I have had nearly all of the Southern generals in high command in front of me, and Joe Johnston gave me more anxiety than
any of the others. I was never half so anxious about Lee." Grant in John R. Young,
Around the World with General Grant, II, 212–213.   1024 *the Nelson-way*: remi-
niscent of the devotion typical of Lord Nelson, who, as he lay dying at Trafalgar,
asked and received the farewell kiss of his chaplain, Captain Hardy.   1025 *cheer
him after six-weeks retreating*: as they would in 1864 during the long withdrawal
that preceded the siege of Atlanta.

The crows have been scared from their nests by the strange crashing,
  they circle in the sky like a flight of blackened leaves, wheeling
  and calling.

———

Back at Centerville, there are three-months' men,
A Pennsylvania regiment, a New York Battery.°   1050
They hear the spent wave of the roar of the opening guns,
But they are three-months' men, their time is up today.
They would have fought yesterday or a week ago,
But then they were still enlisted—today they are not—
Their time is up, and there can't be much use or sense   1055
In fighting longer than you've promised to fight.
They pack up their things and decide they'd better go home,
And quietly march away from that gathering roar.°

———

Luke Breckinridge, crouched by the Warrentown pike,
Saw stuffed dolls in blue coats and baggy trousers   1060
Go down like squirrels under the rifle-cracks.
His eyes glowed as a bullet ripped his sleeve
And he felt well. Armies weren't such a much,
Too damn many orders, too damn much saluting,
Too many damn officers you weren't allowed   1065
To shoot when they talked mean to you because
They were your officers, which didn't make sense.
But this was something he could understand,
Except for those dirty stinkers of big guns,
It wasn't right to shoot you with big guns   1070
But it was a good scrap except for that—
Carried a little high, then . . . change it . . . good . . .
Though men were hard to miss when you were used
To squirrels. His eyes were narrow. He hardly heard
The officer's voice. The woods in front of him   1075
Were full of Kelceys he was going to kill,
Blue-coated Kelcey dolls in baggy trousers.
It was a beautiful and sufficing sight.

———

1050 A *Pennsylvania regiment, a New York Battery:* the 4th Pennsylvania Infantry
and a light artillery battery of the 8th New York State Militia.   1058 *quietly march
away from that gathering roar:* In McDowell's own words, they "marched to the
rear to the sound of the enemy's cannon," *Battles and Leaders,* I, 179.

The first blue wave of Burnside is beaten back from the pike to stumble a little way and rally against Porter's fresh brigade.

Bee and Bartow° move down from the Henry House plateau—grey and butternut° lines trampling the bullet-cut oak-leaves, splashing across Young's Branch.

Tall, black-bearded Bee rides by on his strong horse, his long black hair fluttering.

Imboden's° red-shirted gunners unlimber by the Henry House to answer the Parrotts° and howitzers of Ricketts and Griffin. The air is a sheet of iron, continually and dully shaken.

Shippy, the little man with the sharp rat-eyes,
Saw someone run in front of them waving a sword;
Then they were going along toward a whining sound
That ran like cold spring-water along his spine.
God, he was in for it now! His sharp rat-eyes
Flickered around and about him hopelessly.
If a fellow could only drop out, if a fellow could only
Pretend he was hurt a little and then drop out
Behind a big, safe oak-tree—no use—no use—
He was in for it, now. He couldn't get away.
"Come on, boys—come on, men—clean them out with the bayonet!"
He saw a rail-fence ahead, a quiet rail-fence,
But men were back of it—grey lumps—a million bees
Stinging the air—Oh Jesus, the corporal's got it—
He couldn't shoot, even—he was too scared to shoot—
His legs took him on—he couldn't stop his legs
Or the weak urine suddenly trickling down them.

Curly Hatton, toiling along the slow
Crest of the Henry Hill, over slippery ground,
Glanced at the still-blue sky that lay so deep
Above the little pines, so pooled, so calm.
He thought, with the slow drowsiness of fatigue,
Of Lucy feeding the white, greedy swans
On the blue pool by Weatherby's Retreat.

1081 *Bee and Bartow:* Brigadier General B. E. Bee and Colonel F. S. Bartow, commanding the Third and Second Brigades, respectively, of the Army of the Potomac.   1082 *butternut:* Some Confederate uniforms were light brown, colored by a dye made from butternut hulls. The dye was also used to color homespun material for other clothing.   1086 *Imboden's:* Captain (later Brigadier General) John D. Imboden.   1087 *the Parrotts:* a rifled cannon, designed by Robert P. Parrott, manufactured beginning in 1860, and used by both Union and Confederate forces.

They stretched their necks, and clattered with their wings.
There was a fragrance sleeping in her hair.
"Close up, folks—don't straggle—we're going into action!"   1115
His butterball-legs moved faster—Lucy—Lucy—

Bee and Bartow's brigades are broken in their turn—it is fight
and run away—fight and run away, all day—the day will go to whichever of the untried wrestlers can bear the pain of the grips an instant
longer than the other.   1120
Beauregard and Johnston hurry toward the firing°—McDowell has
already gone—
The chessplayers have gone back to little pieces on the shaken
board—little pieces that cannot see the board as a whole.
The block-plan is lost—there is no plan any more—only the blood- 1125
stained, fighting blocks, the bloodstained and blackened men.

Jack Ellyat heard the guns with a knock at his heart
When he first heard them. They were going to be in it, soon.
He wondered how it would feel. They would win, of course,
But how would it feel? He'd never killed anything much.   1130
Ducks and rabbits, but ducks and rabbits weren't men.
He'd never even seen a man killed, a man die,
Except Uncle Amos, and Uncle Amos was old.
He saw a red sop spreading across the close
Feathers of a duck's breast—it had been all right,   1135
But now it made him feel sick for a while, somehow.
Then they were down on the ground, and they were firing,
And that was all right—just fire as you fired at drill.
Was anyone firing at them? He couldn't tell.
There was a stone bridge.° Were there rebels beyond the bridge?   1140
The shot he was firing now might go and kill rebels
But it didn't feel like it.
                              A man down the line
Fell and rolled flat, with a minor coughing sound
And then was quiet. Ellyat felt the cough
In the pit of his stomach a minute.   1145

1121 *Beauregard and Johnston hurry toward the firing*: from Mitchell's Ford. See
map, p. 92. "After weighing attentively the firing . . . , it appeared to me that
the troops on the right would be unable to get into position before the Federal
offensive. . . . General Johnston and I now set out at full speed for the point of
conflict," Beauregard in *Battles and Leaders*, I, 209–210.   1140 *a stone bridge*:
See note, lines 955–959, above.

But, after that, it was just like a man falling down.
It was all so calm except for their guns and the distant
Shake in the air of cannon. No more men were hit,
And, after a while, they all got up and marched on.
If Rebels had been by the bridge, the rebels were gone,   11
And they were going on somewhere, you couldn't say where,
Just marching along the way that they always did.
The only funny thing was, leaving the man
Who had made that cough, back there in the trampled grass
With the red stain sopping through the blue of his coat   11
Like the stain on a duck's breast. He hardly knew the man
But it felt funny to leave him just lying there.

The wreckage of Bee, Bartow and Evans' commands streams back into a shallow ravine below a little wood—broken blocks hammered into splinters by war—two thousand confused men reeling past their 11 staggering flags and the hoarse curses and rallying cries of their officers, like sheep in a narrow run.

Bee tries to halt them furiously—he stands up in his stirrups, tree-tall, while the blue flood of the North trickles over the stream and pours on and on.   11

He waves his sword—the toyish glitter sparkles—he points to a grey dyke at the top of the ravine—a grey dyke of musket-holding Virginians, silent and ready.

"Look, men, there's Jackson's brigade! It stands there like a stone wall. Rally behind the Virginians!"   1

They rally behind them—Johnston and Beauregard are there —the Scotch dominie plucks a flag and carries it forward to rally the Fourth Alabama—the French hussar-sword rallies them with bursting rockets of oratory—his horse is shot under him, but he mounts again.   1

And the grey stone wall holds like a stiff dyke while the tired men get their breath behind it—and the odd, lemon-sucking, ex-professor of tactics who saw John Brown hung° in his carpetslippers and prayed a Presbyterian prayer for his damned soul, has a new name that will last as long as the face they cut for him on Stone 1 Mountain,° and has the same clang of rock against the chisel-blade.

1177–1178 *ex-professor . . . who saw John Brown hung:* See Book I, line 1386.
1180–1181 *Stone Mountain:* memorial to the Confederate Army near Atlanta.

Judith Henry, Judith Henry, they have moved you back at last, in
    doubt and confusion, to the little house where you know every
    knothole by heart.
It is not safe, but now there is no place safe, you are between the
    artillery and the artillery, and the incessant noise comes to your
    dim ears like the sea-roar within a shell where you are ly-
    ing.
The walls of the house are riddled, the brown clock in the kitchen
    gouged by a bullet, a jar leaks red preserves on the cupboard
    shelf where the shell-splinter came and tore the cupboard apart. 1185
The casual guns do not look for you, Judith Henry, they find you in
    passing merely and touch you only a little, but the touch is
    enough to give your helpless body five sudden wounds° and
    leave you helplessly dying.

    Wingate gentled Black Whistle's pawing
    With hand and wisdom and horseman's play
    And listened anew to the bulldogs gnawing
    Their bone of iron, a mile away.   1190
    There was a wood that a bonfire crowned
    With thick dark smoke without flame for neighbor,
    And the dull, monotonous, heavy sound
    Of a hill or a woman in too-long labor,
    But that was all for the Black Horse Troop   1195
    And had been all since the day's beginning,
    That stray boy beating his metal hoop
    And the tight-lipped wonder if they were winning.
    Wainscott Bristol, behind his eyes,
    Was getting in bed with a sweet-toothed wench,   1200
    Huger Shepley felt for his dice
    And Stuart Cazenove swore in French
    "*Mille diables*° and Yankee blood!
    How long are we going to stick in the mud?"
    While a Cotter hummed with a mocking sigh,   1205
    " 'If you want a good time, jine the cavalry!' "
    "Stuart's in it, Wade Hampton's in it." °
    "The Yanks'll quit in another minute!"

1186 *The casual guns . . . five sudden wounds:* "For a time the house was in the
line of the artillery fire from both sides. Mrs. Henry received five wounds from fragments . . . and died two hours after the battle," editor's note, *Battles and Leaders*,
I, 234. See also *Four Brothers in Blue*, p. 18.   1203 *Mille diables:* literally, a thousand devils or curses.   1207 *"Stuart's in it, Wade Hampton's in it":* Colonel J. E. B.
Stuart, commanding the 1st Virginia Cavalry, and Colonel Wade Hampton, commanding Hampton's (South Carolina) Legion.

"General Beau's° just lost us!"

            "Steady!"

"And he won't find us until he's ready!"   12

"It must be two—we've been here since six."

"It's Virginia up to her old-time tricks!

They never did trust a Georgia man,

But Georgia'll fight while Virginia can!" °

The restless talk was a simmering brew   12

That made the horses restless too;

They stamped and snuffed and pricked their ears—

There were cheers, off somewhere—but which side's cheers?

Had the Yankees whipped? Were the Yankees breaking?

The whole troop grumbled and wondered, aching   12

For fighting or fleeing or fornicating

Or anything else except this bored waiting.

An aide rode up on a sweating mare

And they glowered at him with hostile stare.

He had been in it and they had not.   1

He had smelt the powder and heard the shot,

And they hated his soul and his martial noise

With the envious hate of little boys.

Then "Yaaih! Yaaih!"

           —and Wingate felt

The whole troop lift° like a lifted dart   1

And loosened the sabre at his belt,

And felt his chest too small for his heart.

Curly Hatton was nothing any more

But a dry throat and a pair of burnt black hands

That held a hot gun he was always firing   1

Though he no longer remembered why he fired.

They ran up a cluttered hill and took hacked ground

And held it for a while and fired for a while,

And then the blue men came and they ran away,

To go back, after a while, when the blue men ran.   1

1209 *General Beau's:* Beauregard's.   1212–1214 *Virginia . . . never did trust . . . Georgia . . . :* Throughout the poem, the fictional Georgia Black Horse Troop (see Benét's "Note," p. xiii) plays the role of one of the separate cavalry troops attached to Stuart's command.   1230 *The whole troop lift . . . :* A troop of Confederate cavalry did in fact charge the Fire-Zouaves shortly after 2 P.M. (see line 1211, above) in the first significant cavalry action of the day.

There was a riddled house and a crow in a tree,
There was uneven ground. It was hard to run.
The gun was heavy and hot. There once had been
A person named Lucy and a flag and a star
And a cane chair beside wistarias   1245
Where a nigger brought you a drink. These had ceased to exist.
There was only very hot sun and being thirsty.
Yells—crashings—screams from black lips—a dead, tattered crow
In a tattered tree. There had once been a person named Lucy
Who had had an importance. There was none of her now.   1250

Up the hill again. Damn tired of running up hill.
And then he found he couldn't run any more,
He had to fall down and be sick. Even that was hard,
Because somebody near kept making a squealing noise—
The dolefully nasty noise of a badly-hurt dog.   1255
It got on his nerves and he tried to say something to it,
But it was he who made it, so he couldn't stop it.

Jack Ellyat, going toward the battle again,
Saw the other side of the hill ° where Curly was lying,
Saw, for a little while, the two battered houses,°   1260
The stuffed dead stretched in numb, disorderly postures,
And heard for a while again that whining sound
That made you want to duck, and feel queer if you did.

To him it was noise and smoke and the powder-taste
And, once and again, through the smoke, for a moment seen,   1265
Small, monstrous pictures, gone through the brain like light,
And yet forever bitten into the brain;
A marsh, a monstrous arras° of live and dead
Still shaking under the thrust of the weaver's hand,
The crowd of a deadly fair.
                           Then, orders again.   1270
And they were going away from the smoke once more.

The books say "Keyes' brigade° made a late and weak
Demonstration in front of the Robinson house
And then withdrew to the left, by flank, down Young's Branch,

1259 *the other side of the hill*: Henry House Hill; see map, p. 92. 1260 *two battered houses*: Henry and Robinson houses. 1268 *arras*: tapestry. 1272–1274 *The books say "Keyes' brigade . . .":* Compare: "Keyes's brigade . . . made a feeble advance . . . toward the Robinson house, and then . . . filed off by flank to its left . . . down Young's Branch . . . and took no further part in the engagement," Fry in *Battles and Leaders,* I, 188.

Taking no further part in the day."

                To Jack Ellyat   12'

It was a deadly fair in a burning field
Where strange crowds rushed to and fro and strange drunkards lay
Sprawled in a stupor deeper than wine or sleep,
A whining noise you shrank from and wanted to duck at,
And one dead cough left behind them in the tall grass   12
With the slow blood sopping its clothes like the blood on a shot
      duck's breast.

Imboden is wounded, Jackson is shot through the hand, the guns of Ricketts and Griffin, on the Henry House plateau, are taken and retaken; the gunners shot down at their guns while they hold their fire, thinking the advancing Thirty-Third Virginia is one of their own 12 regiments,° in the dimness of the battle-cloud.

It is nearly three o'clock—the South gathers for a final charge —on the left, Elzey's brigade,° new-come from the Shenandoah, defiles through the oaks near the Sudley Road to reinforce the grey wrestler —the blue wrestler staggers and goes back, on unsteady heels. 12

The charge sweeps the plateau—Bartow is killed, black-haired Bee mortally wounded, but the charge goes on.

For a moment, the Union line is a solid crescent again—a crescent with porcupine-pricks of steel—and then a crescent of sand—and then spilt sand, streaming away. 12

There is no panic at first. There is merely a moment when men have borne enough and begin to go home. The panic comes later, when they start to jostle each other.

Jefferson Davis, riding from Manassas, reaches the back-wash of the battle. A calm grey-bearded stranger tells him calmly that the 1 battle is lost and the South defeated.° But he keeps on, his weak eyes stung with the dust, a picture, perhaps, of a Plutarch death on a shield ° in his schooled mind—and is in time to see the last blue troops disappear beyond Bull Run, and hear the last sour grumble of their guns. 1

1285–1286 *one of their own* . . . : presumed to be "a regiment sent by Colonel Heintzelman to support the battery," Griffin as quoted in *Battles and Leaders*, I, 189. 1288 *Elzey's brigade*: Colonel Arnold Elzey took command of the Fourth Brigade of the Army of the Shenandoah when Brigadier General Kirby Smith was wounded. 1301 *grey-bearded stranger tells him calmly* . . . : "He asked a grey-bearded man whose calm face . . . inspired confidence, how the battle had gone. 'Our line was broken . . . and the battle lost,' " Jefferson Davis, *The Rise and Fall of the Confederate Government*, p. 349. 1302–1303 *Plutarch death on a/shield: The* slain Spartan warriors celebrated in Plutarch's writings were carried from the field of battle on a shield.

Judith Henry, Judith Henry, your body has born its ghost at last,
　　there are no more pictures of peace or terror left in the broken
　　machine of the brain that was such a cunning picture-maker:
Terrified ghost, so rudely dishoused by such casual violence, be at rest;
　　there are others dishoused in this falling night, the falling night is
　　a sack of darkness, indifferent as Saturn to wars or generals,° in-
　　different to shame or victory.
War is a while but peace is a while and soon enough the earth-colored
　　hands of the earth-workers will scoop the last buried shells and the
　　last clotted bullet-slag from the racked embittered acre,
And the rustling visitors drive out fair Sundays to look at the monument
　　near the rebuilt house, buy picture postcards and wonder dimly
　　what you were like when you lived and what you thought when you
　　knew you were going to die.

Wingate felt a frog in his throat   1310
As he patted Black Whistle's reeking coat
And reined him in for a minute's breath.
He was hot as the devil and tired to death,
And both were glad for the sun in the West
And a panting second of utter rest,   1315
While Wingate's mind went patching together
Like a cobbler piecing out scraps of leather
The broken glimmers of what they'd done
Since the sun in the West was a rising sun,
The long, bored hours of shiftless waiting   1320
And that single instant of pure, fierce hating
When the charge came down like a cataract
On a long blue beach of broken sand
And Thought was nothing but all was Act
And the sabre seemed to master the hand.   1325
Wainscott Bristol, a raging terrier
Killing the Yankee that shot Phil Ferrier
With a cut that spattered the bloody brains
Over his saddle and bridle-reins,
One Cotter cursing, the other praying,   1330
And both of them slashing like scythes of slaying,
Stuart Cazenove singing "Lord Randall" °
And Howard Brooke as white as a candle,

1307 *indifferent as Saturn to wars or generals*: During the ancient Roman Saturnalia,
seven days in December, military operations were suspended and war could not be
declared.   1332 *"Lord Randall"*: a Scottish border ballad of a young man about to
die after being poisoned by his "true love."

While Father fought like a fiend in satin,
And killed as he quoted tag-ends of Latin,   13
The prisoners with their sick, dazed wonder
And the mouths of children caught in a blunder
And over it all, the guns, the thunder,
The pace, the being willing to die,
The stinging color of victory.   13

He remembered it all like a harsh, tense dream.
It had a color. It had a gleam.
But he had outridden and lost the rest
And he was alone with the bloody West
And a trampled road, and a black hill-crest.°   13

The road and the bushes all about
Were cluttered with relics of Yankee rout,
Haversacks spilling their shirts and socks,
A burst canteen and a cartridge-box.
Rifles and cups trampled underfoot,   1
A woman's locket, a slashed black boot
Stained and oozing along the slash
And a ripe pear crushed to a yellow mash.
Who had carried the locket and munched the pear,
And why was a dead cat lying there,   1
Stark and grinning, a furry sack,
With a red flannel tongue and a broken back?
You didn't fight wars with a tabby-cat. . . .
He found he was telling the Yankees that,
They couldn't hear him of course, but still . . .   1
He shut his eyes for a minute until
He felt less dizzy. There, that was better,
And the evening wind was chilly and keen—
—He'd have to write Mother some sort of letter—
—He'd promised Amanda a Yank canteen,   1
But he didn't feel like getting it here,
Where that dead cat snickered from ear to ear—

Back in the pinewoods, clear and far,
A bugle sang like a falling star.

1345 *a trampled road, and a black hill-crest:* probably the Manassas-Sudley Road
and the high ground beyond the Henry House. See map, p. 92. By late afternoon (see line 1314, above), Stuart's cavalry had begun pursuit of the Union troops
to the west and north.

He shivered, turned Black Whistle around   1370
And galloped hastily toward the sound.

Curly Hatton opened his eyes again.
A minute ago he had been marching, marching,
Forever up and down enormous hills
While his throat scratched with thirst and something howled—   1375
But then there was a clear minute—and he was lying
In a long, crowded, strangely-churchly gloom
Where lanterns bobbed like marshlights in a swamp
And there was a perpetual rustling noise
Of dry leaves stirred by a complaining wind.   1380
No, they were only voices of wounded men.
"Water. Water. Water. Water. Water."
He heard the rain on the roof and sucked his lips.
"Water. Water. Water. Water. Water."
Oh, heavy sluices of dark, sweet, Summer rain,   1385
Pour down on me and wash me free again,
Cleanse me of battles, make my flesh smell sweet,
I am so sick of thirst, so tired of pain,
So stale with wounds and the heat!
Somebody went by, a doctor with red sleeves;   1390
He stared at the red sleeves and tried to speak
But when he spoke, he whispered. This was a church.
He could see a dim altar now and a shadow-pulpit.
He was wounded. They had put the wounded men in a church.
Lucy's face came to him a minute and then dissolved,   1395
A drowned face, ebbing away with a smile on its mouth.
He had meant to marry that face in another church.
But he was dying instead. It was strange to die.

All night from the hour of three, the dead man's hour, the rain falls
   in heavy gusts, in black irresistible streams as if the whole sky were
   falling in one wet huddle.
All night, living and dead sleep under it, without moving, on the
   field; the surgeons work in the church; the wounded moan; the
   dissevered fragments of companies and regiments look for each
   other, trying to come together.   1400
In the morning, when the burial-parties go out, the rain is still falling,
   damping the powder of the three rounds fired over the grave; before the grave is well-dug, the bottom of the grave is a puddle.

All day long the Southern armies bury their dead to the sodden drums
   of the rain; all day the bugle calls a hoarse-throated "Taps" °; the
    bugler lets the water run from his bugle-mouth and wipes it clean
   again and curses the rainy weather.

All night the Union army fled in retreat
Like horses scared by a shadow—a stumbling flood
Of panicky men who had been brave for a while   14•
And might be brave again on another day
But now were merely children chased by the night
And each man tainting his neighbor with the same
Blind fear.
         When men or horses begin to run
Like that, they keep on running till they tire out   14
Unless a strong hand masters a bridle-rein.
Here there was no hand to master, no rein to clutch,
Where the riderless horses kicked their way through the crowd
And the congressmen's carriages choked Cat Hairpin Bend.
Sykes and the regulars covered the retreat,   14•
And a few brigades were kept in some sort of order,
But the rest—They tried to stop them at Centerville.
McDowell and his tired staff held a haggard conference.
But before the officers could order retreat
The men were walking away.
         They had fought and lost.   1
They were going to Washington, they were going back
To their tents and their cooking-fires and their letters from Susie.
They were going back home to Maine or Vermont or Ohio,
And they didn't care who knew it, and that was that.°

Meanwhile, on the battlefield, Johnston and Beauregard,   1
Now joined by the dusty Davis, found themselves
As dazed by their victory as their foes by defeat.
They had beaten one armed mob with another armed mob

1402 *a hoarse-throated "Taps"*: a final tribute, but not the bugle call now known
as "Taps," which was composed by Union General Daniel Butterfield in July 1862,
a year after First Bull Run.   1418–1424 *a haggard conference/But . . . The men
were walking away . . .* : Compare Fry's recollection of this scene: "McDowell
consulted the . . . commanders who were at hand . . . but a decision of officers
. . . was of no moment; the men . . . were streaming away. . . . Their tents,
provisions, baggage, and letters from home were upon the banks of the Potomac,"
Battles and Leaders, I, 192.

And Washington was theirs for the simple act
Of stretching a hand to the apple up on the bough,   1430
If they had known. But they could not know it then.
They too saw spectres—unbroken Union reserves
Moving to cut their supply-line near Manassas.
They called back the pursuit, such scattered pursuit as it was.
Their men were tired and disordered. The chance went by   1435
While only the stiff-necked Jackson saw it clear
As a fighting-psalm or a phrase in Napoleon's tactics.
He said to the surgeon who was binding his wound,
With a taciturn snap, "Give me ten thousand fresh troops
And I will be in Washington by tomorrow."   1440
But they could not give him the troops while there yet was time.
He had three days' rations cooked for the Stonewall Brigade
And dourly awaited the order that never came.
He had always been at God's orders, and God had used him
As an instrument in winning a certain fight.   1445
Now, if God saw fit to give him the men and guns,
He would take Washington for the glory of God.
If He didn't, it was God's will and not to be questioned.

Meanwhile he could while the hours of waiting away
By seeing the Stonewall Brigade was properly fed,   1450
Endeavoring, with that rigid kindness of his
To show Imboden his error in using profanity
—In the heat of battle many things might be excused,
But nothing excused profanity, even then—°
And writing his Pastor° at Lexington a letter   1455
Enclosing that check for the colored Sunday-school
Which he'd promised, and, being busy, had failed to send.
There is not one word of Bull Run in all that letter
Except the mention of "a fatiguing day's service."
It would not have occurred to Jackson there might have been.   1460

1451–1454 *nothing excused profanity, even then*: Imboden tells of apologizing to
Jackson for swearing during the battle, to which the Colonel replied, "Nothing can
justify profanity," *Battles and Leaders*, I, 238.   1455–1459 *writing his Pastor . . .*:
"My dear pastor, in my tent last night, after a fatiguing day's service, I remembered
that I had failed to send you my contribution for our colored Sunday-school. Enclosed
you will find my check . . . yours faithfully, T. J. Jackson," quoted by Mary Anna
Jackson, *Memoirs of Stonewall Jackson*, p. 182.

Walt Whitman,° unofficial observer to the cosmos, reads of the defeat in a Brooklyn room. The scene rises before him, more real than the paper he stares upon. He sees the defeated army pouring along Pennsylvania Avenue in the drizzling rain, a few regiments in good order, marching in silence, with lowering faces—the rest a drenched, 146° hungry mob that plods along on blistered feet and falls asleep on the stoops of houses, in vacant lots, in basement-areas huddled, too tired to remember battle or be ashamed of flight.

Nothing said—no cries or cheers from the windows, no jeers from the secessionists in the watching crowd—half the crowd is secessionist 147 at heart, even now, more than ever now.

Two old women, white-haired, stand all day in the rain, giving coffee and soup and bread to the passing men. The tears stream down their faces as they cut the bread and pour out the coffee.

Whitman sees it all in his mind's eye—the tears of the two women 147 —the strange look on the men's faces, awake or asleep—the dripping, smoke-colored rain. Perplexed and deep in his heart, something stirs and moves—he is each one of them in turn—the beaten men, the tired women, the boy who sleeps there quietly with his musket still clutched tightly to him. The long lines of a poem begin to lash them- 148 selves against his mind, with the lashing surge and long thunder of Montauk° surf.

Horace Greeley has written Lincoln an hysterical letter°—he has not slept for seven nights—in New York, "on every brow sits sullen, scorching, black despair." 14

He was trumpeting "On to Richmond!" ° two weeks ago. But then the war was a thing for an editorial—a triumphal parade of Unionists over rebels. Now there has been a battle and a defeat. He pleads for an armistice—a national convention—anything on almost any terms to end this war. 14

1461–1482 *Walt Whitman* . . . : In *Specimen Days and Collect*, Whitman describes Washington after the battle. (See Benét's "Note," p. xiii.) Comapre Fry, *Battles and Leaders*, I, 193, whose account also concludes with Whitman's description.   1482 *Montauk*: the eastern tip of Long Island.   1483 *an hysterical letter* . . . : July 29, 1861; "This is my seventh sleepless night—yours too, doubtless. . . . If it is best . . . that we make peace with the rebels at once and on their own terms, do not shrink even from that . . . ," John G. Nicolay and John Hay, *Abraham Lincoln, A History,** IV, 365–366.   1486 *trumpeting "On to Richmond!"*: *The Tribune* had been carrying the motto "Forward to Richmond" on its editorial page since June 26.

Many think as he does; many fine words ring hollow as the skull
of an orator, the skull of a maker of war. They have raised the Devil
with slogans and editorials, but where is the charm that will lay him?
Who will bind the Devil aroused?

Only Lincoln, awkwardly enduring, confused by a thousand coun-   1495
sels, is neither overwhelmed nor touched to folly by the madness that
runs along the streets like a dog in August scared of itself, scaring
everyone who crosses its path.

Defeat is a fact and victory can be a fact. If the idea is good, it will
survive defeat, it may even survive the victory.   1500

His huge, patient, laborious hands start kneading the stuff of the
Union together again; he gathers up the scraps and puts them together;
he sweeps the corners and the cracks and patches together the lost
courage and the rags of belief.

The dough didn't rise that time—maybe it will next time. God   1505
must have tried and discarded a lot of experiment-worlds before he
got one even good enough to whirl for a minute—it is the same with a
belief, with a cause.

It is wrong to talk of Lincoln and a star together—that old rubbed
image is a scrap of tinsel, a scrap of dead poetry—it dries up and blows   1510
away when it touches a man. And yet Lincoln had a star, if you will
have it so—and was haunted by a prairie-star.

Down in the South another man, most unlike him but as steadfast, is haunted by another star that has little to do with tinsel, and
the man they call "Evacuation" Lee° begins to grow taller and to cast   1515
a longer shadow.

1515 *"Evacuation" Lee:* Such names as "Evacuation" Lee and "Granny" Lee had
grown out of minor failures in earlier operations in West Virginia.

❧ BOOK THREE ❧

By Pittsburg Landing,° the turbid Tennessee
Sucks against black, soaked spiles° with soil-colored waters.
That country is huge and disorderly, even now.
—This is Ellyat's tune, this is no tune but his—
Country of muddy rivers, sombre and swollen,   5
Country of bronze wild turkeys and catfish-fries
And brushpile landings going back to the brush.
A province of mush and milk, a half-cleared forest,
A speckled guinea-cock that never was cooped
But ran away to grow his spurs by himself.   10
Neither North nor South, but crunching a root of its own
Between strong teeth—perhaps a wild-onion-root,
Perhaps a white stalk of arbutus, hardier there,
Than any phantom-arbutus of Eastern Springs.°
A mudsill man° with the river-wash in his ears,   15
Munching the coarse, good meal of a johnny-cake
Hot from the hob°—even now it tastes of the brush,
The wilderness, the big lost star in the pines,
The brown river-dirt, the perpetual river-sound,
In spite of the sidewalks, in spite of the trolley-cars.   20
No trolley-car-bell can drown that river-sound,
Or take the loneliness out of the lost moon,
The night too big for a man, too lonesome and wide.
The vastness has been netted in railroad tracks
But it is still vast, uneasy.
                  And when the brief   25
Screech of the railway-whistle stabs at the trees
That grow so thick, so unplanned, so untidily strong
On either side of the two planned ribs of steel,
Ghost-steamboats answer it from the sucking brown water.
In Sixty-two, it was shaggy with wilderness still   30

1 *Pittsburg Landing:* in Hardin County, southwestern Tennessee. 2 *spiles:* pilings.
14 *phantom-arbutus of Eastern Springs:* The early, white blossoms of the evergreen
trailing arbutus native to the eastern United States are, according to Algonquin Indian legend, an assurance that winter has gone away. 15 *mudsill man:* one at the
bottom of the social order. "[Some] assume that whoever is once a hired laborer, is
fatally fixed in that condition for life . . . , that his condition is as bad as, or worse
than, that of a slave. This is the 'mudsill' theory," Lincoln, in Milwaukee on September 30, 1859, *Abraham Lincoln, Complete Works,** ed. John G. Nicolay and
John Hay, I, 581. 17 *hob:* hearth.

For stretches and stretches of close-packed undergrowth,
Wild as a muskrat, ignorant of the axe;
Stretches and stretches where roughly-chinked log-cabins,
Two shouts and a holler away from the nearest neighbors,
Stood in a wisp of open. All night long
The cabin-people heard the chant of the trees,
The forest, hewn away from the painful clearing
For a day or a year, with sweat and back-breaking toil,
But waiting to come back, to crush the crude house
And the planted space with vines and trailers of green,
To quench the fire on the hearth with running green saps,
With a chant of green, with tiny green tendrils curling,
—This is Ellyat's tune, this is no tune but his—
The railway-train goes by with a shrill, proud scream
And the woman comes to the door in a butternut dress
Hair tousled up in a knot on the back of her head,
A barefoot child at her skirt.
                                The train goes by.
They watch it with a slow wonder that is not pathos
Nor heroism but merely a slow wonder.

Jack Ellyat, in camp above Pittsburg Landing,
Speck in Grant's Army of the Tennessee,
Thought of old fences in Connecticut
With a homesick mind.
                        This country was too new,
Too stragglingly-unplanned, too muddy with great,
Uncomfortable floods, too roughly cut
With a broad hatchet out of a hard tree.

It had seemed fine when he was mustered out°
After Bull Run, to wear a veteran air,
And tell pink Ellen Baker about war
And how, as soon as he could re-enlist
He'd do it where he got a chance to fight—
Wet mouth of tears—he hadn't wanted to kiss her
At first, but it was easier later on.
Why had he ever gone out to Chicago?
Why had he ever heard that shallow band

---

57 *he was mustered out*: Ellyat had been a "three-month" man. See note, Book II,
line 259.

Whanging its brass along a Western street
And run to sign the muster-roll again?
Why had he ever talked about Bull Run
To these green, husky boys from Illinois
And Iowa, whose slang was different slang,   70
Who called suspenders galluses and swore
In the sharp pops of a mule-driver's whip?
Bull Run—it had impressed them for a week
But then they started to call him "Bull Run Jack." . . .

Henry Fairfield marching along with his sword,   75
All the old company marching after him
Back in McClellan's army, back by the known
Potomac, back in the safe and friendly East;
All the papers telling how brave they were
And how, as soon as the roads dried up in the spring,   80
"The little Napoleon" ° would hammer the South to bits
With a blue thunderbolt.
                                And here he was
A lost pea, spilt at random in a lost war;
A Tennessee war that had no *Tribunes* or polish
Where he was the only Easterner in the whole   85
Strange-swearing regiment of Illinois farmers,
Alien as Rebels, and rough as all outdoors.

He wanted to get transferred, he wanted to be
Back with the company, back with the Eastern voices,
Back where nobody called him "Bull Run Jack"   90
And snickered at him for shaving every two days.
He'd written about it and Father knew a congressman
But nothing would happen— he'd never get away,
He'd stay being Bull Run Jack till the end of the war
And march through acres of hostile Tennessee mud   95
Till his legs dropped off, and never get to be Corporal.
He was sick of the war and the mud and the Western faces.
He hated the sight of his Illinois uniform.
He was sorry for himself. He felt with a vague
Soft blur of self-pity that he was really quite brave,   100
And if people only knew, they'd do something about it.

81 *"The little Napoleon"*: "Little Mac," Major General George B. McClellan, was
five feet eight inches tall; see note, line 119, below.

This is Ellyat's tune, this is no tune but his.
Nine months have passed ° since McDowell reddened Bull Run,
Nine strong-hoofed months, but they have meant little to Ellyat.
What means the noise of the wind to the dust in the wind?   105
But the wind calls strange things out, calls strange men out,
A dozen pictures flash in front of the eyes
And are gone in a flash—
                                rough-bearded Tecumseh Sherman,
Who had tried most things, but being cursed with a taste
For honesty, had found small luck in his stars;   110
Ex-soldier, banker, lawyer, each in its turn,
Ex-head of a Southern military-school,
Untidy ex-president of a little horse-railroad;°
Talkative, nervous, salty, Scotch-Irish fighter,
High-strung, quick-tempered, essentially modern-minded,   11
Stamping the length of the dusty corridors
Of a Western hotel with a dead cigar in his teeth,
Talking the war to himself, till the word goes round
The new general is crazy—
                                neat, handsome McClellan,
Ex-railroad president too,° but a better railroad;   12
The fortunate youth, the highly-modern boy-wonder,
The snapping-eyed, brisk banner-salesman of war
With all the salesman's gifts and the salesman's ego;
Great organizer, with that magnetic spark
That pulls the heart from the crowd—and all of it spoiled   12
By the Napoleon-complex that haunts such men.
There never has been a young banner-salesman yet
That did not dream of a certain little cocked-hat
And feel it fit. McClellan felt that it fitted.
—After a year and a day,° the auditors come,   13
Dry auditors, going over the books of the company,

103 *Nine months have passed:* It is now April 1862.   108–113 *Sherman, . . .*
Ex-soldier, banker, lawyer . . . : Major General William Tecumseh Sherman
(USMA, 1840); resigned his commission, 1853; was partner in a San Francisco
bank, an unsuccessful lawyer in Leavenworth, Kansas, Superintendent of Louisiana
State Seminary, and President, St. Louis Street Railway; returned to uniform as
Colonel, 31st Infantry, May 1861.   119–120 *McClellan,/Ex-railroad president too:*
George Brinton McClellan (USMA, 1846), three times breveted in the Mexican
War; resigned his commission, 1857; was president of the Ohio and Mississippi Rail-
road, 1860; and returned to uniform as a Major General of Ohio Volunteers, 1861.
130 *After a year and a day:* McClellan, who was made Commander-in-Chief of land
forces on November 1, 1861, was relieved November 5, 1862.

Sad auditors, with groups of red and black figures
That are not moved by a dream of precious cocked hats.
And after the auditors go, the board of directors
Decides, with a sigh, to do without banner-salesmen—   135
It is safer to dream of a rusty Lincoln stovepipe.°
That dream has more patience in it.
                                        And yet, years later
Meeting the banner-salesman in some cheap street
With the faded clippings of old success in his pocket,
One cannot help feeling sorry for the cocked hat   140
So briefly worn in a dream of luck and the ego.
One cannot help feeling sorry for George McClellan,
He should have been a hero by every rule.
He looked the part—he could have acted the part
Word perfectly. He looked like an empire-maker.   145
But so few empire-makers have looked the part.

Fate has a way of picking unlikely material,
Greasy-haired second lieutenants of French artillery,
And bald-headed, dubious, Roman rake-politicians.°
Her stiff hands were busy now with an odd piece of wood,   150
Sometime Westpointer, by accident more than choice,
Sometime brevet-captain in the old Fourth Infantry,
Mentioned in Mexican orders for gallant service
And, six years later, forced to resign from the Army
Without enough money to pay for a stateroom home.   155
Turned farmer on Hardscrabble Farm, turned bill-collector,
Turned clerk in the country-store that his brothers ran,
The eldest-born of the lot, but the family-failure,
Unloading frozen hides from a farmer's sleigh
With stoop-shouldered strength, whittling beside the stove,   160
And now and then turning to whiskey to take the sting
From winter and certain memories.
                                        It didn't take much.°

136 *a rusty Lincoln stovepipe:* Lincoln's untidy top hat was one of his political trademarks.   148–149 *Greasy-haired second lieutenants . . . Roman rake-politicians:* The allusions are to Napoleon Bonaparte and Julius Caesar.   151–162 *Sometime Westpointer . . . :* General (Brigadier General at Shiloh) Ulysses S. Grant. Grant had reluctantly accepted a West Point appointment, which his father had arranged; he graduated with the Class of 1843; resigned his commission in 1854; settled near St. Louis on land belonging to his father-in-law, and built a four-room log house on the farm he called "Hardscrabble." After a series of failures, he returned to the Grant family's leather business in Galena, Illinois, in May 1860.

A glass or two would thicken the dogged tongue
And flush the fair skin beneath the ragged brown beard.
Poor and shabby—old "Cap" Grant of Galena,   16
Who should have amounted to something but hadn't so far
Though he worked hard and was honest.
                               A middle-aged clerk,
A stumpy, mute man in a faded army overcoat,
Who wrote the War Department after Fort Sumter,
Offering them such service as he could give   1?
And saying he thought that he was fit to command
As much as a regiment, but getting no answer.
So many letters come to a War Department,
One can hardly bother the clerks to answer them all—
Then a Volunteer colonel,° drilling recruits with a stick,   1'
A red bandanna instead of an officer's sash;
A brigadier-general, one of thirty-seven,
Snubbed by Halleck and slighted by fussy Frémont;°
And then the frozen February gale
Over Fort Henry and Fort Donelson,   1
The gunboats on the cold river—the brief siege—
"Unconditional surrender" °—and the newspapers.

Major-General Grant, with his new twin-stars,
Who, oddly, cared so little for reading newspapers,
Though Jesse Grant wrote dozens of letters to them   1
Pointing out all the wonders his son had done
And wringing one dogged letter° from that same son

---

175 *Volunteer colonel*: with the 21st Illinois Volunteers, June 1861.   178 *Snubbed by Halleck and slighted by . . . Frémont*: Benét has here reversed the order of events. Major General John C. Frémont gave Grant command of the District of Southeastern Missouri, but only after keeping him waiting for hours for an interview and gratuitously instructing him to procure and wear a proper uniform. Five months later, when Grant rode to St. Louis to seek authority to attack the Confederate forces in Tennessee at Forts Henry and Donelson, Major General Henry W. Halleck, who had succeeded Frémont temporarily, "refused permission, and snubbed Grant so badly that he returned very much crestfallen." See William C. Church, *Ulysses S. Grant*, pp. 82–83, 99.   182 *"Unconditional surrender"*: At Fort Donelson, February 16, 1862, Grant responded to Confederate armistice proposals by writing, "No terms except an unconditional and immediate surrender can be accepted," *Battles and Leaders*, I, 427.   187 *one dogged letter*: From Corinth, Mississippi, September 17, 1862, Grant wrote his father: "I have not an enemy in the world who has done me so much damage as you in your efforts in my defence. I require no defenders and for my sake let me alone. . . . Do nothing to correct what you have already done but for the future keep quiet on this subject," *Letters of Ulysses S. Grant*, edited by Jesse Grant Cramer, pp. 90–91.

That should have squelched anybody but Jesse Grant.
It did not squelch him. He was a business man,
And now Ulysses had astonished Galena   190
By turning out to be somebody after all;
Ulysses' old father was going to see him respected
And, incidentally, try to wangle a contract
For army-harness and boom the family tannery.
It was a great surprise when Ulysses refused,   195
The boy was so stubborn about it.°
                            And everywhere
Were business-people, picking up contraband cotton,
Picking up army-contracts, picking up shoddy,°
Picking up shoes and blankets, picking up wagons,
Businesslike robins, picking up juicy earthworms,   200
Picking up gold all over Tom Tiddler's Ground,°
And Ulysses wouldn't see it.
                            Few people have been
More purely Yankee, in essence, than Jesse Grant.

More pictures—Jefferson Davis, in dripping Spring rain,
Reading a chilly inauguration-address   205
To an unstirred crowd. He is really President now.°
His eyes are more tired, his temper beginning to fray.
A British steamer in the Bahama Channel
Stopped by a Captain Wilkes and a Union cruiser.
They take two men, and let the steamer puff on   210
—And light a long hissing fuse that for a month
Nearly brings war with England. Lincoln and Seward
Stamp out the fuse, and let the Confederates go—°
Wooden frigates at anchor in Hampton Roads

196 *so stubborn about it:* Concerning his father's solicitations, Grant wrote his sister Mary on October 25, 1861: "I do not want to be importuned for places. I have none to give and want to be placed under no obligation to any one. . . . I want always to be in a condition to do my duty without partiality, favor, or affection," *Letters of Ulysses S. Grant,* p. 62.   198 *shoddy:* inferior material rewoven from shredded cloth.   201 *Tom-Tiddler's Ground:* from a children's game in which participants invade the territory of one of the players, exclaiming, "We're on Tom Tiddler's Ground picking up gold and silver."   206 *really President now:* Davis was inaugurated President of the Confederacy, February 18, 1862.   212–213 *Nearly brings war with England* . . . : historically, the "Trent Affair." On November 8, 1861, James Mason and John Slidell, Confederate agents en route to seek European alliances for the South, were taken from the British packet *Trent* on the initiative of U.S. Navy Captain Charles Wilkes and held on board his frigate *San Jacinto.* They were released to British control on January 1, 1862, after long and difficult deliberation in the American cabinet.

Burning and sinking with tattered banners apeak   2

Under the strange new, armadillo-bite

Of something plated with iron that yet can float,

The *Merrimac*—and all Washington and the North

In a twenty-four-hours' panic—then, next day—

As Lincoln stares from the window of the White House   2

For the sooty sign in the sky that means defeat—

The armadillo, smoking back in her pride

To crunch up another meal of weak wooden ships,

Is beaten off by another leaky prodigy

A tin-can cylinder on a floating shingle,

The *Monitor*—the first fight of iron-clads,°   2

The sinking of all the world's old sea-bitten names,°

Temeraire, Victory, and *Constellation,*

Serapis, Bon Homme Richard, Golden Hind,

Galleys of Antony, galleys of Carthage,   2

Galleons with gilded Virgins, galleasses,

Viking long-serpents, siren-haunted galliots,

Argos and argosies and the Achæan pride,

Moving to sea in one long wooden wall

Behind the huge ghost-flagship of the Ark   2

In such a swelling cloud of phantom sail

They whitened Ocean—going down by the head,

Green water seeping through the battened ports,

Spreading along the scrubbed and famous decks,

Going down—going down—going down—to mermaid-pools,   2

To Fiddler's Green—to the dim barnacle-thrones,

Where Davy Jones° drinks everlasting rum

With the sea-horses of his sunken dreams.

But this is Ellyat's tune—and if the new

Army of the Potomac stands astrain   2

To end Secession with its "little Napoleon;"

If Lee is just about to find his hour;

If, among many mirrors and gilt chairs,

Under the flare of the gas-chandeliers

226 *the first fight of iron-clads:* The engagement between the Confederate *Virginia* (known in the North as the *Merrimac*) and the Union *Monitor* took place in Hampton Roads, March 8–9, 1862.   227 *old sea-bitten names:* There follows a list of wooden ships famous by name and type, made passé by the success of the iron-clad.   241–242 *Fiddler's Green . . . Davy Jones:* In nautical folklore, "Fiddler's Green" is the sailors' elysium; Davy Jones, less benevolent than Benét implies here, is master of the graveyard of those who perish at sea.

A sallow-faced and puffy Emperor°   250
With waxed mustachios and a slick goatee
Gave various Southern accents, talking French,
Evasive answers and no definite help,
Ready enough to recognize the South
If he were sure of profit in the scheme   255
But not yet finding such a profit sure;
If in the foggy streets of Westminster,
The salty streets of Liverpool and Hull,
The same mole-struggle in the dark went on
Between Confederate and Unionist—   260
The *Times* raved at the North—Mr. Gladstone thought
England might recognize the South next year,
While Palmerston° played such a tangled game
It is illegible yet—and Henry Adams
Added one more doubt to his education   265
By writing propaganda for the North,°
It is all mist to Ellyat.
               And when he sleeps,
He does not dream of Grant or Lee or Lincoln.
He only dreams that he is back at home
With a heroic wound that does not hurt,   270
A uniform that never stings with lice,
And a sword like Henry Fairfield's to show Ellen Baker.

As far as the maps and the blocks on the maps have meaning
The situation is this.°
              A wide Western river,
A little lost landing,° with a steamboat-store,   275
A post office where the roads from the landings meet,
A plank church three miles inland called Shiloh Chapel,
An undulating and broken table-land
Roughed into a triangle by bordering creeks.

250 *puffy Emperor:* Napoleon III of France.   261–263 *The Times . . . Mr. Glad-stone . . . Palmerston: The London Times.* William Gladstone, Chancellor of the Exchequer at the time, openly favored the Confederacy. Viscount Palmerston, the Prime Minister, was less outspoken concerning his position on recognition.   264–266 *Henry Adams . . . writing propaganda for the North:* Adams was in London as secretary to his father, Charles Francis Adams, United States Minister to England. While there, he wrote a number of unsigned inflammatory letters for anonymous publication in England and America. See *The Education of Henry Adams,* Chapter VIII.   274 *The situation is this:* before the Battle of Shiloh, April 6–7, 1862.   275 A *little lost landing:* Pittsburg Landing. See note, line 1, above.

ADAMSVILLE

CRUMP

Crump's Landing

SAVANNAH
[TENNESSEE]

BUELL
Army of the Ohio
25,000

Lew Wallace's Division

Snake Creek

GRANT
Army of the Tennessee
33,000

STANTONVILLE

Creek

Owl Creek

Pittsburg Landing

GUNBOATS

SHILOH

CORINTH PITTSBURG ROAD

BARK ROAD

Tennessee River

A.S. JOHNSTON
Army of the Mississippi
40,000

Lick Creek

HAMBURG

to CORINTH

Johnston killed during the
afternoon of April 6,
Beauregard then in command.

SHILOH

SITUATION AT THE CLOSE OF THE
FIRST DAY'S BATTLE, APRIL 6, 1862

0   1   2   3
SCALE OF MILES

Each side of the triangle runs about four miles long   280
And, scattered in camps from the tip of the triangle
To the base at the landing, are thirty-three thousand men,
Some fairly seasoned in war, but many green sticks,
Grant's Army of the Tennessee.
                              Down the river
Don Carlos Buell ° has twenty-five thousand more   285
In the Army of the Ohio.
                        Opposing these
Are Albert Sidney Johnston and Beauregard °
With something like forty thousand butternut fighters,
Including a martial bishop.°
                          Johnston plans
To smash Grant's army to bits, before Buell can join it,   290
And water his wagon-trains in the Tennessee.
He has sneaked his army along through wilderness roads
Till now they are only a mile and a half away
Tonight from the Union lines.
                            He is tall and active.
Light brown hair streaked with grey feathers, blue claymore° eyes   295
That get steel shadows in battle, a face like Hamilton's,
Old Westpointer, old cavalry-colonel, well-schooled in war.
Lincoln offered to make him a major-general
And rumor says that he could have had the command
Of the Union armies, once.
                          But he resigned °   300
And later, went with his State. It is hard to say
What he might have been.
                        They called him the *"preux chevalier"* °
At times, as they called and were to call many others
With that Waverley-streak° that was so strong in the South.

---

285 *Don Carlos Buell:* On April 5, General Buell was moving to join Grant against
the Confederate Army of the Mississippi; his division nearest Grant was in Savannah,
seven miles downstream; see map, facing.   287 *Albert Sidney Johnston and
Beauregard:* General A. S. Johnston (not to be confused with Joseph E. Johnston)
was killed the afternoon of April 6, the first day of the battle; General Beauregard
(see note, Book II, line 8) then took command of the Confederate forces.
289 *a martial bishop:* Leonidas Polk (USMA, 1827), Episcopal Bishop of Louisiana,
Lieutenant General, CSA.   295 *claymore:* double-edged Scottish sword.   298–300
Lincoln offered . . . But he resigned: Johnston, then a Brevet Brigadier General
commanding the Department of the Pacific, declined preferment in the Union forces
and resigned in April 1861, shortly after Texas, his adopted state, seceded.   302
"preux chevalier": gallant knight.   304 *Waverley-streak:* The allusion is to Sir Walter Scott's Waverley novels. See note, Book I, line 991.

They also called him one of Davis's pets,   305
One of the tin Westpointers that Davis favored °
Above good politicians and courtesy colonels.
The Richmond *Enquirer* didn't think so much of him,
His soldiers thought rather more.
        Only this can be said.
He caught Grant napping in some strange flaw of skill   310
Which happened once and did not happen again.
And drove his unprepared, unwatchful brigades
Back almost into the river.
       And in the heat
Of seeing his lines go forward, he bled to death
From a wound that should not have been mortal.
         After which,   315
While the broken Union stragglers under the bluff
Were still howling that they were beaten, Buell came up,°
Lew Wallace° came up, the knife half-sunk in the wound
Was not thrust home,° the night fell, the battle lagged.
The bulldog got the bone in his teeth again   320
And next day, reinforced, beat Beauregard back
And counted a Union victory.
      In the books
Both sides claim victory on one day or the other
And both claims seem valid enough.
       It only remains
To take the verdict of the various dead   325
In this somewhat indecisive meeting of blocks.
There were thirty-five hundred dead when the blocks had met.
But, being dead, their verdict is out of court.
They cannot puzzle the books with their testimony.

Now, though, it is only the evening before the day.   330
Johnston and Beauregard meet with their corps-commanders
By the wagon-cut Pittsburg road. The march has been slow.
The marching men have been noisy and hard to manage.

---

306 *tin Westpointers that Davis favored:* Jefferson Davis was himself a graduate of
West Point, Class of 1828.   316–317 *stragglers under the bluff . . . Buell came up:*
"The face of the bluff was crowded with stragglers. . . . The number at nightfall
would not have fallen short of fifteen thousand," Buell in *Battles and Leaders*, I,
494.   318 *Lew Wallace:* Major General Lew Wallace, commanding Grant's Third
Division, later remembered as the author of *Ben Hur*.   319 *Was not thrust home:*
There was no pursuit by Confederate forces.

By every rule of war, Grant must have been warned
Long before now, and is planning an ambush for them.   335
They are being marched into an open Union trap.
So Beauregard thinks° and says—and is perfectly right
According to rules. There is only one difficulty.
There is no ambush.
                    Sherman has just reported
The presence of enemy troops in front of his lines   340
But says he expects nothing more than some picket-firing
And Grant that evening° telegraphs General Halleck,
"I have scarcely the faintest idea of an attack."

So much for the generals. Beauregard makes his point
And is overruled.
                    The April night comes down.   345
The butternut men try to get some sleep while they can.
They are to be up and fighting by five in the morning.

Jack Ellyat, least of any, expected attack.
He woke about five with a dazzle struck in his eyes
Where a long dawn-ray slid through a crack in the tent.   350
He cursed at the ray and tried to go back to sleep
But he couldn't do it, although he was tired enough,
Something ate at his mind as soon as he wakened
And kept on eating.
                    This morning was Sunday morning.
The bells would be jangling for church back home, pretty soon,   355
The girls would be going to church in white Sunday dresses.
No, it was too early for that—they'd be muffled up
In coats and galoshes. Their cheeks would be pink as apples.
He wanted to see a girl who washed her hair,
Not a flat old woman sucking a yellow snuffstick   360
Or one of the girls in the dirty blue silk wrappers
With flags on their garters. He wanted to see a girl.

He wondered idly about the flags on the garters.
Did they change them to Rebel flags when the Rebels came?
Some poor whore down the river had had herself   365
Tattooed with a Secesh° flag. She was patriotic.

336–337 *into an open Union trap./So Beauregard thinks:* "I could not believe the
enemy was still ignorant of our near presence . . . ," Beauregard in *Battles and
Leaders*, I, 583.   342 *that evening:* April 5, 1862.   366 *Secesh:* secessionist.

She cried so hard when the Union troops were landed
That the madam had to hide her down in the cellar.
He must be bad to be thinking of things like that
On Sunday morning. He'd better go to church   370
If they had any kind of church, and make up for it—
O frosty churchbells jangling across the thin
Crust of packed frost, under Connecticut sky,
Put snow on my tongue, and the grey, cool flower of rain—
He had to get up. He couldn't lie here and listen   375
To Bailey and the rest of them, snoring away.
His throat was dry. He needed a drink of water
But not from a muddy river—put rain on my tongue!
Souse me with chilly, sweet flaws° of Puritan rain—
He started to put on his boots, looking over at Bailey.   380
Bailey was bearded, Bailey was thirty-two,
Bailey had been a teamster and was a corporal.
The waking Bailey looked like a stupid horse,
The sleeping Bailey looked like a dirty sack,
Bailey called him "Colonel" and didn't mean it,   385
Bailey had had him tossed in a blanket once,
Bailey had told the tale of the tattooed whore,
Somehow he hated Bailey worse than the rest.
He managed to leave the tent without waking Bailey.
It was very early still. The sun was just up.   390
A fair sky, a very fair day. The air still held
That bloom which is not the bloom on apple or peach
But the bloom on a fruit made up of pure water and light,
The freshness of dawn, still trembling, being new-born.
He sucked at it gratefully.
                          The camp was asleep.   395
All that length of tents still asleep. He could see through the tents.
He could see all those sleeping, rough, lousy, detested men
Laden with sleep as with soft leaden burdens laden,
Movelessly lying between the brown fawns of sleep
Like infants nuzzled against the flanks of a doe,   400
In quietness slumbering, in a warm quietness,
While sleep looked at them with her fawn's agate eyes
And would not wake them yet.
                          And he was alone,
And for a moment, could see this, and see them so

379 *flaws*: sudden gusts.

And, being free, stand alone, and so being free   405
To love or hate, do neither, but merely stand
Above them like sleep and see them with untouched eyes.
In a while they would wake, and he would hate them again.
But now he was sleep. He was the sun on the coat
Of the halted fawn at the green edge of the wood   410
Staring at morning.
                    He could not hate them yet.

Somebody near by, in the woods, took a heap of dry sticks,
And began to break them quickly, first one by one,
Then a dozen together, then hard-cracking axe-helves° breaking.
Ellyat was running. His mouth felt stiff with loud words   415
Though he heard no sound from his mouth. He could see the white
Fine pine-splinters flying from those invisible axe-helves. . . .

For a minute all of them were tangled together
In the bucking tent like fish in a canvas scoop,
Then they were out of it somehow—falling in line—   420
Bailey's hair looked angry and sleepy. The officers
Were yelling the usual things that officers yelled.
It was a surprise. They were going to be licked again.
It did not matter yet. It would matter soon.
Bailey had lost his blouse and his pants weren't buttoned.   425
He meant to tell Bailey about it. There wasn't time.
His eyes felt bald as glass but that was because
He kept looking for flying pine-splinters in the air.
Now they were setting off firecrackers under a boiler
And a man ran past with one hand dripping red paint,   430
Holding the hand with his other hand and talking
As if the hurt hand were a doll.
                        An officer hit him
With the flat of a sword. It spanked some dust from his coat
And the man's face changed from a badly-fitting mask
Of terror, cut into ridges of sallow wax,   435
To something pink and annoyed, but he kept on running.
All this happened at once as they were moving.
The dawn had been hit to pieces with a hard mallet.
There were no fawns. There was an increasing noise
Through which he heard the lugubrious voice of Bailey   440

414 *axe-helves:* ax handles.

Singing off-key, like a hymn,
>   "When I was a weaver, I lived by myself,
>   And I worked at the weaver's tra-a-de—" °

The officers were barking like foxes now.

As the last tent dropped behind them, Ellyat saw   4·
A red, puzzled face, looking out from under a tent-flap,
Like a bear from a cave. The face had been drunk last night,°
And it stared at the end of the column with a huge and stupid
>   wisdom.

"When I was a weaver, I lived by myself,
And I worked at the weaver's trade—"   4·

Jack Ellyat found himself back behind somebody's tent
After a while. He had been out in the woods.
He remembered scrouging against a too-porous tree
For a day or a number of minutes while he jerked
A rattling ramrod up and down in a gun.   4
But they couldn't stay in the woods—they had to come back.
They had called him "Bull Run Jack" but they had to come back,
Bailey and all the rest. He had come back with them,
But that was different—that was all right for him.
This red-colored clang of haste was diffcrent for him.   4·
Bailey and all the rest could run where they liked.
He was an old soldier. He would stay here and fight.

442–443 *When I was a weaver* . . . : "The Foggy, Foggy Dew," a folk ballad.

>   When I was a bachelor, I lived by myself
>   I worked at the weaver's trade;
>   The only, only thing I did that was wrong
>   Was to woo a fair young maid.
>   I wooed her in the winter-time
>   And in the summer, too;
>   And the only, only thing I did that was wrong,
>   Was to keep her from the foggy, foggy dew.

>   Oh, I am a bachelor, I live with my son;
>   We work at the weaver's trade;
>   And every single time I look into his eyes
>   He reminds me of the fair young maid. . . .

446–447 *A red, puzzled face . . . drunk last night*: Grant has been popularly regarded as a heavy drinker and was accused of being drunk at Shiloh. He did not,
however, arrive at Pittsburg Landing until after the initial attack here described by
Benét.

Running, he tripped on a rope, and began to fall,
Bailey picked him back on his feet. "Did they get you, Bud?"
"No, they didn't get me."
Ellyat's voice was a snarl.   465
What business had Bailey steadying him like that?
He hadn't been running.
Suddenly he saw
Grey shouting strangers bursting into the tents
And his heart shrank up in a pea.
"Oh hell," he said,
Hopelessly ramming a cartridge. He was an old soldier.   470
He wasn't going to run. He was going to act
Vast fictive heroisms in front of Bailey,
If they only gave him time, just a little time.

A huge horse rose above the wall of the tent
And hung there a second like a bad prodigy,   475
A frozen scream full of hoofs.
He struck at its head
And tried to get out from under as it lunged down
But he wasn't quite quick enough.
As he slipped and fell
He saw the laughter pasted on Bailey's face
But before he could hear the laugh, the horse had fallen,   480
Jarring the world.
After blunt, sickly time
A fat young man with a little pink moustache
Was bawling "Hey, Yank, surrender!" into his ear
And nervously waving a pistol in front of his eyes.
He nodded weakly. "Hey, boys," called the fat young man,   485
"I got two Yanks!" His mouth was childish with pleasure.
He was going to tell everybody he had two Yanks.
"Here, Yank, come and pull the horse off the other Yank."

The prisoner's column straggled along the road
All afternoon. Jack Ellyat marched in it numbly.   490
He was stiff and sore. They were going away from the battle
But they could still hear it, quaking,
The giant stones rolled over the grumbling bridge.

Some of the prisoners tried to joke with the guards,
Some walked in silence, some spoke out now and then,   495
As if to explain to the world why they were there.

One man said, "I got a sore heel." Another said,
"All the same the Tenth Missouri's a damn good regiment."
Another said, "Listen, boys, don't it beat all hell?
I left my tobacco behind me, back in the tent,   5
Don't it beat all hell to lose your tobacco like that?"

Bailey kept humming the "Weaver," but now and then
He broke it off, to say, with a queer satisfaction,
"Well, we surely did skedaddle—we surely did."
Jack Ellyat had said nothing for a long time.   5
This was war, this was Phaëton,° this was the bronze chariot
Rolling the sky. If he had a soul any more
It felt scrawny and thin as a sick turkey-poult.
It was not worth the trouble to fatten. He tried to fatten it
With various thoughts, now and then, but the thoughts were spoilt   5
Corn. They had damn well skedaddled. They damn well had.
That was all. The rest of the army could win or lose
They had surely skedaddled. They had been whipped again.
He had been whipped again.
                            He was no longer
The old soldier—no longer even "Bull Run Jack."   5
He had lost a piece of himself. It had ragged edges
That piece. He could see it left behind in the tents
Under a dirty coat and a slab of tobacco.

After a while he knocked against Bailey's arm.
"Where are we going?" he said, in a shy voice.
Bailey laughed, not badly, "Well, Colonel, Corinth° I guess,
Corinth first—and then some damn prison-camp."
He spat in the road. "It won't be good grub," he said.
"Bacon and hominy-grits. They don't eat right.
They don't eat nothing but bacon and hominy-grits.
God, I'm goin' to get tired of bacon and hominy-grits!"

Ellyat looked. There was something different about him.
He stated a fact. "You've buttoned your pants," he said.
"I remember you didn't have 'em buttoned this morning."

"That's so," said Bailey, impressed, "Now when did I button 'em?"
They chewed at the question, trying to puzzle it out.
It seemed very important to both for quite a long time.

------

506 *this was Phaëton:* See note, Book I, line 1058.   521 *Corinth:* Corinth, Mississippi, the Confederate base of operations.

It was night now. The column still marched. But Bailey and Ellyat
Had dropped to the rear of the column, planning escape.
There were few guards and the guards were as tired as they.   535
Two men could fall in a ditch by the side of the road
And get away, perhaps, if they picked a good time.
They talked it over in stupid whispers of weariness.
The next bend—no, the guard was coming along.
The next bend after—no, there was light for a moment   540
From a brief star, then clouded—the top of the hill—
The bottom of the hill—and they still were marching.
Rain began to fall, a drizzle at first, then faster.
Ellyat's eyes were thick. He walked in a dream,
A heavy dream, cut from leaden foil with blunt shears.   545
Then Bailey touched him—he felt the tired bones of his skull
Click with a sudden spark—his feet stopped walking—
He held his breath for an instant,
And then wearily slumped in the ditch with enormous noise,
Hunching his shoulders against a phantom bayonet.   550

But when he could raise his head, the column had gone.
He felt fantastic. They couldn't escape like this.
You had to escape like a drawing in *Harper's Weekly*
With stiff little men on horses like sickle-pears°
Firing round frozen cream-puffs into your back.   555
But they had escaped.
                    Life came back to him in a huge
Wave of burnt stars. He wanted to sing and yell.
He crackled out of the ditch and stood beside Bailey.
Had he ever hated Bailey? It could not have been.
He loved Bailey better than anything else in the world.   560

They moved slyly toward the woods, they were foxes escaped.
Wise foxes sliding away to a hidden earth
To a sandy floor, to the warm fawn-flanks of sweet sleep. . . .
And then an awful molasses-taffy voice
Behind them yelled "Halt!" and "Halt!" and—sudden explosion   565
Of desultory popcorn in iron poppers—
Wild running at random—a crash among broken boughs—
A fighting sound—Bailey's voice, half-strangled but clear,
"Run like hell, Jack, they'll never catch you!"
                                        He ran like hell.

Time passed like the rain. Time passed and was one with the rain.   570

---

554 *sickle-pears:* Seckel pears, stubby, asymmetrical fruit; compare Book II, line 920.

Ellyat woke from a nightmare and put out his hand
To touch the wall by his bed, but there was no wall.
Then he listened for Bailey's snoring.

> And he heard

The gorged, sweet pouring of water through infinite boughs,
The hiss of the big spilt drop on the beaten leaf,   57
The bird-voiced and innumerable rain,
A wet quail piping, a thousand soaked black flutes
Building a lonely castle of sliding tears,
Strange and half-cruel as a dryad's° bright grief.

Ellyat huddled closer under the tree,   58
Remembering what he could. He had run for years,
He had slept for years—and yet it was still not dawn.
It seemed cruel to him that it should never be dawn.
It seemed cruel that Bailey was lost. He had meant to show
Some fictive heroisms in front of Bailey.   58
He had not. Bailey had saved his skin instead,
And Bailey was lost. And in him something was lost,
Something worse than defeat or this rain—some piece of himself.
Some piece of courage.

> Now the slant rain began

To creep through his sodden heart. He thought, with wild awe,   59
"This is Nibelung Hall.° I am lying in Nibelung Hall.
I am long dead. I fell there out of the sky
In a wreck of horses, spilling the ball of the sun,°
And they shut my eyes with stone runes° and put me to sleep
On a bier where the living stream perpetually flows   59
Past Ygdrasil ° and waters the roots of the world.
I can hear the ravens scream from the cloudy roof.
I can hear the bubbles rising in the clear stream.
I can hear the old gods shout in the heathen sky
As the hawk-Valkyrie carry the stiffened lumps   60
Of corpse-faced heroes shriekingly to Valhalla.°

---

579 *dryad's:* wood nymph's.   591 *Nibelung Hall:* gathering place of the gods and supernatural beings of Teutonic mythology. Benét has derived the name from the traditions of the *Nibelungenlied.*   592–593 *I fell . . . spilling the ball of the sun:* See line 506, above, and note, Book I, line 1058.   594 *runes:* characters from the ancient Teutonic alphabet, often regarded as magical or mysterious.   596 *Ygdrasil:* in Teutonic legend, the perennially green "world-tree," a three-rooted ash sheltering all living beings.   600–601 *As the hawk-Valkyrie carry . . . heroes shriekingly to Valhalla:* The Valkyries chose those warriors to be admitted to Odin's feasts and carried them to Valhalla, the hall of bravely fallen heroes.

This is Nibelung Hall. I must break the runes from my eyes.
I must escape it or die."

He slept. The rain fell.

Melora Vilas, rising by candlelight,
Looked at herself in the bottom of the tin basin   605
And wished that she had a mirror.

Now Spring was here,
She could kneel above the well of a forest pool
And see the shadow hidden under the water,
The intent brown eyes, the small face cut like a heart.
She looked at the eyes and the eyes looked back at her,   610
But just when it seemed they could start to talk to each other—
"What are you like? Who are you?"—

a ripple flawed
The deep glass and the shadow trembled away.

If she only had a mirror, maybe she'd know
Something, she didn't know what, but something important,   615
Something like knowing your skin and you were alive
On a good day, something as drenched as sleep,
As wise as sleep, as piercing as the bee's dagger.
But she'd never know it unless she could get a mirror
And they'd never get a mirror while they were hiders.   620
They were bound to be hiders as long as the war kept on.
Pop was that way. She remembered roads and places.
She was seventeen. She had seen a lot of places,
A lot of roads. Pop was always moving along.
Everybody she'd ever known was moving along.   625
—Dusty wagons full of chickens and children,
Full of tools and quilts, Rising Sun and Roses of Sharon,°
Mahogany dressers out of Grandmother's house,
Tin plates, cracked china, a couple of silver spoons,
Moving from State to State behind tired, scuffed horses   630
Because the land was always better elsewhere.

Next time they'd quit. Next stop they'd settle right down.
Next year they'd have time to rub up the mahogany dresser.
Next place, Mom could raise the flowers she wanted to raise.
But it never began. They were always moving along.   635

627 *Rising Sun and Roses of Sharon:* quilt patterns.

She liked Kansas best. She wished they'd go back to Kansas.
She liked the smell of the wind there.
But Pop hadn't wanted to join with the Free-Soilers
And then the slavery men° had shot up the town
And killed the best horse they had. That had settled Pop. 64
He said something about a plague on both of your houses°
And moved along. So now they were hiders here
And whenever you wanted to ask Pop about the war
All he said was that same old thing about the plague.
She mustn't call him Pop—that was movers'-talk. 64
She must call him Father, the way Mom, Mother wanted.
But it was hard to remember. Mom talked a lot
About old times back in the East and Grandmother's house.
She couldn't remember an East. The East wasn't real.
There was only the dusty road and moving along. 65
Although she knew that Mom had worn a silk dress
And gone to a ball, once. There was a picture of Pop
And Mom, looking Eastern, in queer old Eastern clothes.
They weren't white trash. She knew how to read and figure.
She'd read *Macbeth* and *Beulah* and *Oliver Twist.*° 65
She liked *Beulah* best but *Macbeth* would have suited Pop.
Sometimes she wondered what had happened to them,
When Mother used to live in Grandmother's house
And wear silk dresses, and Father used to read Latin—
When had they started to go just moving along, 66
And how would it feel to live in Grandmother's house?

But it was so long ago, so hard to work out
And she liked it this way—she even liked being hiders.
It was exciting, especially when the guns
Coughed in the sky as they had all yesterday, 66
When Bent hid out in the woods to keep from recruiters,
And you knew there were armies stumbling all around you,
Big, blundering cows of armies, snuffling and tramping
The whole scuffed world with their muddy, lumbering hoofs,
Except the little lost brushpile where you were safe. 6
There were guns in the sky again today. Big armies.

638–639 *Free-Soilers . . . slavery men:* See note, John Brown's Prayer, Book I, line 385.   641 *a plague on both your houses:* Mercutio's curse, *Romeo and Juliet,* Act III, Scene 1.   655 *Macbeth and Beulah and Oliver Twist: Beulah,* Augusta J. Wilson's novel (1819), is listed with Shakespeare's play and Dickens' novel. The Vilas' pigs (lines 677–707, below) are named for characters from these works.

An army must be fine to look at.
　　　　　　　　But Pop
Would never let her do it or understand.

An army or a mirror. She didn't know
Which she'd rather find, but whenever she thought of it   675
The mirror generally won. You could keep a mirror yourself.

———————

She had to call the hogs that afternoon.
You had to call them once or twice a month
And give them food or else they ran too wild
And never came for butchering in the Fall,   680
Though they lived well enough without your calling,
Fat in the forest, feeding on beech mast°,
Wild muscadines° and forest provender
That made their flesh taste sweet as hazelnuts.

She liked the hogs, they weren't tame, sleepy hogs   685
Grunting in a black wallow, they were proud
Rapid and harsh and savage as Macbeth.
There was a young boar that she called Macbeth,
She'd seen him fight grey-bristled, drowsy Duncan
And drive him from the trough.
　　　　　　　　Fagin was there,   690
Bill Sikes was there and Beulah the black sow,
And Lady Macduff whose grunt was half a whine.
You could learn lots about a book from hogs.
She poured the swill and cupped her hands to call.
Sometimes they'd help her with it, Pop or Bent,   695
But Pop was off with Bent this afternoon
And Mom was always busy.
　　　　　　　　Slim and straight
She stood before the snake-rail pen that kept
Macbeths on their own proper side of the fence.
"Piggy," she called, "Here, piggy, piggy, piggy!"   700
It wasn't the proper call, but the hogs knew
That sweet clear loudness with its sleepy silver
Trembling against a chanter° of white ash.
"Here, piggy, piggy, piggy, piggy, piggy!

703 *chanter*: chantry, a chapel. 682 *beech mast*: beechnuts. 683 *muscadines*: grapes.

Here, piggy, piggy!" There was a scrambling noise   7

At the edge of the woods. "Here, piggy!"

It was Banquo.

Greedy, but hesitant.

The Artful Dodger

Slim, black and wicked, had two feet in the trough

Before that obese indecision moved.

"Here, piggy! Here, piggy, piggy!"

The gleaming call   7

Floated the air like a bright glassy bubble,

Far, far, with its clean silver and white ash.

And Ellyat, lost and desperate in the wood,

Heard it, desirous as the elvish blast

Wound on a tiny horn of magic grass   7

To witch steel riders into a green hill.

He stumbled toward its music.

"Piggy, piggy,

Here, piggy, piggy!"

The swine grunted and jostled.

Melora watched them, trying to count them up

With grave eyes, brown as nuts in rainwater.

They were all there, she thought—she must be sure.

She called again. No, something moved in the woods.

She stared past the clearing, puzzled. So Ellyat saw her

Beyond the swine, head lifted like a dark foal

That listens softly for strangeness.

And she saw

An incoherent scarecrow in blue clothes

Stagger on wooden feet from the deep wood.

She called to him to keep away from the hogs,

Half-frightenedly.

He did not hear or obey.

He was out of Nibelung Hall.

She put one hand

On the rail of the fence to steady herself and waited.

"You can't come in here," she said, fiercely. "The hogs'll kill you."

But he was past the fed hogs and over the fence.

She saw a queer look on his face. "You're hungry," she said.

He grinned, made a noise in his throat, and fell, trying to
     touch her.

Now that I am clean again,
Now I've slept and fed,
How shall I remember when
I was someone dead?

Now the balm has worked its art   740
And the gashes dry,
And the lizard at my heart
Has a sleepy eye,

How shall I remember yet
Freezing underground,   745
With the wakened lizard set
To the living wound? °

Do not ponder the offence
Nor reject the sore,
Do not tear the cerements°   750
Flesh may need once more.

Cold comes back and pain comes back
And the lizard, too.
And the burden in the sack
May be meant for you.   755

Do not play the risen dunce
With unrisen men.
Lazarus was risen once°
But earth gaped again.

So Ellyat swam back to life, swam back to warmth   760
And the smell of cooking food. It was night. He heard
Impenetrable rain shake a low roof
And hiss stray, scattering drops on an open fire.
But he was safe. That rain was caged in the sky.

746–747 *lizard set/To the living wound:* In folk tradition, the lizard, which sheds
its skin, is variously the dwelling place of the soul, a manifestation of a healing deity,
or a source of rejuvenating powders and potions.   750 *cerements:* funeral wrappings.
758 *Lazarus was risen once:* For the account of Christ's raising Lazarus from the
dead, see John 11.

It could not fall on him.
                        He lay in a lax
Idleness, warm and hungry, not wanting to move.
A grub in a close cocoon neither bold nor wise, but content.

A tall woman was cooking mush in an iron pot.
The smell of the mush was beautiful, the shape of the pot
More beautiful than an urn by sea-nymphs carved
From sunken marbles stained with the cold sea-rose.
The woman was a great Norn,° in her pot she cooked a new world,
Made of pure vapors and the juices of unspoilt light,
A new globe of sulliless amber and grains of white corn,
An orbed perfection. All life was beautiful now.

A girl came into the room upon light, quick feet.
He stared at her, solemnly. She was young and thin.
The small, just head was set on the slender neck
With a clean sureness. The heavy hair was a helm
Of bronze cooled under a ripple, marked by that flowing.
It was not slight but it could not weight her down.
Her hands and feet were well made and her body had
That effortless ease, that blood that flies with the bird.
She saw his open eyes and came over to him,
Not shyly but not concernedly.
                                Their eyes met.
The older woman kept stirring her melted world.
"Well," said the girl, "You look better." He nodded, "Yes."
Their eyes said, "I have seen a new thing. In the deep cells
Below the paltry clockwork of the ticked heart,
I have seen something neither light nor night,
A new thing, a new picture. It may mean
The lifting of a shut latch. It may mean nothing."

She made an escaping gesture with her right hand.
"You didn't say who you were," she said. "You just fell.
You better tell who you are, Pop'll want to know."
A shadow crossed her. "Pop won't want to keep you," she said.
"But I reckon we'll have to keep you here for a piece,
You're not fit to travel yet and that's a fact.
You look a little bit like Young Seward,° " she said

772 *Norn:* The Norns were the Three Fates of Scandinavian mythology.   799
Young Seward: son of the Earl of Northumberland in *Macbeth.*

Reflectively, "But sometimes you look more like Oliver.°   800
I dunno. What's your name?"
                      Ellyat put forth his hand
Toward being alive again, slowly, hauling it down.
He remembered. He was Jack Ellyat. He had been lost.
He had lain with hel-shoes° on in Nibelung Hall
For twenty years. This was the girl with the swine   805
Whose loud sweet calling had come to him in the wood
And lifted him back to warmth and a cooking world.
He had lost a piece of himself, a piece of life,
He must find it, but now—
               "What's your name?" he said in a whisper.

———

This is the hidden place that hiders know.   810
This is where hiders go.
Step softly, the snow that falls here is different snow,
The rain has a different sting.
Step softly, step like a cloud, step softly as the least
Whisper of air against the beating wing,   815
And let your eyes be sealed
With two blue muscadines
Stolen from secret vines,
Or you will never find in the lost field
The table spread, the signs of the hidden feast.   820

This is where hiders live.
This is the tentative
And outcast corner where hiders steal away
To bake their hedgehogs in a lump of clay,
To raise their crops and children wild and shy,   825
And let the world go by
In accidental marches of armed wrath
That stumble blindly past the buried path.
Step softly, step like a whisper, but do not speak
Or you will never see   830
The furriness curled within the hollow tree,
The shadow-dance upon the wilderness-creek.

800 *Oliver:* Oliver Twist.   804 *hel-shoes:* shoes provided the dead for the difficult journey to the afterworld (Hel).

This is the hiders' house.
This is the ark of pine-and-willow-boughs.
This is the quiet place.
You may call now, but let your call be sweet
As clover-honey strained through silver sieves
And delicate as the dust upon the moth
Or you will never find your fugitives.
Call once, and call again,
Then, if the lifted strain
Has the true color and substance of the wild,
You may perceive, if you have lucky eyes,
Something that ran away from being wise
And changed silk ribbons for a greener cloth,
Some budding-horned and deer-milk-suckled child
Some lightness, moving toward you on light feet,
Some girl with indolent passion in her face.

———

Jack Ellyat wondered about things, six days later.
The world had come back to its shape. He was well and strong.
He had seen the old man with the burnt dreams in his eyes,
Who had fallen from something years ago in his youth
Or risen from something with an effort too stark;
The runaway who had broken the pasture-bars
To test the figments of life on a wild stone.
You could see the ultimate hardness of that strange stone
Cut in his face—but then, there was something else,
That came at moments and went, and answered no questions.
Had the feel of the stone been worth it, after all?
It puzzled Ellyat.
                        He couldn't figure it out.
Going West to get fat acres was common enough,
But, once you got the acres, you settled down,
You sent your children to school. You put up a fence.
When a war came along, you fought on your proper side;
You didn't blast both sides with Mercutio's curse°
And hide in a wilderness.
                        The man was all wrong,

865 *Mercutio's curse:* See note, line 641, above.

And yet the man was not weak. It was very strange.
If the man had been weak, you could understand him all right.

The woman was more easy to understand.
He liked the woman—he liked the rough shaggy boy   870
Who had lived so much in the woods to keep from the armies
That his ears were sharp as a squirrel's, and all his movements
Had something untamed about them, something leafy and strange.
Of course he ought to be fighting for the North,
He was really a skulk—but things were different here.   875
You couldn't reason about the difference in words
But you felt it inside your skin.
                              Things were different here.
Like Nibelung Hall in the rain of his fever-dream,
But with no terror, with an indolent peace.

He'd have to get back to the regiment pretty soon.   880
He couldn't stay here. They none of them wanted him here.
He'd have to get back. But he didn't know where to go.
They could tell him how to get back to Pittsburg Landing
But how did he know if the army was there or not?
He didn't even know who'd won in the battle,   885
And, if the Rebs had won, he'd be captured again
As soon as he got on a road.
                              Well, he'd have to chance it.
He couldn't stay here and fall in love with Melora.
Melora came walking down the crooked path
With a long shadow before her. It was the hour   890
When the heat is out of the gold of afternoon
And the cooled gold has not yet turned into grey,
The hour of the paused tide, neither flow nor ebb,
The flower beginning to close but not yet closed.

He saw her carry her fairy head aloft   895
Against that descending gold,
He saw the long shadow that her slight body made.

When she came near enough to him, she heard him humming
A tune he had thought forgotten, the weaver's tune.

"And the only harm that I've ever done,
Was to love a pretty maid." °

She halted, trying to listen. He stopped the tune.
"What's that you were singing?" she said.
                              "Oh, just trash," he said.
"I liked it. Sing it some more."
                              But he would not sing it.

They regarded each other a foot or so apart.
Their shadows blotted together into one shadow.

She put her hand to both cheeks, and touched them lightly,
As if to cool them from something.
                              A soft, smooth shock
Inexplicable as the birth of a star
And terrible as the last cry of the flesh
Ran through his cords and struck.
                              He stared at the shadows.
Then she took her shadow into the house with her
But he still stood looking where the shadows had touched.

———————

John Vilas watched them go off through the wood
To get the water from the other spring,
The big pail clanking between them.
                              His hard mouth
Was wry with an old nursery-rhyme,° but his eyes
Looked somewhere beyond hardness.
                              Let them go.
Harriet said and Harriet always said
And Harriet was right, but let them go.
Men who go looking for the wilderness-stone
And find it, should not marry or beget,
But, having done so, they must take the odds
As the odds are.
                              Faustus and I are old.
We creep about among the hollow trees
Where the bright devils of our youth have gone
Like a dissolving magic, back to earth.
But in our tarnished and our antique wands

900–901 "And the only harm . . .": See note, line 442, above.   917 an old nursery-
rhyme: "Jack and Jill."

And in the rusty metal of our spells
There still remain such stubbornness and pith   930
As may express elixirs from a rock
Or pick a further quarrel with the gods
Should we find cause enough.
                              I know this girl,
This boy, this youth, this honey in the blood,
This kingly danger, this immediate fire.   935
I know what comes of it and how it lies
And how, long afterwards, at the split core
Of the prodigious and self-eaten lie,
A little grain of truth lies undissolved
By all the acids of philosophy.   940
Therefore, I will not seek a remedy
Against a sword but in the sword itself
Nor medicine life with anything but life.
I am too old to try the peddler's tricks,
Too wise, too foolish, too long strayed in the wood,   945
The custom of the world is not my custom,
Nor its employments mine.
                              I know this girl
As well as if I never lay with her mother.
I know her heart touched with that wilderness-stone
That turns good money into heaps of leaves   950
And builds an outcast house of apple-twigs
Beside a stream that never had a name.
She will forget what I cannot forget,
And she may learn what I shall never learn,
But, while the wilderness-stone is strong in her,   955
I'd have her use it for a touchstone yet
And see the double face called good and bad
With her own eyes. So, if she stares it down,
She is released, and if it conquers her,
She was not weighted with a borrowed shield.   960

We are no chafferers,° my daughter and I.
We give what pleases us and when we choose,
And, having given, we do not take back.
But once we shut our fists upon a star
It will take portents to unloose that grip   965

961 *chafferers:* bargainers.

And even then the stuff will keep the print.
It is a habit of living.
                                For the boy
I do not know but will not stand between.
He has more toughness in him than he thinks.
—I took my wife out of a pretty house.
—I took my wife out of a pleasant place.
—I stripped my wife of comfortable things.
—I drove my wife to wander with the wind.
—And we are old now, Faustus.
                                    Let it be so.
There was one man who might have understood,
Because he was half-oriole and half-fox,
Not Emerson, but the man by Walden Pond.°
But he was given to the birds in youth
And never had a woman or a daughter.

The filled pail stood on a stone by the lip of the spring,
But they had forgotten the pail.
                            The spring was a cool
Wavering mirror that showed them their white, blurred faces
And made them wonder to see the faces so like
And yet so silent and distant.
                            Melora turned.
"We ought to go back," she said in a commonplace voice.
"Not yet, Melora."
                            Something, as from the spring
Rising, in silver smoke, in arras of silvers,
Drifting around them, pushed by a light, slow wind.
"Not yet, Melora."
                            They sat on a log above.
Melora's eyes were still looking down at the spring.
Her knees were hunched in her arms.
                                    "You'll be going," she said,
Staring at the dimmed glass. "You'll be going soon."
The silver came closer, soaking into his body,
Soaking his flesh with bright, impalpable dust.
He could smell her hair. It smelt of leaves and the wind.
He could smell the untaken whiteness of her clean flesh,
The deep, implacable fragrance, fiercer than sleep,

977 *the man by Walden Pond:* Henry David Thoreau.

Sweeter than long sleep in the sun.

He touched her shoulder.

She let the hand stay but still she gazed at the spring.
Then, after a while, she turned.

The mirrored mouths   1000

Fused in one mouth that trembled with the slow waters.

Melora, in the room she had to herself
Because they weren't white-trash and used to be Eastern,
Let the rain of her hair fall down,
In a stream, in a flood, on the white birch of her body.   1005
She was changed, then. She was not a girl any more.
She was the white heart of the birch,
Half hidden by a fleece that a South wind spun
Out of bronze air and light, on a wheel of light.
Her sharp clear breasts   1010
Were two young victories in the hollow darkness
And when she stretched her hands above her head
And let the spun fleece ripple to her loins,
Her body glowed like deep springs under the sun.

She had no song to sing herself asleep   1015
Tonight, but she would need no song to sing.
A thousand thoughts ran past her in a brief
Unhurrying minute, on small, quiet feet
But did not change her. Nothing could change her now.
—Black winter night against the windowpane   1020
And she, a child, singing her fear to sleep
With nursery-rhymes and broken scraps of tunes.
How well she could remember those old songs.
But this night she would sleep without a song
Except the song the earth knows in the night   1025
After the huge embrace of the bright day,
And that was better.

She thought to herself.

"I don't know. I can't think. I ought to be scared.
I ought to have lots of maybes. I can't find them.
It's funny. It's different. It's a big pair of hands   1030
Pushing you somewhere—but you've got to go.
Maybe you're crazy but you've got to go.
That's why Mom went. I know about Mom now.
I know how she used to be. It's pretty sweet.

It's rhymes, it's hurting, it's feeling a bird's heart
Beat in your hand, it's children growing up,
It's being cut to death with bits of light,
It's wanting silver bullets in your heart,
It's not so happy, but it's pretty sweet,
I've got to go."
                     She passed her narrow hands
Over her body once, half-wonderingly.

"Divide this transitory and temporal flesh
Into twelve ears of red and yellow corn
And plant each ear beside a different stream.
Yet, in the summer, when the harvesters
Come with their carts, the grain shall change again
And turn into a woman's body again
And walk across a heap of sickle-blades
To find the naked body of its love." °

She slipped her dress back on and stole downstairs.
The bare feet, whispering, made little sound.
A sleeper breathed, a child turned in its sleep.
She heard the tiny breathings. She shut the door.

The moon rode a high heaven streaked with cloud.
She watched it for a moment. Then she drank
That moon from its high heaven with her mouth
And felt the immaculate burning of that frost
Run from her fingers in such corporal silver
Her whole slight body was a corposant°
Of hollow light and the cold sap of the moon.

She knew the dark grass cool beneath her feet.
She knew the opening of the stable door.
It shut behind her. She was in darkness now.

1042–1049 *"Divide this transitory and temporal flesh . . . of its love.":* Benét here draws upon a number of American Indian folk legends connected with the corn maiden or corn goddess; the passage also recalls the mutilation and resurrection of Osiris and the fertility of the earth-mother, Demeter. 1059 *corposant:* a ball of light appearing about the masts of a ship in a storm; St. Elmo's fire.

Jack Ellyat, lying in a warm nest of hay,
Stared at the sweet-smelling darkness with troubled eyes.   1065
He was going tomorrow. He couldn't skulk any more.
—Oh, reasonless thirst in the night, what can slake your thirst,
Reasonless heart, why will you not let me rest?
I have seen a woman wrapped in the grace of leaves,
I have kissed her mouth with my mouth, but I must go—   1070
He was going back to find a piece of himself
That he had lost in a tent,° in a red loud noise,
Under a sack of tobacco. Until he found it
He could never be whole again

                —but the hunger creeps
Like a vine about me, crushing my narrow wisdom,   1075
Crushing my thoughts—

            He couldn't stay with Melora.
He couldn't take her back home. If he were Bailey
He would know what to do. He would follow the weaver's tune
He would keep Melora a night from the foggy dew
And then go off with the sunrise to tell the tale   1080
Sometime for a campfire yarn. But he wasn't Bailey.
He saw himself dead without ever having Melora
And he didn't like it.

             Maybe, after the war.
Maybe he could come back to the hider's place,
Maybe—it is a long time till after the war   1085
And this is now—you took a girl when you found her—
A girl with flags on her garters or a new girl—
It didn't matter—it made a good campfire yarn—
It was men and women—Bailey—the weaver's tune—

He heard something move and rustle in the close darkness   1090
"What's that?" he said. He got no answering voice
But he knew what it was. He saw a light-footed shadow
Come toward the nest where he lay. For a moment then
He felt weak, half-sickened almost.

                Then his heart began
To pound to a marching rhythm that was not harsh   1095
Nor sweet, but enormous cadence.

                "Melora," he said.
His hand went out and touched the cup of her breast.

1071–1072 *a piece of himself . . . lost in a tent:* Compare lines 516–518, above.

What things shall be said of you,
Terrible beauty in armor?
What things shall be said of you, 110
Horses riding the sky?
The fleetness, the molten speed,
The rhythm rising like beaten
Drums of barbaric gold
Until fire mixes with fire? 111

The night is a sparkling pit
Where Time no longer has power
But only vast cadence surging
Toward an instant of tiny death.
Then, with the slow withdrawal 11
Of seas from a rock of moonlight,
The clasping bodies unlock
And the lovers have little words.

What is this spear, this burnished
Arrow in the deep waters 11
That is not quenched by them
Until it has found its mark?
What is this beating of wings
In the formless heart of the tempest?
This wakening of a sun 11
That was not wakened before?

They have dragged you down from the sky
And broken you with an ocean
Because you carried the day,
Phaëton,° charioteer. 11
But still you loose from the cloud
The matched desires of your horses
And sow on the ripened earth
The quickened, the piercing flame.

What things shall be said of you,
Terrible beauty in armor? 11
Dance that is not a dance,
Brief instant of welded swords.

1125 *Phaëton:* Compare Book I, line 1058.

For a moment we strike the black
Door with a fist of brightness.   1135
And then it is over and spent,
And we sink back into life.

Back to the known, the sure,
The river of sleep and waking,
The dreams floating the river,   1140
The nearness, the conquered peace.
You have come and smitten and passed,
Poniard,° poniard of sharpness.
The child sleeps in the planet.
The blood sleeps again.   1145

He wasn't going away when he went to the wood.
He told himself that. They had broken the dime together.°
They had cut the heart on the tree.
       The jack-knife cut
Two pinched half-circles of white on the green bark.
The tree-gum bled from the cuts in sticky, clear drops,   1150
And there you were.
     And shortly the bark would dry
Dead on the living wood and leave the white heart
All through the winter, all through the rain and snow,
A phantom-blaze to guide a tall phantom-hunter
Who came in lightness along a leaf-buried path.   1155
All through the snowing winter it would be white.
It would take many springs to cover that white again.
What have I done in idleness, in sweet idleness,
What have I done to the forest?
       I have marked
A tree to be my own with a jack-knife blade   1160
In idleness, in sweet idleness. I have loosed
A dryad out of the tree to chain me with wild
Grapevines and forest trailers forever and ever
To the hider's place, to the outcast house of the lost,
And now, when I would be free, I am free no more.   1165
He thought of practical matters. There ought to be
A preacher and a gold ring and a wedding-dress,

1143 *Poniard:* dagger. 1147 *broken the dime together:* the custom of dividing a
coin with each party carrying half as a remembrance.

Only how could there be?
                He rolled hard words
Over his tongue. "A shotgun wedding," he said.
It wasn't like that, it never could be like that,
But there was a deadly likeness.
               He saw the bored
Shamefaced seducer in the clean Sunday collar,
The whining, pregnant slut in the cheesecloth veil.
They weren't like that—but the picture colored his mind.

If he only could go away without going away
And have everything turn out just as it ought to be
Without rings or hiding!
            He told himself "I'm all right.
I'm not like Bailey. I wouldn't sleep with a girl
Who never slept with anybody before
And then just go off and leave her."
               But it was Melora.
It wasn't seducing a girl. It was all mixed up.
All real where it ought to be something told in a sermon,
And all unreal when you had to do something about it,
His thoughts went round and round like rats in a cage,
But all he knew was—
             he was sick for a room
And a red tablecloth with tasselled fringes,
Where a wife knitted on an end of a scarf,
A father read his paper through the same
Unchanging spectacles with the worn bows
And a young girl beneath a nickeled lamp
Soundlessly conjugated Latin verbs,
"Amo, amas, amat," and still no sound—

Slight dryad, trailing the green, curled vines of the Spring,
I hate you for this moment, I hate your white breast
And idleness, sweet, hidden idleness—

He started awake. He had been walking through dreams.
How far had he come? He studied the sun and the trees.
Was he lost? No, there was the way.
             He turned back slowly,
To the dryad, the idleness—to the cheesecloth veil,
The incredible preacher, the falling out of life.

He'd ask her this evening where you could find such preachers.
The old man mustn't know till the thing was done
Or he would turn to a father out of a cheap
Play, a cheap shotgun father with a wool beard
Roaring gilt rhetoric—and loading a musket.   1205
He got the dry grins.
          If the property-father shot him
Would they carve his name on the soldiers' monument
After the war?
          There should be a special tablet.
"Here lies John Ellyat Junior, shot and killed
By an angry father for the great cause of Union.   1210
'How sleep the brave.' "
          He stumbled and looked around him.
"Well, I might go on as far as the road," he said.

A little while later he burst through the screen of brush.
And saw the highroad below him.
          He wiped his face.
The road dipped down a hill to a little bridge.   1215
He was safe enough now.
          What was it Melora had said?
The highroad was six miles away from the farm,
Due west, and he could tell the west by the sun.
He must have covered a dozen, finding the road,
But getting back would be easy.
          The sun was high.   1220
He ought to be starting soon. But he lay down
And stared for a while at the road. It was good to see
A road in the open again, a dust-bitten road
Where people and horses went along to a town.
—Dryad, deep in the woods, your trails are small,   1225
Winding and faint—they run between grass and flowers—
But it is good once more to come on a road
That is not drowsy with your idleness—

He looked down toward the bridge. There were moving blobs of dust
Crossing it—men on horses. His heart gave a strange   1230
Throb of desire. What were they? They looked like soldiers.
Blue coats or grey? He could not tell for the dust.
He'd have to get back in the woods before they passed,
He was a hider now. But he kept on staring

A long two minutes, trying to make them out,
Till his eyes stung. One man had a yellow beard
And carried his rifle slung the Missouri way°
But there were Missouri troops on either side.
In a minute he could tell—and wriggle away—

A round stick jabbed in his back.

                    A slow voice said
"Reach for the sky, Yank, or I'll nachully drill yuh."
His hands flew up.

               "Yuh're the hell of a scout," said the voice
With drawling scorn. "Yuh h'ain't even got a gun.
I could have picked yuh off ten minutes ago,
Yuh made more noise than a bear, bustin' thru' that bresh.
What'd yuh use to work at—wrappin' up corsets?
Yeah—yuh kin turn around."

                  Jack Ellyat turned
Incredulously.

            "Well, I'll be damned," said the boy
In butternut clothes with the wrinkled face of a leaf.
"Yuh're a young 'un all right—aw, well, don't take it so hard.
Our boys get captured, too. Hey, Billy!" he called,
"Got a Yankee scout."

              The horse-hoofs stopped in the road.
"Well, bring him along," said a voice.

                Jack Ellyat slid
Down a little bank and stood in front of the horses.
He was dazed. This was not happening. But the horses
Were there, the butternut men on the horses were there.

A gaunt old man with a sour, dry mouth was talking,
"He's no scout," he said, "He's one of their lousy spies.
Don't he look like a spy? Let's string him up to a tree."
His eye roved, looking for a suitable branch,
His mouth seemed pleased.

              Ellyat saw two little scooped dishes,
Hung on a balance, wavering in the air.
One was bright tin and carried his life and breath,
The other was black. They were balanced with dreadful evenness.
But now the black dish trembled, starting to fall.

1237 *slung the Missouri way:* the barrel cradled in the crook of the left arm, the
small of the rifle stock in the right hand.

"Hell, no," said the boy with the face like a wrinkled leaf.
"He's a scout all right. What makes yuh so savage, Ben?
Yuh're always hankerin' after a necktie-party.
Who captured the bugger anyhow?"
                              "Oh, well,"
Said the other man. "Oh, well." He spat in the dust.   1270
"Anyhow," he said, with a hungry look at Ellyat,
"He's got good boots."
                    The boy with the wrinkled face
Remarked that, as for the boots, no Arkansaw catfish
Was going to take them away from their lawful captor.

The rest sat their horses loosely and looked at him   1275
With mild curiosity, ruminating tobacco.
Ellyat tried to think. He could not think.
                                    He was free,
These stuffless men on stuffless horses had freed him
From dryads and fathers, from cheesecloth veils and Melora.
He began to talk fast. He didn't hear what he said.   1280
"But I've got to get back," he said. Then he stopped. They laughed.
"Oh, yuh'll get over it, Bub," said the wrinkled boy,
"It ain't so bad. You won't have to fight no more.
Maybe yuh'll git exchanged. Git up on that horse.
No, take off them boots first, thanks."
                                He slung the boots   1285
Around his neck. "Now I got some good boots," he said.
And grinned at the gaunt man with the sour mouth.
"Now, Bub, I'll just tie yuh a little with this yere rope
And then you won't be bustin' loose from the gang.
Grab the pommel as well as yuh kin."
                                The gaunt man coughed.   1290
"I tell you," he said, in a disappointed voice,
"If we just strung him up it'd make things a hull lot easier.
He's a spy for sure, and everyone strings up spies.
We got a long piece to go yet and he's a nuisance."

"Aw, shut yore face," said Jim Breckinridge in a drawl,   1295
"Yuh kin hang any Yanks yuh ketch on a piece uh dishrag,
Yuh ain't caught no armies yit."
                            The gaunt man was silent.
Ellyat saw the little tin dish that carried the life
Slowly sink down, to safety, the black dish rise.

"Come on," said Billy. The horses started to move,
Stirring a dust that rose for a little while
In a faint cloud. But after the horses had gone,
The cloud settled, the road went to sleep again.

❧ BOOK FOUR ❧

Strike up, strike up for Wingate's tune,
Strike up for Sally Dupré!
Strike up, strike up for the April moon,
And the rain on the lilac spray!
For Wingate Hall in its pride once more,   5
For the branch of myrtle over the door,°
Because the men are back from the war;
For the clean bed waiting the dusty rider
And the punchbowl cooling for thirsty throttles,°
For the hot cooks boiling the hams in cider   10
And Cudjo grinning at cobwebbed bottles—
The last of the wine, the last of the wine,
The last of the '12 and the '29!
Three times voyaged around the Cape
Till old Judge Brooke, with an oath oracular,   15
Pronounced it the living soul of the grape,
And the veriest dregs to be supernacular!

Old Judge Brooke with his double chins
Sighing over his hoarded claret
And sending the last of his cherished bins   20
To the hospital-doctors with "I can spare it
But if you give it to some damned layman
Who doesn't know brandy from licorice-water
And sports a white ribbon,° by fire and slaughter,
I'll hang the lot of you higher than Haman!"°   25

The Wingate cellars are nearly bare
But Miss Louisa is doing her hair
In the latest style of Napoleon's court.
(A blockade-runner brought the report,
A blockade-runner carried the silk,   30
Heavy as bullion and white as milk,
That makes Amanda a gleaming moth.
For the coasts are staked with a Union net
But the dark fish slip through the meshes yet,

---

6 *myrtle over the door*: in English tradition, to keep love and peace within. 9
throttles: throats. 24 *white ribbon*: badge of temperance. 25 *higher than Haman*:
In the Old Testament, Haman, a Persian courtier, was hanged on a gallows fifty
cubits high, a gallows which he had intended for Mordecai, a Jew. Esther 7:9–10.

Shadows sliding without a light, 35
Through the dark of the moon, in the dead of night,
Carrying powder, carrying cloth,
Hoops for the belle and guns for the fighter,
Guncotton, opium, bombs and tea.
Fashionplates, quinine and history. 40
For Charleston's corked with a Northern fleet
And the Bayou City lies at the feet
Of a damn-the-torpedoes commodore;°
The net draws tighter and ever tighter,
But the fish dart past till the end of the war, 45
From Wilmington to the Rio Grande,
And the sandy Bahamas are Dixie Land
Where the crammed, black shadows start for the trip°
That, once clean-run, will pay for the ship.
They are caught, they are sunk with all aboard. 50
They scrape through safely and praise the Lord,
Ready to start with the next jammed hold
To pull Death's whiskers out in the cold,
The unrecorded skippers and mates
Whom even their legend expurgates, 55
The tough daredevils from twenty ports
Who thumbed their noses at floating forts
And gnawed through the bars of a giant's cage
For a cause or a laugh or a living-wage,
Who five long years on a sea of night, 60
Pumped new blood to the vein bled white
—And, incidentally, made the money
For the strangely rich of the after years—
For the flies will come to the open honey,
And, should war and hell have the same dimensions, 65
Both have been paved with the best intentions
And both are as full of profiteers.)

The slaves in the quarters are buzzing and talking.
—All through the winter the ha'nts went walking,

42–43 *Bayou City lies at the feet/Of a . . . commodore:* New Orleans fell to Captain (later Admiral) David G. Farragut's fleet on April 25, 1862; but it was not until 1865 that he gave his "damn the torpedoes" order at Mobile Bay. 47–48 *Bahamas are Dixie Land/Where . . . shadows start for the trip:* Throughout the war, the Bahamas enjoyed extraordinary prosperity as a supply base for blockade runners. Slavery, however, had been abolished there since 1838, and the plantation economy was decaying.

Ha'nts the size of a horse or bigger,   70
Ghost-patrollers, scaring a nigger,
But now the winter's over and broken,
And the sun shines out like a lovin' token,
There's goin' to be mixin's and mighty doin's,
Chicken-fixin's and barbecuin's,   75
Old Marse Billy's a-comin' home!
He's slewn a brigade with a ha'nt's jaw-bone,°
He's slewn an army with one long sabre,
He's scared old Linkum 'most to death,
Now he's comin' home to rest from he labor,   80
Play on he fiddle and catch he breath!

The little black children with velvet eyes
Tell each other tremendous lies.
They play at Manassas with guns of peeled
Willow-stalks from the River Field,   85
Chasing the Yanks into Kingdom Come
While one of them beats on a catskin drum.
They are happy because they don't know why.
They scare themselves pretending to die,
But all through the scare, and before and after,   90
Their voices are rich with the ancient laughter,
The negro laughter, the blue-black rose,
The laughter that doesn't end with the lips
But shakes the belly and curls the toes
And prickles the end of the fingertips.   95

Up through the garden, in through the door,
That undercurrent of laughter floats,
It mounts like a sea from floor to floor,
A dark sea, covering painted boats,
A warm sea, smelling of earth and grass,   100
It seeps through the back of the cheval-glass°
Where Amanda stares at her stately self
Till her eyes are bright with a different spark,
It sifts like a dye, where Louisa's peering
In a shagreen°-case for a garnet ear-ring   105

77 *slewn a brigade with a ha'nt's jaw-bone*: as Samson slew the thousand Philistines with the jawbone of an ass. Judges 15:15.   101 *cheval-glass*: a full-length mirror mounted on swivels in a standing frame.   105 *shagreen*: untanned, pebble-grained rawhide.

Till the little jewels shine in the dark,
It spills like a wave in the crowded kitchen
Where the last good sugar of Wingate Hall
Is frosting a cake like a Polar Highland
And fat Aunt Bess in her ice-wool shawl   11(
Spends the hoarded knowledge her heart is rich in
On oceans of trifle° and floating-island.°

Fat Aunt Bess is older than Time
But her eyes still shine like a bright, new dime,
Though two generations have gone to rest   11!
On the sleepy mountain of her breast.
Wingate children in Wingate Hall,
From the first weak cry in the bearing-bed
She has petted and punished them, one and all,
She has closed their eyes when they lay dead.   12
She raised Marse Billy when he was puny,
She cared for the Squire when he got loony,
Fed him and washed him and combed his head,
Nobody else would do instead.
The matriarch of the weak and the young,   12
The lazy crooning, comforting tongue.
She has had children of her own,
But the white-skinned ones are bone of her bone.
They may not be hers, but she is theirs,
And if the shares were unequal shares,   13
She does not know it, now she is old.
They will keep her out of the rain and cold.
And some were naughty, and some were good,
But she will be warm while they have wood,
Rule them and spoil them and play physician   1?
With the vast, insensate force of tradition,
Half a nuisance and half a mother
And legally neither one nor the other,
Till at last they follow her to her grave,
The family-despot, and the slave.   14

—Curious blossom from bitter ground,
Master of masters who left you bound,

---

112 *trifle:* a dessert of sponge cake, jam, and crumbled macaroons, soaked in wine.
floating-island: custard in whipped egg whites.

Who shall unravel the mingled strands
Or read the anomaly of your hands?
They have made you a shrine and a humorous fable,   145
But they kept you a slave while they were able,
And yet, there was something between the two
That you shared with them and they shared with you,
Brittle and dim, but a streak of gold,
A genuine kindness, unbought, unsold,   150
Graciousness founded on hopeless wrong
But queerly living and queerly strong. . . .

There were three stout pillars that held up all
The weight and tradition of Wingate Hall.
One was Cudjo and one was you   155
And the third was the mistress, Mary Lou.
Mary Lou Wingate, as slightly made
And as hard to break as a rapier-blade.
Bristol's daughter and Wingate's bride,
Never well since the last child died   160
But staring at pain with courteous eyes.
When the pain outwits it, the body dies,
Meanwhile the body bears the pain.
She loved her hands and they made her vain,
The tiny hands of her generation   165
That gathered the reins of the whole plantation;
The velvet sheathing the steel demurely
In the trained, light grip that holds so surely.

She was at work by candlelight,
She was at work in the dead of night,   170
Smoothing out troubles and healing schisms
And doctoring phthisics° and rheumatisms,
Guiding the cooking and watching the baking,
The sewing, the soap-and-candle-making,
The brewing, the darning, the lady-daughters,   175
The births and deaths in the negro-quarters,
Seeing that Suke had some new, strong shoes
And Joe got a week in the calaboose,
While Dicey's Jacob escaped a whipping
And the jellybag dripped with its proper dripping,   180

172 *phthisics:* respiratory ailments; pronounced *tiz' iks.*

And the shirts and estrangements were neatly mended,
And all of the tasks that never ended.
Her manner was gracious but hardly fervent
And she seldom raised her voice to a servant.
She was often mistaken, not often blind,
And she knew the whole duty of womankind,
To take the burden and have the power
And seem like the well-protected flower,
To manage a dozen industries
With a casual gesture in scraps of ease,
To hate the sin and to love the sinner
And to see that the gentlemen got their dinner
Ready and plenty and piping-hot
Whether you wanted to eat or not.
And always, always, to have the charm
That makes the gentlemen take your arm
But never the bright, unseemly spell
That makes strange gentlemen love too well,
Once you were married and settled down
With a suitable gentleman of your own.

And when that happened, and you had bred
The requisite children, living and dead,
To pity the fool and comfort the weak
And always let the gentlemen speak
To succor your love from deep-struck roots
When gentlemen went to bed in their boots,
And manage a gentleman's whole plantation
In the manner befitting your female station.

This was the creed that her mother taught her
And the creed that she taught to every daughter.°
She knew her Bible—and how to flirt
With a swansdown fan and a brocade skirt.
For she trusted in God but she liked formalities
And the world and Heaven were both realities.
—In Heaven, of course, we should all be equal,
But, until we came to that golden sequel,
Gentility must keep to gentility

203–210 *To pity the fool . . . the creed that she taught to every daughter:* Compare with the creed of Elspeth Mackay, Book I, lines 252–254.

Where God and breeding had made things stable,
While the rest of the cosmos deserved civility
But dined in its boots at the second-table.   220
This view may be reckoned a trifle narrow,
But it had the driving force of an arrow,
And it helped Mary Lou to stand up straight,
For she was gentle, but she could hate
And she hated the North with the hate of Jael   225
When the dry hot hands went seeking the nail,°
The terrible hate of women's ire,
The smoky, the long-consuming fire.
The Yankees were devils, and she could pray,
For devils, no doubt, upon Judgment Day,   230
But now in the world, she would hate them still
And send the gentlemen out to kill.

The gentlemen killed and the gentlemen died,
But she was the South's incarnate pride
That mended the broken gentlemen   235
And sent them out to the war again,
That kept the house with the men away
And baked the bricks where there was no clay,
Made courage from terror and bread from bran
And propped the South on a swansdown fan   240
Through four long years of ruin and stress,
The pride—and the deadly bitterness.

Let us look at her now, let us see her plain,
She will never be quite like this again.
Her house is rocking under the blast   245
And she hears it tremble, and still stands fast,
But this is the last, this is the last.
The last of the wine and the white corn meal,
The last high fiddle singing the reel,
The last of the silk with the Paris label,   250
The last blood-thoroughbred safe in the stable
—Yellow corn meal and a jackass colt,
A door that swings on a broken bolt,

225–226 *Jael . . . seeking the nail*: Jael, the wife of Heber, an Israelite, first
sheltered Sisera, the fleeing captain of the Canaanites, and then killed him by driving
a tent nail through his head. Judges 4, 5.

Brittle old letters spotted with tears
And a wound that rankles for fifty years—
This is the last of Wingate Hall,
The last bright August before the Fall,
Death has been near, and Death has passed,
But this is the last, this is the last.
There will be hope, and a scratching pen,
There will be cooking for tired men,
The waiting for news with shut, hard fists,
And the blurred, strange names in the battle-lists,
The April sun and the April rain,
But never this day come back again.

But she is lucky, she does not see
The axe-blade sinking into the tree
Day after day, with a slow, sure stroke
Till it chops the mettle from Wingate oak.
The house is busy, the cups are filling
To welcome the gentlemen back from killing,
The hams are boiled and the chickens basting,
Fat Aunt Bess is smiling and tasting,
Cudjo's napkin° is superfine,
He knows how the gentlemen like their wine,
Amanda is ready, Louisa near her,
Glistering girls from a silver mirror,
Everyone talking, everyone scurrying,
Upstairs and downstairs, laughing and hurrying,
Everyone giving and none denying,
There is only living, there is no dying.
War is a place but it is not here,
The peace and the victory are too near.
One more battle, and Washington taken,
The Yankees mastered, the South unshaken,
Fiddlers again, and the pairing season,
The old-time rhyme and the old-time reason,
The grandchildren, and the growing older
Till at last you need a gentleman's shoulder,
And the pain can stop, for the frayed threads sever,
But the house and the courtesy last forever.

274 *napkin:* here, service.

So Wingate found it, riding at ease,
The cloud-edge lifting over the trees,
A white-sail glimmer beyond the rise,
A sugar-castle that strained the eyes,   295
Then mounting, mounting, the shining spectre
Risen at last from the drop of nectar,
The cloud expanding, the topsails swelling,
The doll's house grown to a giant's dwelling,
Porches and gardens and ells and wings   300
Linking together like puzzle-rings,
Till the parts dissolved in a steadfast whole,
And Wingate saw it, body and soul.

Saw it completely, and saw it gleam,
The full-rigged vessel, the sailing dream,   305
The brick and stone that were somehow quick
With a ghost not native to stone and brick,
The name held high and the gift passed on
From Wingate father to Wingate son,
No longer a house but a conjur-stone   310
That could hate and sorrow and hold its own
As long as the seed of Elspeth Mackay°
Could mix its passion with Wingate clay
And the wind and the river had memories. . . .

Wingate saw it all—but with altered eyes.   315
He was not yet broken on any wheel,
He had no wound of the flesh to heal,
He had seen one battle, but he was still
The corn unground by the watermill,
He had ridden the rainy winter through   320
And he and Black Whistle were good as new,
The Black Horse Troop still carried its pride
And rode as the Yankees could not ride,
But, when he remembered a year-old dawn,
Something had come and something gone,   325
And even now, when he smelt the Spring,
And his heart was hot with his homecoming,
There was a whisper in his ear

312 *the seed of Elspeth Mackay*: See Book I, lines 227 ff.

That said what he did not wish to hear,
"This is the last, this is the last,   330
Hurry, hurry, this is the last,
Drink the wine before yours is spilled,
Kiss the sweetheart before you're killed,
She will be loving, and she will grieve,
And wear your heart on her golden sleeve   335
And marry your friend when he gets his leave.
It does not matter that you are still
The corn unground by the watermill,
The stones grind till they get their will.
Pluck the flower that hands can pluck,   340
Touch the walls of your house for luck,
Eat of the fat and drink the sweet,
There is little savor in dead men's meat.
It does not matter that you once knew
Future and past and a different you,   345
That went by when the wind first blew.
There is no future, there is no past,
There is only this hour and it goes fast,
Hurry, hurry, this is the last,
This is the last,   350
This is the last."

He heard it and faced it and let it talk.
The tired horses dropped to a walk.
And then Black Whistle lunged at the bit
And whinnied because he was alive,   355
And he saw the porch where the evenings sit
And the tall magnolias shading the drive,
He heard the bell of his father's mirth,
"Tallyho, Yanks—we've gone to earth!
Home, boy, home to Wingate Hall,   360
Home in spite of them, damn them all!"
He was stabbed by the rays of the setting sun,
He felt Black Whistle break to a run,
And then he was really there again,
Before he had time to think or check,   365
And a boy was holding his bridle-rein,
And Mary Lou's arms were around his neck.

Sally Dupré and Wingate talk with the music. . . .
The dance. Such a lovely dance. But you dance so lightly.
Amanda dances so well. But you dance so lightly.   370
(Do you remember the other dance?)
Phil Ferrier was here, remember, last year.
(He danced with me. He could dance rather well. He is dead.)
We were all so sorry when we heard about Phil.
(How long will you live and be able to dance with me?)   375
Yes. Phil was a fine fellow. We all liked Phil.
(Do not talk of the dead.
At first we talk of the dead, we write of the dead,
We send their things to their people when we can find them,
We write letters to you about them, we say we liked him,   380
He fought well, he died bravely, here is his sword,
Here is his pistol, his letters, his photograph case;
You will like to have these things, they will do instead.
But the war goes on too long.
After a while you still want to talk of the dead.   385
But we are too tired. We will send you the pistol still,
The photograph-case, the knickknacks, if we can find them,
But the war has gone on too long.
We cannot talk to you still, as we used to, about the dead.)
Nancy Huguenot's here tonight. Have you danced with her yet?   390
She didn't want to come. She was brave to come.
(Phil Ferrier was Nancy's lover.
She sent him off. She cut her hair for a keepsake.
They were going to be married as soon as he came back.
For a long time she dressed in black.   395
Then one morning she rose, and looked at the sun on the wall,
She put on a dress with red sleeves and a red, striped shawl,
She said "Phil was my beau. He wouldn't have liked me in black."
She used to cry quite a lot but she hasn't cried much since then.
I think she'll get well and marry somebody else.   400
I think she's right. If I had to wear grief for a lover,
I wouldn't wear black.
I would wear my best green silk and my Empire sacque°
And walk in the garden at home and feel the wind
Blow through my rags of honor forever and ever.   405
And after that, when I married some other beau,
I would make a good wife and raise my children on sweet

403 *sacque:* jacket.

Milk, not on poison, though it might have been so.
And my husband would never know
When he turned to me, when I kissed him, when we were kind,   41●
When I cleaned his coat, when we talked about dresses and weather,
He had married something that belonged to the wind
And felt the blind
And always stream of that wind on her too-light bones,
Neither fast nor slow, but never checked or resigned,   41
Blowing through rags of honor forever and ever.)

They are calling for partners again. Shall we dance again?
(Why do we hate each other so well, when we
Are tied together by something that will not free us?
If I see you across a room, I will go to you,   42
If you see me across a room, you will come to me,
And yet we hate each other.)

Not yet, for a minute. I want to watch for a minute.
(I do not hate you. I love you. But you must take me.
I will not take your leavings nor you my pity.   42
I must break you first for a while and you must break me.
We are too strong to love the surrendered city.
So we hate each other.)

That's a pretty girl over there. Beautiful hair.
(She is the porcelain you play at being.)   4
Yes, isn't she. Her name is Lucy Weatherby.
(I hate her hair. I hate her porcelain air.)
She can't be from the county or I'd remember her.
(I know that kind of mouth. Your mouth is not that.
Your mouth is generous and bitter and sweet.   4
If I kissed your mouth, I would have to be yours forever.
Her mouth is pretty. You could kiss it awhile.)
No, they're kin to the Shepleys. Lucy comes from Virginia.
(I know that kind of mouth. I know that hair.
I know the dolls you like to take in your hands,   4
The dolls that all men like to take in their hands,
I will not fight with a doll for you or any one.)

We'd better dance now.
(Lucy Weatherby.

When this dance is done, I will leave you and dance with her.   445
I know that shallow but sufficient mouth.)
As you please.
(Lucy Weatherby.
I will make an image of you, a doll in wax.
I will pierce the little wax palms with silver bodkins.   450
No, I will not.)
That's good music. It beats in your head.
(It beats in the head, it beats in the head,
It ties the heart with a scarlet thread,
This is the last,   455
This is the last,
Hurry, hurry, this is the last.
We dance on a floor of polished sleet,
But the little cracks are beginning to meet,
Under the play of our dancing feet.   460
I do not care. I am Wingate still.
The corn unground by the watermill.
And I am yours while the fiddles spill,
But my will has a knife to cut your will,
My birds will never come to your hill.   465

You are my foe and my only friend,
You are the steel I cannot bend,
You are the water at the world's end.

But Wingate Hall must tumble down,
Tumble down, tumble down,   470
A dream dissolving, a ruined thing,
Before we can melt from the shattered crown
Gold enough for a wedding-ring.
And Wingate Hall must lie in the dust,
And the wood rot and the iron rust   475
And the vines grow over the broken bust,
Before we meet without hate or pride,
Before we talk as lover and bride,
Before the daggers of our offence
Have the color of innocence,   480
And nothing is said and all is said,
And we go looking for secret bread,
And lie together in the same bed.)
Yes, it's good music, hear it lift.

(It is too mellow, it is too swift,
I am dancing alone in my naked shift,
I am dancing alone in the snowdrift.
You are my lover and you my life,
My peace and my unending strife
And the edge of the knife against my knife.
I will not make you a porcelain wife.

We are linked together for good and all,
For the still pool and the waterfall,
But you are married to Wingate Hall.
And Wingate Hall must tumble down,
Tumble down, tumble down,
Wingate Hall must tumble down,
An idol broken apart,
Before I sew on a wedding gown
And stitch my name in your heart.
And Wingate Hall must lie in the grass,
And the silk stain and the rabbits pass
And the sparrows wash in the gilded glass,
Before the fire of our anger smothers,
And our sorrows can laugh at their lucky brothers,
Before the knives of our enmity
Are buried under the same green tree
And nothing is vowed and all is vowed
And we have forgotten how to be proud,
And we sleep like cherubs in the same cloud.)

Lucy Weatherby, cuddled up in her bed,
Drifted along toward sleep with a smile on her mouth,
"I was pretty tonight," she thought, "I was pretty tonight.
Blue's my color—blue that matches my eyes.
I always ought to wear blue. I'm sorry for girls
Who can't wear that sort of blue. Her name is Sally
But she's too dark to wear the colors I can,
I'd like to give her my blue dress and see her wear it,
She'd look too gawky, poor thing.
                                        He danced with her
For a while at first but I hadn't danced with him then,
He danced with me after that. He's rather a dear.

I wonder how long he'll be here. I think I like him.
I think I'm going to be pretty while I am here.

Lucy Weatherby—Lucy Shepley—Lucy Wingate—
Huger's so jealous, nearly as jealous as Curly,   525
Poor Curly—I ought to answer his mother's letter
But it's so hard answering letters."
                              She cried a little,
Thinking of Curly. The tears were fluent and warm,
They did not sting in her eyes. They made her feel brave.
She could hardly remember Curly any more   530
But it was right to cry for him, now and then,
Slight tears at night and a long, warm, dreamless sleep
That left you looking pretty.
                              She dried the tears
And thought to herself with a pleasant little awe,
"You really are mighty brave, dear. You really are.   535
Nobody would think your beau was killed at Manassas." °
—She could hardly remember Curly any more—
She tried to make Curly's face come out of the darkness
But it was too hard—the other faces kept coming—
Huger Shepley and all the Virginia boys   540
And now this new boy's face with the dark, keen eyes.

Boys who were privates, boys who were majors and captains,
Nice old Generals who patted your shoulder,
Darling convalescents who called you an angel—
A whole, great lucky-bag° of nice, thrilling boys,   545
Fighting for you—and the South and the Cause, of course.
You were a flame for the Cause. You sang songs about it.
You sent white feathers° to boys who didn't enlist
And bunches of flowers to boys who were suitably wounded.
You wouldn't dream of making peace with the North   550
While a single boy was left to fight for the Cause
And they called you the Dixie Angel.
                              They fought for the Cause
But you couldn't help feeling, too, that they fought for you,
And when they died for you—and the Cause and the flag—

536 *Manassas:* First Bull Run.   545 *lucky-bag:* at fairs, a bag which contained a variety of articles to be drawn by chance.   548 *white feathers:* symbol of cowardice.

Your heart was tender enough. You were willing to say
You had been engaged to them, even when you hadn't
And answer their mothers' letters in a sweet way,
Though answering letters was hard.
                                        She cuddled closer,
"Pillow, tell me I'm pretty, tell me I'm lovely,
Tell me I'm nicer than anybody you know,
Tell me that nice new boy is thinking about me,
Tell me that Sally girl couldn't wear my blue,
Tell me the war won't end till we've whipped the Yankees,
Tell me I'll never get wrinkles and always have beaus."

———————

The slave got away from Zachary's place that night.
He was a big fellow named Spade with one cropped ear.
He had splay feet and sometimes walked with a limp.
His back was scarred. He was black as a pine at night.
He'd tried to run away a couple of times
—That was how he got some of the marks you could tell him by—
But he'd been pretty quiet now for a year or so
And they thought he had settled down.
                                        When he got away
He meant to kill Zachary first but the signs weren't right.
He talked to the knife but the knife didn't sweat or heat,
So he just got away instead.
                                        When he reached the woods
And was all alone, he was pretty scared for a while,
But he kept on going all night by the big soft stars,
Loping as fast as he could on his long splay feet
And when morning broke, he knew he was safe for a time.

He came out on a cleared place, then. He saw the red
Sun spill over the trees.
                                        He threw his pack
Down on the ground and started to laugh and laugh,
"Spade, boy, Spade, you's lucky to git dis far.
You never managed to git dis far before,
De Lawd's sho'ly with you, Spade."
                                        He ate and drank.
He drew a circle for Zachary's face in the ground
And spat in the circle. Then he thought of his woman.
"She's sho'ly a grievin' woman dis mawnin', Spade."
The thought made him sad at first, but he soon cheered up.

"She'll do all right as soon as she's thu with grievin'.   590
Grievin' yaller gals always does all right.
Next time I'se gwine to git me a coal-black gal.
I'se tired of persimmon-skins.
                            I'se gwine to break loose.
De signs is right dis time. I'se gwine to be free,
Free in de Norf."
                            He saw himself in the North.   595
He had a stovepipe hat and a coal-black gal.
He had a white-folks' house and a regular mule.
He worked for money and nobody ever owned him.
He got religion and dollars and lucky dice
And everybody he passed in the white folks' street   600
Said "Good mawnin', Mr. Spade—Mr. Spade, good mawnin'."
He chuckled aloud. "Good mawnin', Mistuh Spade,
Gwine to be free, Mistuh Spade—yes, suh, Mistuh Spade!"
For a lazy moment, he was already there—
Then he stiffened, nostrils flaring, at a slight sound.   605
It couldn't be dogs already.
                            "Jesus," he whispered,
"Sweet, lovin' Jesus, don't let 'em git me again,
Burn me up, but don't let 'em git me again,
Dey's gwine to cut me apart."
                            The rabbit ran past.
He stared at it for a moment with wild, round eyes,   610
Started a yell of laughter—and choked it off.
"Dat ain't no nachul rabbit dere, Spade, boy.
Dat's a sign. Yes, suh. You better start makin' tracks.
Take your foot in your hand, Mistuh Spade."
                            He swung the bundle
Up on his shoulders and slid along through the trees.   615
The bundle was light. He was going to be hungry soon
And the big splay feet would soon be bleeding and sore,
But, as he went, he shook with uncanny chuckles.
"Good mawnin', Mr. Spade—glad to see you dis mawnin'
How's Mrs. Spade, Mr. Spade?"   620

———————

Sally Dupré, from the high porch of her house
Stared at the road.
                    They would be here soon enough.
She had waved a flag the last time they went away.
This time she would wave her hand or her handkerchief.

That was what women did. The column passed by
And the women waved, and it came back and they waved,
And, in between, if you loved, you lived by a dull
Clock of long minutes that passed like sunbonneted women
Each with the same dry face and the same set hands.
I have read, they have told me that love is a pretty god
With light wings stuck to his shoulders.
                              They did not tell me
That love is nursing a hawk with yellow eyes,
That love is feeding your heart to the beak of the hawk
Because an old woman, gossiping, uttered a name.°

They were coming now.
She remembered the first time.
They were different now. They rode with a different rein.
They rode all together. They knew where they were going.
They were famous now,° but she wondered about the fame.
And yet, as she wondered, she felt the tears in her blood
Because they could ride so easily.
                              He was there.
She fed her heart to the hawk and watched him ride.

She thought, "But they like this, too. They are like small boys
Going off to cook potatoes over a fire
Deep in the woods, where no women can ever come
To say how blackened and burnt the potatoes are
And how you could cook them better back in a house.
Oh, they like to come home. When they're sick they like to come home,
They dream about home—they write you they want to come back,
And they come back and live in the house for a while
And raise their sons to hear the same whistle-tune
Under the window, the whistle calling the boys
Out to the burnt potatoes.
                              O whistler Death,
What have we done to you in a barren month,
In a sterile hour, that our lovers should die before us?"
Then she thought. "No, no, I can't bear it. It cannot be borne."
And knowing this, bore it.
                              He saw her. He turned his horse.

---

634 *because an old woman . . . uttered a name:* See Book I, lines 933 ff.   639
They were famous now: Benét's Black Horse Troop is fictional, but "The Black
Horse" was a cognomen frequently applied to crack Confederate cavalry units, and
Company H of the 4th Virginia Cavalry, for example, was specifically known as
"The Black Horse Troop."

"If he comes here, I can't keep it back, I can't keep it back,
I can't stand it, don't let him come." He was coming now.
He rides well, she thought, while her hands made each other cold.   660
I will have to remember how. And his face is sharper.
The moustache quite changes his face. The face that I saw
While he was away was clean-shaven and darker-eyed.
I must change that, now. I will have to remember that.
It is very important.
                          He swung from Black Whistle's back.   665
His spurs made a noise on the porch. She twisted her hands.
"If I shut my eyes, I can make him kiss me. I will not."

They were saying good-by, now. She heard polite voices saying it.
Then the voices ended. "No, no, it is not to be borne,
It is the last twist of the vise."
                                   Her will snapped then.   670
When she looked at him, she knew that the knives were edgeless.
In an instant life would begin, life would be forever.

His eyes wavered. There was a thin noise in her ears,
A noise from the road.
                        The instant fell and lay dead
Between them like something broken.   675

She turned to see what had killed it.

Lucy Weatherby, reining a bright bay mare,
Played with the braided lash of a riding-whip
And talked to Wingate's father with smiling eyes,
While Huger Shepley tried to put in a word   680
And the whole troop clustered about her.
                                          Her habit was black
But she had a knot of bright ribbons pinned at her breast,
Red and blue—the Confederate colors.
                                      They had cheered her.
They had cheered her, riding along with her colored ribbons.
It was that which had killed the instant.
                                          Sally looked   685
At the face with the new moustache she had to remember.
"Good-by," she said. The face bent over her hand
And kissed it acceptably.
                          Then the face had gone.
He was back with the others now. She watched for a minute.

Lucy was unpinning her knot of ribbons.   6
She saw a dozen hands go up for the knot
And Lucy laugh her sweet laugh and shake her bright head,
Glance once at Huger Shepley and once at Clay,
And then toss the colored knot to the guidon-bearer
Who grinned and tied the ribbons around the staff   6
While some of them cheered again.
                           Then the horses moved.
They went by Lucy. Lucy was waving her hand.
She had tears in her eyes and was saying brave words to the soldiers.
Sally watched a back and a horse go out of sight.
She was tired, then.
When the troop had quite disappeared
Lucy rode up to the house.
                     The two women kissed
And talked for a while about riding-habits and war.
"I just naturally love every boy in the Black Horse Troop,
Don't you, Sally darling? They're all so nice and polite,
Quite like our Virginia boys, and the Major's a dear,
And that nice little one with the guidon is perfectly sweet.
You ought to have heard what he said when I gave him the knot.
Though, of course, I can tell why you didn't come down to the road,
War's terrible, isn't it? All those nice boys going off—
I feel just the way you do, darling—we just have to show them
Whenever we can that we know they are fighting for us,
Fighting for God and the South and the cause of the right—
'Law, Chile, don't you fret about whether you's pretty or plain,
You just do what you kin, and the good Lawd'll brighten your tracks.'
That's what my old mammy would tell me when I was knee-high
And I always remember and just try to do what I can
For the boys and the wounded and—well, that's it, isn't it, dear?
We've all got to do what we can in this horrible war."
Sally agreed that we had, and drank from a cup.
She thought. "Lucy Weatherby. Yes. I must look for a doll.
I must make a doll with your face, an image of wax.
I must call that doll by your name."

———————

Now the scene expands, we must look at the scene as a whole.
How are the gameboards chalked and the pieces set?
There is an Eastern game and a Western game.°

726 *There is an Eastern game and a Western game:* See end papers.

In the West, blue armies try to strangle the long
Snake of the Mississippi with iron claws;
Buell and Grant against Bragg and Beauregard.
They have hold of the head of the snake where it touches the Gulf,   730
New Orleans is taken, the fangs of the forts drawn out,
The ambiguous Butler wins ambiguous fame
By issuing orders stating that any lady
Who insults a Union soldier in uniform
Shall be treated as a streetwalker plying her trade.   735
The orders are read and hated. The insults stop
But the ladies remember Butler for fifty years
And make a fabulous devil with pasteboard horns
—"Beast" Butler, the fiend who pilfered the silver spoons—
From a slightly-tarnished, crude-minded, vain politician   740
Who loved his wife and ached to be a great man.
You were not wise with the ladies,° Benjamin Butler,
It has been disproved that you stole New Orleans spoons
But the story will chime at the ribs of your name and stain it,
Ghost-silver, clinking against the ribs of a ghost,   745
As long as the ladies have tongues.
                              Napoleon was wiser
But he could not silence one ugly, clever De Staël.°
Make war on the men—the ladies have too-long memories.

The head of the snake is captured—the tail gripped fast—
But the body in between still writhes and resists,   750
Vicksburg is still unfallen—Grant not yet master—
Sheridan, Sherman, Thomas still in the shadow.°

732–742 *ambiguous Butler . . . not wise with the ladi.*: Major General Benjamin
Butler, successful lawyer but inept tactician, the harshly efficient commander of New
Orleans, despised for such measures as confiscating the property ("stealing the silver") of those fighting against the Union. His General Order 28 (May 15, 1862)
read, "When any female shall by word, gesture or movement insult or show contempt
for any officer or soldier of the United States she shall . . . be treated as a woman
of the town plying her avocation," *Official Records,** Series I, Vol. XV, 426.   747
ugly, clever De Staël: Madame Anne Louise Germaine de Staël, plain and buxom
daughter of Necker, Louis XVI's finance minister; an author and social theorist
whose continuing verbal duel with Napoleon led to her exile from Paris.   752
Sheridan, Sherman, Thomas still in the shadow: General Philip Henry Sheridan
would in 1863 gain Grant's attention at the Battle of Chattanooga, reorganize the
Union cavalry in 1864, and subsequently command the Army of the Shenandoah
Valley. Sherman: see note, Book III, lines 108–113. General George H. Thomas,
a southerner who remained with the Union Army, would become a hero in the
Union defeat at Chickamauga in September 1863, and the victorious commander
at Chattanooga two months later.

The eyes of the captains are fixed on the Eastern game,
The presidents—and the watchers oversea—
For there are the two defended kings of the board,   7
Muddy Washington, with its still-unfinished Capitol,
Sprawling, badly-paved, beset with sharp hogs
That come to the very doorsteps and grunt for crumbs,
Full of soldiers and clerks, full of all the baggage of war,
"Bombproof" ° officers, veterans back on leave,   7
Recruits, spies, spies on the spies, politicians, contractors,
Reporters, slackers, ambassadors, bands and harlots,
Negro-boys who organize butting-matches
To please the recruits, tattooers and fortune-tellers,
Rich man, poor man, soldier, beggarman, thief,   7
And one most lonely man in a drafty White House
Whose everlasting melancholy runs
Like a deep stream under the funny stories,
The parable-maker, humble in many things
But seldom humble with his fortitude,   7
The sorrowful man who cracked the sure-fire jokes,
Roared over Artemus Ward and Orpheus C. Kerr°
And drove his six cross mules° with a stubborn hand.
He has lost a son,° but he has no time to grieve for him.
He studies tactics now till late in the night
With the same painful, hewing industry
He put on studying law.
                          McClellan comes,
McClellan goes, McClellan bustles and argues,
McClellan is too busy to see the President,°
McClellan complains of this, complains of that,
The Government is not supporting him,
The Government cannot understand grand strategy,
The Government—
                          McClellan feels abused.
McClellan is quite sincere and sometimes right.
They come to the lonely man about McClellan

760 *"Bombproof"*: contemptuous term for noncombatants.   772 *Artemus Ward and Orpheus C. Kerr*: contemporary humorists. Artemus Ward was the pen name of Charles Farrar Browne; Orpheus C. Kerr that of Robert Henry Newell.   773 *drove his six cross mules*: the Cabinet. See Book II, line 240.   774 *He has lost a son*: William ("Willie") died in February 1862 at the age of eleven.   779 *too busy to see the President*: McClellan once left Lincoln waiting in the sitting room and retired to his bed. See *Abraham Lincoln: A History*, IV, 468–469.

With various tales.
        McClellan lacks respect,
McClellan dreams about a dictatorship,
McClellan does that and this.
          The lonely man
Listens to all the stories and remarks,
"If McClellan wins, I will gladly hold his horse." °   790

A hundred miles away in an arrow-line
Lies the other defended king of the giant chess,
Broad-streeted Richmond.
         All the baggage of war
Is here as well, the politicians, the troops,
The editors who scream at the government,   795
The slackers, the good and the bad, but the flavor is different:
There is something older here, and smaller and courtlier,
The trees in the streets are old trees used to living with people,
Family-trees that remember your grandfather's name.
It is still a clan-city, a family-city, a city   800
That thinks of the war, on the whole, as a family-matter,
A woman city, devoted and fiercely jealous
As any of the swan-women who ruled it then—
Ready to give their lives and hearts for the South,
But already a little galled by Jefferson Davis   805
And finding him rather too much of a doctrinaire
With a certain comparative touch of the parvenu.
He is not from Virginia, we never knew his grandfather.

The South is its husband, the South is not quite its master.
It has a soul while Washington is a symbol,   810
Beautiful, witty, feminine, narrow and valiant,
Unwisely-chosen, perhaps, for a king of the game,
But playing the part with a definite air of royalty
Until, in the end, it stands for the South completely
And when it falls, the sword of the South snaps short.   815

789–790 *Listens . . . and remarks, ". . . I will gladly hold his horse.":* "On one occasion he had made an engagement for a conference . . . to which [McClellan] did not come. After long waiting, at which the other gentlemen may have shown some irritation, the President said, 'Never mind; I will hold McClellan's horse if he will only bring us success,' " *Abraham Lincoln, A History,* IV, 469.

At present, the war has not yet touched it home.
McClellan has landed, on the Peninsula,
But his guns are still far away.
                              The ladies go
To Mrs. Davis's parties in last year's dresses.°
Soon they are to cut the green and white chintz curtains   8
That shade their long drawing-rooms from the lazy sun
To bandage° the stricken wounded of Seven Pines.

The lonely man with the chin like John Calhoun's
Works hard and is ill at ease in his Richmond White House.
His health was never too strong—it is tiring now   8
Under a mass of detail, under the strain
Of needless quarrels with secretaries and chiefs
And a Congress already beginning to criticize him.
He puts his trust in God with a charmed devotion
And his faith, too often, in men who can feed his vanity.   8
They mock him for it. He cannot understand mocking.
There is something in him that prickles the pride of men
Whom Lincoln could have used, and makes them his foes.
Joe Johnston and he have been at odds from the first.
Beauregard and he are at odds and will be at odds,°   8
One could go through a list—
                              He is quite as stubborn as Lincoln
In supporting the people he trusts through thick and thin,
But—except for Lee—the people he trusts so far
Seldom do the work that alone can repay the trust.
They fail in the end and his shoulders carry the failure,   8
And leave him, in spite of his wife, in spite of his God,

819 Mrs. Davis's parties in last year's dresses: "I attended Mrs. Davis's last reception. . . . As we don't often wear our evening gowns, they are still quite passable.
I wore the gray . . . made for Mrs. Douglas's last reception . . . ," from a letter
to Mrs. Roger A. Pryor, Reminiscences of Peace and War, pp. 227–228.   820–822
green and white chintz . . . bandage . . . : "My springlike green and white chintz
bandages appeared on many a manly arm and leg," Pryor, p. 184.   834–835 at odds
from the first./Beauregard . . . : Johnston's and Davis' personal differences were
aggravated early in the war by Davis' placing officers formerly junior to Johnston
above him, and by publicly giving Beauregard almost total credit for the victory at
Bull Run. But Davis' relationship with Beauregard soon became strained, as well.
As Beauregard put it, "Mr. Davis's friendship, warm at the early period of the war,
was changed, sometime after the battle of Manassas, to a corresponding hostility,"
Battles and Leaders, I, 224.

Lonely, beginning and end, with that other's loneliness.
The other man could have understood him and used him.
He could never have used or comprehended the other.
It is their measure.
                        And yet, a deep loneliness,   845
A deep devotion, a deep self-sacrifice,
Binds the strange two together.
                            He, too, is to lose
A child ° in his White House, ere his term is accomplished.
He, too, is to be the scapegoat for all defeat.
And he is to know the ultimate bitterness,   850
The cause lost after every expense of mind,
And bear himself with decent fortitude
In the prison where the other would not have kept him.°
One cannot balance tragedy in the scales
Unless one weighs it with the tragic heart.   855
The other man's tragedy was the greater one
Since the blind fury tore the huger heart,
But this man's tragedy is the more pitiful.
Thus the Eastern board and the two defended kings.
But why is the game so ordered, what crowns the kings?   860
They are cities of streets and houses like other cities.
Baltimore might be taken, and war go on,
Atlanta will be taken and war go on,
Why should these two near cities be otherwise?
We do not fight for the real but for shadows we make.   865
A flag is a piece of cloth and a word is a sound,
But we make them something neither cloth nor a sound,
Totems of love and hate, black sorcery-stones,
So with these cities.
                      And so the third game is played,
The intricate game of the watchers oversea,   870
The shadow that falls like the shadow of a hawk's wing
Over the double-chessboard until the end—
The shadow of Europe, the shadows of England and France,
The war of the cotton against the iron and wheat.
The shadows ponder and mutter, biding their time;   875

847–848 *He, too, is to lose/A child:* Davis' favorite, Joe, age four, was killed at his
Richmond home by falling from an upstairs balcony April 30, 1864.   853 *In the
prison . . . :* Under the harsh reconstruction attitudes that prevailed after Lincoln's
death, Davis was kept in prison at Fort Monroe for two years.

If the knights and bishops that play for the cotton-king
Can take the capital-city of wheat and iron,
The shadow-hands will turn into hands of steel
And intervene for the cotton that feeds the mills.
But if the fable throned on a cotton-bale   88
Is checkmated by the pawns of iron and wheat,
The shadows will pause, and cleave to iron and wheat,
They will go their ways and lift their eyes from the game,
For iron and wheat are not to be lightly held.
So the watchers, searching the board.

       And so the game.   8
The blockade grips, the blockade-runners break through,
There are duels and valors, the Western game goes on
And the snake of the Mississippi is tamed at last,°
But the fight in the East is the fight between the two kings.
If Richmond is threatened, we threaten Washington,   8
You check our king with McClellan or Hooker or Grant,
We will check your king with Jackson or Early or Lee
And you must draw back strong pieces to shield your king,
For we hold the chord of the circle and you the arc°
And we can shift our pieces better than you.   8

So it runs for years until Jubal Early, riding,
A long twelve months after Gettysburg's high tide,
Sees the steeples° of Washington prick the blue June sky
And the Northern king is threatened for the last time.
But, by then, the end is too near, the cotton is withered.   9
Now the game still hangs in the balance—the cotton in bloom—
The shadows of the watchers long on the board.
McClellan has moved his men from their camps at last
In a great sally.

    There are many gates he can try.
The Valley gate and the old Manassas way,

§88 *the Mississippi is tamed at last*: With the fall of Vicksburg in July 1863, Lincoln remarked, "The Father of Waters again goes unvexed to the sea." See John B. McMaster, A *History of the People of the United States During Lincoln's Administration,** p. 395.   894 *we hold the chord . . . and you the arc*: In military parlance, the South had the advantage of interior lines for troop movement, supply, and communication.   896–898 *Jubal Early . . . Sees the steeples*: In midsummer 1864, Major General Jubal Anderson Early led a diversionary raid which brought him within sight of Washington.

But he has chosen to ferry his men by sea,
To the ragged half-island between the York and the James
And thrust up a long, slant arm from Fortress Monroe
Northwest toward Richmond.
                            The roads are sticky and soft,
There are forts at Yorktown and unmapped rivers to cross.   910
He has many more men than Johnston or John Magruder
But the country hinders him, and he hinders himself
By always thinking the odds on the other side°
And that witches of ruin haunt each move he makes.
But even so—he has boarded that jutting deck   915
That is the Peninsula, and his forces creep
Slowly toward Richmond, slowly up to the high
Defended captain's cabin of the great ship.
—There was another force that came from its ships°
To take a city set on a deck of land,   920
The cause unlike, but the fighting no more stark,
The doom no fiercer, the fame no harder to win.
There are no gods to come with a golden smoke
Here in the mud between the York and the James
And wrap some high-chinned hero away from death.   925
There are only Bibles and buckles and cartridge belts
That sometimes stop a bullet before it kills
But oftener let it pass.
                        And when Sarpedon°
Falls and the heavy darkness stiffens his limbs
They will let him lie where he fell, they will not wash him   930
In the running streams of Scamander,° the half-divine,
They will bury him in a shallow and cumbered pit.
But, if you would sing of fighters, sing of these men,

911–913 *more men than Johnston or John Magruder . . . always thinking the odds
on the other side:* In April 1862, the leading elements of the Army of the Potomac
were seriously delayed by the much smaller force of Major General John Bankhead
Magruder, who by repeatedly shifting his troop positions to simulate the presence
of a strong force, bluffed McClellan into overcautiousness. Before Richmond, a
month later, McClellan again gave up the initiative even though his force outnumbered Johnston's command five to three. See map, p. 205. 919 *another force
that came from its ships:* the Greeks at Troy. 928 *Sarpedon:* the son of Zeus and
Europa, one of the strongest Trojan fighters. After he was killed, Zeus ordered Apollo
to carry the body from the battlefield, wash him in a running river, anoint him in
ambrosia, and so prepare him for due burial in a tomb. 931 *Scamander:* river on
which Troy was built.

Sing of Fair Oaks and the battered Seven Days,°
Not of the raging of Ajax,° the cry of Hector.°   93
These men were were not gods nor shielded by any gods,
They were men of our shape: they fought as such men may fight
With a mortal skill: when they died it was as men die.

Army of the Potomac, advancing army,
Alloy of a dozen disparate, alien States,   94•
City-boy, farm-hand, bounty-man, first volunteer,
Old regular, drafted recruit, paid substitute,
Men who fought through the war from First Bull Run,
And other men, nowise different in look or purpose,
Whom the first men greeted at first with a ribald cry   94
"Here they come! Two hundred dollars and a ka-ow!" °
Rocks from New England and hickory-chunks from the West,
Bowery boy and clogging Irish adventurer,
Germans who learnt their English under the shells
Or didn't have time to learn it before they died.   95
Confused, huge weapon, forged from such different metals,
Misused by unlucky swordsmen till you were blunt
And then reforged with anguish and bloody sweat
To be blunted again by one more unlucky captain
Against the millstone of Lee.
                              Good stallion,   95•
Ridden and ridden against a hurdle of thorns
By uncertain rider after uncertain rider.°
The rider fails and you shiver and catch your breath,
They plaster your wounds and patch up your broken knees,
And then, just as you know the grip of your rider's hands   9€
And begin to feel at home with his horseman's tricks,
Another rider comes with a different seat,
And lunges you at the bitter hurdle again,
And it beats you again—and it all begins from the first,
The patching of wounds, the freezing in winter camps,   9•

934 *Fair Oaks* . . . *Seven Days:* major battles in McClellan's Peninsular Campaign: Fair Oaks (or Seven Pines), May 31–June 1, 1862; Seven Days, June 25–July 1, 1862.   935 *the raging of Ajax:* Greek warrior and hero who killed himself in anger when Achilles' armor was awarded to Ulysses.   *Hector:* field captain of the Trojans and their greatest warrior.   946 *Two hundred dollars and a ka-ow!:* Because of the bonus they received, new enlistees were derisively called two hundred dollar men.   957 *uncertain rider after uncertain rider:* Within a year the Army of the Potomac was commanded without notable success by a series of leaders: McClellan, Pope, Burnside, and Hooker.

The vain mud-marches, the diarrhea, the wastage,
The grand reviews, the talk in the newspapers,
The sour knowledge that you were wasted again,
Not as Napoleons waste for a victory
But blindly, unluckily—
                              until at last   970
After long years, at fish-hook Gettysburg,°
The blade and the millstone meet and the blade holds fast.
And, after that, the chunky man from the West,
Stranger to you, not one of the men you loved
As you loved McClellan,° a rider with a hard bit,   975
Takes you and uses you as you could be used,
Wasting you grimly but breaking the hurdle down.
You are never to worship him as you did McClellan,
But at the last you can trust him. He slaughters you
But he sees that you are fed. After sullen Cold Harbor°   980
They call him a butcher and want him out of the saddle,
But you have had other butchers who did not win
And this man wins in the end.
                              You see him standing,
Reading a map, unperturbed, under heavy fire.
You do not cheer him as the recruits might cheer   985
But you say "Ulysses doesn't scare worth a darn.°
Ulysses is all right. He can finish the job."
And at last your long lines go past in the Grand Review°
And your legend and his begins and are mixed forever.

Now, though, he is still just one of the Western leaders,   990
And Little Mac is your darling.
                              You are unshaken
By the ruin of Fredericksburg, the wounds of Antietam.

971 *at fish-hook Gettysburg:* The deployment of the Union forces at the Battle of
Gettysburg resembled a fishhook. See map, p. 301.   975 *As you loved McClellan:* In spite of his lack of success, McClellan remained a favorite with his troops,
and there was considerable dismay and debate within the ranks when Lincoln relieved him. See, for example, *Four Brothers in Blue,* pp. 172–174.   980 *sullen Cold
Harbor:* where, in June 1864, Grant lost 7000 men in an hour.   986 *Ulysses
doesn't scare worth a darn:* "A shell exploded directly in front of him. . . . Without the slightest change of countenance [Grant] went on writing. . . . One of [the
wounded being carried past] made the remark: 'Ulysses don't scare worth a d—n,' "
Horace Porter, *Campaigning with Grant,* pp. 96–97.   988 *the Grand Review:* On
May 23–24, 1865, six weeks after Lee surrendered, the Union armies marched in a
Grand Review in Washington before the President and his Cabinet.

Chancellorsville is a name in the Wilderness,°
Your pickets, posted in front of the Chickahominy,
Hear the churchbells of Richmond, ringing;   9
Listen well to those bells, they are very near tonight,
But you will not hear them again° for three harsh years.

Black months of war, hard-featured, defeated months
Between Fair Oaks and Gettysburg,°
What is your tale for this army?   10
What do the men,
So differently gathered for your word to devour,
Say to your ears, deaf with cannon? What do they bring
In powder-pocked hands to the heart of the burst shell?
Let us read old letters awhile,   1
Let us try to hear
The thin, forgotten voices of men forgotten
Crying out of torn scraps of paper, notes scribbled and smudged
On aces, on envelope-backs, on gilt-edged cards stolen out of a dead
    man's haversack.

—Two brothers lay on the field of Fredericksburg°   1
After the assault had failed.
They were unwounded but they could not move,
The sharpshooters covered that patch of ground too well.
They had a breastwork to hide them from the bullets,
A shelter of two dead men. One had lost his back,   1
Scooped out from waist to neck with a solid shot.
The other's legs were gone. They made a good breastwork.
The brothers lay behind them, flat in the mud,
All Sunday till night came down and they could creep off.
They did not dare move their hands for fourteen hours.   1

992–993 *Fredericksburg . . . Antietam/Chancellorsville . . . in the Wilderness:*
major battles to come: Antietam in September 1862; Fredericksburg in December
1862; and Chancellorsville, in a heavily forested sector of Virginia known as "The
Wilderness," in May 1863.   997 *you will not hear them again:* McClellan's advance
to a point on the Chickahominy River about five miles from Richmond was the
closest that major Union forces came to Richmond until 1865.   998–999 *Black
months . . . Between Fair Oaks and Gettysburg:* from June 1862 to July 1863.
1010–1139 The voices and stories in this section are largely drawn from incidents and
letters in *Four Brothers in Blue.* For the story of the two brothers at Fredericksburg,
see pp. 200 ff.; for Asa Fletcher, the sharpshooter from Massachusetts, see pp. 113–
115.

—A middle-aged person named Fletcher from Winchester
Enlisted in the Massachusetts Sharpshooters.
He was a crack-duckshooter, skilful and patient.
They gave him the wrong sort of rifle and twenty rounds
And told him to join his company.   1025
It took him days to find it. He had no rations,
He begged bread and green corn and peaches and shot a hog;
So got there at last. He joined just before Antietam.
He'd never been drilled but he knew how to shoot,
Though at first his hands kept shaking.   1030
"It was different kind of gunning from what I was used to,
I was mad with myself that I acted so like a coward."
But as soon as they let him lie down and fight on his own,
He felt all right. He had nineteen cartridges now.
The first five each killed a man—he was a good shot—   1035
Then the rifle fouled. He began to get up and fix it,
Mechanically. A bullet went through his lung.
He lay on the field all day. At the end of the day
He was captured, sent to prison, paroled after weeks,
Died later, because of the wound.   1040
That was his war—

Other voices, rising out of the scraps of paper,
Till they mix in a single voice that says over and over
"It is cold. It is wet. We marched till we couldn't stand up.
It is muddy here. I wish you could see us here.   1045
I wish everybody at home could see us here.
They would know what war is like. We are still patriotic.
We are going to fight. We hope this general's good.
We hope he can make us win. We'll do all we can.
But I wish we could show everybody who stays at home   1050
What this is like."
Voices of tired men,
Sick, convalescent, afraid of being sick.
"The diarrhea is bad. I hope I don't get it
But everybody seems to get it sometime.   1055
I felt sick last night. I thought I was going to die,
But Jim rubbed me and I feel better. There's just one thing
I hope I never get sent to the hospital,
You don't get well when you go to the hospital.
I'd rather be shot and killed quick."   1060
(Nurses and doctors, savagely, tenderly working,

Trying to beat off death without enough knowledge,
Trying and failing.
Clara Barton,° Old Mother Bickerdyke,°
Overworked evangels of common sense,
Nursing, tending, clearing a ruthless path
Through the cant and red tape, through the petty jealousies
To the bitter front, bringing up the precious supplies
In spite of hell and high water and pompous fools,
To the deadly place where the surgeons' hands grew stiff
Under the load of anguish they had to deal,
Where they bound men's wounds and swabbed them with green corn
  leaves,
There being no other lint.
Whitman, with his sack of tobacco and comfits,
Passing along the terrible, crowded wards,
Listening, writing letters, trying to breathe
Strong life into lead-colored lips.
He does what he can.° The doctors do what they can.
The nurses save a life here and another there,
But the sick men die like flies in the hospitals.)

Voices of boys and men,
Homesick, stubborn, talking of little things,
"We get better food. I'm getting to be a good cook.
The food's bad. The whole company yelled 'Hard Bread!' ° today.
There are only three professed Christians in my whole regiment,
I feel sad about that.
I wish you could see the way we have to live here,
I wish everybody at home could see what it's like.
It's muddy. It's cold. My shoes gave out on the march.
We lost the battle. The general was drunk.
This is the roughest life that you ever saw.

1064 *Clara Barton:* later the founder of the American Red Cross, famous for her work as a field nurse and for her continuing effort to supply hot food and other comforts to the Union troops. *Old Mother Bickerdyke:* Mary Ann Ball Bickerdyke (1817–1901), colorful hospital worker and forager, was in nineteen battles, including the siege of Vicksburg and service on Union gunboats. 1074–1078 *Whitman . . . does what he can:* During most of the war years, the poet, then in his forties, lived in Washington working at various jobs while also serving as a volunteer helper in the hospitals. 1084 *The whole company yelled 'Hard Bread!':* Compare Grant in *Battles and Leaders,* III, 518: "A soldier, recognizing me, said in rather a low voice, but yet so that I heard him, 'Hard-tack.' In a moment the cry was taken up all along the line, 'Hard-tack! Hard-tack!' " See also *Four Brothers in Blue,* p. 190.

If I ever get back home—"
And, over and over, in stiff, patriotic phrases,
"I am resigned to die for the Union, mother.
If we die in this battle, we will have died for the right,   1095
We will have died bravely—you can trust us for that.
It is only right to die for our noble Union.
We will save it or die for it. There's just one thing.
I hope I die quick. I hope I don't have to die
In the hospital.   1100
There is one thought that to me is worse than death.
(This, they say over and over) it is the thought
Of being buried as they bury us here
After a battle. Sometimes they barely cover us.
I feel sick when I think of getting buried like that,   1105
Though if nothing except our death will rescue our Union,
You can trust us to die for it."
And, through it all, the deep diapason swelling,
"It is cold. We are hungry. We marched all day in the mud.
We could barely stand when we got back into camp.   1110
Don't believe a thing the newspapers say about us.
It's all damn lies.
                        We are willing to die for our Union,
But I wish you could all of you see what this is like,
Nobody at home can imagine what it is like.
We are ready to fight. We know we can fight and win.   1115
But why will they waste us in fights that cannot be won?
When will we get a man that can really lead us?"
These are the articulate that write the letters.
The inarticulate merely undergo.
There are times of good food and times of campfire jokes,   1120
Times of good weather, times of partial success
In those two years.
                        "The mail came. Thanks for the papers.
We had a good feed at Mrs. Wilson's place.
I feel fine today. We put on a show last night.
You ought to have seen Jim Wheeler in 'Box and Cox.' °   1125
Our little band of Christians meets often now
And the spirit moves in us strongly, praise be to God.
The President reviewed us two days ago.

1125 'Box and Cox': a popular farce adapted from the French by J. M. Morton,
1847.

You should have seen it, father, it was majestic.
I have never seen a more magnificent sight.
It makes me proud to be part of such an army.
We got the tobacco. The socks came. I'm feeling fine."
All that—but still the deep diapason throbs
Under the rest.
                    The cold. The mud. The bleak wonder.
The weakening sickness—the weevils tainting the bread—
We were beaten again in spite of all we could do.
We don't know what went wrong but something went wrong.
When will we find a man who can really lead us?
When will we not be wasted without success?

Army of the Potomac, army of brave men,
Beaten again and again but never quite broken,
You are to have the victory in the end
But these bleak months are your anguish.
                                Your voice dies out.
Let us hear the voice of your steadfast enemy.

Army of Northern Virginia, fabulous army,
Strange army of ragged individualists,
The hunters, the riders, the walkers, the savage pastorals,
The unmachined, the men come out of the ground,
Still for the most part, living close to the ground
As the roots of the cow-pea,° the roots of the jessamine,°
The lazy scorners, the rebels against the wheels,
The rebels against the steel combustion-chamber
Of the half-born new age of engines and metal hands.
The fighters who fought for themselves in the old clan-fashion.
Army of planters' sons and rusty poor-whites,
Where one man came to war with a haircloth trunk
Full of fine shirts and a body-servant to mend them,
And another came with a rifle used at King's Mountain°
And nothing else but his pants and his sun-cracked hands,
Aristo-democracy armed with a forlorn hope,
Where a scholar turned the leaves of an Arabic grammar
By the campfire-glow, and a drawling mountaineer

1150 *cow-pea:* the black-eyed pea, a legume cultivated in the South.   *jessamine:*
jasmine, a flowering shrub native to the South.   1158 *King's Mountain:* in North
Carolina hill country, the site of a British defeat in the American Revolution on
October 7, 1780.

Told dirty stories old as the bawdy world,
Where one of Lee's sons worked a gun with the Rockbridge Battery°
And two were cavalry generals.°
                        Praying army,   1165
Full of revivals, as full of salty jests,
Who debated on God and Darwin° and Victor Hugo,
Decided that evolution might do for Yankees
But that Lee never came from anything with a tail,
And called yourselves "Lee's miserables faintin' "   1170
When the book came out that tickled your sense of romance,°
Army of improvisators of peanut-coffee
Who baked your bread on a ramrod stuck through the dough,
Swore and laughed and despaired and sang "Lorena,"
Suffered, died, deserted, fought to the end.   1175
Sentimental army, touched by "Lorena,"
Touched by all lace-paper-valentines of sentiment,
Who wept for the mocking-bird on Hallie's grave°
When you had better cause to weep for more private griefs,
Touched by women and your tradition-idea of them,   1180
The old, book-fed, half-queen, half-servant idea,
False and true and expiring.
                       Starving army,
Who, after your best was spent and your Spring lay dead,
Yet held the intolerable lines of Petersburg°
With deadly courage.
                  You too are a legend now   1185
And the legend has made your fame and has dimmed that fame,
—The victor strikes and the beaten man goes down
But the years pass and the legend covers them both,

1164 *one of Lee's sons . . . with the Rockbridge Battery:* At Antietam, the Rockbridge Battery "galloped by [and] . . . Robert E. Lee, Jr., a private at the guns,
black with the grime and powder of a long day's fight, stopped a moment to salute
his father and then rushed after his gun," H. K. Douglas in *Battles and Leaders,* II,
629. 1165 *two were cavalry generals:* Major General George Washington Custis
Lee (USMA, 1854) and Brigadier General William Henry Fitzhugh Lee (Harvard,
1858). 1167 *Darwin:* Although American reaction to Charles Darwin's *Origin of
Species* (1859) was muted by the press of events leading to the Civil War, his
theories were debated in intellectual circles before the war. 1167–1171 *Victor
Hugo . . . "Lee's miserables faintin' "* . . . : "The soldiers are all reading it. They
calmly walk into the bookstores, . . . and ask for 'Lee's Miserables faintin'!'—the
first volume being 'Fantine,'" Pryor, p. 226. 1174–1178 *"Lorena" . . . the
mocking-bird on Hallie's grave:* "Lorena" and "Listen to the Mocking Bird" were sad
and sentimental songs popular in the South. 1184 *Petersburg:* Petersburg, Virginia, under attack by Union forces from June 15, 1864, to April 4, 1865.

The beaten cause turns into the magic cause,
The victor has his victory for his pains—
So with you—and the legend has made a stainless host
Out of the dusty columns of footsore men
Who found life sweet and didn't want to be killed,
Grumbled at officers, grumbled at Governments.
That stainless host you were not. You had your cowards,
Your bullies, your fakers, your sneaks, your savages.
You got tired of marching. You cursed the cold and the rain.
You cursed the war and the food—and went on till the end.
And yet, there was something in you that matched your fable.
What was it? What do your dim, faint voices say?
"Will we ever get home? Will we ever lick them for good?
We've got to go on and fight till we lick them for good.
They've got the guns and the money and lots more men
But we've got to lick them now.
We're not fighting for slaves.
Most of us never owned slaves and never expect to,
It takes money to buy a slave and we're most of us poor,
But we won't lie down and let the North walk over us
About slaves or anything else.
                         We don't know how it started
But they've invaded us now and we're bound to fight
Till every last damn Yankee goes home and quits.
We used to think we could lick them in one hand's turn.
We don't think that any more.
                         They keep coming and coming.
We haven't got guns that shoot as well as their guns,
We can't get clothes that wear as well as their clothes,
But we've got to keep on till they're licked and we're independent,
It's the only thing we can do.
                         Though some of us wonder—
Some of us try and puzzle the whole thing through,
Some of us hear about Richmond profiteers,
The bombproofs who get exempted and eat good dinners,
And the rest of it, and say, with a bitter tongue,
'This is the rich man's war and the poor man's fight.'
And more of us, maybe, say that, after a while,
But most of us just keep on till we're plumb worn out,
We just keep on.
                         We've got the right men to lead us,

It doesn't matter how many the Yankees are,
Marse Robert and Old Jack° will take care of that,
We'll have to march like Moses° and fight like hell
But we're bound to win unless the two of them die
And God wouldn't be so mean as to take them both,   1230
So we just keep on—and keep on—"
                                   To the Wilderness,
To Appomattox, to the end of the dream.

Army of Northern Virginia, army of legend,
Who were your captains that you could trust them so surely?
Who were your battle-flags?
                              Call the shapes from the mist,   1235
Call the dead men out of the mist and watch them ride.
Tall the first rider, tall with a laughing mouth,
His long black beard is combed like a beauty's hair,
His slouch hat plumed with a curled black ostrich-feather,
He wears gold spurs and sits his horse with the seat   1240
Of a horseman born.
                     It is Stuart of Laurel Hill,
"Beauty" Stuart,° the genius of cavalry,
Reckless, merry, religious, theatrical,
Lover of gesture, lover of panache,°
With all the actor's grace and the quick, light charm   1245
That makes the women adore him—a wild cavalier
Who worships as sober a God as Stonewall Jackson,
A Rupert° who seldom drinks, very often prays,
Loves his children, singing, fighting, spurs, and his wife.
Sweeney his banjo-player° follows him.   1250

1227 *Marse Robert and Old Jack:* Lee and Jackson.   1228 *march like Moses:* as
he led the Jews from Egypt. Exodus 13, 14.   1241–1242 *Stuart of Laurel Hill,/*
"Beauty" Stuart: "Jeb" Stuart (see note, Book I, line 752) was born at Laurel Hill
plantation, Patrick County, Virginia. He acquired the nickname "Beauty" while a
cadet at West Point.   1244 *panache:* a feathered plume for a helmet; here, an
emblem of flamboyant leadership.   1248 *Rupert:* Prince Rupert (Count Palatine
of the Rhine and Duke of Bavaria), who served Charles I against Cromwell as
general of the cavalry. "[Stuart] had the fire, zeal, and capacity of Prince Rupert,
but, like him, lacked caution," Fitzhugh Lee, *General Lee,* p. 152.   1250 *Sweeney*
his banjo-player: Joseph Sweeney, who enlisted in the 9th Virginia Cavalry in the
autumn of 1861 from a minstrel show stranded in Richmond. Stuart transferred
him to his headquarters where he played on the march, for dances, and for religious
services until he died of pneumonia during the winter of 1863–1864.

And after them troop the young Virginia counties,
Horses and men, Botetort, Halifax,
Dinwiddie, Prince Edward, Cumberland, Nottoway,
Mecklenburg, Berkeley, Augusta, the Marylanders,°
The horsemen never matched till Sheridan came.°   12
Now the phantom guns creak by. They are Pelham's guns.
That quiet boy with the veteran mouth is Pelham.°
He is twenty-two. He is to fight sixty battles
And never lose a gun.
     The cannon roll past,
The endless lines of the infantry begin.   12
A. P. Hill leads the van.° He is small and spare,
His short, clipped beard is red as his battleshirt, .
Jackson and Lee are to call him in their death-hours.°
Dutch Longstreet° follows, slow, pugnacious and stubborn,
Hard to beat and just as hard to convince,   12
Fine corps commander, good bulldog for holding on,
But dangerous when he tries to think for himself,
He thinks for himself too much at Gettysburg,°
But before and after he grips with tenacious jaws.
There is D. H. Hill°—there is Early and Fitzhugh Lee°—   12

1251–1254 *Virginia counties . . . Botetort* [*sic*] *. . . Augusta, the Marylanders:*
Stuart's Virginia cavalry was largely made up of companies drawn from Virginia
counties and so designated: Botetourt, Halifax, *et al.* Company K of the 1st Virginia
Cavalry was composed of Marylanders. 1255 *never matched till Sheridan came:*
The Confederate cavalry was undisputedly superior at first, but a number of factors
served to shift the balance. By 1864, the Union cavalry under Sheridan was often
able to best, if not destroy, the Southern cavalry—as at Yellow Tavern, where Stuart
was killed. 1257 *Pelham:* John C. Pelham, captain and "boy-major," commanding
the Virginia Battery of horse artillery attached to Stuart's cavalry. 1261 *A. P. Hill
leads the van:* Lieutenant General Ambrose Powell Hill, commander of the famed
Light Division and later of Lee's Third Corps, was almost continuously in front-line
action. 1263 *call him in their death-hours:* Though Jackson and A. P. Hill had
serious differences (Jackson brought court-martial charges several times), together
they won outstanding victories, and Hill's name was the last Jackson mentioned in
his death throes in 1863. See Book VI, lines 1156–1157. Seven years later Lee's final
words, in delirium, were, "Tell Hill he must come up." See Fitzhugh Lee, p. 412.
1264 *Dutch Longstreet:* Lieutenant General James Longstreet was of Dutch descent;
the original spelling of the family name was Langenstraat. 1267–1268 *dangerous
when he tries to think for himself . . . :* Longstreet had failed on earlier independent missions, but Lee aptly characterized him as "my old war horse." Because
his corps was slow to execute Lee's order to attack at Gettysburg, however, he has
frequently been blamed for the Confederate defeat. See Book VII, lines 605 ff.
1270 *D. H. Hill:* Lieutenant General Daniel Harvey Hill, a division and corps
commander. *Early and Fitzhugh Lee:* cavalry generals under Stuart. Fitzhugh Lee
was Robert E. Lee's nephew; W. H. Fitzhugh Lee (line 1165, above), his son.

Yellow-haired Hood with his wounds and his empty sleeve,
Leading his Texans, a Viking shape of a man,
With the thrust and lack of craft of a berserk sword,°
All lion, none of the fox.
                        When he supersedes
Joe Johnston, he is lost,° and his army with him,   1275
But he could lead forlorn hopes with the ghost of Ney.°
His bigboned Texans follow him into the mist.
Who follows them?
                        These are the Virginia faces,
The Virginia speech. It is Jackson's foot-cavalry,°
The Army of the Valley,   1280
It is the Stonewall Brigade, it is the streams
Of the Shenandoah, marching.
                        Ewell goes by,
The little woodpecker, bald and quaint of speech,
With his wooden leg stuck stiffly out from his saddle,
He is muttering, "Sir, I'm a nervous Major-General,   1285
And whenever an aide rides up from General Jackson
I fully expect an order to storm the North Pole."
He chuckles and passes, full of crotchets and courage,
Living on frumenty° for imagined dyspepsia,
And ready to storm the North Pole° at a Jackson phrase.   1290
Then the staff—then little Sorrel °—and the plain
Presbyterian figure in the flat cap,

1271–1273 Hood . . . a berserk sword: General John Bell Hood earned fame as the fearless commander of the Texas Brigade; he lost an arm at Gettysburg and a leg at Chickamauga, yet continued as a field commander.   1274–1275 supersedes/Joe Johnston, he is lost: When the aggressive Hood replaced Johnston, who had been fighting a wily delaying action before Atlanta (1864), he predictably counterattacked and met a series of defeats.   1276 Ney: Napoleon's marshal, known as "the bravest of the brave."   1279–1280 Jackson's foot-cavalry: In the Valley Campaign of 1862, Jackson "sometimes made thirty miles in twenty-four hours with his entire army, thus gaining for his infantry the sobriquet of 'Jackson's foot cavalry.' " Imboden in Battles and Leaders, II, 289: See map, p. 205.   1289 frumenty: hulled wheat boiled with milk, sugar, raisins, etc.   1282–1290 Ewell . . . ready to storm the North Pole: Lieutenant General Richard Stoddert Ewell, who lost his leg on the eve of Second Bull Run. He was convinced that Jackson was a bit mad, but followed his orders faithfully. "He told me that he never saw one of Jackson's couriers approach without expecting an order to assault the north pole," Richard Taylor, Destruction and Reconstruction, pp. 36–37.   1291 little Sorrel: Jackson's horse, which he bought from a trainload of Union horses captured at Harper's Ferry, July 1861.

Throwing his left hand out in the awkward gesture
That caught the bullet° out of the air at Bull Run,
Awkward, rugged and dour, the belated Ironside°
With the curious, brilliant streak of the cavalier
That made him quote Mercutio in staff instructions,
Love lancet windows,° the color of passion-flowers,
Mexican sun and all fierce, taut-looking fine creatures;
Stonewall Jackson, wrapped in his beard and his silence,
Cromwell-eyed and ready with Cromwell's short
Bleak remedy° for doubters and fools and enemies,
Hard on his followers, harder on his foes,
An iron sabre vowed to an iron Lord,
And yet the only man of those men who pass
With a strange, secretive grain of harsh poetry
Hidden so deep in the stony sides of his heart
That it shines by flashes only and then is gone.
It glitters in his last words.°

                    He is deeply ambitious,
The skilled man, utterly sure of his own skill
And taking no nonsense about it from the unskilled,
But God is the giver of victory and defeat,
And Lee, on earth, vicegerent under the Lord.
Sometimes he differs about the mortal plans
But once the order is given, it is obeyed.
We know what he thought about God. One would like to know
What he thought of the two together, if he so mingled them.
He said two things about Lee it is well to recall.
When he first beheld the man that he served so well,
"I have never seen such a fine-looking human creature."
Then, afterwards, at the height of his own fame,
The skilled man talking of skill, and something more.

1293–1294 *gesture/That caught the bullet*: "He had a way of throwing up his left hand with the open palm toward the person he was addressing. . . . As he spoke he jerked down the hand, and I saw that blood was streaming from it," Imboden, describing Jackson at First Bull Run, *Battles and Leaders*, I, 236. 1295–1304 *Ironside* . . . : Oliver Cromwell. "[Jackson] impressed me always as a man of the Cromwell stamp, a Puritan, . . . whatever he believed in became a deep religious duty, a duty he would discharge at any cost," Grant quoted by John R. Young, *Around the World with General Grant*, p. 212. 1298 *lancet windows*: high, narrow, pointed windows without tracery. 1301–1302 *Cromwell's short/Bleak remedy*: death by the sword. 1306–1309 *poetry . . . in his last words*: "Let us pass over the river, and rest under the shade of the trees," as quoted by Reverend (Captain) James Power in *Battles and Leaders*, III, 214. Compare Book VI, line 1163.

"General Lee is a phenomenon,
He is the only man I would follow blindfold."
Think of those two remarks and the man who made them   1325
When you picture Lee as the rigid image in marble.
No man ever knew his own skill better than Jackson
Or was more ready to shatter an empty fame.
He passes now in his dusty uniform.
The Bible jostles a book of Napoleon's Maxims   1330
And a magic lemon° deep in his saddlebags.

And now at last,
Comes Traveller and his master. Look at them well.
The horse is an iron-grey, sixteen hands high,
Short back, deep chest, strong haunch, flat legs, small head,   1335
Delicate ear, quick eye, black mane and tail,°
Wise brain, obedient mouth.
                         Such horses are
The jewels of the horseman's hands and thighs,
They go by the word and hardly need the rein.
They bred such horses in Virginia then,   1340
Horses that were remembered after death
And buried not so far from Christian ground
That if their sleeping riders should arise
They could not witch them from the earth again
And ride a printless course along the grass   1345
With the old manage and light ease of hand.
The rider, now.
                He too, is iron-grey,
Though the thick hair and thick, blunt-pointed beard
Have frost in them.
                Broad-foreheaded, deep-eyed,
Straight-nosed, sweet-mouthed, firm-lipped, head cleanly set,   1350
He and his horse are matches for the strong
Grace of proportion that inhabits both.
They carry nothing that is in excess

1330–1331 *The Bible . . . Napoleon's Maxims . . . a magic lemon:* The two
books were his constant companions, and Jackson's habit of sucking lemons added to
the mystique that built up with his continuing victories. 1333–1336 *Traveller
. . . :* In Lee's own words: "If I were an artist . . . I would draw a true picture
of Traveller— . . . deep chest and short back, strong haunches, flat legs, small
head, broad forehead, delicate ears, quick eye, small feet, and black mane and tail,"
Recollections and Letters of General Robert E. Lee, by his son R. E. Lee, p. 83.

And nothing that is less than symmetry,
The strength of Jackson is a hammered strength,
Bearing the tool marks still. This strength was shaped
By as hard arts but does not show the toil
Except as justness, though the toil was there.
—And so we get the marble man again,
The head on the Greek coin, the idol-image,
The shape who stands at Washington's left hand,
Worshipped, uncomprehended and aloof,
A figure lost to flesh and blood and bones,
Frozen into a legend out of life,
A blank-verse statue—

                How to humanize
That solitary gentleness and strength
Hidden behind the deadly oratory
Of twenty thousand Lee Memorial days,
How show, in spite of all the rhetoric,
All the sick honey of the speechifiers,
Proportion, not as something calm congealed
From lack of fire, but ruling such a fire
As only such proportion could contain?

The man was loved, the man was idolized,
The man had every just and noble gift.
He took great burdens and he bore them well,
Believed in God but did not preach too much,
Believed and followed duty first and last
With marvellous consistency and force,
Was a great victor, in defeat as great,
No more, no less, always himself in both,
Could make men die for him but saved his men
Whenever he could save them—was most kind
But was not disobeyed—was a good father,
A loving husband, a considerate friend:
Had little humor, but enough to play
Mild jokes that never wounded, but had charm,
Did not seek intimates, yet drew men to him,
Did not seek fame, did not protest against it,
Knew his own value without pomp or jealousy
And died as he preferred to live—sans phrase,
With commonsense, tenacity and courage,
A Greek proportion—and a riddle unread.
And everything that we have said is true

And nothing helps us yet to read the man,   1395
Nor will he help us while he has the strength
To keep his heart his own.
                    For he will smile
And give you, with unflinching courtesy,
Prayers, trappings, letters, uniforms and orders,
Photographs, kindness, valor and advice,   1400
And do it with such grace and gentleness
That you will know you have the whole of him
Pinned down, mapped out, easy to understand—
And so you have.
              All things except the heart.
The heart he kept himself, that answers all.   1405
For here was someone who lived all his life
In the most fierce and open light of the sun,
Wrote letters freely, did not guard his speech,
Listened and talked with every sort of man,
And kept his heart a secret to the end   1410
From all the picklocks of biographers.

He was a man, and as a man he knew
Love, separation, sorrow, joy and death.
He was a master of the tricks of war,
He gave great strokes and warded strokes as great.   1415
He was the prop and pillar of a State,
The incarnation of a national dream,
And when the State fell and the dream dissolved
He must have lived with bitterness itself—
But what his sorrow was and what his joy,   1420
And how he felt in the expense of strength,
And how his heart contained its bitterness,
He will not tell us.
              We can lie about him,
Dress up a dummy in his uniform
And put our words into the dummy's mouth,   1425
Say "Here Lee must have thought," and "There, no doubt.
By what we know of him, we may suppose
He felt—this pang or that—" but he remains
Beyond our stagecraft, reticent as ice,
Reticent as the fire within the stone.   1430

Yet—look at the face again—look at it well—
This man was not repose, this man was act.

This man who murmured "It is well that war
Should be so terrible, if it were not
We might become too fond of it—" ° and showed
Himself, for once, completely as he lived
In the laconic balance of that phrase;
This man could reason, but he was a fighter,
Skilful in every weapon of defence
But never defending when he could assault,
Taking enormous risks again and again,
Never retreating while he still could strike,
Dividing a weak force on dangerous ground
And joining it again to beat a strong,
Mocking at chance and all the odds of war
With acts that looked like hairbreadth recklessness
—We do not call them reckless, since they won.
We do not see him reckless for the calm
Proportion that controlled the recklessness—
But that attacking quality was there.
He was not mild with life or drugged with justice,
He gripped life like a wrestler with a bull,
Impetuously. It did not come to him
While he stood waiting in a famous cloud,
He went to it and took it by both horns
And threw it down.
                    Oh, he could bear the shifts
Of time and play the bitter loser's game,
The slow, unflinching chess of fortitude,
But while he had an opening for attack
He would attack with every ounce of strength.
His heart was not a stone but trumpet-shaped
And a long challenge blew an anger through it
That was more dread for being musical
First, last, and to the end.
                    Again he said
A curious thing to life.
"I'm always wanting something."
                    The brief phrase
Slides past us, hardly grasped in the smooth flow
Of the well-balanced, mildly-humorous prose

1433–1435 *murmured ". . . war/Should be so terrible . . .":* after his forces had
inflicted severe casualties on Burnside's troops at Fredericksburg.

That goes along to talk of cats and duties,
Maxims of conduct, farming and poor bachelors,   1470
But for a second there, the marble cracked
And a strange man we never saw before
Showed us the face he never showed the world
And wanted something—not the general
Who wanted shoes and food for ragged men,   1475
Not the good father wanting for his children,
The patriot wanting victory—all the Lees
Whom all the world could see and recognize
And hang with gilded laurels—but the man
Who had, you'd say, all things that life can give   1480
Except the last success—and had, for that,
Such glamor as can wear sheer triumph out,
Proportion's son and Duty's eldest sword
And the calm mask who—wanted something still,
Somewhere, somehow and always.
                              Picklock biographers,   1485
What could he want that he had never had?

He only said it once—the marble closed—
There was a man enclosed within that image.
There was a force that tried Proportion's rule
And died without a legend or a cue   1490
To bring it back. The shadow-Lees still live.
But the first-person and the singular Lee?

The ant finds kingdoms in a foot of ground
But earth's too small for something in our earth,
We'll make a new earth from the summer's cloud,   1495
From the pure summer's cloud.
                              It was not that,
It was not God or love or mortal fame.
It was not anything he left undone.
—What does Proportion want that it can lack?
—What does the ultimate hunger of the flesh   1500
Want from the sky more than a sky of air?

He wanted something. That must be enough.

Now he rides Traveller back into the mist.

Continual guns, be silent for a moment,
Be silent, now.
We know your thirst. We hear the roll of your wheels
Crushing down tangled June,
Virginia June,
With tires of iron, with heavy caissons creaking,
Crushing down maidenhair and wilderness-seal,°
Scaring the rabbit and the possum-children,
Scaring the redbird and the mockingbird
As McClellan's army moves forward.
We know your bloody thirst so soon to be slaked
With the red burst-grape juices.
But now, we would have you silent, a little moment,
We would have you hold your peace and point at the moon
For when you speak, we can hear no sound but your sound,
And we would hear the voices of men and women
For a little while.

Jake Diefer, the barrel-chested Pennsylvanian,
Shippy, the little man with the sharp rat-eyes,
Luke Breckinridge, the gawky boy from the hills,
Clay Wingate, Melora Vilas, Sally Dupré,
The slaves in the cabins, ragged Spade in the woods,
We have lost these creatures under a falling hammer.
We must look for them now, again.

Jake Diefer is with the assault that comes from the ships,
He has marched, he has fought at Fair Oaks, but he looks the same:
A slow-thought-chewing Clydesdale horse of a man
Who doesn't think much of the way that they farm down here.
The sun may be good, if you like that sort of sun,
But the barns and the fields are different, they don't look right,
They don't look like Pennsylvania.
                              He spits and wonders.
Whenever he can, he reads a short, crumpled letter
And tries to puzzle out from the round, stiff writing
How things are back on the farm.
                              The boy's a good boy
But the boy can't do it all, or the woman either.
He knows too much about weather and harvest-hands

1510 *maidenhair and wilderness-seal:* ferns and wild flowers.

—It's all right fighting the Rebels to save the Union   1540
But they ought to get through with it quicker, now they've begun,
They don't take the way the crops are into account,
You can't go off and leave a farm like a store,
And you can't expect a boy to know everything,
Or a hired man. No, sir.
        He walks along like an ox.   1545
—He'd like to see the boy and the woman again,
Eat pancakes and sleep in a bed and look at the hay—
This business comes first but after it's finished up—
He can't say he's bothered exactly most of the time.
The weather bothers him more than anything.   1550
He knows it's not the same sort of weather down here,
But every day when he wakes, he looks at the sky
And tries to figure out what it's like back home.

Shippy, the little man with the sharp rat-eyes,
Creeps into an old house in beleaguered Richmond   1555
And meets a woman dressed in severe black silk
With a gentle voice, soft delicate useless hands,
A calm, smooth, faded, handsome mask of a face
And an incredible secret under her brooches.
You would picture her with ivory crochet-needles   1560
Demurely tatting,° demurely singing mild hymns
To an old melodeon° before a blurred mirror.
She is to live in Richmond throughout the war,
A Union spy, never caught, never once suspected,°
And when she dies, she dies with a shut prim mouth   1565
Locked on her mystery.
      Shippy is afraid.
She gives him instructions, he tries to remember them.
But his hands are sweating, his eyes creep around the floor.
He is afraid of the rustle of the black silk.
He wishes he were back in Pollet's Hotel   1570
With Sophy, the chambermaid.
       The woman talks
And he listens, while the woman looks through and through him.

1561 *tatting:* making lace. 1562 *melodeon:* a small parlor organ worked by bel-
lows. 1564 *A Union spy, . . . never once suspected:* Elizabeth L. Van Lew, a
prim spinster who, because she was an open sympathizer with the North, was considered a traitor but never seriously considered to be a spy.

Melora Vilas, rising by crack of dawn,
Looked at herself in the bottom of her tin basin
And wished that she had a mirror.
                        She thought dully,
"He's been gone two months. I can't get used to it yet.
I've got to get used to it. Maybe I'll die instead.
No, I'd know if he'd died."

Sally Dupré was tired of scraping lint°
But her hands kept on. The hours, sunbonneted women,
Passed and passed. "If he ever comes back to me!"
She finished her scraping and wondered how to make coffee
Out of willow-bark and life from a barren stick. . . .
Spade the fugitive stared at the bleak North Star. . . .
Luke Breckinridge, on picket out in the woods,
Remembered a chambermaid at Pollet's Hotel.
And wanted a fight. He hadn't been lucky, of late.
Jim, his cousin, was lucky, out in the West,
Riding a horse and capturing Yankee scouts.°
But his winter here had been nothing but work and mud,
He'd nearly got courtmartialed a dozen times,
Though they knew how he could shoot.
                          The chambermaid's name
Was Sophy. She was little and scared and thin,
But he liked her looks and he liked the size of her eyes,
He'd like to feed her up and see how she looked,
If they ever got through with fighting the Yankees here.
The Yankees weren't all Kelceys. He knew that now,
But he always looked for Kelceys whenever he fought. . . .
Clay Wingate slept in his cloak and dreamed of a girl
With Sally's face and Lucy Weatherby's mouth
And waked again
To know today there would be continual guns.
Continual guns, silent so brief a moment,
Speak again, now,
For now your ignorance
Drowns out the little voices of human creatures.

1579 *scraping lint*: carding worn cloth to be respun and woven into low quality material called "shoddy."　1588–1589 *Jim . . . capturing Yankee scouts*: See Book III, line 1295.

Jackson slips from the Valley° where he has played
A dazzling game against Banks and Shields and Frémont°
And threatened the chess-game-king of Washington
Till strong pieces meant to join in McClellan's game   1610
Are held to defend that king.
                And now the two,
Jackson and Lee, strike hard for Seven Days°
At the host come up from its ships, come up from the sea
To take the city set on a deck of land,
Till the deck is soaked and red with a bloody juice.   1615
And the host goes back.
             You can read in the histories
How the issue wavered, the fog of tiny events,
How here, at one dot, McClellan might have wrung
A victory, perhaps, with his larger force,
And there, on the other hand, played canny and well;   1620
How Jackson, for once, moved slowly, how Porter held,°
And the bitter, exhausted wrestling of Malvern Hill.°
What we know is this.
           The host from the ships went back,
Hurt but not broken, hammered but undestroyed,
To find a new base far up the crook of the James   1625
And rest there, panting.
          Lincoln and Halleck come.°
The gaunt, plain face is deeper furrowed than ever,
The eyes are strained with looking at books of tactics
And trying to understand.

1607 *slips from the Valley:* on June 24, 1862. After a classic campaign that diverted sizable Union forces in the Shenandoah Valley, Jackson—on orders from Lee—moved quickly to assist in the defense of Richmond. 1608 *Banks and Shields and Frémont:* Major General Nathaniel P. Banks, Brigadier General James Shields, and Major General John C. Frémont. 1612 *Seven Days:* the series of battles (June 26–July 2, 1862) around Richmond (including Mechanicsville, Gaines's Mill, Frayser's Farm, and Malvern Hill) that terminated McClellan's unsuccessful Peninsular Campaign. 1621 *moved slowly . . . Porter held:* On June 26, 1862, Jackson failed to take part in an attack with A. P. Hill designed to turn the Union right flank held by Major General Fitz-John Porter's corps. 1622 *exhausted wrestling of Malvern Hill:* After six days of running battles, the Confederates made a mismanaged attempt to destroy McClellan's army just before it withdrew from the vicinity of Richmond. 1626 *Lincoln and Halleck come:* Major General Henry Halleck, called from the Army of the West to be General-in-Chief. Lincoln and Halleck visited McClellan's headquarters at Harrison's Landing on separate dates in July. For the actions described in lines 1607–1626, see map, p. 205.

There is so much
For one man to understand, so many lies,
So much half-truth, so many counselling voices,
So much death to be sown and reaped and still no end.
The dead of the Seven Days. The four months dead
Boy° who used to play with a doll named Jack,
Was a bright boy as boys are reckoned and now is dead.
The doll named Jack° was sometimes a Union soldier,
Sometimes a spy.
                    The boy and his brother held
A funeral in the White House flower-beds
After suitably executing the doll named Jack
But then they thought of a different twist to the game.
The gaunt man signed a paper.
                                "The doll named Jack
Is pardoned. By order of the President.
A. Lincoln."
                    So Jack was held in honor awhile
But next day the boy and his brother forgot the pardon
And the doll named Jack was shot and buried once more.
So much death to be sown and reaped.
                            So much death to be sown
By one no sower of deaths.
                        And still no end.

The council is held. The chiefs and captains debate.
McClellan clings to his plan of storming the deck
From the water ways. He is cool now. He argues well.
He has written Lincoln° "From the brink of eternity"
—A strained, high-flown, remarkable speech of a letter
Of the sort so many have written and still will write—
Telling how well he has done in saving his army,
No thanks to the Government, or to anything else
But the pith of his fighting-men and his own craft.
Lincoln reads and pockets the speech and thanks him.
There had been craft and courage in that retreat
And much was due to McClellan.
                            The others speak.

1633–1634 *The four months dead/Boy*: Lincoln's son "Willie." See line 774, above.
1636 *doll named Jack*: given to Tad Lincoln by The Sanitary Commission of New
York. Dressed in Zouave uniform, "Jack" was a favorite toy of the two younger
Lincoln boys.   1651 *He has written Lincoln*: McClellan gave the letter to Lincoln
when he visited the troops at Harrison's Landing.

Some corps commanders agree and some demur,
The Peninsula-stroke has failed and will fail again.
Elbow-rubbing Halleck, newly-made chief of staff,
Called "Old Brains," ° for reasons that history
Still tries to fathom, demurs. He urges withdrawal.
Washington must be defended first and last—
Withdraw the army and put it in front of Washington.
Lincoln listens to all as he tries to sift
The mustardseed from the twenty barrels of chaff
With patient hands.
     There has been a growth in the man,
A tempering of will in these trotting months
Whose strong hoofs striking have scarred him again and again.
He still rules more by the rein than by whip or spur
But the reins are fast in his hands and the horses know it.
He no longer says "I think," but "I have decided."
And takes the strength and the burden of such decision
For good or bad on himself.
      He will bear all things
But lack of faith in the Union and that not once.
Now at last he decides to recall McClellan's army
For right or wrong.
     We see the completed thing,
Long afterward, knowing all that was still to come,
And say "'He was wrong." °
      He saw the incomplete,
The difficult chance that might turn a dozen ways
And say "He was wrong." °
      He saw the incomplete,

So the deck is cleared and the host goes back to its ships.
The bells in the Richmond churches, clanging for Sunday,
Clang as if silver were mixed in their sweet bell-metal,
The dark cloud lifts, the girls wear flowers again.
Virginia June,
Crushed under cannon, under the cannon ruts,
The trampled grass lifts up its little green guidons,

1663 *"Old Brains"*: There is disagreement as to when Halleck acquired the nickname, but it seems to have been suggested by his high forehead and large, popping eyes.   1681 *"He was wrong."*: not only in his choice of new commanders (Pope and Halleck), but tactically as well. Critics have since generally agreed that leaving the Army of the Potomac in place and providing it with more able leadership would have been a better course of action.

The honeysuckle and the eglantine°
Blow on their tiny trumpets,
Blow out "Dixie,"
Blow out "Lorena," blow the "Bonnie Blue Flag" °
—There are many dead, there are many too many dead,   1695
The hospitals are crowded with broken dolls—
But cotton has won again, cotton is haughty,
Cotton is mounting again to a sleepy throne,
Wheat and iron recoil from the fields of cotton,
The sweet grass grows over them, the cotton blows over them,   1700
One more battle and free, free, free forever.
Cotton moves North in a wave, in a white-crested
Wave of puff-blossoms—in a long grey coil
Of marching men with tongues as dry as cotton.
Cotton and honeysuckle and eglantine   1705
Move North in a drenching wave of blossom and guns
To wash out wheat and iron forever and ever.
There will be other waves that set toward the North,
There will be a high tide,
But this is the high hour.   1710
Jackson has still three hammerstrokes° to strike,
Lee is still master of the attacking sword,
Stuart still carries his black feather high.
Put silver in your bell-metal, Richmond bells,
The wave of the cotton goes North to your sweet ringing,   1715
The first great raiding wave of the Southern dream.

Jack Ellyat, in prison deep in the South,
Gaunt, bearded, dirty old man with the captive eyes,
Lay on his back and stared at the flies on the wall
And tried to remember, through an indifferent mist,   1720
A green place lost in the woods and a herd of black swine.
They came and went and the mist moved round them again.
The mist was not death. He was used to death by now,
But the mist still puzzled him, sometimes.
It was curious—being so weak and yet used to death.   1725

1691 eglantine: sweetbrier. 1693–1694 "Dixie" . . . "Lorena" . . . "Bonnie Blue
Flag": Confederate war songs. "Dixie" is attributed to Dan Emmett (1859);
"Lorena" was an adaptation of a folk song; "Bonnie Blue Flag," by Harry McCarthy
(1861), saluted the first flag of the Confederacy, a blue field with a single white
star. 1711 Jackson has still three hammerstrokes: Second Bull Run, Fredericksburg,
and Chancellorsville.

When you were strong, you thought of death as a strong
Rider on a black horse, perhaps, or at least
As some strong creature, dreadful because so strong.
But when you were weak and lived in a place like this,
Things changed. There was nothing strong about death any more.   1
He was only the gnawed rat-bone on the dirty floor,
That you stumbled across and hardly bothered to curse.
That was all.
             The two Michigan men had died last night.
The Ohio brothers were going to die this week,
You got pretty soon so you knew when people would die,   1
It passed the time as well as carving bone-rings,
Playing checkers with straws or learning Italian nouns
From the lanky schoolteacher-sergeant from Vermont.
Somewhere, sometime, in a tent, by a red loud noise,
Under a dirty coat and a slab of tobacco,   1
He had lost a piece of himself,° a piece of life.
He couldn't die till he got that piece of him back
And felt its ragged edges fit in his heart.
Or so he thought. Sometimes, when he slept, he felt
As if he were getting it back—but most of the time   1
It was only the mist and counting the flies that bothered him.
He heard a footstep near him and turned his head.
"Hello, Charley," he said, "Where you been?"
                              Bailey's face looked strange,
The red, hot face of a hurt and angry boy,
"Out hearing the Rebs," he said. He spat on the floor   1
And broke into long, blue curses. When he was through,
"Did you hear them?" he asked. Jack Ellyat tried to remember
A gnat-noise buzzing the mist. "I guess so," he said.
"What was it? Two-bottle Ed on another tear?"
"Hell," said Bailey. "They cheered. They've licked us again.   1
The news just come. It happened back at Bull Run."
"You're crazy," said Ellyat. "That was the start of the war.
I was in that one."
             "Oh, don't be a fool," said Bailey,
"They licked us again, I tell you, the same old place.
Pope's army's ruined." °

1741 *a piece of himself*: See Book III, line 516.   1755–1760 *licked us again . . .*
Pope's army's ruined: At Second Bull Run, August 29–30, 1862, Lee defeated Pope's
newly formed Army of Virginia.

"Who's he?" said Ellyat wearily.   1760
"Aw, we had him out West—he's God Almighty's pet horse,
He came East and told all the papers how good he was,°
'Headquarters in the saddle'! ° " Bailey snickered.
"Well, they snaffled his saddle and blame near snaffled him,
Jackson and Lee—anyhow they licked us again."   1765

"What about Little Mac?"
                    "Well, Gawd knows what's happened to *him*,"
Said Bailey, flatly, "Maybe he's captured, too,
Maybe they captured Old Abe and everyone else.
I don't know—you can't tell from those lyin' Rebs."

There was a silence. Ellyat lay on his back   1770
And watched the flies on the wall for quite a long time.
"I wish I had a real newspaper," said Bailey,
"Not one of your Richmond wipers. By God, you know, Jack,
When we get back home, I'll read a newspaper, sometimes.
I never was much at readin' the newspaper   1775
But I'd like to read one now, say once in a while."
Ellyat laughed.
            "You know, Charley," he said at last,
"We've got to get out of this place."
                              Bailey joined in the laugh.
Then he stopped and stared at the other with anxious eyes.
"You don't look crazy," he said, "Stop countin' those flies." 1780
Ellyat raised himself on one arm.
                        "No, honest, Charley,
I mean it, damn it. We've got to get out of here.
I know we can't but we've got to. . . ."
                              He swallowed dryly.
"Look here—" he said, "It just came over me then.
I've got a girl and she doesn't know where I am.   1785
I left her back in a tent—no, that wasn't a girl—

1762 *told . . . how good he was:* In his initial address (July 14, 1862), Pope
bluntly stated that "I have come to you from the West where we have always seen
the backs of our enemies," *Battles and Leaders,* II, 530. 1763 *'Headquarters in the
saddle':* Pope's reply to a reporter's question about where his headquarters would be.
It led to the quip that his headquarters were where his hindquarters should have
been.

And you say we got licked again. But that's just it, Charley.
We get licked too much. We've got to get out of here."

He sank back to the floor and shut his ghost-ridden eyes.
Bailey regarded him for a long, numb moment.
"You couldn't walk a mile and a half," he muttered,
"And, by God, I couldn't carry you twenty feet,
And, by God, if we could, there ain't no way to get out,
But all the same—"
                "If there was any use tryin',"
He said, half-pleadingly, half-defiantly,
"I tell you, Jack, if there was any use tryin'—"
He stopped. Ellyat's eyes were shut. He rose with great care.
"I'll get you some water," he muttered. "No, let you sleep."
He sat down again and stared at the sleeping face.
"He looks bad," he thought. "I guess I look bad myself.
I guess the kid's goin' to die if we don't get out.
I guess we're both goin' to die. I don't see why not."
He looked up at the flies on the ceiling and shook his fist.
"Listen, you dirty Rebs," he said, under his breath,
"Flap your goddam wings—we're goin' to get out of here!"

John Brown lies dead in his grave and does not stir,
It is nearly three years since he died and he does not stir,
There is no sound in his bones but the sound of armies
And that is an old sound.

He walks, you will say, he walks in front of the armies,
A straggler met him, going along to Manassas,
With his gun on his shoulder, his phantom-sons at heel,
His eyes like misty coals.

A dead man saw him striding at Seven Pines,
The bullets whistling through him like a torn flag,
A madman saw him whetting a sword on a Bible,
A cloud above Malvern Hill.

But these are all lies. He slumbers. He does not stir.
The spring rains and the winter snows on his slumber
And the bones of his flesh breed armies and yet more armies
But he himself does not stir.

It will take more than cannon to shake his fortress,
His song is alive and throbs in the tramp of the columns,
His song is smoke blown out of the mouth of a cannon,
But his song and he are two.   1825

The South goes ever forward, the slave is not free,
The great stone gate of the Union crumbles and totters,
The cotton-blossoms are pushing the blocks apart,
The roots of cotton grow in the crevices,
(John Brown's body lies a-mouldering in the grave.)   1830
Soon the fight will be over, the slaves will be slaves forever.
(John Brown's body lies a-mouldering in the grave.)
You did not fight for the Union or wish it well,
You fought for the single dream of a man unchained
And God's great chariot rolling. You fought like the thrown   1835
Stone, but the fighters have forgotten your dream.
(John Brown's body lies a-mouldering in the grave.)
You fought for a people you did not comprehend,
For a symbol chained by a symbol in your own mind,
But, unless you arise, that people will not be free.   1840
Are there no seeds of thunder left in your bones
Except to breed useless armies?
(John Brown's body lies a-mouldering in the grave.)
Arise, John Brown,
Call up your sons from the ground,   1845
In smoky wreaths, call up your sons to heel,
Call up the clumsy country boys you armed
With crazy pikes and a fantastic mind.
Call up the American names,
Kagi, the self-taught scholar, quiet and cool,   1850
Stevens, the cashiered soldier, bawling his song,
Dangerfield Newby, the freed Scotch-mulatto,
Watson and Oliver Brown and all the hard-dying.°
Call up the slug-riddled dead of Harper's Ferry
And cast them down the wind on a raid again.   1855
This is the dark hour,
This is the ebb-tide,
This is the sunset, this is the defeat.
The cotton-blossoms are growing up to the sky,

1849–1853 *Call up . . . Kagi . . . Stevens . . .* : John Brown's raiders at Harper's Ferry. See note, Book I, line 428.

The great stone gate of the Union sinks beneath them,
And under the giant blossoms lies Egypt's land,
The dark river,
The ground of bondage,
The chained men.
If the great gate falls, the cotton grows over your dream.
Find your heart, John Brown,
(A-mouldering in the grave.)
Call your sons and get your pikes,
(A-mouldering in the grave.)
Your song goes on, but the slave is still a slave,
And all Egypt's land rides Northward while you moulder in the grave!
Rise up, John Brown,
(A-mouldering in the grave.)
Go down, John Brown,
(Against all Egypt's land)
Go down, John Brown,
Go down, John Brown,
Go down, John Brown, and set that people free!

❧ BOOK FIVE ❧

It was still hot in Washington, that September,°
Hot in the city, hot in the White House rooms,
Desiccate heat, dry as a palm-leaf fan,
That makes hot men tuck cotton handkerchiefs
Between their collars and their sweaty necks,   5
And Northern girls look limp at half-past-four,
Waiting the first cool breath that will not come
For hours yet.
       The sentinel on post
Clicks back and forth, stuffed in his sweltering coat,
And dreams about brown bottles of cold beer   10
Deep in a cellar.
       In the crowded Bureaus
The pens move slow, the damp clerks watch the clock.
Women in houses take their corsets off
And stifle in loose gowns.
         They could lie down
But when they touch the bed, the bed feels hot,   15
And there are things to do.
         The men will want
Hot food when they come back from work.
           They sigh
And turn, with dragging feet, to the hot kitchens.

Sometimes they pause, and push a window up
To feel the blunt, dry buffet of the heat   20
Strike in the face and hear the locust-cry
Of shrilling newsboy-voices down the street,
"News from the army—extra—ter-ble battle—
Terr-r-ble vic'try—ter-r-ble defeat—
Lee's army trapped invading Maryland—   25
McClellan—Sharpsburg°—fightin'—news from the front—"
The women at the windows sigh and wonder
"I ought to buy a paper—No, I'll wait
Till Tom gets home—I wonder if it's true—
Terrible victory—terrible defeat—   30
They're always saying that—when Tom gets home

1 *that September:* September 1862. 26 *Sharpsburg:* Sharpsburg, Maryland, scene
of the Battle of Antietam, September 16–17, 1862.

He'll have some news—I wonder if the army—
No, it's too hot to buy a paper now—"

A hot, spare day of waiting languidly
For contradictory bits of dubious news.

It was a little cooler, three miles out,
Where the tall trees shaded the Soldiers' Home.°
The lank man, Abraham Lincoln, found it so,
Glad for it, doubtless, though his cavernous eyes
Had stared all day into a distant fog
Trying to pierce it.
                        "General McClellan
Is now in touch with Lee in front of Sharpsburg
And will attack as soon as the fog clears." °

It's cleared by now. They must be fighting now.

We can't expect much from the first reports.
Stanton and Halleck° think they're pretty good
But you can't tell. Nobody here can tell.
We're all too far away.
                        You get sometimes
Feeling as if you heard the guns yourself
Here in the room and felt them shake the house
When you keep waiting for the news all day.
I wish we'd get some news.
                        Bull Run was first.
We got the news of Bull Run soon enough.
First that we'd won, hands down, which was a lie,
And then the truth.

37 *Soldiers' Home:* the President's country place a few miles northeast of the White House. Lincoln used one of two mansions there; the other was a rest home for retired volunteers. Described by Nathaniel W. Stephenson in *Lincoln,* p. 364. 40–43 *all day into a distant fog . . . :* At noon September 16, Lincoln telegraphed Governor Curtin of Pennsylvania, "What do you hear from General McClellan's army?"; and later the same day, "Since telegraphing you, despatch came from General McClellan. . . . This morning he was up with the enemy at Sharpsburg, and was waiting for heavy fog to rise," *Abraham Lincoln, Complete Works,* II, 236–237. 46 *Stanton and Halleck:* Edwin M. Stanton, Lincoln's Secretary of War, and General Henry W. Halleck, General-in-Chief of the Army.

It may be that to-day.   55
I told McClellan not to let them go,
Destroy them if he could—but you can't tell.
He's a good man in lots of different ways,
But he can't seem to finish what he starts
And then, he's jealous, like the rest of them,   60
Lets Pope get beaten,° wanted him to fail,
Because he don't like Pope.
                          I put him back
Into command.° What else was there to do?
Nobody else could lick those troops in shape.
But, if he wins, and lets Lee get away,   65
I'm done with him.
                      Bull Run—the Seven Days—
Bull Run again°—and eighteen months of war—
And still no end to it.
                     What is God's will?

They come to me and talk about God's will
In righteous deputations and platoons,   70
Day after day, laymen and ministers.
They write me Prayers From Twenty Million Souls
Defining me God's will and Horace Greeley's.°
God's will is General This and Senator That,
God's will is those poor colored fellows' will,   75
It is the will of the Chicago churches,°
It is this man's and his worst enemy's.
But all of them are sure they know God's will.
I am the only man who does not know it.

61 *Lets Pope get beaten:* "Unquestionably, [McClellan] has acted badly toward Pope; he wanted him to fail," Lincoln, quoted in Stephenson, p. 275.   62–63 *I put him back/Into command:* During August 1862, units were shifted from McClellan's Army of the Potomac to Pope's Army of Virginia, leaving McClellan the Washington defenses, but only nominal control of field operations. After Pope's defeat at Second Bull Run, Lincoln returned McClellan to full command.   66–67 *Bull Run—the Seven Days—/Bull Run again:* major battles: First Bull Run, July 21, 1861; Seven Days, June 26–July 2, 1862; Second Bull Run, August 29, 1862. 72–73 *Prayers From Twenty Million Souls . . . :* "The Prayer of Twenty Millions" was printed in Horace Greeley's *New York Tribune,* August 20, 1862.   76 *the will of the Chicago churches:* On September 13, 1862, an interdenominational gathering of Christians in Chicago forwarded to the President a resolution demanding a proclamation of emancipation.

And, yet, if it is probable that God
Should, and so very clearly, state His will
To others, on a point of my own duty,
It might be thought He would reveal it me
Directly, more especially as I
So earnestly desire to know His will.

The will of God prevails. No doubt, no doubt—
Yet, in great contests, each side claims to act
In strict accordance with the will of God.
Both may, one must be wrong.
                              God could have saved
This Union or destroyed it without war
If He so wished. And yet this war began,
And, once begun, goes on, though He could give
Victory, at any time, to either side.°
It is unfathomable. Yet I know
This, and this only. While I live and breathe,
I mean to save the Union if I can,
And by whatever means my hands can find
Under the Constitution.°
                              If God reads
The hearts of men as clearly as He must
To be Himself, then He can read in mine
And has, for twenty years, the old, scarred wish
That the last slave should be forever free
Here, in this country.
                              I do not go back
From that scarred wish and have not.
                              But I put
The Union, first and last, before the slave.
If freeing slaves will bring the Union back
Then I will free them; if by freeing some
And leaving some enslaved I help my cause,
I will do that—but should such freedom mean

86–93 *The will of God . . . to either side:* Compare Lincoln's "Meditation on the
Divine Will," which he wrote for himself only, September 30, 1862, *Complete
Works,* II, 243–244.   96–98 *to save the Union if I can . . . Under the Constitution:* "I would save it in the shortest way, under the Constitution," from Lincoln's
reply to Horace Greeley, published in the *National Intelligencer,* August 22, 1862.

The wreckage of the Union that I serve   110
I would not free a slave.°
           O Will of God,
I am a patient man, and I can wait
Like an old gunflint buried in the ground
While the slow years pile up like moldering leaves
Above me, underneath the rake of Time,   115
And turn, in time, to the dark, fruitful mold
That smells of Sangamon° apples, till at last
There's no sleep left there, and the steel event
Descends to strike the live coal out of me
And light the powder that was always there.   120

That is my only virtue as I see it,
Ability to wait and hold my own
And keep my own resolves once they are made
In spite of what the smarter people say.
I can't be smart the way that they are smart.   125
I've known that since I was an ugly child.
It teaches you—to be an ugly child.
It teaches you—to lose a thing you love.
It sticks your roots down into Sangamon ground
And makes you grow when you don't want to grow   130
And makes you tough enough to wait life out,
Wait like the fields, under the rain and snow.

I have not thought for years of that lost grave°
That was my first hard lesson in the queer
Thing between men and women we call love.   135
But when I think of it, and when I hear
The rain and snow fall on it, as they must,
It fills me with unutterable grief.

105–111 *The Union . . . before the slave . . . :* Lincoln to Greeley, "If I could
save the Union without freeing any slave, I would do it; . . . and if I could
save it by freeing some and leaving others alone, I would also do that," *Complete
Works*, II, 227–228.   117 *Sangamon:* The Sangamon River runs through Menard
and Sangamon Counties, Lincoln's home country in Illinois.   133 *that lost grave:*
the grave of Ann Rutledge, Lincoln's sweetheart, who died of fever in August 1835
at the age of 22.

We've come a good long way, my hat and I,
Since then, a pretty lengthy piece of road,   14
Uphill and down but mostly with a pack.
Years of law-business, years of cracking jokes,
And watching Billy Herndon° do his best
To make me out, which seemed to be a job;
Years trying how to learn to handle men,   14
Which can be done, if you've got heart enough,
And how to deal with women or a woman
And that's about the hardest task I know.
For, when you get a man, you've got the man
Like a good big axehandle in your fist,   1
But you can't catch a woman like an axe.
She'll run like mercury between your hands
And leave you wondering which road she went,
The minute when you thought you knew her ways.

I understand the uses of the earth.   1
And I have burned my hands at certain fires
Often enough to know a use for fire,
But when the genius of the water moves,
And that's the woman's genius, I'm at sea
In every sense and meaning of the word,   1
With nothing but old patience for my chart,
And patience doesn't always please a woman.

Bright streams of water, watering the world,
Deep seas of water that all men must sail
Or rest half-men and fill the narrow graves,   1
When will I understand or comprehend
Your salt, sweet taste, so different from the taste
Of Sangamon russets,° weighing down the bough?
You can live with the water twenty years
And never understand it like the earth   1
But that's the lesson I can't seem to learn.

143 *Billy Herndon:* Lincoln's law partner in Springfield; later one of his biographers.
168 *russets:* apples.

"Abraham Lincoln, his hand and pen,
He will be good, but God knows when." °
He will be wise, but God knows when.

It doesn't matter. If I had some news—   175
News from that fog—
                    I'll get the hypo,° sure,
Unless I watch myself, waiting for news.
I can't afford to get the hypo now,
I've got too much to do.
                    Political years,
Housekeeping years of marrying and begetting   180
And losing, too, the children and the town,
The wife, the house, the life, the joy and grief,
The profound wonder still behind it all.°

I had a friend who married and was happy.
But something haunted him that haunted me°   185
Before he did, till he could hardly tell
What his own mind was, for the brooding veil
And immaterial horror of the soul
Which colors the whole world for men like that.

I do not know from whence that horror comes   190
Or why it hangs between us and the sun
For some few men, at certain times and days,
But I have known it closer than my flesh,
Got up with it, lain down and walked with it,
Scotched it awhile, but never killed it quite,   195
And yet lived on.

172–173 *"Abraham Lincoln . . . God knows when"*: Lincoln wrote these lines in
his "sum book" in the early 1820s; see Lord Charnwood, *Abraham Lincoln,** p. 12.
176 *the hypo*: depression, hypochondria. The term appears in Lincoln's letters.
179–183 *Political years,/Housekeeping years . . .* : In February 1861, upon leaving
Springfield to be inaugurated, Lincoln remarked, "Here I have lived a quarter of a
century, and have passed from a young to an old man. Here my children have been
born and one is buried. I now leave, not knowing when or whether ever, I may
return. . . ." Quoted in Stephenson, p. 123.   184–185 *a friend . . . something
haunted him that haunted me*: Joshua Speed of Salem, Illinois, a confidant whose
uncertain engagement to Fanny Henning was contemporary with Lincoln's equally
uncertain engagement to Mary Todd. See Stephenson, p. 39.

                              I wrote him good advice,
        The way you do, and told him this, for part,
        "Again you fear that that Elysium
        Of which you've dreamed so much is not to be.
        Well, I dare swear it will not be the fault
        Of that same black-eyed Fanny, now your wife.
        And I have now no doubt that you and I,
        To our particular misfortune, dream
        Dreams of Elysium far exceeding all
        That any earthly thing can realize." °

        I wrote that more than twenty years ago,
        At thirty-three, and now I'm fifty-three,
        And the slow days have brought me up at last
        Through water, earth and fire, to where I stand,
        To where I stand—and no Elysiums still.

        No, no Elysiums—for that personal dream
        I dreamt of for myself and in my youth
        Has been abolished by the falling sledge
        Of chance and an ambition so fulfilled
        That the fulfillment killed its personal part.

        My old ambition was an iron ring
        Loose-hooped around the live trunk of a tree.
        If the tree grows till bark and iron touch
        And then stops growing, ring and tree are matched
        And the fulfillment fits.
                                But, if by some
        Unlikely chance, the growing still keeps on,
        The tree must burst the binding-ring or die.

        I have not once controlled the circumstances.
        They have controlled me. But with that control

196–205 *I wrote him good advice . . . "exceeding all/That any earthly thing can realize"*: From Springfield, February 25, 1842, Lincoln wrote, "Our forebodings (for which you and I are peculiar) are all the worst sort of nonsense. . . . You say you much fear that that elysium of which you have dreamed so much is never to be realized. Well, if it shall not, I dare swear it will not be the fault of her who is now your wife. I have no doubt that it is the peculiar misfortune of both you and me to dream dreams of elysium far exceeding all that anything earthly can realize." See Stephenson, pp. 41–42.

They made me grow or die. And I have grown.   225
The iron ring is burst.
                    Three elements,°
Earth, water and fire. I have passed through them all,
Still to find no Elysium for my hands,
Still to find no Elysium but growth,
And the slow will to grow to match my task.   230

Three elements, I have not sought the fourth
Deeply, till now—the element of air,
The everlasting element of God,
Who must be there in spite of all we see,
Who must be there in spite of all we bear,   235
Who must exist where all Elysiums
Are less than shadows of a hunter's fire
Lighted at night to scare a wolf away.

I know that wolf—his scars are in my hide
And no Elysiums can rub them out.   240
Therefore at last, I lift my hands to You
Who Were and Are and Must Be, if our world
Is anything but a lost ironclad
Shipped with a crew of fools and mutineers
To drift between the cold forts of the stars.   245

I've never found a church that I could join°
Although I've prayed in churches in my time
And listened to all sorts of ministers
Well, they were good men, most of them, and yet—
The thing behind the words—it's hard to find.   250
I used to think it wasn't there at all
Couldn't be there. I cannot say that, now.
And now I pray to You and You alone.
Teach me to know Your will. Teach me to read
Your difficult purpose here, which must be plain   255
If I had eyes to see it. Make me just.

226 *Three elements:* of the four basic elements of medieval science.   246 *I've never found a church that I could join:* "I have never united myself to any church because I have found difficulty in giving my assent, without mental reservation, to the long, complicated statements of Christian doctrine." Lincoln as quoted in Stephenson, p. 265.

There was a man I knew near Pigeon Creek°
Who kept a kennel full of hunting dogs,
Young dogs and old, smart hounds and silly hounds.
He'd sell the young ones every now and then,
Smart as they were and slick as they could run.
But the one dog he'd never sell or lend
Was an old half-deaf foolish-looking hound
You wouldn't think had sense to scratch a flea
Unless the flea were old and sickly too.
Most days he used to lie beside the stove
Or sleeping in a piece of sun outside.
Folks used to plague the man about that dog
And he'd agree to everything they said,
"No—he ain't much on looks—or much on speed—
A young dog can outrun him any time,
Outlook him and outeat him and outleap him,
But, Mister, that dog's hell on a cold scent
And, once he gets his teeth in what he's after,
He don't let go until he knows he's dead."
I am that old, deaf hunting-dog, O Lord,
And the world's kennel holds ten thousand hounds
Smarter and faster and with finer coats
To hunt your hidden purpose up the wind
And bell upon the trace° you leave behind.
But, when even they fail and lose the scent,
I will keep on because I must keep on
Until You utterly reveal Yourself
And sink my teeth in justice soon or late.
There is no more to ask of earth or fire
And water only runs between my hands,
But in the air, I'll look, in the blue air,
The old dog, muzzle down to the cold scent,
Day after day, until the tired years
Crackle beneath his feet like broken sticks
And the last barren bush consumes with peace.

I should have tried the course with younger legs,

257 *There was a man I knew near Pigeon Creek*: The Pigeon Creek settlement was in southern Indiana, where the Lincoln family lived from 1816 to 1830. The ensuing story (lines 257–320) follows the usual pattern of Lincoln's homespun parables. 280 *bell upon the trace*: bay while following a trail.

This hunting-ground is stiff enough to pull
The metal heart out of a dog of steel;
I should have started back at Pigeon Creek   295
From scratch, not forty years behind the mark.
But you can't change yourself, and, if you could,
You might fetch the wrong jack-knife in the swap.
It's up to you to whittle what you can
With what you've got—and what I am, I am   300
For what it's worth, hypo and legs and all.
I can't complain. I'm ready to admit
You could have made a better-looking dog
From the same raw material, no doubt,
But, since You didn't, this'll have to do.   305

Therefore I utterly lift up my hands
To You, and here and now beseech Your aid.
I have held back when others tugged me on,
I have gone on when others pulled me back
Striving to read Your will, striving to find   310
The justice and expedience of this case,
Hunting an arrow down the chilly airs
Until my eyes are blind with the great wind
And my heart sick with running after peace.
And now, I stand and tremble on the last   315
Edge of the last blue cliff, a hound beat out,
Tail down and belly flattened to the ground,
My lungs are breathless and my legs are whipped,
Everything in me's whipped except my will.
I can't go on. And yet, I must go on.   320

I will say this. Two months ago I read
My proclamation° setting these men free
To Seward and the rest. I told them then
I was not calling on them for advice
But to hear something that I meant to do.   325

321–322 *Two months ago I read/My proclamation:* Lincoln read a draft of the
Emancipation Proclamation to his Cabinet on July 22, 1862; the final version was
released to the public September 22, to become effective on January 1, 1863. The
comment from Seward (lines 329–335) is a close paraphrase of his actual statement.
See Stephenson, p. 270.

We talked about it. Most of them approved
The thing, if not the time. Then Seward said
Something I hadn't thought of, "I approve
The proclamation—but, if issued now
With our defeats in everybody's mouth   330
It may be viewed as a last shriek for help
From an exhausted, beaten government.
Put it aside until a victory comes,
Then issue it with victory."
                              He was right.
I put the thing aside—and ever since   335
There has been nothing for us but defeat,
Up to this battle now—and still no news.

If I had eyes to look to Maryland!
If I could move that battle with my hands!
No, it don't work. I'm not a general.
All I can do is trust the men who are.   340

I'm not a general, but I promise this,
Here at the end of every ounce of strength
That I can muster, here in the dark pit
Of ignorance that is not quite despair
And doubt that does but must not break the mind!   345
The pit I have inhabited so long
At various times and seasons, that my soul
Has taken color in its very grains
From the blind darkness, from the lonely cave   350
That never hears a footstep but my own
Nor ever will, while I'm a man alive
To keep my prison locked from visitors.

What if I heard another footstep there,
What if, some day—there is no one but God,   355
No one but God who could descend that stair
And ring his heavy footfalls on the stone.
And if He came, what would we say to Him?

That prison is ourselves that we have built,
And, being so, its loneliness is just,   360
And, being so, its loneliness endures.
But, if another came,

What would we say?
What can the blind say, given back their eyes?

No, it must be as it has always been.
We are all prisoners in that degree   365
And will remain so, but I think I know
This—God is not a jailor . . . .
                   And I make
A promise now to You and to myself.
If this last battle° is a victory
And they can drive the Rebel army back   370
From Maryland, back over the Potomac,
My proclamation shall go out at last
To set those other prisoners and slaves
From this next year, then and forever free.

So much for my will. Show me what is Yours!   375

That must be news, those footsteps in the hall,
Good news, or else they wouldn't come so fast.

What is it, now? Yes, yes, I'm glad of that.
I'm very glad. There's no mistake this time?
We have the best of them? They're in retreat?   380
This is a great day, Stanton . . . .
. . . . If McClellan
Can only follow up the victory now!

Lord, I will keep my promise and go on,
Your will, in much, still being dark to me,   385
But, in this one thing, as I see it, plain.

And yet—if Lee slips from our hands again
As he well may from all those last reports
And the war still goes on—and still no end—
Even after this Antietam—not for years—   390

I cannot read it but I will go on,
Old dog, old dog, but settled to the scent
And with fresh breath now from this breathing space,

369 *this last battle:* the Battle of Antietam.

Almighty God.
         At best we never seem
To know You wholly, but there's something left,   395
A strange, last courage.
             We can fail and fail,
But, deep against the failure, something wars,
Something goes forward, something lights a match,
Something gets up from Sangamon County ground
Armed with a bitten and a blunted axe   400
And after twenty thousand wasted strokes
Brings the tall hemlock crashing to the ground.

Spade saw the yellow river rolling ahead
His sore, cracked lips curled back in a death's head grin
And his empty belly ceased to stick to his sides.   405
He sat on the bank a minute to rest his legs
And catch his breath. He had lived for the last three days
On a yam, two ears of horse-corn and the lame rabbit
That couldn't run away when he threw the stick.

He was still a big man but the ribs stuck into his skin   410
And the hard, dry muscles were wasted to leather thongs.
"Boy, I wisht we had a good meal," he thought with a dull
Fatigue. "Dat's Freedom's lan' ovah dere fer sho',
But how we gwine to swim it without a good meal?
I wisht we had even a spoonful of good hot pot-licker°   415
Or a smidgin' of barbecued shote.°
               Dat river's cold.
Colder'n Jordan. I wisht we had a good meal."

He went down to the river and tested it with his hand.
The cold jumped up his arm and into his heart,
Sharp as the toothache. His mouth wried up in a queer   420
Grimace. He felt like crying. "I'se tired," he said.
"Flow easy, river," he said.
            Then he tumbled in.
The hard shock of the plunge took his breath away.

415 *pot-licker:* gravy from boiled beans and bacon. 416 *shote:* a young hog.

So stinging at first that his arms and legs moved fast,
But then the cold crept into his creaking bones   425
And he rolled wild eyes.
                    "Oh, God," he thought as he struggled,
"I'se weak as a cat. I ust to be a strong man."

The yellow flood sucked round him, pulling him down,
The yellow foam had a taste like death in his mouth,
"We ought to of had a good meal," he thought with a weak   430
Wonder, as he fought weakly. "A good hot meal.
Dis current, she's too strong for a hungry mouth.
We'se done our best, but she fights like a angel would
Like wrestlin' with a death-angel."
                              He choked and sank
To come up gasping and staring with bloodshot eyes.   435
His brain had a last, clear flash. "You're drowned," said the brain.
Then it stopped working.
                    But the black, thrashing hands
Caught hold of something solid and hard and rough
And hung to it with a last exhausted grip.
—He had been fighting an angel for seven nights   440
And now he hung by his hands to the angel's neck,
Lost in an iron darkness of beating wings.
If he once let go, the angel would push him off
And touch him across the loins with a stony hand
In the last death-trick of the wrestle.°
                    He moaned a little.   445
The blackness began to lighten. He saw the river
Rolling and rolling. He was clutched to a log
Like a treetoad set afloat on a chip of wood,
And the log and he were rushing downstream together,
But the current pulled them both toward the freedom side.   450

He hunched up a little higher. An eddy took
The log and him and spun them both like a top
While he prayed and sickened.
                    Then they were out of the eddy
And drifting along more slowly, straight for the shore.

434–445 *wrestlin' with a death-angel* . . . : Compare Jacob's wrestling with the
angel. Genesis 32:24–26.

He hauled himself up the bank with enormous care,
Vomited and lay down.
                              When he could arise
He looked at his hands. They were still hooked into a curve.
It took quite a time to straighten them back again.

He said a prayer as he tried to dry his clothes,
Then he looked for a stone and threw it into the river.
"You'se a mean and hungry river," he said. "You is.
Heah's a present for you. I hope it busts up your teef.
Heah's a present fum Mistah Spade."
                              He felt better then,
But his belly started to ache. "Act patient," he said,
Rubbing it gently, "We'se loose in Freedom's land,
Crossed old Jordan—bound to get vittles now."

He started out for the town. The town wasn't far
But he had to go slow. Sometimes he fell on the way.
The last time he fell was in front of a little yard
With a white, well-painted fence. A woman came out.
"Get along," she said. "You can't get sick around here.
I'm tired of you nigger tramps. You're all of you thieves."
Spade rose and said something vague about swimming rivers
And vittles. She stamped her foot. "Get along!" she said,
"Get along or I'll call the dog and——"
                              Spade got along.

The next house, the dog was barking out in the yard,
He went by as fast as he could, but when he looked back
A man had come out with a hostile stick in his hand.
Spade shook his head. "Freedom's land," he thought to himself,
"They's some mighty quick-actin' people in Freedom's land,
Some mighty rash-tempered dogs."
                              He swayed as he walked.
Here was another house. He looked for the dog
With fright in his eyes. Then a swimming qualm came over him.
A deathly faintness. His hands went out to the fence.
He gripped two palings, hung, and stared at his shoes.
Somebody was talking to him. He tried to move on
But his legs wouldn't walk. The voice was a woman's voice.

She'd be calling the dog in a minute. He shivered hard.
"Excuse me ma'am, but I'se feelin' poorly," he said.
"I just crossed over—I'll go as soon as I kin." 490
A man's voice now. They were taking him under the arms.
He didn't care what they did. He let himself walk.

Then he was sitting up in a bentwood chair
In a tidy kitchen that smelt of frying and ham;
The thick, good smell made him strangely sick at first 495
But it soon passed off. They fed him little by little
Till at last he could tell his tale and ask about them.

They were churchgoing people and kind to runaway slaves.
She wore a blue dress. They had two sons in the war.
That was all that he knew and all that he ever knew. 500
But they let him sleep in the garret and gave him some shoes
And fifty cents when he left.
     He wanted to stay
But times were bad and they couldn't afford to keep him.
The town was tired of runaway negroes now.

All the same, when he left, he walked with a different step. 505
He went down town. He was free. He was Mister Spade.
The President had written a letter about it
And the mule and the coal-black gal might come any day.

He hummed a tuneless whistle between his teeth
And fished a piece of paper out of his pants, 510
They'd written him down a boss's name and address
But he'd have to get somebody to read it again.
He approached a group of three white men on a corner
Holding the paper.
     " 'Scuse me, boss, can you tell me——"
The white men looked at him with hard, vacant eyes. 515
At last one of them took the paper. "Oh, Hell," he said,
Spitting, and gave Spade a stare. Then he seemed to think
Of something funny. He nudged the other two men.
"Listen, nigger," he said. "You want Mr. Braid.
You'll find him two blocks down at the Marshal's office, 520
Tell him Mr. Clarke sent you there—Mr. William Clarke—

He'll fix you up all right."
                                        The other men grinned,
Adding directions. Spade thanked them and went away.
He heard them laugh as he went.
                                        Another man took him
To a red-faced person who sat in a tilted chair,
Reading a paper, his feet cocked up on his desk.
He looked at Spade and his feet came down with a slam.
"Take that God damn smile off," he said. "Who let you come in?
You contraband niggers think that you own this town
And that all you've got to do is cross over here
For people to feed you free the rest of your lives.
Well it don't go down with me—just understand that."

Spade brought out his paper, dumbly. The man looked at it.
"Hell, this ain't for me," he said.
                                        Spade started to go.

"Come back here, nigger," ordered the red-faced man.
"Hey, Mike!" he yelled, "Here's another of Lincoln's pets.
Send him out with the rest of the gang."
                                        "But, boss——" said Spade.
"Don't get lippy with me," said the man, "Mike, take him along."
The pimply boy named Mike jerked a sallow thumb.
"Come on, black beauty," he said. "We got you a job."
Spade followed him, dazed.
                                        When they were out in the street
The boy turned to him. "Now, nigger, watch out," he said,
Patting a heavy pistol swung at his belt,
With puppy-fierceness, "You don't get away from me.
I'm a special deputy, see?"
                                        "All right, boss," said Spade.
"I ain't aimin' to get away from nobody now,
I just aims to work till I gets myself a good mule."
The boy laughed briefly. The conversation dropped.
They walked out of the town till they came to a torn-up road
Where a gang of negroes was working.
                                        "Say, boss—" said Spade.
The boy cut him off. "Hey, Jerry," he called to the foreman,
"Here's another one."
                                        The foreman looked up and spat.
"Judas!" he said, "Can't they keep the bastards at home?

I'd put a gun on that river if I was Braid.
Well, come along, nig, get a move on and find a shovel.   555
Don't stand lookin' at me all day."
                      The boy went away.
Spade found a shovel and started work on the road.
The foreman watched him awhile with sarcastic eyes,
Spade saw that he, too, wore a pistol.
                "Christ," said the foreman,
Disgustedly, "Try and put some guts in it there.   560
You're big enough. That shovel'll cost five dollars.
Remember that—it comes out of your first week's pay.
You're a free nigger now."
          He chuckled. Spade didn't answer
And, after a while, the foreman moved away.

Spade turned to the gingerskinned negro who worked beside him.   565
"You fum de Souf?" he mouthed at him.
                 Ginger nodded.
"I been here a month now. They fotched me here the first day.
Got any money?"
         "Nuthin' but fifty cents."
"You better give it to him," said Ginger, stealing
A glance at the foreman. "He'll treat you bad if you don't.   570
He's a cranky man."
          Spade's heart sank into his boots.
"Don't we uns get paid? We ain't none of us slaves no more,
The President said so. Why we wuhkin' like dis?"
Ginger snickered. "Sho' we uns get paid," he said,
"But we got to buy our stuff at de company sto'   575
And he sells his old shovels a dozen times what dey's wuth.
I only been here a month but I owes twelve dollars.
Dey ain't no way to pay it except by wuhk,
And de more you wuhk de more you owe at the sto'.
I kain't figure it out exactly but it's dat way."   580
Spade worked for a while, revolving these things in his mind.
"I reckoned I sho' was gwine to be sassy and free
When I swum dat river," he said.
          Ginger grinned like a monkey,
"Swing your shubbel, boy, and forget what you ain't.
You mought be out on de chain-gang, bustin' up rocks,   585
Or agin, you mought be enlisted."
             "Huh?" said Spade.

"Sho', dey's gwine enlist us all when we finish dis road.
All excep' me. I got bad sight in my eyes
And dey knows about it."
                              "Dey kain't enlist me," said Spade.
"I ain't honin' to go an' fight in no white-folks war,   5
I ain't bust loose into Freedom's land fer dat,
All I want is a chance to git me a gal and a mule.
If I'se free, how kin dey enlist me, lessen I want?"

"You watch 'em," said Ginger. They worked on for a time.
The foreman stood on the bank and watched them work,   5
Now and then he drank from a bottle.
                              Spade felt hungry.

Autumn is filling his harvest-bins
    With red and yellow grain,
Fire begins and frost begins
    And the floors are cold again.   6

Summer went when the crop was sold,
    Summer is piled away,
Dry as a faded marigold
    In the dry, long-gathered hay.

It is time to walk to the cider-mill   6
    Through air like apple wine
And watch the moon rise over the hill,
    Stinging and hard and fine.

It is time to cover your seed-pods deep
    And let them wait and be warm,   6
It is time to sleep the heavy sleep
    That does not wake for the storm.

Winter walks from the green, streaked West
    With a bag of Northern Spies,°
The skins are red as a robin's breast,   6
    The honey chill as the skies.

---

614 *Northern Spies:* apples.

Melora Vilas walked in the woods that autumn
And heard the dry leaves crackle under her feet,
Feeling, below the leaves, the blunt heavy earth.
"It's getting-in time," she thought. "It's getting-in time,   620
Time to put things in barns and sit by the stove,
Time to watch the long snow and remember your lover.

He isn't dead. I know that he isn't dead.
Maybe they've changed his body into a tree,
Maybe they've changed his body into a cloud   625
Or something that sleeps through the Winter.
                              But I'll remember.
I'll sleep through the Winter, too. We all sleep then
And when the Spring freshet drums in the narrow brooks
And fills them with a fresh water, they'll let him come
Out of the cloud and the tree and the Winter-sleep.   630

The winter falls and we lie like beleaguered stones
In the black, cramped ground.
                              And then you wake in the morning
And the air's got soft and you plant the narrow-edged seeds,
They grow all Summer and now we've put them in barns
To sleep again for a while.   635
I am the seed and the husk.° I have sown and reaped.
My heart is a barn full of grain that my work has harvested.
My body holds the ripe grain. I can wait my time."

She walked on farther and came to the lip of the spring,
The brown leaves drifted the water. She watched them drift.   640

"I am satisfied," she thought, "I am satisfied.
I can wait my time in spite of Mom being sad
And Pop looking fierce and sad when he sees me walk
So heavy and knows I'll have to walk heavier still
Before my time comes. I'm sorry to make them sad,   645
I'm sorry I did a bad thing if it was a bad thing;
But I'm satisfied.
                  We cut the heart on the tree.
I've got my half of the dime° and he's got his,

636 *I am the seed and the husk*: Compare Book III, lines 1042–1049.   648 *my half of the dime*: See Book III, line 1147.

He'll come back when Winter's over or else I'll find him,
When you can push up the windows, when the new colts
Come out in the Spring, when the snake sheds his winter coat,
When the old, shed coat of Winter lies on the ground
Grey as wasp-paper under the green, slow rain,
When the big barn door rolls open.

I was worried to death at first and I couldn't tell.
But as soon as I knew what it was—it was different then—
It made things all right.
                              I can't tell why it did that."

She awkwardly stooped and put her hand on the ground,
Under the brittle leaves the soil was alive,
Torn with its harvest, turned on its side toward sleep,
But stripped for battle, too, for the unending
Battle with Winters till the Spring is born
Like a tight green leaf uncurling, so slightly, so gently,
Out of the husk of ice and the blank, white snows.

The wind moved over it, blowing the leaves away,
Leaving the bare, indomitable breast.
She felt a wind move over her heavy body,
Stripping it clean for war.
                              She felt the blind-featured
Mystery move, the harmonics of the quick grain,
The battle and the awakening for battle,
And the salt taste of peace.

A flight of geese passed by in a narrow V,
Honking their cry.
                              That cry was stuck in her heart
Like a bright knife.
                              She could have laughed or wept
Because of that cry flung down from a moving wing,
But she stood silent.
                              She had touched the life in the ground.

———————

Love came by from the riversmoke,
    When the leaves were fresh on the tree,

But I cut my heart on the blackjack oak
    Before they fell on me.   680

The leaves are green in the early Spring,
    They are brown as linsey° now,
I did not ask for a wedding-ring
    From the wind in the bending bough.

Fall lightly, lightly, leaves of the wild,   685
    Fall lightly on my care,
I am not the first to go with child
    Because of the blowing air.

I am not the first nor yet the last
    To watch a goosefeather sky,   690
And wonder what will come of the blast
    And the name to call it by.

Snow down, snow down, you whitefeather bird,
    Snow down, you winter storm,
Where the good girls sleep with a gospel word   695
    To keep their honor warm.

The good girls sleep in their modesty,
    The bad girls sleep in their shame,
But I must sleep in the hollow tree
    Till my child can have a name.   700

I will not ask for the wheel and thread
    To spin the labor plain,
Or the scissors hidden under the bed
    To cut the bearing-pain.°

I will not ask for the prayer in church   705
    Or the preacher saying the prayer,
But I will ask the shivering birch
    To hold its arms in the air.

682 *linsey:* coarse homespun cloth.   701–704 *wheel and thread* . . . *scissors* . . . :
superstitions calculated to ease the pain of childbirth.

Cold and cold and cold again,
   Cold in the blackjack limb
The winds of the sky for his sponsor-men
   And a bird to christen him.

Now listen to me, you Tennessee corn,
   And listen to my word,
This is the first child ever born
   That was christened by a bird.

He's going to act like a hound let loose
   When he comes from the blackjack tree,
And he's going to walk in proud shoes
   All over Tennessee.

I'll feed him milk out of my own breast
   And call him Whistling Jack.
And his dad'll bring him a partridge nest,
   As soon as his dad comes back.

John Brown's raid has gone forward, the definite thing is done,
Not as we see it done when we read the books,
A clear light burning suddenly in the sky,
But dimly, obscurely, a flame half-strangled by smoke,
A thing come to pass from a victory not a victory,
A dubious doctrine dubiously received.
The papers praise, but the recruiting is slow,
The bonds sell badly, the grind of the war goes on—
There is no sudden casting off of a chain,
Only a slow thought working its way through the ground,
A slow root growing, touching a hundred soils,
A thousand minds—no blossom or flower yet.

It takes a long time to bring a thought into act
And when it blossoms at last, the gardeners wonder—
There have been so many to labor this patch of ground,
Garrison, Beecher, a dozen New England names,
Courageous, insulting Sumner,° narrow and strong,

740–741 *Garrison, Beecher . . . Sumner:* William Lloyd Garrison, editor of the
Liberator; Henry Ward Beecher, celebrated Congregationalist preacher; and Charles
Sumner, U.S. Senator from Massachusetts, all militant abolitionists.

With his tongue of silver and venom and his wrecked body,
Wendell Phillips, Antinous of Harvard°—
But now that the thought has arisen, they are not sure
It was their thought after all—it is good enough—   745
The best one could expect from a man like Lincoln,
But this and that are wrong, are unshrewdly planned,
We could have ordered it better, we knew the ground,
It should have been done before, in a different way,
And our praise is grudging.
                    Pity the gardeners,   750
Pity Boston, pity the pure in heart,
Pity the men whom Time goes past in the night,
Without their knowledge. They worked through the heat of the day.

Let us even pity
Wendell Phillips, Antinous of Harvard,   755
For he was a model man and such men deserve
A definite pity at times.
                  He too did his best.
Secure in his own impenetrable self-knowledge,
He seldom agreed with Lincoln or thought him wise;
He sometimes thought that a stunning defeat would give   760
A needed lesson to the soul of the nation,
And, before, would have broken the Union as blithely as Yancey°
For his own side of abolition, speaking about it
In many public meetings where he was heckled
But usually silenced the hecklers sooner or later   765
With his mellifluous, masculine, well-trained accents.
War could hardly come too soon for a man like that
And when it came, he was busy. He did his part,
Being strong and active, blessed with a ready mind,
And the cause being one to which he professed devotion,   770
He spoke. He spoke well, with conviction, and frequently.

So much for the banner-bearers of abolition,
The men who carried the lonely flag for years

---

743 *Wendell Phillips, Antinous of Harvard*: wealthy, handsome abolitionist, noted
orator (Harvard, 1831), here identified with Antinous, page to the Roman Emperor
Hadrian and a model of masculine beauty. See Book I, line 179. 762 *Yancey*:
William Lowndes Yancey, one of three Special Commissioners seeking recognition
in Europe for the Confederacy.

And could bear defeat with the strength of the pure in heart
But could not understand the face of success.

The other dissenters are simpler to understand.
They are ready to fight for the Union but not for niggers,
They don't give a damn for niggers and say so now
With a grievous cry.
       And yet the slow root-thought works
Gradually through men's minds.
         The Lancashire spinners,
Thrown out of work because no cotton can come
To feed their mills through the choking Union blockade,
Yet hold starvation meetings and praise the Union.°
The tide has begun to turn in some English minds,
The watchers overseas feel their hands grow numb,
Slidell and Mason and Huse° still burrow and argue,
But a cold breath blows through the rooms with the chandeliers.
A door is beginning to close.
        Few men perceive
The turn of the tide, the closing of the door.
Lincoln does not perceive it. He sees alone
The grind of the war, the lagging of the recruits,
Election after election going against him,°
And Lee back safe in Virginia after Antietam
While McClellan sticks for five weeks and will not move.
He loses patience at last and removes McClellan.°
Burnside succeeds him—
       and the grimly bewildered
Army of the Potomac has a new rider,
Affable, portly, whiskered and self-distrusting,°

780–783 *The Lancashire spinners . . . praise the Union:* Workers in the mills in the English Midlands petitioned "the House to address Her Majesty not to recognize the American insurgents 'who keep three million human persons in the condition of cattle,'" Edward Channing, *A History of the United States,** VI, 361.   786 *Slidell and Mason and Huse:* Confederate emissaries seeking European support for the South. Caleb Huse was an arms buyer. For the Union capture and release of Slidell and Mason, see note, Book III, line 212.   792 *Election after election . . . :* A majority of the congressional elections of 1862 went to Lincoln's opponents, suggesting a general repudiation of his policies.   795 *removes McClellan:* November 5, 1862; see Book III, lines 130–135.   796–798 *Burnside . . . self-distrusting:* Major General Ambrose E. Burnside, who had twice refused the offer of command of the Army of the Potomac. "[He] was utterly unfit, knew he was unfit and did not wish it. . . . He was ordered to assume it and reluctantly did so [November 7, 1862]," McMaster, p. 264.

Who did not wish the command and tried to decline it,
Took it at last and almost wept when he did.   800
A worried man who passes like a sad ghost
Across November, looking for confidence,
And beats his army at last against stone walls
At Fredericksburg in the expected defeat
With frightful slaughter.°
                  The news of the thing comes back.   805
There are tears in his eyes. He never wanted command.
"Those men over there," he groans, "Those men over there"
—They are piled like cordwood in front of the stone wall—

He wants to lead a last desperate charge himself,
But he is restrained.°
                  The sullen army draws back,   810
Licking its wounds. The night falls. The newspapers rave.
There are sixty-three hundred dead in that doomed attack
That never should have been made.
                  His shoulders are bowed.
He tries a vain march in the mud and resigns at last
The weapon he could not wield.
                  Joe Hooker succeeds him.°   815
The winter clamps down, cold winter of doubt and grief.

The sun shines, the wind goes by,
The prisoners and captives lie
In a cell without an eye.

Winter will not touch them more   820
Than the cold upon a sore
That was frozen long before.

Summer will not make them sweet
Nor the rainy Springs refresh

---

805 *frightful slaughter*: "The total loss, killed, wounded and missing [December 13, 1862], on the Union side was 12,653; on the Confederate, 5,309," McMaster, p. 266. 807–810 *"Those men over there,"* . . . *He wants to lead a last desperate charge* . . . : " 'Oh, those men, those men over there. I am thinking of them all the time.' He thought seriously of leading in person still another attack [but] his officers finally dissuaded him," McMaster, p. 266.   815 *Joe Hooker succeeds him*: President Lincoln relieved Burnside on January 25, 1863, and replaced him with Major General "Fighting Joe" Hooker.

That extremity of heat
In the self-corrupting flesh.

The band blares, the bugles snort,
They lose the fort or take the fort,
Someone writes a wise report.

Someone's name is Victory.
The prisoners and captives lie
Too long dead before they die.

For all prisoners and captives now,
For the dark legion,
The Andersonvillers, the Castle Thunder men,°
The men who froze at Camp Morton° and came from the dungeons
With blood burst out on their faces.
The men who died at Salisbury and Belle Isle,
Elmira, St. Louis, Camp Douglas°—the Libby tunnellers°—
The men in the fetid air.

There are charges back and forth upon either side,
Some true, some false.
                    You can read the official reports,
The dozen thick black-bound volumes of oaths and statements,
A desert of type, a dozen black mummy-cases
Embalming the long-forgotten, building again
The cumbrous machine of guards and reports and orders,
"Respectfully submitted" . . . "I beg to state" . . .
"State of kitchen good." . . . "Food, quality of—quite good." . . .
"Police of hospital—good except Ward 7" . . .
"Remarks—we have ninety-five cases of smallpox now." . . .
"Remarks—as to general health of prisoners, fair." . . .
"Remarks" . . . "Remarks" . . . "Respectfully submitted" . . .
Under this type are men who used to have hands
But the creaking wheels have respectfully submitted them

835 *Andersonvillers, the Castle Thunder men*: prisoners held at the Andersonville (Georgia) camp and at the Richmond penitentiary. 836 *Camp Morton*: at Indianapolis. 838–839 *Salisbury and Belle Isle,/Elmira, St. Louis, Camp Douglas*: Salisbury (North Carolina) and Belle Isle (Virginia) were Confederate prisons; Elmira (New York) and St. Louis were sites of Union prison camps, as was Chicago (Camp Douglas). 839 *the Libby tunnellers*: 109 Union prisoners escaped (February 9, 1864) via a tunnel from Libby prison in Richmond.

Into a void, embalmed them in mummy-cases,   855
With their chills and fever, their looks and plans of escape.
They called one "Shorty," they called another "The Judge,"
One man wore the Virgin's medal around his neck,
One had a broken nose and one was a liar,
"Respectively submitted—"
                      But, now and then,   860
A man or a scene escapes from the mummy-cases,
Like smoke escaping, blue smoke coiling into pictures,
Stare at those coils—
             and see in the hardened smoke,
The triple stockade of Andersonville the damned,
Where men corrupted like flies in their own dung   865
And the gangrened sick were black with smoke and their filth.
There were thirty thousand Federal soldiers there
Before the end of the war.
              A man called Wirtz,°
A Swiss, half brute, half fool, and wholly a clod,
Commanded that camp of spectres.
                   One reads what he did   870
And longs to hang him higher than Haman° hung,
And then one reads what he said when he was tried
After the war—and sees the long, heavy face,
The dull fly buzzing stupidly in the trap,
The ignorant lead of the voice, saying and saying,   875
"Why, I did what I could, I was ordered to keep the jail.
Yes, I set up deadlines, sometimes chased men with dogs,
Put men in torturing stocks, killed this one and that,
Let the camp corrupt till it tainted the very guards
Who came there with mortal sickness.   880
But they were prisoners, they were dangerous men,
If a hundred died a day—how was it my fault?
I did my duty. I always reported the deaths.
I don't see what I did different from other people.
I fought well at Seven Pines and was badly wounded.   885
I have witnesses here to tell you I'm a good man
And that I was really kind. I don't understand.
I'm old. I'm sick. You're going to hang me. Why?" °

868 *Wirtz* [*sic*]: Captain Henry Wirz.   871 *Haman:* See note, Book IV, line 25.
876–888 *"Why, . . . You're going to hang me. Why?":* Wirz was convicted by
court-martial and hanged November 10, 1865. Benét's version of his plea is taken
from official records. See *Official Records*, Series II, Vol. VIII, 538–539, 775–791.

Crush out the fly with your thumb and wipe your hand,
You cannot crush the leaden, creaking machine,
The first endorsement, the paper on the desk
Referred by Adjutant Feeble to Captain Dull
For further information and his report.

Some men wish evil and accomplish it
But most men, when they work in that machine,
Just let it happen somewhere in the wheels.
The fault is no decisive, villainous knife
But the dull saw that is the routine mind.

Why, if a man lay dying on their desk
They'd do their best to help him, friend or foe,
But this is merely a respectfully
Submitted paper, properly endorsed
To be sent on and on, and gather blood.

Stare at the smoke again for a moment's space
And see another live man in another prison.

A colored trooper named Woodson° was on guard
In the prison at Newport News, one night around nine.
There was a gallery there, where the privy was,
But prisoners weren't allowed in it after dark.

The colored soldier talked with the prisoners
At first, in a casual, more or less friendly way;
They tried to sell him breastpins and rings they had
And bothered him by wanting to go to the privy.

At last, he fired on a man
Who went in the gallery, but happened to miss him.
A lieutenant came down to ask the cause of the shot.
Woodson told him.
                    A second prisoner went
On the same errand, a shadow slipping through shadows.

906 *Woodson:* Private Harrison Woodson, Company G, 122d U.S. Colored Troops.
Benét's account of the incident that follows is very nearly a verbatim transcription
of Woodson's testimony before a board of inquiry.

Woodson halted him twice but he kept on moving.
"There's a man in the gallery now," said the young lieutenant.   920
"Well, I reckon it's one of the men makin' water again,"
Said Woodson, uneasily. The lieutenant stiffened.
He was officer of the guard and orders were orders.
"Why don't you use the bayonet on him?" he said.
Woodson jumped forward. The bayonet hunched and struck.   925
The man ran into the privy and fell like a log. . . .
A prisoner said "You've killed him dead," in a voice.
"Yes, by God!" said Woodson, cleaning his bayonet,
"They buried us alive at Fort Pillow." °

                                       The court
Found the sentry a trifle hasty,° but on the whole   930
Within his instructions, the officer's orders lawful;
One cannot dispute the court.
                            And yet the man
Who went to the privy is inconveniently dead.
It seems an excessive judgment for going there.

The little pictures wreathe into smoke again.   935
The mummy-cases close upon the dark legion.
The papers are filed away.
                        If they once were sent
To another court for some last word of review,
They are back again. It seems strange that such tidy files
Of correspondence respectfully submitted   940
Should be returned from God with no final endorsement.

The slow carts hitched along toward the place of exchange
Through a bleak wind.°
                    It was not a long wagon train,
Wagons and horses were too important to waste

929 *buried us alive at Fort Pillow:* Losses among the Union Negro troops were extremely heavy during the Confederate assault and capture of Fort Pillow, Tennessee, April 12, 1864. It was variously reported and denied that Confederate burial parties buried the wounded with the dead.   929–930 *The court/Found the sentry a trifle hasty:* "The Board were of the opinion that although the sentinel acted hastily, yet he was justifiable," *Official Records*, Series II, Vol. VIII, 693.   942–943 *the place of exchange/Through a bleak wind:* probably Aiken's Landing, Virginia, on the James River. City Point, the second exchange point in the East, was closed during the summer of 1862 after being open less than one month.

On prisoners for exchange, if the men could march.
Many did march and some few died on the way
But more died up in the wagons, which was not odd.
If a man was too sick to walk, he was pretty sick.

They had been two days on the road.
                              Jack Ellyat lay
Between a perishing giant from Illinois
Who raved that he was bailing a leaky boat
Out on the Lakes, and a slight, tubercular Jew
Who muttered like a sick duck when the wagon jounced.
Bailey marched. He still was able to march
But his skin hung on him. He hummed to the Weaver's tune.

They got to the river at last.
                              Jack Ellyat saw
A yellow stream and slow boats crossing the stream.
Bailey had helped him out. He was walking now
With his arm around Bailey's neck. Their course was a crab's.
The Jew was up and staring with shoe-button eyes
While his cough took him. The giant lay on a plank,
Some men were trying to lift him.
                              The wind blew
Over a knife of frost and shook their rags.
The air was a thawing ice of most pure, clear gold.
They stared across the river and saw the flag
And the tall, blue soldiers walking in thick, warm coats
Like strong, big men who fed well. And then they cheered,
A dry thin cheer, pumped up from exhausted lungs
And yet with a metal vibrance.
                              The bright flag flapped.
"I can smell 'em frying meat," said the coughing Jew.
He sniffed, "Oh God, I hope it ain't ham," he said
With his mouth puckered. A number of scarecrows laughed.
And then they heard the echo of their own cheer
Flung back at them, it seemed, in a high, shrill wail
With that tongue of metal pulsing its feebleness.
But it did not end like an echo, it gathered and rose,
It was the Confederate sick on the other side,
Cheering their own.
                    The two weak crowd-voices met

In one piping, gull-like cry.
                    Then the boats began
To take the weak men on board.
                              Jack Ellyat walked   980
To his boat on stuffless legs. "Keep quiet," he thought,
"You're not through yet—you won't be through till you land.
They can jerk you back, even now, if you look too pleased.
Look like a soldier, damn you, and show them how."
The thought was childish but it stiffened his back   985
And got him into the boat.
                    In the midst of the stream
They passed a boat with Confederate prisoners
So near they could yell at each other.
                              "Hello there, Yank."
"Hello Reb" . . . "You look pretty sick—don't we feed you good?" . . .
"You don't look so damn pretty, yourself" . . . "My, ain't that a
     shame!" . . .   990
"You'll look a lot sicker when Hooker gets after you" . . .
"Hell, old Jack'll take Hooker apart like a coffee-pot" . . .
"Well, good-by, Yank" . . . "Good-by, Reb" . . . "Get fat if you kin."

So might meet and pass, perhaps, on a weedier stream
Other boats, no more heavily charged, to a wet, black oar.   995
Bailey watched the boat move away with its sick grey men
Still yelling stingless insults through tired lips.
He cupped his hands to his mouth. "Oh——" he roared,
Then he sank back, coughing.
                    "They look pretty bad," he said,
"They look glad to get back. They ain't such bad Rebs at that."   1000

The boat's nose touched the wharf. It swung and was held.
They got out. They didn't move toward the camp at first.
They looked back at the river first and the other side,
Without saying words. They stood there thus for a space
Like a row of tattered cranes at the edge of a stream,   1005
Blinking at something.

"All right, you men," said an officer. "Come along."
Jack Ellyat's heart made a sudden lump in his chest.
It was a blue officer. They were back in their lines,
Back out of prison.
               Bailey whirled out his arm   1010

In a great wheel gesture. "Hell," he said in a low,
Moved voice, thumbed his nose across at the Stars and Bars
And burst into horrible tears. Jack Ellyat held him.
"Captain, when do we eat?" said the Jew in a wail.

❧ BOOK SIX ❧

Cudjo breathed on the silver urn
And rubbed till his hand began to burn,
With his hoarded scrap of chamois-skin.
The metal glittered like bright new tin
And yet, as he labored, his mouth was sad—   5
"Times is gettin' almighty bad.
Christmas a-comin', sure and swif',
But no use hollerin' 'Christmas Gif!' °
No use keepin' the silver fittin',
No use doin' nothin' but sittin'.   10
Old Marse Billy stayin' away,
Yankees shootin' at Young Marse Clay,
Grey hairs in Miss Mary's brush,
And a-whooin' wind in de berry-bush,
Dat young red setter done eat her pups,   15
We was washin' de tea set an' bust two cups,
Just come apart in Liza's han'—
Christmas, where has you gwine to, man?
Won't you never come back again?
I feels like a cat in de outdoors rain."   20
Christmas used to come without fail,
A big old man with a raccoon tail,°
So fine and bushy it brushed the ground
And made folks sneeze when he waltzed around.
He was rolling river and lucky sun   25
And a laugh like a double-barrelled gun,
And the chip-straw° hat on his round, bald head
Was full of money and gingerbread.
"Come in, Christmas, and have a cheer!
But, if he's comin', he won't stop here,   30
He likes folks cheerful and dinners smokin'
And famblies shootin' off caps and jokin',
But he won't find nothin' on dis plantation,
But a lot of grievin' conversation.

8 'Christmas Gif!': traditional southern greeting on Christmas Day. 22 A *big old man* . . . : in the English tradition of the Lord of Misrule, who led the revels of the Christmas season. 27 *chip-straw*: made from thin strips of palm leaf or the like.

Dey's tooken de carpets and window-weights 3⁵
To go and shoot at de Yankee States,
Dey's tooken Nelly, de cross-eye mule,
And whoever took her was one big fool;
Dey's tooken dis an' dey's tooken dat,
Till I kain't make out what dey's drivin' at. 4●
But if Ole Marse Billy could see dis place
He'd cuss all Georgia blue in de face.
To see me wuhkin with dis ole shammy
Like a field-hand-nigger fum Alabammy,
And Ole Miss wearin' a corn-husk hat, 4⁴
Dippin' ole close in de dyein' vat,
Scrapin' her petticoats up for lint
An' bilin' her tea out of julep-mint.

Young Marse Clay he'd feel mighty sad
If he'd seed de weddin' his sisters had. 5
De grooms was tall and de brides was fine,
But dey drunk de health in blackberry wine,
And supper was thu at half-past-nine.

Weddin's ust to last for a week,
But now we's rowin' up Hard Times Creek. 5
Somethin's conjured dis white-folks' South.
Somethin' big with a hongry mouth,
Eatin' an' eatin'—I done my bes',
Scattered de fedders and burnt de nes',
Filled de bottle an' made de hand 6
An' buried de trick in Baptis' land,
An' dat trick's so strong, I was skeered all night,
But, somehow or udder, it don' wuhk right.
Ef I got me a piece of squinch-owl's tail
An' some dead-folks' yearth fum de county jail,° 6
It mout wuhk better—but I ain't sho',
And de wind keeps scrabblin' under de do',
Scratchin' and scratchin' his buzzard-claws,
Won't nuthin' feed you, hongry jaws?

59–65 *Scattered de fedders . . . An' buried de trick in Baptis' land . . .* : Negro superstition in the South often fused voodoo (Haitian) and Protestant elements.

Field hands keeps on hoein' de corn,   70
Stupidest niggers ever born,
All dey's good for is gravy-lickin',
Ram-buttin' ° and cotton-pickin';
Dey don't hear de wind in de slew,°
But dat wind's blowin' over 'em too,   75
An' dat wind's res'less an' dat wind's wile,
An' dat wind aches like a motherless chile,
Won't nuthin' feed you, achin' wind?"

The hand stopped rubbing. The spoons were shined.
He put them back in the flannel bag   80
And stared at his scrap of chamois-rag.
War was a throat that swallowed things
And you couldn't cure it with conjurings.

———————

Sally Dupré watched over her dyeing-pots,
Evening was setting in with a light slow rain   85
That marched like a fairy army—there being nothing
From the white fog on the hill to the soaked door-stone
But a moving grey and silver hurry of lances,
Distinct yet crowded, thin as the edge of the moon,
Carried in no fleshed hand.
                      She thought to herself,   90
"I have stained my arms with new colors, doing this work,
The red is pokeberry-juice, the grey is green myrtle,
The deep black is queen's delight.°
                          If he saw me now
With my hands so parti-colored he would not know them.
He likes girls' hands that nothing has stained but lotions,   95
This is too fast a dye.
                    I will dye my heart
In a pot of queen's delight, in the pokeberry sap,
I will dye it red and black in the fool's old colors°
And send it to him, wrapped in a calico rag,
To keep him warm through the rain.

73 *Ram-buttin'*: head-butting contests.   74 *de slew*: slough, swampland.   92–93
pokeberry-juice . . . queen's delight: native herb dyes.   98 *the fool's old colors*:
Pantalone, the classical clown of Italian *commedia dell'arte*, was traditionally dressed
in red and black; costuming of French and English fools varied.

                             It will keep him warm 10
And women in love do better without a heart.
What fools we are to wait the wheel of the year,
The year will not help our trouble.
                        What fools we are
To give our parti-colored hearts to the rain.

I am tired of the slogans now and tired of the saving, 10
I want to dance all night in a brand-new dress
And forget about wars and love and the South and courage.

The South is an old high house full of charming ladies,
The war is a righteous war full of gallant actions,
And love is a white camellia worn in the hair. 1

But I am tired of talking to charming ladies
And the smell of the white camellia, I will dye
My hands twice as black as ink in the working waters
And wait like a fool for bitter love to come home.

He was wounded this year. They hurt him. They hurt you, darling. 1
I have no doubt she came with a bunch of flowers
And talked to your wound and you like a charming lady.
I have no doubt that she came.

Her heart is not parti-colored. She'll not go steeping
Her gentle hands in the pulp and the dead black waters 1
Till the crooked blot lies there like a devil's shadow,
And the heart is stained with the stain.

If I came to the bed where you lay sick and in fever,
I would not come with little tight-fisted flowers
But with the white heron's plume° that lay in the forest 1
Till it was cooler than sleep.

The living balm would touch on your wound less gently,
The Georgia sun less fierce than my arms to hold you,
The steel bow less stubborn than my curved body
Strung against august death.

125 *white heron's plume:* The heron plume is a symbol of silence; herons, a symbol of fertility and regeneration.

They hurt you, darling, they hurt you and I not with you,
I nowhere there to slit the cloth from your burning,
To find the head of the man who fired the bullet
And give his eyes to the crows.

House, house, house, it is not that my friend was wounded,   135
But that you kept him from me while he had freedom,
You and the girl whose heart is a snuffed white candle—
Now I will curse you both.

Comely house, high-courteous house of the gentle,
You must win your war for my friend is mixed in your quarrel,   140
But then you must fall, you must fall, for your walls divide us,
Your worn stones keep us apart.

I am sick of the bland camellias in your old gardens,
Your pride and passion are not my pride and my passion,
I am strangling to death in your cables of honeysuckle,   145
Your delicate lady-words.

I would rather dig in the earth than learn your patience,
I have need of a sky that never was cut for dresses
And a rough ground to tear my hands on like lion's clothing,
And a hard wheel to move.   150

The low roof by the marches of rainy weather,
The sharp love that carries the fool's old colors,
The bare bed that is not a saint's or a lady's,
The strong death at the end.

They hurt you, darling, they hurt you, and I not with you,   155
I nowhere by to see you, to touch my darling,
To take your fever upon me if I could take it
And burn my hands at your wound.

If I had been there—oh, how surely I would have found you,
How surely killed your foe—and sat by your bedside   160
All night long, like a mouse, like a stone unstirring,
Only to hear your slow breath moving the darkness,
Only to hear, more precious than childish beauty,
The slow tired beat of your heart."

Wingate sat by a smoky fire
Mending a stirrup with rusty wire.
His brows were clenched in the workman's frown,
In a day or a week they'd be back in town,
He thought of it with a brittle smile
That mocked at guile for its lack of guile
And mocked at ease for its lack of ease.
It was better riding through rainy trees
And playing tag with the Union spies
Than telling ladies the pleasant lies,
And yet, what else could you do, on leave?

He touched a rent in his dirty sleeve,
That was the place that the bullet tore
From the blue-chinned picket whose belt he wore,
The man who hadn't been quick enough,
And the powder-burn on the other cuff
Belonged to the fight with the Yankee scout
Who died in Irish when he went out.
He thought of these things as a man might think
Of certain trees by a river-brink,
Seen in a flash from a passing train,
And, before you could look at them, gone again.
It was more important to eat and drink
Than give the pain or suffer the pain
And life was too rapid for memory.

"There are certain things that will cling to me,
But not the things that I thought would cling,
And the wound in my body cannot sting
Like the tame black crow with the bandaged wing,
The nervous eye and the hungry craw
That picked at the dressing-station straw
Till I was afraid it would pick my eyes
And couldn't lift hand to beat it off.
I can tell the ladies the usual lies
Of the wild night-duels when two scouts clash
And your only light is his pistol-flash;
But I remember a watering-trough
Lost in a little brushwood town
And the feel of Black Whistle slumping down

Under my knees in the yellow air,
Hit by a bullet from God knows where . . .   205
Not the long, mad ride round the Union lines°
But the smell of the swamp at Seven Pines,
The smell of the swamp by Gaines's Mill,
And Lee in the dusk before Malvern Hill,°
Riding along with his shoulders straight   210
Like a sending out of the Scæan Gate,°
The cold intaglio° of war.
'This is Virginia's *Iliad*,'
But Troy was taken° nevertheless—
I remember the eyes my father had   215
When we saw our dead in the Wilderness—°
I cannot remember any more—

Lucy will wear her English gown
When the Black Horse Troop comes back to town,
Pin her dress with a silver star   220
And tell our shadows how brave we are.
Lucy I like your white-and-gold—"

He blew on his hands for the day was cold,
And the damp, green wood gave little heat:
There was something in him that matched the sleet   225
And washed its hands in a rainy dream,
Till the stirrup-strap and the horses' steam
And Shepley and Bristol behind his back,
Playing piquet° with a dog-eared pack
And the hiss of the sap in the smoky wood   230

---

206 *the long, mad ride round the Union lines*: On June 12, 1862, Lee dispatched Stuart's cavalry to gain information about the Union forces threatening Richmond. Stuart converted this into a four-day foray encircling the entire Army of the Potomac. 207–209 *Seven Pines . . . Gaines's Mill . . . Malvern Hill*: battles around Richmond (May 31, June 28, July 1, 1862) which were characterized by heavy close fighting, not spectacular cavalry sweeps.   211 *the Scæan Gate*: western gate of Troy, through which the warriors passed to fight the Greeks.   212 *intaglio*: scenes or figures incised in stone or metal.   213–214 *'This is Virginia's Iliad,'/But Troy was taken*: Like the Greek invaders, the Army of the Potomac was driven back to its ships, but eventually conquered the city.   216 *our dead in the Wilderness*: a reference to the "Wilderness" section of Virginia; however, operations known as the Wilderness Campaign did not take place there until more than one year later (May 1864).   229 *piquet*: a card game.

Mixed for a moment in something good,
Something outside of peace or war
Or a fair girl wearing a silver star,
Something hardly as vain as pride
And gaunt as the men he rode beside.
It made no comments but it was there,
Real as the color of Lucy's hair
Or the taste of Henry Weatherby's wine.
He thought "These people are friends of mine.
And we certainly fooled the Yanks last week,
When we caught those wagons at Boiling Creek,
I guess we're not such a bad patrol
If we never get straight with the muster-roll,
I guess, next Spring, we can do it again—"

Bristol threw down a flyspecked ten,
"Theah," he said, in the soft, sweet drawl
That could turn as hard as a Minie-ball,°
"This heah day is my lucky day,
And Shepley nevah could play piquet."
He stretched his arms in a giant yawn,
"Gentlemen, when are we movin' on?
I have no desire for a soldier's end,
While I still have winnin's that I can spend
And they's certain appointments with certain ladies
Which I'd miss right smart if I went to Hades,
Especially one little black-eyed charmer
Whose virtue, one hopes, is her only armor,
So if Sergeant Wingate's mended his saddle
I suggest that we all of us now skedaddle,
To employ a term that the Yankees favor—"
He tasted his words, for he liked the flavor.
"And yet, one dreads to be back," said he,
"One knows how tippled° one well may be
If one meets with the oppor-tun-ity.
And even the charmers can likewise raise
Unpleasant doubts that may last for days—
And as one," he sighed, "of our martial lads,
I'd rather be chargin' Columbiads,°

247 *Minie-ball*: a conical rifle bullet. 263 *tippled*: drunk. 268 *Columbiads*: long-chambered guns designed to fire shells at high angles.

Than actin' sweet to some old smooth-bore°
When he tells me how he could win the War   270
By burnin' the next Yank crossroads-store.
The Yanks aren't always too blame polite,
But they fight like sin when they've got to fight,
And after they've almost nailed your hide
To your stinkin' saddle in some ole ride,   275
It makes you mad when some nice home-guard
Tells you they nevah could combat hard.
I have no desire to complain or trouble
But I'd find this conflict as comfortable
As a big green pond for a duck to swim in,   280
If it wasn't for leave, and the lovin' women."

The snow lay hard on the hills. You could burn your eyes
By too-long-looking into the cold ice-lens
Of infinite, pure, glittering, winter air.
It was as cold as that, as sparkling as that,   285
Where the crystal trees stood up like strange, brittle toys
After the sleet storm passed, till the setting sun
Hung the glass boughs with rainbows frozen to gems
And the long blue shadows pooled in the still hill-hollows.

The white and the purple lilacs of New England   290
Are frozen long, they will not bloom till the rains,
But when you look from the window, you see them there,
A great field of white lilacs.
                          A gathered sheaf
Of palest blossoms of lilac, stained with the purple evening.

Jack Ellyat turned away from the window now,   295
The frosty sleighbell of winter was in his ears,
He saw the new year, a child in a buffalo-robe,
Dragged in a sleigh whose runners were polished steel
Up the long hill of February, into chill light.
The child slept in the robe like a reindeer-colt,   300
Nuzzled under the winter. The bright bells rang.

269 *smooth-bore:* here, a veteran of the days of unrifled weapons.

He warmed his hands at the stove and shivered a little
Hearing that ice-sweet chime.
                              He was better now,
But his blood felt thin when he thought of skating along
Over black agate floors in the bonfire light
Or beating a girl's red mittens free of the snow,
And he slept badly at times, when his flesh recalled
Certain smells and sights that were prison.

He stared at the clock where Phaëton's horses lunged
With a queer nod of recognition. The rest had altered,
People and winter and nightmares and Ellen Baker,
Or stayed in a good dimension that he had lost,
But Phaëton was the same. He said to himself,
"I have met you twice, old, drunken charioteer,
Once in the woods, and once in a dirty shack
Where Death was a coin of spittle left on the floor.°
I suppose we will meet again before there's an end,
Well, let it happen.
                     It must have been cold last year
At Fredericksburg. I'm glad I wasn't in that.
Melora, what's happened to you?"
                                  He saw Melora
Walking down from the woods in the low spring light.
His body hurt for a minute, but then it stopped.
He was getting well. He'd have to go back pretty soon.
He grinned, a little dryly, thinking of chance,
Father had seen the congressman after all,
Just before Shiloh. So now, nearly ten months later,
The curious wheels that are moved by such congressmen
Were sending him back to the Army of the Potomac,
Back with the old company, back with the Eastern voices,
Henry Fairfield limping along with his sticks,
Shot through both hips at Antietam.
                                    He didn't care,
Except for losing Bailey, which made it tough.
He tried to puzzle out the change in his world
But gave it up. Things and people looked just the same,
You could love or like or detest them just the same way,

But whenever you tried to talk of your new dimension
It didn't sound right, except to creatures like Bailey.
"I have met you twice, old, drunken charioteer,
The third time you may teach me how to be cool."

Ned, asleep by the stove, woke up and yawned,   340
"Hello Ned," said his master, with a half-smile,
"I told a girl about you, back in a wood,
You'd like that girl. She'd rub the back of your ears.
And Bailey'd like you too. I wish Bailey was here.
Want to go to war, Ned?" Ned yawned largely again.   345
Ellyat laughed. "You're right, old fella," he said,
"You get too mixed up in a war. You better stay here.
God, I'd like to sleep by a stove for a million years,
Turn into a dog and remember how to stand cold."
The clock struck five. Jack Ellyat jumped at the sound   350
Then he sank back. "No, fooled you that time," he said,
As if the strokes had been bullets.
                                    Then he turned
To see his mother, coming in with a lamp,
And taste the strange tastes of supper and quietness.

John Vilas heard the beating of another   355
Sleet at another and a rougher wall
While his hands knotted together and then unknotted.
Each time she had to moan, his hands shut down,
And now the moans were coming close together,
Close as bright streaks of hail.
                                  The younger children   360
Slept the uneasy sleep of innocent dogs
Who know there's something strange about the house,
Stranger than storms, and yet they have to sleep,
And someone has to watch them sleeping now.

"Harriet's right and Harriet's upstairs,   365
And Harriet cried like this when she gave birth,
Eighteen years back, in that chintz-curtained room,
And her long cry ran like an icicle
Into my veins. I can remember yet
The terrible old woman with the shawl   370
Who sat beside me, like deserted Fate,

Cursing me with those eyes each time she cried,
Although she must, one time, have cried like that
And been the object of as wild a cry,
And so far back,—and on—and always that,   37
The linked, the agonizing chain of cries
Brighter than steel, because earth will be earth
And the sun strike it, and the seed have force.
And yet no cry has touched me like this cry.

Harriet's right and Harriet's upstairs   38
And Harriet would have kept her from today,
And now today has come, I look at it,
Under the icicle, and wish it gone,
Because it hurts me to be sitting here,
Biting my fingers at my daughter's cry   38
And knowing Harriet has the harder task
As she has had for nearly twenty years.
And yet, what I have sought that I have sought
And cannot disavouch for my own pang,
Or be another father to the girl   3
Than he who let her run the woods alone
Looking for stones that have no business there.
For Harriet sees a dozen kinds of pain.
And some are blessed, being legitimate,
And some are cursed, being outside a law: 3
But she and I see only pain itself
And are hard-hearted with our epitaphs,
And yet I wish I could not hear that cry.
I know that it will pass because all things
Pass but the search that only ends with breath,   4
And, even after that, my daughter and I
May still get up from bondage, being such
Smoke as no chain of steel-bright cries can chain
To walk like Indian Summer through the woods
And be the solitaries of the wind   4
Till we are sleepy as old clouds at last.

She has a lover and will have a child
And I'm alone. I had forgotten that,
Though you'd not think it easy to forget.
No, we'll not go together.

                    The cries beat   410
Like hail upon the cold panes of my heart
Faster and faster, till they crack the glass
And I can know at last how old I am.

That is my punishment and my defence,
My ecstasy and my deep-seated bane.   415
I prayed to life for life once, in my youth,
Between the rain and a long stroke of cloud
Till my soaked limbs felt common with the sky
And the black stone of heaven swung aside,
With a last clap of water, to reveal   420
Lonely and timid, after all that wrath,
The small, cold, perfect flower of the new moon
And now, perhaps, I'll pray again tonight,
Still to the life that used me as a man
Uses and wears a strong and riotous horse,   425
Still to the vagrants of no fortunate word.

Men who go looking for the wilderness-stone,
Eaters of life who run away from bread
And are not satisfied with lucky days!
Robbers of airy gold, skin-changing men   430
Who find odd brothers when the moon is full,
Stray alchemics who entertain an imp
And feed it plums within a hollow tree
Until its little belly is sufficed,
Men who have seen the bronze male-partridge beat   435
His drum of feathers not ten feet away,
Men who have listened to wild geese at night
Until your hearts were hollowed with that sound,
Moth-light and owl-light and first-dayspring men,
Seekers and seldom-finders of the woods,   440
But always seekers till your eyes are shut;
I have an elder daughter that I love
And, having loved from childhood, would not tame
Because I once was tamed.
                    If you're my friends,
Then she's your friend.
                    I do not ask for her   445
Refusal or compunction or the safe

Road between little houses and old gates
Where Death lies sleepy as a dog in the sun
And the slow cows come home with evening bells
Into the tired peace that's good for pain.
Those who are never tired of eating life
Must immolate themselves against a star
Sooner or late, as she turns crucified
Now, on that flagellating wheel of light
Which will not miss one revolution's turn
For any anguish we can bring to it,
Because it is our master and our stone,
Body of pain, body of sharpened fire,
Body of quenchless life, itself, itself,
That safety cannot buy or peddlers sell
Or the rich cowards leave their silly sons.
But, oh,
She's tired out, she's broken, she's athirst.
Wrap her in twilights now, she is so torn,
And mask again the cold, sweat-runnelled mask
With the deep silence of a leafy wood
So cool and dim its birds are all asleep
And will not fret her. Wipe her straining hands
With the soft, gleaming cobwebs April spins
Out of bright silver tears and spider silk
Till they are finer than the handkerchiefs
Of a young, wild, spear-bearing fairy-queen.
Soothe her and comfort her and let her hear
No harshness but the mumbling peaceful sound
The fed bee grumbles to his honey-bags
In the red foxglove's throat.
                              Oh, if you are
Anything but lost shadows, go to her!"

Melora did not make such words for herself,
Being unable, and too much in pain.
If wood-things were beside her, she did not see them,
But only a lamp, and hands.
                              The pains came hard now,
A fist that hardly opened before it shut,
A red stair mounting into an ultimate
Flurry of misty conflict, when it seemed

As if she fought against the earth itself 485
For mere breath and something other than mere breath.
She heard the roar of the tunnel, drowned in earth.
Earth and its expulsive waters, tearing her, being born.
Then it was yellow silence and a weak crying.

After the child was washed, they showed her the child, 490
Breakable, crumpled, breathing, swathed and indignant,
With all its nails and hands that moved of themselves—
A queer thing to come out of that, but then it was there.
"Looks healthy enough," said her mother in a tired voice.
Melora stared. "He's got blue eyes," she said finally. 495
Her mother sniffed. "A lot of 'em start out blue."
She looked at the child as if she wanted to tell it,
"You aren't respectable. What are you doing here?"
But the child began wailing. She rocked it mechanically.
The rain kept on through the night but nobody listened. 500
The parents talked for a while, then they fell asleep.
Even the new child slept with its fists tight shut.
Melora heard the rain for a single moment
And then deep, beautiful nothing. "Over," she thought.
She slept, handfasted to the wilderness-stone. 505

Now the earth begins to roll its wheel toward the sun,
The deep mud-gullies are drying.
                         The sluggish armies
That have slept the bear months through in their winter camps,
Begin to stir and be restless.
                         They're tired enough
Of leaky huts and the rain and punishment-drill. 510
They haven't forgotten what it was like last time,
But next time we'll lick 'em, next time it won't be so bad,
Somehow we won't get killed, we won't march so hard.
"These huts looked pretty good when we first hit camp
But they look sort of lousy now—we might as well git— 515
Fight the Rebs—and the Yanks—and finish it up."
So they think in the bored, skin-itching months
While the roads are drying. "We're sick of this crummy place,
We might as well git, it doesn't much matter where."
But when they git, they are cross at leaving the huts, 520
"We fixed up ours first rate. We had regular lamps.

We knew the girls at the Depot. It wasn't so bad.
Why the hell do we have to git when we just got fixed?
Oh, well, we might as well travel." °
                              So they go on,
The huts drop behind, the dry road opens ahead. . . .

Fighting Joe Hooker° feels good when he looks at his men.
A blue-eyed, uncomplex man with a gift for phrase.
"The finest army on the planet," he says.
The phrase is to turn against him with other phrases°
When he is beaten—but now he is confident.
Tall, sandy, active, sentimental and tart,
His horseman's shoulder is not yet bowed by the weight
Of knowing the dice are his and the cast of them,
The weight of command, the weight of Lee's ghostly name.
He rides, preparing his fate.
                              In the other camps,
Lee writes letters, is glad to get buttermilk,
Wrings food and shoes and clothes from his commissariat,
Trusts in God and whets a knife on a stone.°
Jackson plays with his new-born daughter, waiting for Spring,
His rare laugh clangs as he talks to his wife and child.
He is looking well. War always agrees with him,
And this, perhaps, is the happiest time of his life.
He has three months of it left.°
                              By the swollen flood
Of the Mississippi, stumpy Grant is a mole

508–524 *winter-camps,/Begin to stir* . . . : Spring 1863. Compare descriptions of
Union forces breaking winter camps, *Four Brothers in Blue*, pp. 241 ff.   526 *Fighting Joe Hooker:* Hooker took command of the Army of the Potomac following Burnside's failure at Fredericksburg: See notes, Book II, line 927, and Book V, line 815.
529 *to turn against him with other phrases:* Compare, for example, Hooker's General Order 47 of April 30, 1863, "It is with heartfelt satisfaction the commanding
general announces to the army . . . that our enemy must either ingloriously fly or
come out from behind his defenses . . . where certain destruction awaits him,"
and Hooker's message to President Lincoln three days later, "We have had a desperate fight yesterday and today . . . which resulted in no success to us," *Official Records*, Series I, Vol. XXV, Part 1, 170–171.   536–538 *glad to get buttermilk* . . . :
Such details appear in Lee's personal correspondence. See, for example, *Recollections
and Letters of General Robert E. Lee* by his son Captain Robert E. Lee, *passim*.
543 *He has three months of it left:* Jackson saw the five-month-old Julia for the first
time on April 20, 1863. He died on May 10, three weeks, not three months, later.
See Mary Anna Jackson, *Memoirs of Stonewall Jackson*, pp. 408–411.

Gnawing at Vicksburg. He has been blocked four times   545
But he will carry that beaver-dam at last.
There is no brilliant lamp in that dogged mind
And no conceit of brilliance to shake the hand,
But hand and mind can use the tools that they get
This long way out of Galena.°
                    Sherman is there   550
And Sherman loves him and finds him hard to make out,
In Sherman's impatient fashion—the quick, sharp man
Seeing ten thousand things where the slow sees one
And yet with a sort of younger brother awe
At the infinite persistence of that slow will   555
—They make a good pair of hunting dogs, Grant and Sherman,
The nervous, explosive, passionate, slashing hound
And the quiet, equable, deadly holder-on,
Faded-brown as a cinnamon-bear in Spring—
See them like that, the brown dog and the white dog,   560
Calling them back and forth through the scrubby woods
After the little white scut° of Victory,
Or see them as elder brother and younger brother,
But remember this. In their time they were famous men
And yet they were not jealous,° one of the other.   565
When the gold has peeled from the man on the gilded horse,
Riding Fifth Avenue, and the palm girl's blind;°
When the big round tomb° gapes empty under the sky,
Vacant with summer air, when it's all forgotten,
When nobody reads the books, when the flags are moth dust,   570
Write up that. You won't have to write it so often.
It will do as well as the railway-station tombs.

So with the troops and the leaders of the bear armies,
The front-page-newspaper-things.
                      Tall Lincoln reviews
Endless columns crunching across new snow.   575

---

550 *Galena:* Grant's home. See note, Book III, line 151.   562 *scut:* rabbit's tail.
565 *they were not jealous:* "There never was and never can be raised a question of
rivalry or claim between us. . . . We were as brothers," Sherman in *Battles and
Leaders,* IV, 250.   566–567 *When the gold has peeled . . . and the palm-girl's
blind:* The gilded equestrian statue of Sherman at Fifth Avenue and 59th
Street in New York City is preceded by an allegorical female figure carrying palms.
568 *big round tomb:* Grant's Tomb. See note, Book II, line 989.

They pass uncheering at the marching-salute.
Lincoln sits on his horse with his farmer's seat,
Watching the eyes go by and the eyes come on.
The gaunt, long body is dressed in its Sunday black,
The gaunt face, strange as an omen, sad and foreboding.
The eyes look at him, he looks back at the eyes;
They pass and pass. They go back to their camps at last.
"So that was him," they say. "So that's the old man.
I'm glad we saw him. He isn't so much on looks
But he looks like people you know. He looks sad all right,
I never saw nobody look quite as sad as that
Without it made you feel foolish. He don't do that.
He makes you feel—I dunno—I'm glad we could see him.
He was glad to see us but you could tell all the same
This war's plumb killin' him. You can tell by his face.
I never saw such a look on any man's face.
I guess it's tough for him. Well, we saw him, for once." °

That day in Richmond, a mob of angry women
Swarm in the streets and riot for bread or peace.
They loot some shops, a few for the bread they need,
A few for thieving, most because they are moved
By discontent and hunger to do as the rest.
The troops are called out. The troops are about to fire,
But Davis gets on a wagon and calms the crowd
Before the tumbled bodies clutter the street.
He never did a better thing with his voice
And it should be told. Next day they riot again,
But this time the fire is weaker. They are dispersed,
A few arrested. Bread grows dearer than ever.
The housewives still go out with their market-baskets,
But coffee's four dollars a pound and tea eleven.°
They come back with a scraping of this and a scrap of that
And try to remember old lazy, lagnappe° days,

574–592 *Lincoln reviews/Endless columns . . . He looks sad . . . :* Compare separate observations in *Four Brothers in Blue*, pp. 235–237: "There is no end of reviews for him." "Abraham looks poorly . . . I could but pity." "That sad, anxious face, so full of melancholy foreboding." 593–606 *That day . . . a mob . . . :* April 3, 1863. Davis' actions are described by McMaster, pp. 333–334. For a description of the Richmond bread riots, see also Mrs. Roger A. Pryor, *Reminiscences of Peace and War*, p. 239. 608 *lagnappe days:* days of plenty, when merchants gave customers an extra something (lagnappe) with purchases.

The slew-foot negro chanting his devilled crabs
Along the street, and the market-women piling   610
The wicker baskets with everything good and fresh;
Topping it off with a great green fist of parsley
That you used to pretty the sides of the serving-dish
And never bothered to eat.
                    They improvise dishes,
"Blockade pudding" . . . "Confederate fricassee,"   615
Serve hominy grits on the Royal Derby china
And laugh or weep in their cups of willow-bark tea.

Davis goes back from the riot, his shoulders stooped,
The glow of speech has left him and he feels cold.
He eats a scant meal quickly and turns to the endless   620
Papers piled on his desk, the squabbles and plans.
A haggard dictator, fretting the men he rules
And being fretted by them.
                  He dreams, perhaps,
Of old days, riding wild horses beside his wife°
Back in his youth, on a Mississippi road.   625
That was a good time. It is past. He drowns in his papers.

The curtain is going up on that battlesmoked,
Crowded third act° which is to decide this war
And yet not end it for years.
                  Turn your eyes away
From these chiefs and captains, put them back in their books.   630
Let the armies sleep like bears in a hollow cave.
War is an iron screen in front of a time,
With pictures smoked upon it in red and black,
Some gallant enough, some deadly, but all intense.
We look at the pictures, thinking we know the time,   635
We only know the screen.
                  Look behind it now
At the great parti-colored quilt of these patchwork States.
This part and that is vexed by a battle-worm,

624 *old days, riding wild horses beside his wife:* In his youth Davis was a social
favorite especially known for daring horsemanship. He married (then Colonel)
Zachary Taylor's daughter in 1824 and settled in Mississippi; his bride died three
months later.   628 *Crowded third act:* 1863, which would see the high tide of
Confederate success at Chancellorsville recede with the Union victories at Vicksburg, Gettysburg, and Chattanooga.

But the ploughs go ahead, the factory chimneys smoke,
A new age curdles and boils in a hot steel caldron
And pours into rails and wheels and fingers of steel,
Steel is being born like a white-hot rose
In the dark smoke-cradle of Pittsburg—

        a man with a crude
Eye of metal and crystal looks at a smear
On a thin glass plate and wonders°—

        a shawled old woman
Sits on a curbstone calling the evening news.
War, to her, is a good day when papers sell
Or a bad day when papers don't. War is fat black type.
Anything's realer than war.

      By Omaha
The valleys and gorges are white with the covered wagons°
Moving out toward the West and the new, free land.
All through the war they go on.

        Five thousand teams
Pass Laramie in a month in the last war-year,
Draft-evaders, homesteaders, pioneers,
Old soldiers, Southern emigrants, sunburnt children. . . .
Men are founding colleges, finding gold,
Selling bad beef to the army and making fortunes,
Ploughing the stone-cropped field that their fathers ploughed.
(Anything's realer than war.)

       A moth of a woman,
Shut in a garden, lives on scraps of Eternity
With a dog, a procession of sunsets and certain poems
She scribbles on bits of paper. Such poems may be
Ice-crystals, rubies cracked with refracted light,
Or all vast death like a wide field in ten short lines.
She writes to the tough, swart-minded Higginson
Minding his negro troops in a lost bayou,
"War feels to me like an oblique place." °

643–645 *a man with a crude/Eye of metal and crystal* . . . : Consider here John
William Draper (1811–1882), pioneer in microscopy, medicine, and photography.
His *Human Physiology* (1856) contained the first photomicrography ever published;
his work in various fields carried well beyond the Civil War.   650 *white with the*
covered wagons: "We read of the wagons of the migrants whitening the plains,"
Channing, VI, 583.   659–667 A *moth of a woman* . . . "*War feels to me.* . . .":
Emily Dickinson. The quotation is from her letter (February 1863) to T. W. Higginson, then commanding a regiment of South Carolina volunteers, the first Negro
regiment in the United States Army. See note, Book I, line 189.

A man
Dreams of a sky machine° that will match the birds
And another, dusting the shelves of a country store,
Saves his pennies until they turn into dimes.°   670
(Anything's realer than war.)
A dozen men
Charter a railroad to go all across the Plains°
And link two seas with a whistling iron horse.
A whiskered doctor stubbornly tries to find
The causes of childbed-fever°—and, doing so,   675
Will save more lives than all these war-months have spent,
And never inhabit a railway-station tomb.

All this through the war, all this behind the flat screen. . . .

I heard the song of breath
Go up from city and country,   680
The even breath of the sleeper,
The tired breath of the sick,
The dry cough in the throat
Of the man with the death-sweat on him,
And the quiet monotone   685
We breathe but do not hear.

The harsh gasp of the runner,
The long sigh of power
Heaving the weight aloft,
The grey breath of the old.   690
Men at the end of strength
With their lungs turned lead and fire,

668 *Dreams of a sky machine:* probably Samuel Pierpont Langley (1834–1906),
who later constructed the first heavier-than-air machine capable of sustained flight.
669–670 *another, dusting the shelves . . . :* Consider here Aaron Montgomery
Ward (1843–1913), who at nineteen went to work in a St. Joseph, Michigan general store for five dollars a month and his board; at the end of three years, he was
managing the store at $100 a month. 672 *a railroad . . . across the Plains:* the
Union Pacific. 674–675 *A whiskered doctor stubbornly tries . . . :* Oliver Wendell Holmes had, since 1843, suggested that puerperal fever was transmitted in the
hospitals. In Vienna in 1846, I. P. Semmelweiss located the primary cause yet was
ignored; but in America, due largely to Holmes' influence, the disinfection of doctor's
and midwife's hands became common practice.

Panting like thirsty dogs;
A child's breath, blowing a flame.

The breath that is the voice,
The silver, the woodwinds speaking,
The dear voice of your lover,
The hard voice of your foe,
And the vast breath of wind,
Mysterious over mountains,
Caught in pines like a bird
Or filling all hammered heaven.

I heard the song of breath,
Like a great strand of music,
Blown between void and void,
Uncorporal as the light.
The breath of nations asleep,
And the piled hills they sleep in,
The word that never was flesh
And yet is nothing but life.

What are you, bodiless sibyl,°
Unseen except as the frost-cloud
Puffed from a silver mouth
When the hard winter's cold?
We cannot live without breath,
And yet we breathe without knowledge,
And the vast strand of sound
Goes on, eternally sighing,
Without dimension or space,
Without beginning or end.

I heard the song of breath
And lost it in all sharp voices,
Even my own voice lost
Like a thread in that huge strand,
Lost like a skein° of air,
And with it, continents lost
In the great throat of Death.
I trembled, asking in vain,

---

711 *sibyl:* prophetess.   725 *skein:* a loosely coiled length of thread or yarn.

Whence come you, whither art gone?
The continents flow and melt   730
Like wax in the naked candle,
Burnt by the wick of time—
Where is the breath of the Chaldees,°
The dark, Minoan° breath?
I said to myself in hate,   735
Hearing that mighty rushing,
Though you raise a new Adam up
And blow fresh fire in his visage,
He has only a loan of air,
And gets but a breathing-space.   740
But then I was quieted.

I heard the song of breath,
The gulf hollow with voices,
Fused into one slow voice
That never paused or was faint.   745
Man, breathing his life,
And with him all life breathing,
The young horse and the snake,
Beetle, lion and dove,
Solemn harps of the fir,   750
Trumpets of sea and whirlwind
And the vast, tiny grass
Blown by a breath and speaking.
I heard these things. I heard
The multitudinous river.   755
When I came back to my life,
My voice was numb in my ears,
I wondered that I still breathed.

———

Sophy, scared chambermaid in Pollet's Hotel,
Turned the cornhusk mattress and plumped the pillow   760
With slipshod hands.
                    Then she picked the pillow up
And sniffed it greedily.
                    Something in it smelt sweet.

733 *the Chaldees:* a Semitic people of ancient Babylonia.   734 *Minoan:* of ancient
Crete.

The bright, gold lady had slept there the night before—
Oh, her lovely, lovely clothes! and the little green bottle
That breathed out flowers when you crept into the room
And pulled out the silver stopper just far enough
To get the sweetness, not far enough to be caught
If anyone came.
     It made her thin elbows ache
To think how fine and golden the lady was
And how sweet she smelled, how sweet she looked at the men,
How they looked at her.
       "I'd like to smell sweet," she thought,
"Smell like a lady."
       She put the hard pillow back.
The lady and the green bottle had gone away.
—If only you had clever hands—after the next sleeper—
—You could steal green bottles—the room would smell stale again—
Hide it somewhere under your dress—as it always did—
Stale cigars and tired bodies—or even say
When they reached to give you the tip, "Don't give me a tip,
Just give me"—unwashed men with their six-weeks' beards,
Trying to hold you back when—"that little green bottle,
I want it so."—but the lady would never do it.
Ladies named Lucy. Lucy was a good name,
Flower-smelling. Sophy was just a name.

She took up her broom and swept ineffectively,
Thinking dim thoughts.
      The ladies named Lucy came,
Sometimes in the winter, and then all the men got shaved
And you could look through the door at the people dancing.
But when battles drew near, the ladies went home to stay.
It was right they should. War wasn't a thing for ladies.

War was an endless procession of dirty boots.
Filling pitchers and emptying out the slops,
And making the cornhusk beds for the unshaved men
Who came in tired—but never too tired to wonder—
Look in the eyes—and hands—and suppose you didn't,
They didn't like it—and if you did, it was nothing—
But they always—and rough sometimes—and drunk now and then—
And a couple of nice ones—well, it didn't mean nothing.
It was merely hard to carry the heavy pails

When you didn't get fed enough and got up so soon.
But, now the army was moving, there wouldn't be   800
So many men or beds or slops for a while
And that meant something.
                    She sighed and dabbed with her broom.

Shippy, the little man with the sharp rat-eyes,
Came behind her and put his hands on her waist.
She let him turn her around. He held her awhile   805
While his eyes tried to look at her and over his shoulder
At once and couldn't.
                    She felt his poor body shake
But she didn't think much about it.
                              He murmured something
She shook her head with the air of a frightened doll
And he let her go.
                    "Well, I got to go anyway,"   810
He said, in a gloomy voice. "I'm late as it is,
But I thought that maybe—" He let the sentence trail off.

"What do you want, next time I come back?" he said.
Her face was sharper. "You bring me a bottle, Charley,
The kind that lady had, with the Richmond scent.   815
Hers has got a big silver stopper."
                              He pursed his mouth.
"I don't know," he said. "I'll try. I'd like to all right.
You be a good girl now, Soph. Do you love me, Sophy?"

"Uh-huh," she said, in a tired voice, thinking of pitchers.

"Well, I—you're a good girl, Soph." He held her again.   820
"I'm late," he muttered. She looked at him and felt mean.
He was skimpy like her. They ought to be nice to each other.
She didn't like him much but she sort of loved him.
"You be a good girl till Charley comes back," he mumbled
Kissing her nervously. "I'll bring you the scent."   825

"It's got a name called French Lilies," she said. "Oh, Charley!"
They clung together a moment like mournful shadows.
He was crying a little, the wet tears fell on her chin,
She cried herself when he'd gone, she didn't know why,

But when she thought of the scent with the silver stopper   8
She felt more happy. She went to make the next bed.

———————

Luke Breckinridge, washing his shirt in a muddy pool,
Chewed on a sour thought.
                              Only yesterday
He had seen the team creak by toward Pollet's Hotel
With that damn little rat-eyed peddler driving his mules   8
As if he was God Almighty.
                              He conjured up
A shadow-Shippy before him to hate and bruise
As he beat his shirt with a stone.
                              "If we-uns was home,
I could just lay for him and shoot him out of the bresh,
Goin' to see my girl with his lousy mules.   8
Tryin' to steal my girl with his peddler's talk!"

But here, in the war, you could only shoot at the Yanks,
If you shot other folks, they found out about it and shot you,
Just like you was a spyer or something mean
Instead of a soldier. There wasn't no sense to it.   8
"Teach him to steal my girl—if I had him home,
Back in the mountains—I told her straight the last time,
You be a good girl, Soph, and I'll buy you a dress—
We can fix the cabin up fine—and if we have kids
We'll get ourselves married. Couldn't talk fairer than that,   8
And she's a good girl—but women's easy to change—
God-damn peddler, givin' her Richmond trash,
And we-uns movin' away to scrimmage the Yanks
Before I git a chance to see her agin
And find out if she's been good—He'll come back this way,   8
Drivin' his mules—plumb easy to lay for him,
But they'd catch me, shore."
                              His mouth had a bitter twist,
His slow mind grubbed for a plan to settle his doubts.
At last he dropped his stone with a joyous whoop.
"Hey, Billy," he called to his neighbor. "Got your shirt dry?   8
Well, lend it here for a piece until mine's wrung out,
I got to go see the Captain."
                              Billy demurred.
"I got friends enough in this shirt," he said with a drawl.

"I ain't hankerin' after no visitors out of yours.
I'm a modest man and my crawlies is sort of shy,   865
They don't mix well with strangers. They's Piedmont crawlies.°
Besides, this shirt, she's still got more shirt than hole,
Yours ain't a shirt—it's a doughnut."
                              They swore for a while
But finally Luke went off with the precious shirt,
Whistling the tuneless snatch of a mountain jig,   870
"Gawd help you, peddler," he thought, as he looked for the Captain.

Shippy drove his rattletrap cart along
Through the dusty evening, worried and ill at ease.
He ought to have taken the other road by the creek
But he'd wasted too much time at Pollet's Hotel   875
Looking for Sophy—and hardly seen her at that—
And now she wanted a bottle of scent.
                              His soul
Shivered with fear like a thin dog in the cold,
Raging in vain at the terrible thing called Life.
—There must be a corner somewhere where you could creep,   880
Curl up soft and be warm—but he'd never found it.
The big boys always stole his lunch at the school
And rubbed his nose in the dirt—and when he grew up
It was just the same.
                       There was something under his face,
Something that said, "Come, bully me—I won't bite."   885
He couldn't see it himself, but it must be there.
He was always going places and thinking, "This time,
They won't find out." But they always did find out
After a while.
                  It had been that way at the store,
That way in the army, that way now as a spy.   890
Behind his eyes he built up a super-Shippy
Who ordered people around, loved glittering girls,
Threw out his chest and died for a bloody flag
And then revived to be thanked by gilt generals,
A schoolboy Shippy, eating the big boys' lunch.   895
It was his totem. He visioned that Shippy now,
Reckless Shippy with papers sewed in his boots,
Slyly carrying fate through the Rebel lines

866 *Piedmont crawlies:* from recent operations in the uplands of western Virginia.

To some bright place where—

　　　　　　　　　　The off mule stumbled and brayed.
He cursed it whimperingly and jerked at the reins,　　　　　　90
While his heart jerked, too. The super-Shippy was gone.
He was alone and scared and late on the road.
My God, but he was scared of being a spy
And the mute-faced woman in Richmond ° and war and life!
He had some papers sewn in his boots all right　　　　　　9
And they'd look at the papers while he stood sweating before them,
Crumple them up and bully him with cross speech,
"Couldn't you even find out where Heth's men° are?
Can't you draw a map? You don't know about Stonewall Jackson?
Why don't you know it? What's this ford by the church?　　　9
My God, man, what do you think you are out there for?
You'll have to do better next time, I can tell you that.
We'll send you over Route 7. We had a man there,
But he's been reported killed—"
　　　　　　　　　　He shuddered in vain,
Seeing a rope and a tree and a dangling weight　　　　　　9
And the mute-faced woman sending a paper off
In somebody's else's boots, and somebody saying
In an ice-cream voice to another scared little man,
"Next time, you'll try Route 7. We had a man there,
But he's been reported killed—"
　　　　　　　　　　Oh, there is a hole　　　ç
Somewhere deep in the ground where the rabbits hide,
But I've never found it—
　　　　　　　　They stuck up signs and a flag
And it was war and you went and got scared to death
By the roar and the yells and the people trying to kill you
Till anything else seemed better—and there you were,　　　ç
Driving mules with papers sewn in your boots,
But people still wanting to kill you—and no way out.
If you deserted, the mute-faced woman would know
And that would be the worst—and if you went back,
It would be Bull Run and yelling and all that blood

---

904 *mute-faced woman in Richmond:* See note, Book IV, line 1564.　908 *Heth's men:* Major General Henry Heth's division, moving with the leading elements of Lee's army north into Pennsylvania. See Book VII, lines 255–256.

When it made you sick to your stomach. Even at school
You always had to fight. There was no way out.

Sophy was sweet and Sophy was a good girl
And Sophy was the warm earth where the rabbits hide
Away from danger, letting their hearts go slow;   935
But you couldn't stay with Sophy, you couldn't stay,
And she'd say she'd be a good girl—
      but, in spite of himself,
He saw a big boy tearing a cardboard box
Apart, with greedy hands, in a bare school-yard,
Where a Shippy whimpered—
     "Oh, Soph, I'll get you the scent,   940
Honest I will! Oh God, just let me get through,
Just this one time—and I'll pray—I'll be good—oh God,
Make these papers something they want!"

      He clucked to his mules.
Another mile and he'd be out on the pike
And pretty safe for a while.
     His spirit returned   945
To building the super-Shippy from dust again.
His head began to nod with the sway of the cart. . . .
Half a dozen men rode out from a little clearing
And casually blocked the road. He pulled up his mules,
Staring around. He saw a face that he knew,   950
Now queer with triumph—Sophy filling a pail
And that gangling feller lounging against the pump,
Hungry-eyed—
   It happened too fast to be scary.
You got stopped such a lot. It was only some new patrol.
"All the boys know me," he said. "Yes, I got my pass."   955
They took the pass but they did not give it back.
There was a waver shaking the dusty air,
The feel of a cord grown tauter. How dry his throat was!
He'd be driving on in a minute. "Well boys?" he said,
"Well, fellers?"
    They didn't answer or look at him.   960
"I tell you that's the man," said the mountaineer.

The sergeant-feller looked dubiously at the rest,
Gentlemanly he looked like, a nice young feller

With his little black moustache and his thin, brown face,
He wouldn't do anything mean. It would be all right.   9
Another man was paring his nails with a knife,
His face was merry and reckless—nice feller, too,
Feller to stand you a drink and talk gay with the girls,
Not anybody to hurt you or twist your wrist.
They were all nice fellers except for the mountaineer.   9

They were searching him now, but they didn't do it mean.
He babbled to them all through it.
                                        "Now boys, now boys,
You're making a big mistake, boys. They all know me,
They all know Charley the peddler."
                                        The sergeant looked   9
Disgusted now—wonder why. Go ahead and look,
You'll never find it—Sophy—bottle of scent—

A horrible voice was saying, "Pull off his boots,"
He fought like a frightened rat then, weeping and biting,
But they got him down and found the papers all right.
Luke Breckinridge observed them with startled eyes,   ç
"Christ," he thought, "so the skunk's a spy after all.
Well, I told 'em so—but I didn't reckon he was.
Little feist of a peddler, chasin' my girl,
Wanted to scare him off so he wouldn't come back—
Hell, they ought to make me a corporal now."   ç
He was pleased.
            Clay Wingate looked at the writhing man,
"Get up!" he said, in a hard voice, feeling sick.
But they had to drag it up before it would stand
And even then it still babbled.
                                    His throat was dry
But that was all right—it was going to be all right—   ¢
He was alive—he was Shippy—he knew a girl—
He was going to buy her a bottle of first-class scent.
It couldn't all stop. He wasn't ready to die.
He was willing enough to be friends and call it a joke.
Let them take the mules and the cart and hurt him a lot
Only not that—it was other spies who were hung,
Not himself, not Shippy, not the body he knew
With the live blood running through it, making it warm.
He was real. He wore clothes. He could make all this go away

If he shut his eyes. They'd turn him loose in a minute.   1000
They were all nice fellers. They wouldn't treat a man mean.
They couldn't be going to hang him.
But they were.

Lucy Weatherby spread out gowns on a bed
And wondered which she could wear to the next levee.°
The blue was faded, the rose brocade had a tear,   1005
She'd worn the flowered satin a dozen times,
The apricot had never gone with her hair,
And somebody had to look nice at the evening parties.
But it was hard. The blockade runners of course—
But so few of them had space for gowns any more   1010
And, really, they charged such prices!
Of course it is
The war, and, of course, when one thinks of our dear, brave boys—
But, nevertheless, they like a girl to look fresh
When they come back from their fighting.
When one goes up
To the winter-camps, it doesn't matter so much,   1015
Any old rag will do for that sort of thing.
But here, in Richmond . . .
She pondered, mentally stitching,
Cutting and shaping, lost in a pleasant dream.

Fighting at Chancellorsville and Hooker beaten
And nobody killed that you knew so terribly well   1020
Except Jo Frear's second brother—though it was sad
Our splendid general Jackson's lost his arm,
Such an odd man but so religious.
She hummed a moment
"That's Stonewall Jackson's way" ° in her clear cool voice.
"I really should have trained for nursing," she thought.   1025
She heard a voice say, "Yes, the General's very ill,
But that lovely new nurse will save him if anyone can.
She came out from Richmond on purpose."
The voice stopped speaking.
She thought of last month and the boys and the Black Horse Troop,

---

1004 *levee:* a fashionable party, usually for an honored person. 1024 *"That's Stonewall Jackson's way":* "Stonewall Jackson's Way," written by John Williamson Palmer on September 17, 1862, while the Battle of Antietam was in progress.

And the haggard little room in Pollet's Hotel
Whose slipshod chambermaid had such scared, round eyes.
She was just as glad they were fighting now, after all,
Huger had been so jealous and Clay so wild,
It was quite a strain to be engaged to them both
Especially when Jim Merrihew kept on writing
And that nice Alabama major—

      She heard the bells
Ring for a wedding—but who was the man beside her?
He had a face made up of too many faces.
And yet, a young girl must marry—

      You may dance,
Play in the sun and wear bright gowns to levees,
But soon or late, the hands unlike to your hands
But rough and seeking, will catch your lightness at last
And with strange passion force you. What is this passion,
This injury that women must bear for gowns?
It does not move me or stir me. I will not bear it.
There are women enough to bear it. If I have sweetness,
It is for another service. It is my own.
I will not share it. I'll play in the heat of the sun.
And yet, young girls must marry—what am I thinking?

She stepped from her hoops to try on the rose brocade,
But let it lie for a moment, while she stood up
To look at the bright ghost-girl in the long dark mirror,
Adoringly.

    "Oh, you honey," she thought. "You honey!
You look so pretty—and nobody knows but me.
Nobody knows."

      She kissed her little white shoulders,
With fierce and pitying love for their shining whiteness,
So soft, so smooth, so untarnished, so honey-sweet.
Her eyes were veiled. She swayed in front of the mirror.
"Honey, I love you," she whispered, "I love you, honey.
Nobody loves you like I do, do they, sugar?
Nobody knows but Lucy how sweet you are.
You mustn't get married, honey. You mustn't leave me.
We'll be pretty and sweet to all of them, won't we, honey?
We'll always have beaus to dance with and tunes to dance to,
But you mustn't leave me, honey. I couldn't bear it.
You mustn't ever leave me for any man."

In the dense heart of the thicketed Wilderness,
Stonewall Jackson lies dying for four long days.°
They have cut off his arm, they have tried such arts as they know,
But no arts now can save him.
1070
When he was hit
By the blind chance bullet-spatter from his own lines,
In the night, in the darkness, they stole him off from the field
To keep the men from knowing, but the men knew.
The dogs in the house will know when there's something wrong.
You do not have to tell them.
1075
He marched his men
That grim first day across the whole Union front
To strike a sleepy right wing with a sudden stone
And roll it up—it was his old trick of war
That Lee and he could play like finger and thumb!
It was the last time they played so.
1080
When the blue-coated
Unprepared ranks of Howard saw that storm,
Heralded by wild rabbits and frightened deer,
Burst on them yelling, out of the whispering woods,
They could not face it. Some men died where they stood,
The storm passed over the rest. It was Jackson's storm,°
1085
It was his old trick of war, for the last time played.
He must have known it. He loosed it and drove it on,
Hearing the long yell shake like an Indian cry
Through the dense black oaks, the clumps of second-growth pine,
And the red flags reel ahead through the underbrush.
1090
It was the hour he did not stop to taste,
Being himself. He saw it and found it good,
But night was falling, the Union centre still held,
Another attack would end it. He pressed ahead
Through the dusk, pushing Little Sorrel, as if the horse
1095
Were iron, and he were iron, and all his men
Not men but iron, the stalks of an iron broom
Sweeping a dire floor clean—and yet, as he rode,
A canny captain, planning a ruthless chess
Skilfully as night fell. The night fell too soon.
1100

1068 *dying for four long days:* The amputation of Jackson's left arm was considered successful until pneumonia set in; he died on May 10, eight days after being wounded. 1081–1085 *Unprepared ranks of Howard . . . Jackson's storm:* Major General Oliver Otis Howard's XI Corps, taken by surprise at Chancellorsville when Jackson with 26,000 men made a daring flanking movement across the Union front.

It is hard to tell your friend from your enemy
In such a night. So he rode too far in advance
And, turning back toward his lines, unrecognized,
Was fired upon in the night, in the stumbling darkness,
By his own men. He had ridden such rides before
Often enough and taken the chance of them,
But this chance was his bane.
                              He lay on the bed
After the arm had been lopped from him, grim and silent,
Refusing importunate Death with terrible eyes.
Death was a servant and Death was a sulky dog
And Death crouched down by the Lord in the Lord's own time,
But he still had work to finish that Death would spoil.
He would live in spite of that servant.
                                        Now and then
He spoke, with the old curt justice that never once
Denied himself or his foe or any other
The rigid due they deserved, as he saw that due.
He spoke of himself and his storm. "A successful movement.
I think the most successful I ever made."
—He had heard that long yell shake like an Indian cry
Through the ragged woods and seen his flags go ahead.
Later on, they brought him a stately letter from Lee
That said in Lee's gracious way, "You have only lost
Your left arm, I my right."
                           The dour mouth opened.
"Better ten Jacksons should fall than one Lee," it said
And closed again, while the heart went on with its task
Of beating off foolish, unnecessary Death.

The slow time wore. They had to tell him at last
That he must die. The doctors were brave enough,
No doubt, but they looked awhile at the man on the bed
And summoned his wife to do it. So she told him.
He would not believe at first. Then he lay awhile
Silent, while some slow, vast reversal of skies
Went on in the dying brain. At last he spoke.
"All right," he said.
                      She opened the Bible and read.
It was Spring outside the window, the air was warm,
The rough, plank house was full enough of the Spring.
They had had a good life together, those two middle-aged

Calm people, one reading aloud now, the other silent.
They had passed hard schools. They were in love with each other
And had been for many years. Now that tale was told.   1140
They had been poor and odd, found each other trusty,
Begotten children, prayed, disliked to be parted,
Had family-jokes, known weather and other matters,
Planned for an age: they were famous now, he was dying.

The clock moved on, the delirium began.   1145
The watchers listened, trying to catch the words;
Some awed, one broken-hearted, a few, no doubt,
Not glad to be there precisely, but in a way
Glad that, if it must happen, they could be there.
It is a human emotion.
     The dying man   1150
Went back at first to his battles, as soldiers do.
He was pushing a new advance
With the old impatience and skill, over tangled ground,
A cloudy drive that did not move as he willed
Though he had it clear in his mind. They were slow today.   1155
"Tell A. P. Hill to push them—push the attack—
Get up the guns!"
    The cloudy assault dispersed.
There were no more cannon. The ground was plain enough now.

He lay silent, seeing it so, while the watchers listened.
He had been dying once, but that was a dream.   1160
The ground was plain enough now.
He roused himself and spoke in a different voice.
"Let us cross the river," he said, "and rest under the shade of the trees."

1107–1163 *He lay on the bed* . . . : For details of Jackson's death, see *Battles and Leaders*, III, 203–214, and Mary Anna Jackson's *Memoirs of Stonewall Jackson*, pp. 450–457. The quotations included here are factual, though not always precise.

✦ BOOK SEVEN ✦

They came on to fish-hook Gettysburg in this way, after this fashion.
Over hot pikes heavy with pollen, past fields where the wheat was high.
Peaches grew in the orchards; it was a fertile country,
Full of red barns and fresh springs and dun, deep-uddered kine.

A farmer lived with a clear stream that ran through his very house-room,   5
They cooled the butter in it and the milk, in their wide, stone jars;
A dusty Georgian came there, to eat and go on to battle;
They dipped the milk from the jars, it was cold and sweet in his mouth.

He heard the clear stream's music as the German housewife served him,
Remembering the Shenandoah and a stream poured from a rock;   10
He ate and drank and went on to the gunwheels crushing the harvest.
It was a thing he remembered as long as any guns.°

Country of broad-backed horses, stone houses and long, green meadows,
Where Getty came° with his ox-team to found a steady town
And the little trains of my boyhood ° puffed solemnly up the Valley   15
Past the market-squares and the lindens and the Quaker meetinghouse.

Penn stood under his oak° with a painted sachem beside him,
The market-women sold scrapple° when the first red maples turned;
When the buckeyes slipped from their sheaths, you could gather a pile
   of buckeyes,
Red-brown as old polished boots, good to touch and hold in the hand.   20

5–12 *A farmer . . . A dusty Georgian . . .* : Compare the memoirs of General
John B. Gordon, a Georgian and one, of Early's brigade commanders at Gettysburg:
"He was a staid and laborious farmer of German descent. . . . He had built his
dining-room immediately over this fountain. . . . For many days, we had been
marching over dusty turnpikes, . . . we sat in that cool room, with the hot breakfast served from one side, while from the other the frugal housewife dipped cold
milk and cream from immense jars," *Reminiscences of the Civil War*, pp. 141–142.
14 *Getty* [sic] *came:* James Gettys established the first inn and store in Marsh Creek
Settlement in the 1780s. The village became known as "Gettistown" and eventually
was incorporated in 1806 as Gettysburg.   15 *my boyhood:* Although the Benét
family left Pennsylvania in 1899, the year after Stephen was born, he returned frequently to visit his mother's parents in Carlisle.   17 *Penn stood under his oak:*
In the fall of 1682 under a great tree [probably an elm] at Shackamaxon, now the
Kensington section of Philadelphia, William Penn concluded his initial treaty with
the Indians.   18 *scrapple:* cold cornmeal mush with pork scraps, to be sliced and
fried.

The ice-cream parlor was papered with scenes from *Paul and Virginia*,°
The pigs were fat all year, you could stand a spoon in the cream,
—Penn stood under his oak with a feathered pipe in his fingers,
His eyes were quiet with God, but his wits and his bargain sharp.

So I remember it all, and the light sound of buckeyes falling
On the worn rose-bricks of the pavement, herring-boned, trodden for
 years;
The great yellow shocks of wheat and the dust-white road through
 Summer,
And, in Fall, the green walnut shells, and the stain they left for a while.

So I remember you, ripe country of broad-backed horses,
Valley of cold, sweet springs and dairies with limestone-floors;
And so they found you that year, when they scared your cows with their
 cannon,
And the strange South moved against you, lean marchers lost in the corn.

———

Two months have passed since Jackson died in the woods°
And they brought his body back to the Richmond State House
To lie there, heaped with flowers, while the bells tolled,
Two months of feints and waiting.
     And now,° at length,
The South goes north again in the second raid,
In the last cast for fortune.
     A two-edged chance
And yet a chance that may burnish a failing star;
For now, on the wide expanse of the Western board,
Strong pieces that fought for the South have been swept away
Or penned up in hollow Vicksburg.
     One cool Spring night
Porter's ironclads° run the shore-batteries

21 *Paul and Virginia:* a romance by Bernardin de St. Pierre, 1787.   33 *Jackson
died in the woods:* at Chancellorsville, May 10, 1863.   36 *And now:* July 1863.
42–43 *One cool Spring night/Porter's ironclads:* "It was necessary . . . to have
transports below [Vicksburg], both for the purposes of ferrying troops over the river
and to carry supplies. . . . The night of [April 29, 1863] the batteries of that place
were run by the navy and transports . . . under the direction of Admiral Porter,
and on the following day . . . a landing effected," Grant in *Battles and Leaders*,
III, 494–495.

Through a velvet stabbed with hot flashes.
                              Grant lands his men.
Drives the relieving force of Johnston° away   45
And sits at last in front of the hollow town
Like a huge brown bear on its haunches, terribly waiting.
His guns begin to peck at the pillared porches,
The sleepy, sun-spattered streets. His siege has begun.

Forty-eight days° that siege and those guns go on   50
Like a slow hand closing around a hungry throat,
Ever more hungry.
                    The hunger of hollow towns,
The hunger of sieges, the hunger of lost hope.
As day goes by after day and the shells still whine
Till the town is a great mole-burrow of pits and caves   55
Where the thin women hide their children, where the tired men
Burrow away from the death that falls from the air
And the common sky turned hostile—and still no hope,
Still no sight in the sky when the morning breaks
But the brown bear there on his haunches, steadfastly waiting.   60
Waiting like Time for the honey-tree to fall.

The news creeps back to the watchers oversea.
They ponder on it, aloof and irresolute.
The balance they watch is dipping against the South.
It will take great strokes to redress that balance again.   65
There will be one more moment of shaken scales
When the Laird rams almost alter the scheme of things,°
But it is distant.
                    The watchers stare at the board
Waiting a surer omen than Chancellorsville
Or any battle won on a Southern ground.   70

45 *Johnston:* General Joseph E. Johnston.   50 *Forty-eight days:* May 18 to July 4,
1863.   67 *the Laird rams almost alter the scheme of things:* In the fall of 1863,
the British government, under pressure from the United States, seized two 1800-ton
ironclads, newly built for the Confederate navy by Lairds of Birkenhead. "They were
probably superior to any vessels at the time in possession of the United States. The
main object for which they were intended was the recovery of the Mississippi," J. R.
Soley in *Battles and Leaders*, IV, 597.

Lee sees that dip of the balance and so prepares
His cast for the surer omen and his last stroke
At the steel-bossed Northern shield. Once before he tried
That spear-rush North° and was halted. It was a chance.
This is a chance. He weighs the chance in his hand
Like a stone, reflecting.
                  Four years from Harper's Ferry—
Two years since the First Manassas—and this last year
Stroke after stroke successful—but still no end.

He is a man with a knotty club in his hand
Beating off bulls from the breaks in a pasture fence
And he has beaten them back at each fresh assault,
McClellan—Burnside—Hooker at Chancellorsville—
Pope° at the Second Manassas—Banks in the Valley—°
But the pasture is trampled; his army needs new pasture.
An army moves like a locust, eating the grain,
And this grain is well-nigh eaten. He cannot mend
The breaks in his fence with famine or starving hands,
And if he waits the wheel of another year
The bulls will come back full-fed, shaking sharper horns
While he faces them empty, armed with a hunger-cracked
Unmagic stick.
            There is only this thing to do,
To strike at the shield with the strength that he still can use
Hoping to burst it asunder with one stiff blow
And carry the war up North, to the untouched fields
Where his tattered men can feed on the bulls' own grain,
Get shoes and clothes, take Washington if they can,
Hold the fighting-gauge° in any event.
                    He weighs
The chance in his hand. I think that he weighed it well
And felt a high tide risen up in his heart
And in his men a high tide.
                  They were veterans,

---

74 *That spear-rush North:* Lee's invasion of Maryland in September 1862, which
ended in the stand-off Battle of Antietam.   82–83 *McClellan—Burnside—Hooker
. . . Pope:* See Book V, lines 56–62, 795–815.   83 *Banks in the Valley:* Major
General Nathaniel P. Banks, commander of the Union forces that opposed Jackson
in the Shenandoah Valley, May–June 1862.   97 *fighting-gauge:* initiative.

They had never been beaten wholly and blocked but once,
He had driven four Union armies within a year
And broken three blue commanders from their command.
Even now they were fresh from triumph.

                    He cast his stone
Clanging at fortune, and set his fate on the odds.   105

Lincoln hears the rumor in Washington.
They are moving North.

                The Pennsylvania cities
Hear it and shake, they are loose, they are moving North.
Call up your shotgun-militia, bury your silver,
Shoulder a gun or run away from the State,   110
They are loose, they are moving.

                Fighting Joe Hooker has heard it.
He swings his army back across the Potomac,
Rapidly planning, while Lee still visions him South.
Stuart's horse should have brought the news of that move
But Stuart is off on a last and luckless raid °   115
Far to the East, and the grey host moves without eyes
Through crucial days.

                They are in the Cumberland now,
Taking minor towns, feeding fat for a little while,
Pressing horses and shoes, paying out Confederate bills
To slow Dutch storekeepers who groan at the money.   120
They are loose, they are in the North, they are here and there.
Halleck rubs his elbows and wonders where,
Lincoln is sleepless, the telegraph-sounders click
In the War Office day and night.

                There are lies and rumors,
They are only a mile from Philadelphia now,   125
They are burning York—they are marching on Baltimore—

Meanwhile, Lee rides through the heart of the Cumberland.
A great hot sunset colors the marching men,
Colors the horse and the sword and the bearded face

---

115 *a last and luckless raid:* June 24–July 1. A common opinion: "Stuart, who should
have kept him informed, was off on a useless cavalry raid well to the east of the
Army of the Potomac," McMaster, p. 384.

But cannot change that face from its strong repose.   1.
And—miles away—Joe Hooker, by telegraph
Calls for the garrison left at Harper's Ferry
To join him. Elbow-rubbing Halleck refuses.
Hooker resigns command—and fades from the East
To travel West, fight keenly at Lookout Mountain,   1
Follow Sherman's march as far as Atlanta,
Be ranked by Howard, and tartly resign once more
Before the end and the fame and the Grand Review,
To die a slow death, in bed, with his fire gone out,
A campfire quenched and forgotten.°
                                        He deserved   1
A better and brusquer end that marched with his nickname,
This disappointed, hot-tempered, most human man
Who had such faith in himself except for once,
And the once, being Chancellorsville, wiped out the rest.
He was often touchy and life was touchy with him,   1
But the last revenge was a trifle out of proportion.
Such things will happen—Jackson went in his strength,
Stuart was riding his horse when the bullet took him,
And Custer died to the trumpet°—Dutch Longstreet lived
To quarrel and fight dead battles. Lee passed in silence.   1
McClellan talked on forever in word and print.
Grant lived to be President. Thomas died sick at heart.°

So Hooker goes from our picture—and a spent aide
Reaches Meade's hut at three o'clock in the morning
To wake him with unexpected news of command.°   1

133–140 *Halleck refuses./Hooker resigns . . . :* "Not allowed to manoeuver his
own army in the presence of the enemy," Hooker asked to be relieved. See Hunt in
Battles and Leaders, III, 270. He later led the XX Corps in the Chattanooga and
Atlanta Campaigns (Lookout Mountain, November 24, 1863); but in July 1864,
when Sherman elevated Howard, Hooker's junior, to command the Army of the
Tennessee, Hooker "was incensed, . . . resigned [his command], and went home."
See Howard, *Battles and Leaders,* IV, 321. Hooker did not, however, leave the army
until 1868, when he retired after a paralytic stroke.   149 *Custer died to the
trumpet:* at Little Big Horn against the Sioux, June 25, 1876.   152 *Thomas died
sick at heart:* Major General George H. Thomas, on the whole a well-regarded commander, was unable to dismiss the criticism of his actions, particularly his conduct
of the successful Nashville campaign.   154–155 *three o'clock in the morning . . . :*
"At three o'clock on the morning of the twenty-eighth an officer from Washington
entered the hut of General George Gordon Meade, awoke him and delivered an
order relieving Hooker and placing Meade in command," McMaster, pp. 383–384.

The thin Pennsylvanian puts on his spectacles
To read the order. Tall, sad-faced and austere,
He has the sharp, long nose of a fighting-bird,
A prudent mouth and a cool, considering mind.
An iron-grey man with none of Hooker's panache,   160
But resolute and able, well skilled in war;
They call him "the damned old goggle-eyed snapping-turtle"
At times, and he does not call out the idol-shout
When he rides his lines, but his prudence is a hard prudence,
And can last out storms that break the men with panache,   165
Though it summons no counter-storm° when the storm is done.

His sombre schoolmaster-eyes° read the order well.
It is three days before the battle.
                              He thinks at first
Of a grand review, gives it up,° and begins to act.

That morning a spy brings news to Lee in his tent   170
That the Union army has moved and is on the march.
Lee calls back Ewell and Early from their forays
And summons his host together by the cross-roads
Where Getty came with his ox-cart.
                              So now we see
These two crab-armies fumbling for each other,   175
As if through a fog of rumor and false report,
These last two days of sleepy, hay-harvest June.
Hot June lying asleep on a shock of wheat
Where the pollen-wind blows over the burnt-gold stubble
And the thirsty men march past, stirring thick grey dust   180
From the trodden pikes—till at last, the crab-claws touch
At Getty's town, and clutch, and the peaches fall
Cut by the bullets, splashing under the trees.

That meeting was not willed by a human mind,
When we come to sift it.
                              You say a fate rode a horse   185
Ahead of those lumbering hosts, and in either hand
He carried a skein of omen. And when, at last,

166 *no counter-storm:* no counterattack. See lines 1161–1162, below.   167 *school-master-eyes:* Meade was very near-sighted and habitually wore spectacles.   169 *a grand review, gives it up:* "General Orders Nos. 65 and 66 were published and we escaped a grand review which General Butterfield . . . urged there was no time for," *Four Brothers in Blue,* p. 296.

He came to a certain umbrella-copse of trees
That never had heard a cannon or seen dead men,
He knotted the skeins together and flung them down°   1
With a sound like metal.
                                    Perhaps. It may have been so.
All that we know is—Meade intended to fight
Some fifteen miles away on the Pipe Creek Line.°
And where Lee meant to fight him, if forced to fight,
We do not know, but it was not there where they fought.   1
Yet the riding fate,
Blind and deaf and a doom on a lunging horse,
Threw down his skeins and gathered the battle there.

The buttercup-meadows°
Are very yellow.
A child comes there   2
To fill her hands.
The gold she gathers
Is soft and precious
As sweet new butter   2
Fresh from the churn.

She fills her frock
With the yellow flowers,
The butter she gathers
Is smooth as gold,   2
Little bright cups
Of new-churned sunshine
For a well-behaved
Hoop-skirted doll.

Her frock's full   2
And her hands are mothy
With yellow pollen

185–190 *fate rode a horse . . . knotted the skeins together and flung them down:*
The Three Fates traditionally spun, measured, and cut the thread of life.   192–193
Meade intended . . . : On June 30, Meade "directed the chiefs of engineers
and artillery to select a field of battle . . . indicating the general line of Pipe
Creek as a suitable locality," Hunt in *Battles and Leaders,* III, 274.   199 *but-
tercup-meadows:* "No more glorious sun ever shown than that which . . . revealed
to our eyes that beautiful valley, with its wealth of yellow grain, the meadows tinted
with buttercups, . . . the battlefield of Gettysburg," *Four Brothers in Blue,* p. 305.

But she keeps on.
Down by the fence
They are even thicker.   220
She runs, bowed down with
Buttercup-gold.

She sees a road
And she sees a rider.
His face is grey   225
With a different dust.
He talks loud.
He rattles like tinware.
He has a long sword
To kill little girls.   230

He shouts at her now,
But she does not answer.
"*Where is the town?*"
But she will not hear.
There are other riders   235
Jangling behind him.
"*We won't hurt you, youngster!*"
But they have swords.

The buttercups fall
Like spilt butter.   240
She runs away.
She runs to her house.
She hides her face
In her mother's apron
And tries to tell her   245
How dreadful it was.

Buford came to Gettysburg late that night
Riding West with his brigades of blue horse,
While Pettigrew and his North Carolinians
Were moving East toward the town with a wagon-train,   250
Hoping to capture shoes.
                    The two came in touch.°

---

251 *Hoping to capture shoes. The two came in touch.*: "Pettigrew with a wagon
train approached from the west. He was coming to capture shoes believed to be
in Gettysburg, became aware of the presence of Buford and fell back," McMaster,
p. 384.

Pettigrew halted and waited for men and orders.
Buford threw out his pickets beyond the town.

The next morning was July first. It was hot and calm.
On the grey side, Heth's division° was ready to march
And drive the blue pickets in. There was still no thought
Of a planned and decisive battle on either side
Though Buford had seen the strength of those two hill-ridges
Soon enough to be famous, and marked one down
As a place to rally if he should be driven back.

He talks with his staff in front of a tavern now.
An officer rides up from the near First Corps.
"What are you doing here, sir?"

                         The officer
Explains. He, too, has come there to look for shoes.
—Fabulous shoes of Gettysburg, dead men's shoes,
Did anyone ever wear you, when it was done,
When the men were gone, when the farms were spoiled with the bones,
What became of your nails and leather? The swords went home,
The swords went into museums and neat glass cases,
The swords look well there. They are clean from the war.
You wouldn't put old shoes in a neat glass case,
Still stuck with the mud of marching.

                       And yet, a man
With a taste for such straws and fables, blown by the wind,
Might hide a pair in a labelled case sometime
Just to see how the leather looked, set down by the swords.

The officer is hardly through with his tale
When Buford orders him back to his command.
"Why, what is the matter, general?"

                       As he speaks
The far-off hollow slam of a single gun
Breaks the warm stillness. The horses prick up their ears.
"That's the matter," says Buford and gallops away.°

---

255 See note, Book VI, line 908.   263–281 *"What are you doing here, sir?"* . . . :
"A quartermaster of Reynolds' (First) Corps rode in. . . . Buford turned to him
and said: 'What are you doing here, sir?' The reply was that he had come in to get
some shoes. 'You had better return immediately to your command,' said Buford.
'Why, what is the matter, General?' At that moment a far-off boom of a single gun
was heard, and Buford replied, . . . 'That's the matter!' " *Four Brothers in Blue,*
pp. 294–295.

Jake Diefer, the barrel-chested Pennsylvanian,
Marched toward Getty's town past orderly fences,
Thinking of harvest.
                          The boy was growing up strong
And the corn-haired woman was smart at managing things   285
But it was a shame what you had to pay hired men now
Though they'd had good crops last year and good prices too.
The crops looked pretty this summer.
                                          He stared at the long
Gold of the wheat reflectively, weighing it all,
Turning it into money and cows and taxes,   290
A new horse-reaper, some first-class paint for the barn,
Maybe a dress for the woman.
                                  His thoughts were few,
But this one tasted rough and good in his mouth
Like a spear of rough, raw grain. He crunched at it now.
—And yet, that wasn't all, the paint and the cash,   295
They were the wheat but the wheat was—he didn't know—
But it made you feel good to see some good wheat again
And see it grown up proper.
                                He wasn't a man
To cut a slice of poetry from a farm.
He liked the kind of manure that he knew about   300
And seldom burst into tears when his horses died
Or found a beautiful thought in a bumble-bee,
But now, as he tramped along like a laden steer,
The tall wheat, rustling, filled his heart with its sound.

Look at that column well, as it passes by,   305
Remembering Bull Run and the cocksfeather hats,
The congressmen, the raw militia brigades
Who went to war with a flag and a haircloth trunk
In bright red pants and ideals and ignorance,
Ready to fight like picture-postcard boys   310
While fighting still had banners and a sword
And just as ready to run in blind mob-panic. . . .
These men were once those men. These men are the soldiers,
Good thieves, good fighters, excellent foragers,
The grumbling men who dislike to be killed in war   315
And yet will hold when the raw militia break
And live where the raw militia needlessly die,

Having been schooled to that end.

The school is not
A pretty school. They wear no cocksfeather hats.
Some men march in their drawers and their stocking feet.
They have handkerchiefs round their heads, they are footsore and
  chafed,°
Their faces are sweaty leather.

And when they pass
The little towns where the people wish them godspeed,
A few are touched by the cheers and the crying women
But most have seen a number of crying women,
And heard a number of cheers.

The ruder yell back
To the sincere citizens cool in their own front yards,
"Aw, get a gun and fight for your home yourself!" °
They grin and fall silent. Nevertheless they go on.

Jake Diefer, the barrel-chested Pennsylvanian,
The steer-thewed, first-plank-splitter from Cumberland,
Came through the heat and the dust and the mounting roar
That could not drown the rustle of the tall wheat
Making its growing sound, its windrustled sound,
In his heart that sound, that brief and abiding sound,
To a fork and a road he knew.

And then he heard
That mixed, indocile noise of combat indeed
And as if it were strange to him when it was not strange.
—He never took much account of the roads they went,
They were always going somewhere and roads were roads.
But he knew this road.

He knew its turns and its hills,
And what ploughlands lay beyond it, beyond the town,
On the way to Chambersburg.

He saw with wild eyes
Not the road before him or anything real at all

320–321 *men march . . . footsore and chafed:* "Men became ragged, footsore and chafed. Many were marching in their drawers, and, with handkerchiefs . . . tied about their heads. . . . Some were marching in their 'stocking' feet," *Four Brothers in Blue*, p. 296.   323–328 *people wish them godspeed . . . :* "The people were all astir, and tried to encourage us by stolid cheers and 'God speeds,' to which some of our chronic grumblers . . . [replied,] 'Fall in, take a rifle, and defend your own fireside!' " *Four Brothers in Blue*, p. 298.

But grey men in an unreal wheatfield, tramping it down,   345
Filling their tattered hats with ripe, rough grain
While a shell burst over a barn.
                    "Grasshoppers!" he said
Through stiff dry lips to himself as he tried to gauge
That mounting roar and its distance.
                        "The Johnnies is there!
The Johnnies and us is fighting in Gettysburg,   350
There must be Johnnies back by the farm already,
By Jesus, those damn Johnnies is on my farm!"

———————

That battle of the first day° was a minor battle
As such are counted.
                That is, it killed many men.
Killed more than died at Bull Run, left thousands stricken°   355
With wounds that time might heal for a little while
Or never heal till the breath was out of the flesh.
The First Corps lost half its number in killed and wounded.
The pale-faced women, huddled behind drawn blinds
Back in the town, or in apple-cellars, hiding,   360
Thought it the end of the world, no doubt.
                     And yet,
As the books remark, it was only a minor battle.
There were only two corps engaged on the Union side,
Longstreet had not yet come up, nor Ewell's whole force,
Hill's corps lacked a division till evening fell.   365
It was only a minor battle.
              When the first shot
Clanged out, it was fired from a clump of Union vedettes°
Holding a farm in the woods beyond the town.
The farmer was there to hear it—and then to see
The troopers scramble back on their restless horses   370
And go off, firing, as a grey mass came on.

He must have been a peaceable man, that farmer.
It is said that he died of what he had heard and seen
In that one brief moment, although no bullet came near him

353 *first day:* July 1, 1863.   355 *more than died at Bull Run* . . . : killed and
wounded, Union and Confederate: First Bull Run, 4,553; Gettysburg, first day,
11,037.   367 *a clump of Union vedettes:* mounted sentinels from the 8th Illinois
Cavalry. See *Four Brothers in Blue,* pp. 303–304.

And the storm passed by and did not burst on his farm.
No doubt he was easily frightened. He should have reflected
That even minor battles are hardly the place
For peaceable men—but he died instead, it is said.°
There were other deaths that day, as of Smiths and Clancys,
Otises, Boyds, Virginia and Pennsylvania,
New York, Carolina, Wisconsin, the gathered West,
The tattered Southern marchers dead on the wheat-shocks.
Among these deaths a few famous.

                               Reynolds is dead,
The model soldier, gallant and courteous,
Shot from his saddle in the first of the fight.
He was Doubleday's friend, but Doubleday° has no time
To grieve him, the Union right being driven in
And Heth's Confederates pressing on toward the town.
He holds the onrush back till Howard comes up
And takes command for a while.

                            The fighting is grim.
Meade has heard the news. He sends Hancock up to the field.°
Hancock takes command in mid-combat. The grey comes on.
Five color-bearers are killed at one Union color,°
The last man, dying, still holds up the sagging flag.
The pale-faced women creeping out of their houses,
Plead with retreating bluecoats, "Don't leave us boys,
Stay with us—hold the town." Their faces are thin,
Their words come tumbling out of a frightened mouth.
In a field, far off, a peaceable farmer puts
His hands to his ears, still hearing that one sharp shot
That he will hear and hear till he dies of it.°

369–378 *The farmer was there . . . died of what he heard . . .* : The Union
picket line was established on the Lott farm. "It is said that Lott was so frightened
he died shortly after [they withdrew]," *Four Brothers in Blue*, p. 304.   383–386
Reynolds . . . Doubleday: Major General John F. Reynolds, Major General
Abner Doubleday. When Reynolds was killed by a Confederate sharpshooter,
Doubleday succeeded him as commander of the First Corps. They had been friends
since cadet days at West Point.   391 *He sends Hancock . . . :* "After the death
of General Reynolds, General [Winfield S.] Hancock was assigned to the command
of all the [Second Corps] troops on the field of battle," editor's note, *Battles and
Leaders*, III, 434.   393 *one Union color:* "After five color-bearers of the Twenty-
fourth Michigan Volunteers had fallen, Colonel Morrow took the flag in his own
hands, but was immediately prostrated," Abner Doubleday, *Chancellorsville and
Gettysburg*, p. 146.   399–401 *a peaceable farmer . . . dies of it:* See lines 369–
378, above.

It is Hill and Ewell now against Hancock and Howard
And a confused, wild clamor—and the high keen°
Of the Rebel yell—and the shrill-edged bullet song
Beating down men and grain, while the sweaty fighters   405
Grunt as they ram their charges with blackened hands.

Till Hancock and Howard are beaten away at last,
Outnumbered and outflanked, clean out of the town,
Retreating as best they can to a fish-hook ridge,
And the clamor dies and the sun is going down   410
And the tired men think about food.
                              The dust-bitten staff
Of Ewell, riding along through the captured streets,
Hear the thud of a bullet striking their general.
Flesh or bone? Death-wound or rub of the game?
"The general's hurt!" They gasp and volley their questions.   415
Ewell turns his head like a bird, "No, I'm not hurt, sir,
But, supposing the ball had struck you, General Gordon,
We'd have the trouble of carrying you from the field.
You can see how much better fixed for a fight I am.
It don't hurt a mite to be shot in your wooden leg." °   420

So it ends. Lee comes on the field in time to see
The village taken, the Union wave in retreat.
Meade will not reach the ground till one the next morning.

So it ends, this lesser battle of the first day,
Starkly disputed and piecemeal won and lost   425
By corps-commanders who carried no magic plans
Stowed in their sleeves, but fought and held as they could.
It is past. The board is staked for the greater game
Which is to follow—The beaten Union brigades
Recoil from the cross-roads town that they tried to hold.   430
And so recoiling, rest on a destined ground.
Who chose that ground?
                              There are claimants enough in the books.
Howard thanked by Congress° for choosing it
As doubtless, they would have thanked him as well had he

403 *keen:* shriek.   413–420 *the thud of a bullet* . . . *"No, I'm not hurt. . . . :*
Ewell had lost a leg at Second Bull Run. This conversation appears in Gordon's
Reminiscences of the Civil War, p. 157.   433 *Howard thanked by Congress:* in a
resolution dated January 28, 1864.

Chosen another, once the battle was won,
And there are a dozen ifs on the Southern side,
How, in that first day's evening, if one had known,
If Lee had been there in time, if Jackson had lived,
The heights that cost so much blood in the vain attempt
To take days later, could have been taken then.
And the ifs and the thanks and the rest are all true enough
But we can only say, when we look at the board,
"There it happened. There is the way of the land.
There was the fate, and there the blind swords were crossed."

You took a carriage to that battlefield.
Now, I suppose, you take a motor-bus,
But then, it was a carriage—and you ate
Fried chicken out of wrappings of waxed paper,
While the slow guide buzzed on about the war
And the enormous, curdled summer clouds
Piled up like giant cream puffs in the blue.
The carriage smelt of axle-grease and leather
And the old horse nodded a sleepy head
Adorned with a straw hat. His ears stuck through it.
It was the middle of hay-fever summer
And it was hot. And you could stand and look
All the way down from Cemetery Ridge,
Much as it was, except for monuments
And startling groups of monumental men
Bursting in bronze and marble from the ground,
And all the curious names upon the gravestones. . . .

So peaceable it was, so calm and hot,
So tidy and great-skied.
                  No men had fought
There but enormous, monumental men
Who bled neat streams of uncorrupting bronze,
Even at the Round Tops, even by Pickett's boulder,
Where the bronze, open book could still be read
By visitors and sparrows and the wind:
And the wind came, the wind moved in the grass,
Saying . . . while the long light . . . and all so calm . . .

      "Pickett came
      And the South came

And the end came,
And the grass comes
And the wind blows   475
On the bronze book
On the bronze men
On the grown grass,
And the wind says
'Long ago   480
Long
Ago.' "

Then it was time to buy a paperweight
With flags upon it in decalcomania°
And hope you wouldn't break it, driving home.   485

Draw a clumsy fish-hook now on a piece of paper,
To the left of the shank, by the bend of the curving hook,
Draw a Maltese cross with the top block cut away.
The cross is the town. Nine roads star out from it
East, West, South, North.
            And now, still more to the left   490
Of the lopped-off cross, on the other side of the town,
Draw a long, slightly-wavy line of ridges and hills
Roughly parallel to the fish-hook shank.
(The hook of the fish-hook is turned away from the cross
And the wavy line.)
            There your ground and your ridges lie.   495
The fish-hook is Cemetery Ridge and the North
Waiting to be assaulted—the wavy line
Seminary Ridge whence the Southern assault will come.°

The valley between is more than a mile in breadth.
It is some three miles from the lowest jut of the cross   500
To the button at the far end of the fish-hook shank,
Big Round Top, with Little Round Top not far away.
Both ridges are strong and rocky, well made for war.
But the Northern one is the stronger shorter one.
Lee's army must spread out like an uncoiled snake   505
Lying along a fence-rail, while Meade's can coil
Or halfway coil, like a snake part clung to a stone.

484 *decalcomania*: a transfer picture; decal.   486–498 *Draw a clumsy fish-hook*
. . . : See map, p. 301.

Meade has the more men and the easier shifts to make,
Lee the old prestige of triumph and his tried skill.
His task is—to coil his snake round the other snake
Halfway clung to the stone, and shatter it so,
Or to break some point in the shank of the fish-hook line
And so cut the snake in two.
                              Meade's task is to hold.

That is the chess and the scheme of the wooden blocks
Set down on the contour map.
                              Having learned so much,
Forget it now, while the ripple-lines of the map
Arise into bouldered ridges, tree-grown, bird-visited,
Where the gnats buzz, and the wren builds a hollow nest
And the rocks are grey in the sun and black in the rain,
And the jacks-in-the-pulpit grow in the cool, damp hollows.
See no names of leaders painted upon the blocks
Such as "Hill," or "Hancock," or "Pender" °—
                              but see instead
Three miles of living men—three long double miles
Of men and guns and horses and fires and wagons,
Teamsters, surgeons, generals, orderlies,
A hundred and sixty thousand living men
Asleep or eating or thinking or writing brief
Notes in the thought of death, shooting dice or swearing,
Groaning in hospital wagons, standing guard
While the slow stars walk through heaven in silver mail,
Hearing a stream or a joke or a horse cropping grass
Or hearing nothing, being too tired to hear.
All night till the round sun comes and the morning breaks,
Three double miles of live men.
Listen to them, their breath goes up through the night
In a great chord of life, in the sighing murmur
Of wind-stirred wheat.
                              A hundred and sixty thousand
Breathing men, at night, on two hostile ridges set down.

Jack Ellyat slept that night on the rocky ground
Of Cemetery Hill while the cold stars marched,

522 *"Hill," or "Hancock," or "Pender"*: major commanders in the fight for Seminary Ridge on July 1.

GETTYSBURG

SITUATION JUST PRIOR TO PICKETT'S
CHARGE ON THE AFTERNOON OF JULY
3, 1863, THE THIRD DAY OF THE BATTLE.

1000   0   1000   2000

SCALE OF MILES

And if his bed was harder than Jacob's stone°
Yet he could sleep on it now and be glad for sleep.

He had been through Chancellorsville and the whistling wood,
He had been through this last day. It is well to sleep
After such days.
                    He had seen, in the last four months,
Many roads, much weather and death, and two men fey°
Before they died with the prescience of death to come,
John Haberdeen and the corporal from Millerstown.
Such things are often remembered even in sleep.
He thought to himself, before he lay on the ground,
"We got it hot today in that red-brick town
But we'll get it hotter tomorrow."
                                    And when he woke
And saw the round sun risen in the clear sky,
He could feel that thought steam up from the rocky ground
And touch each man.
                    One man looked down from the hill,
"That must be their whole damn army," he said and whistled,
"It'll be a picnic today, boys. Yes, it'll be
A regular basket-picnic." He whistled again.

"Shut your trap about picnics, Ace," said another man,
"You make me too damn hungry!"
                                He sighed out loud.
"We had enough of a picnic at Chancellorsville,"
He said. "I ain't felt right in my stummick since.
Can you make 'em out?"
                        "Sure," said Ace, "but they're pretty far."

"Wonder who we'll get? That bunch we got yesterday
Was a mean-shootin' bunch."
                            "Now don't you worry," said Ace,
"We'll get plenty."
                    The other man sighed again.

---

541 *Jacob's stone:* Jacob "took the stones of [Bethel] and put them for pillows, and
lay down in that place to sleep." Genesis 28:11.   546 *fey:* here, doomed.

"Did you see that darky woman selling hot pies,
Two days ago, on the road?" he said, licking his lips,
"Blackberry pies. The boys ahead got a lot
And Jake and me clubbed together for three. And then   570
Just as we were ready to make the sneak,
Who comes up with a roar but the provost-guard?
Did we get any pies? I guess you know if we did.
I couldn't spit for an hour, I felt so mad.
Next war I'm goin' to be provost-guard or bust." °   575

A thin voice said abruptly, "They're moving—lookit—
They're moving. I tell you—lookit—"
                          They all looked then.
A little crackling noise as of burning thornsticks
Began far away—ceased wholly—began again—
"We won't get it awhile," thought Ellyat. "They're trying the left.   580
We won't get it awhile, but we'll get it soon.
I feel funny today. I don't think I'm going to be killed
But I feel funny. That's their whole army all right.
I wonder if those other two felt like this,
John Haberdeen and the corporal from Millerstown?   585
What's it like to see your name on a bullet?
It must feel queer. This is going to be a big one.
The Johnnies know it. That house looks pretty down there.
Phaëton, charioteer in your drunken car,
What have you got for a man that carries my name?   590
We're a damn good company now, if we say it ourselves,
And the Old Man knows it—but this one's bound to be tough.
I wonder what they're feeling like over there.

Charioteer, you were driving yesterday,
No doubt, but I did not see you. I see you now.   595
What have you got today for a man with my name?" °

The firing began that morning° at nine o'clock,
But it was three before the attacks were launched.

567–575 *that darky woman selling hot pies* . . . . : " 'Yas, sah! I'se got some blackberry pies right in the oben just now.' . . . A hot, juicy blackberry pie was slipped
into the outspread hands . . . and we scurried around the corner of the old
'ramshackle' house just as the Provost came in on the front," *Four Brothers in Blue*,
pp. 285–286.   589–596 *Phaëton, charioteer* . . . : Compare Book I, line 1058.
597 *that morning*: July 2, 1863.

There were two attacks, one a drive on the Union left
To take the Round Tops, the other one on the right.
Lee had planned them to strike together and, striking so,
Cut the Union snake in three pieces.
                          It did not happen.
On the left, Dutch Longstreet, slow, pugnacious and stubborn,
Hard to beat and just as hard to convince,
Has his own ideas of the battle and does not move°
For hours after the hour that Lee had planned,
Though, when he does, he moves with pugnacious strength.

Facing him, in the valley before the Round Tops,
Sickles thrusts out blue troops in a weak right angle,
Some distance from the Ridge, by the Emmettsburg pike.°
There is a peach orchard there, a field of ripe wheat
And other peaceable things soon not to be peaceful.

They say the bluecoats, marching through the ripe wheat,
Made a blue-and-yellow picture that men remember
Even now in their age, in their crack-voiced age.°
They say the noise was incessant as the sound
Of all wolves howling, when that attack came on.
They say, when the guns all spoke, that the solid ground
Of the rocky ridges trembled like a sick child.
We have made the sick earth tremble with other shakings
In our time, in our time, in our time, but it has not taught us
To leave the grain in the field.
                          So the storm came on
Yelling against the angle.
                          The men who fought there

603–605 *Longstreet . . . does not move:* Longstreet's actions at Gettysburg have
provided one of the perennial controversies of Civil War history. See *Battles and
Leaders,* III, 339–356. For Benét's comments, see Book IV, lines 1264–1269.   609–
610 *Sickles . . . in a weak right angle . . . by the Emmettsburg* [sic] *pike:* Under
attack by Longstreet, late on the second day, Major General Daniel E. Sickles,
commanding Meade's Third Corps, was forced to withdraw from his extended position along the Emmitsburg road to the general lines shown on the map, p. 301.
613–615 *They say . . . :* "Standing waist deep in the beautiful yellow grain, the
blue strongly contrasting, was the Regular Division. . . . It was moving through
the wheat field . . . as upon parade . . . , and the contrast of the tall yellow
grain, so soon to be trampled by succeeding columns, was very striking, and a scene
never to be forgotten," *Four Brothers in Blue,* p. 312.

Were the tried fighters, the hammered, the weather-beaten,
The very hard-dying men.
      They came and died   625
And came again and died and stood there and died,
Till at last the angle was crumpled and broken in,
Sickles shot down, Willard, Barlow and Semmes° shot down,
Wheatfield and orchard bloody and trampled and taken,
And Hood's tall Texans sweeping on toward the Round Tops 630
As Hood ° fell wounded.
      On Little Round Top's height
Stands a lonely figure, seeing that rush come on—
Greek-mouthed Warren, Meade's chief of engineers.
—Sometimes, and in battle even, a moment comes
When a man with eyes can see a dip in the scales   635
And, so seeing, reverse a fortune. Warren has eyes
And such a moment comes to him now. He turns
—In a clear flash seeing the crests of the Round Tops taken,
The grey artillery there and the battle lost—
And rides off hell-for-leather to gather troops   640
And bring them up in the very nick of time,°
While the grey rush still advances, keening its cry.
The crest is three times taken and then retaken
In fierce wolf-flurries of combat, in gasping Iliads
Too rapid to note or remember, too obscure to freeze in a song 645
But at last, when the round sun drops, when the nun-footed night,
Dark-veiled walker, holding the first weak stars
Like children against her breast, spreads her pure cloths there,
The Union still holds the Round Tops and the two hard keys of war.

---

628 *Sickles shot down, Willard, Barlow and Semmes:* Sickles was wounded in the
second day's fighting; Colonel George L. Willard, a brigade commander, was killed.
Brigadier General Francis C. Barlow, a division commander, was wounded the
preceding day and left for dead, but recovered and within a year returned for duty.
Brigadier General Paul J. Semmes, a Confederate brigade commander, was wounded
in the first day's fighting and died the second. 631 *Hood:* Major General John B.
Hood. See note, Book IV, line 1271. 633–641 *Greek-mouthed Warren . . . in
the very nick of time:* Brigadier General Gouverneur Kemble Warren. "Passing
along the lines he found Little Round Top, the key of the position, unoccupied
except by a signal station. . . . Fully comprehending the imminent danger, Warren sent to General Meade for a division. The enemy was already advancing when,
noticing the approach of the Fifth Corps, Warren rode to meet it, caused Weed's
and Vincent's brigades and Hazlett's battery to be detached . . . and hurried them
to the summit. . . . They were barely in time, for the enemy were also climbing
the hill," Hunt in *Battles and Leaders*, III, 307–309.

Night falls. The blood drips in the rocks of the Devil's Den.°
The murmur begins to rise from the thirsty ground
Where the twenty thousand dead and wounded lie.
Such was Longstreet's war, and such the Union defence,
The deaths and the woundings, the victory and defeat
At the end of the fish-hook shank.

And so Longstreet failed
Ere Ewell and Early struck the fish-hook itself
At Culp's Hill and the Ridge and at Cemetery Hill,
With better fortune, though not with fortune enough
To plant hard triumph deep on the sharp-edged rocks
And break the scales of the snake.

When that last attack
Came, with its cry, Jack Ellyat saw it come on.

They had been waiting for hours on that hard hill,°
Sometimes under fire, sometimes untroubled by shells.
A man chewed a stick of grass and hummed to himself.
Another played mumbledeypeg with a worn black knife.
Two men were talking girls till they got too mad
And the sergeant stopped them.

Then they waited again.

Jack Ellyat waited, hearing that other roar
Rise and fall, be distant and then approach.
Now and then he turned on his side and looked at the sky
As if to build a house of peace from that blue,
But could find no house of peace there.

Only the roar,
The slow sun sinking, the fey touch at his mind. . . .

He was lying behind a tree and a chunk of rock
On thick, coarse grass. Farther down the slope of the hill
There were houses, a rough stone wall, and blue loungy men.
Behind them lay the batteries on the crest.

He wondered if there were people still in the houses.

650 *Devil's Den:* See map, p. 301.   662 *that hard hill:* Cemetery Hill.

One house had a long, slant roof. He followed the slant
Of the roof with his finger, idly, pleased with the line.   680

The shelling burst out from the Southern guns again.
Their own batteries answered behind them. He looked at his house
While the shells came down. I'd like to live in that house.
Now the shelling lessened.
                The man with the old black knife
Shut up the knife and began to baby his rifle.   685
They're coming, Jack thought. This is it.
                      There was an abrupt
Slight stiffening in the bodies of other men,
A few chopped ends of words scattered back and forth,
Eyes looking, hands busy in swift, well-accustomed gestures.
This is it. He felt his own hands moving like theirs   690
Though he was not telling them to. This is it. He felt
The old familiar tightness around his chest.
The man with the grass chewed his stalk a little too hard
And then suddenly spat it out.
                Jack Ellyat saw
Through the falling night,° that slight, grey fringe that was war   695
Coming against them, not as it came in pictures
With a ruler-edge, but a crinkled and smudgy line
Like a child's vague scrawl in soft crayon, but moving on
But with its little red handkerchiefs of flags
Sagging up and down, here and there.
                   It was still quite far,   700
It was still like a toy attack—it was swallowed now
By a wood and came out larger with larger flags.
Their own guns on the crest were trying to break it up
—Smoking sand thrown into an ant-legged line—
But it still kept on—one fringe and another fringe   705
And another and—
            He lost them all for a moment
In a dip of ground.
            This is it, he thought with a parched
Mind. It's a big one. They must be yelling all right
Though you can't hear them. They're going to do it this time.

695 *Through the falling night*: July 2, 1863, the second day of the battle.

Do it or bust—you can tell from the way they come—
I hope to Christ that the batteries do their job
When they get out of that dip.
                              Hell, they've lost 'em now,
And they're still coming.
                              He heard a thin gnat-shrieking
"Hold your fire till they're close enough, men!"
                                        The new lieutenant.
The new lieutenant looked thin. "Aw, go home," he muttered,
"We're no militia—What do you think we are?"

Then suddenly, down by his house, the low stone wall
Flashed and was instantly huge with a wall of smoke.
He was yelling now. He saw a red battleflag
Push through smoke like a prow and be blotted out
By smoke and flash.
                    His heart knocked hard in his chest.
"Do it or bust," he mumbled, holding his fire
While the rags of smoke blew off.
                              He heard a thick chunk
Beside him, turned his head for a flicker of time.
The man who had chewed on the grass was injuredly trying
To rise on his knees, his face annoyed by a smile.
Then the blood poured over the smile and he crumpled up.
Ellyat stretched out a hand to touch him and felt the hand
Rasped by a file.
                  He jerked back the hand and sucked it.
"Bastards," he said in a minor and even voice.

All this had occurred, it seemed, in no time at all,
But when he turned back, the smoky slope of the hill
Was grey—and a staggering red advancing flag
And those same shouting strangers he knew so well,
No longer ants—but there—and stumblingly running—
And that high, shrill, hated keen piercing all the flat thunder.

His lips went back. He felt something swell in his chest
Like a huge, indocile bubble.
                              "By God," he said,
Loading and firing, "You're not going to get this hill,
You're not going to get this hill. By God, but you're not!"

He saw one grey man spin like a crazy dancer
And another fall at his heels—but the hill kept growing them.
Something made him look toward his left.
                                        A yellow-fanged face
Was aiming a pistol over a chunk of rock.
He fired and the face went down like a broken pipe   745
While something hit him sharply and took his breath.
"Get back, you suckers," he croaked, "Get back there, you suckers!"
He wouldn't have time to load now—they were too near.
He was up and screaming. He swung his gun like a club
Through a twilight full of bright stabbings, and felt it crash   750
On a thing that broke. He had no breath any more.
He had no thoughts. Then the blunt fist hit him again.

He was down in the grass and the black sheep of night ran over him . . .

That day, Melora Vilas sat by the spring
With her child in her arms and felt the warm wind blow   755
Ruffling the little pool that had shown two faces
Apart and then clung together for a brief while
As if the mouths had been silver and so fused there. . . .

The wind blew at the child's shut fists but it could not open them.
The child slept well. The child was a strong, young child.   760

"Wind, you have blown the green leaf and the brown leaf
And in and out of my restless heart you blow,
Wakening me again.
                    I had thought for a while
My heart was a child and could sleep like any child,
But now that the wind is warm, I remember my lover,   765
Must you blow all summer, warm wind?"

"Divide anew this once-divided flesh
Into twelve shares of mercy and on each
Bestow a fair and succourable child,
Yet, in full summer, when the ripened stalks   770
Bow in the wind like golden-headed men,

Under the sun, the shares will reunite
Into unmerciful and childless love." °

She thought again, "No, it's not that, it's not that,
I love my child with an 'L' because he's little,   7
I love my child with an 'S' because he's strong.
With an 'M' because he's mine.
                            But I'm restless now.
We cut the heart on the tree but the bark's grown back there.
I've got my half of the dime° but I want his.
The winter-sleep is over."   7

The shadows were longer now. The child waked and cried.
She rocked and hushed it, feeling the warm wind blow.
"I've got to find him," she said.

About that time, the men rode up to the house
From the other way. Their horses were rough and wild.   7
There were a dozen of them and they came fast.
Bent should have been out in the woods but he had come down
To mend a split wagon-wheel. He was caught in the barn.
They couldn't warn him in time, though John Vilas tried,
But they held John Vilas and started to search the place   7
While the younger children scuttled around like mice
Squeaking "It's drafters, Mom—it's the drafters again!"
Even then, if Bent had hidden under the hay
They might not have found him, being much pressed for time,
But perhaps he was tired of hiding.
                            At any rate
When Melora reached the edge of the little clearing,
She saw them there and Bent there, up on a horse,
Her mother rigid as wood and her father dumb
And the head man saying, gently enough on the whole,
"Don't you worry, ma'am—he'll make a good soldier yet   8
If he acts proper."
                    That was how they got Bent.

767–773 *"Divide anew this once-divided flesh . . .":* Compare Book III, lines
1042–1049.   779 *my half of the dime:* See Book III, lines 1147–1150.

On the crest of the hill, the sweaty cannoneers,
The blackened Pennsylvanians, picked up their rammers
And fought the charge with handspikes and clubs and stones,
Biting and howling.° It is said that they cried   805
Wildly, "Death on the soil of our native state
Rather than lose our guns." A general says so.°
He was not there. I do not know what they cried
But that they fought, there was witness—and that the grey
Wave that came on them fought, there was witness too.   810
For an instant that wheel of combat—and for an instant
A brief, hard-breathing hush.
                              Then came the hard sound
Of a column tramping—blue reinforcements at last,°
A doomsday sound to the grey.
                              The hard column came
Over the battered crest and went in with a yell.   815
The grey charge bent and gave ground, the grey charge was broken.
The sweaty gunners fell to their guns again
And began to scatter the shells in the ebbing wave.

Thus ended the second day of the locked bull-horns
And the wounding or slaying of the twenty thousand.   820
And thus night came to cover it.
                              So the field
Was alive all night with whispers and words and sighs,
So the slow blood dripped in the rocks of the Devil's Den.
Lincoln, back in his White House, asks for news.
The War Department has little. There are reports   825
Of heavy firing near Gettysburg—that is all.
Davis, in Richmond, knows as little as he.
In hollow Vicksburg, the shells come down and come down
And the end is but two days off.°
                              On the field itself

803–805 *blackened Pennsylvanians . . . Biting and howling:* the 1st Pennsylvania
Artillery at Cemetery Hill. "The cannoneers . . . so summarily ousted, rallied and
recovered their guns by a vigorous attack—with pistols by those who had them, by
others with handspikes, rammers, stones, and even fence-rails," Hunt in *Battles and
Leaders,* III, 313.   807 *A general says so:* General Abner Doubleday in *Chancellorsville and Gettysburg* (1882), p. 182.   813 *blue reinforcements at last:* "The ar-
rival of [Colonel Samuel S.] Carroll's brigade . . . caused the attack to miscarry,"
Hunt in *Battles and Leaders,* III, 313.   829 *the end is but two days off:* Vicksburg
surrendered July 4, 1863.

Meade calls a council and considers retreat.   8
His left has held and the Round Tops still are his.
But his right has been shaken, his centre pierced for a time,
The enemy holds part of his works on Culp's Hill,
His losses have been most stark.

                    He thinks of these things
And decides at last to fight it out where he stands.°   8

Ellyat lay upon Cemetery Hill.
His wounds had begun to burn.

                    He was rising up
Through cold and vacant darknesses into faint light,
The yellow, watery light of a misty moon.
He stirred a little and groaned.

                There was something cool   8
On his face and hands. It was dew. He lay on his back
And stared at a blowing cloud and a moist, dark sky.
"Old charioteer," he thought.

                He remembered dully
The charge. The charge had come. They had beaten the charge.
Now it was moist dark sky and the dew and his pain.

He tried to get his canteen but he couldn't reach it.
That made him afraid.

              "I want some water," he said.
He turned his head through stiff ages.

                Two feet away
A man was lying quietly, fast asleep,
A bearded man in an enemy uniform.
He had a canteen. Ellyat wet his lips with his tongue.
"Hey Johnnie, got some water?" he whispered weakly.
Then he saw that the Johnnie had only half a head,
And frowned because such men could not lend canteens.

He was half-delirious now, and it seemed to him
As if he had two bodies, one that was pain
And one that lay beyond pain, on a couch of dew,

---

835 *decides at last to fight it out* . . . : After a council of war following the second day's fighting, Meade concluded, "Well, gentlemen, the question is settled; we
will remain here, but I wish to say I consider this no place to fight a battle," as
quoted by F. A. Walker, *Battles and Leaders*, III, 412.

And stared at the other with sober wondering eyes.
"Everyone's dead around here but me," he thought,
"And as long as I don't sing out, they'll think that I'm dead   860
And those stretcher-bearers won't find me—there goes their lantern
No, it's the moon—Sing out and tell 'em you're here."
The hot body cried and groaned. The cool watched it idly.
The yellow moon burst open like a ripe fruit
And from it rolled on a dark, streaked shelf of sky   865
A car and horses, bearing the brazen ball
Of the unbearable sun, that halted above him
In full rush forward, yet frozen, a motion congealed,
Heavy with light.
                    Toy death above Gettysburg.°

He saw it so and cried out in a weak, thin voice   870
While something jagged fitted into his heart°
And the cool body watched idly.
                              And then it was
A lantern, bobbing along through the clumped dead men,
That halted now for an instant. He cried again.
A voice said, "Listen, Jerry, you're hearing things,   875
I've passed that feller twice and he's dead all right,
I'll bet you money."
                    Ellyat heard himself piping,
"I'm alive, God damn you! Can't you hear I'm alive?"

Something laughed, quite close now.
                              "All right, Bub," said a cloud,
"We'll take your word for it. My, but the boy's got language!   880
Go ahead and cuss while we get you up on the stretcher—
It helps some—easy there, Joe."
                              Jack Ellyat fell
Out of his bodies into a whispering blackness
Through which, now and then, he could hear certain talking clouds
Cough or remark.
                    One said. "That's two and a half   885
You owe me, Joe. You're pickin' 'em wrong tonight."
"Well, poor suckers," said Joseph. "But all the same,

843–869 *"Old charioteer,"* . . . *A car and horses* . . . : Compare Book I, line 1058.
871 *something jagged fitted into his heart*: See Book III, lines 516–517.

If this one doesn't last till the dressing station
The bet's off—take it slower, Jerry—it hurts him."

———————

Another clear dawn breaks over Gettysburg,   8⁹
Promising heat and fair weather—and with the dawn
The guns are crashing again.
                          It is the third day.°
The morning wears with a stubborn fight at Culp's Hill
That ends at last in Confederate repulse
And that barb-end of the fish-hook cleared of the grey.   8

Lee has tried his strokes on the right and left of the line.
The centre remains—that centre yesterday pierced
For a brief, wild moment in Wilcox's attack,°
But since then trenched, reinforced and alive with guns.
It is a chance. All war is a chance like that.   9
Lee considers the chance and the force he has left to spend
And states his will.
                    Dutch Longstreet, the independent,
Demurs, as he has demurred since the fight began.
He had disapproved of this battle from the first°
And that disapproval has added and is to add   9
Another weight in the balance against the grey.
It is not our task to try him for sense or folly,
Such men are the men they are—but an hour comes
Sometimes, to fix such men in most fateful parts,
As now with Longstreet who, if he had his orders   9
As they were given, neither obeyed them quite
Nor quite refused them, but acted as he thought best,
So did the half-thing, failed as he thought he would,
Felt justified and wrote all of his reasons down°
Later in controversy.
                     We do not need   9
Such controversies to see that pugnacious man
Talking to Lee, a stubborn line in his brow
And that unseen fate between them.

---

892 *the third day:* July 3, 1863.   898 *Wilcox's attack:* an assault on Cemetery
Ridge by Brigadier General Cadmus M. Wilcox's Alabama Brigade.   902–904
Longstreet . . . disapproved . . . from the first: See lines 603–605, above.   914
wrote all of his reasons down: in *From Manassas to Appomattox, Memoirs of the
Civil War in America* (1896).

Lee hears him out
Unmoved, unchanging.
"The enemy is there
And I am going to strike him," says Lee, inflexibly.°   920

Wingate cursed with an equal stress
The guns in the sky and his weariness,
The nightmare riding of yesterday
When they slept in the saddle by whole platoons
And the Pennsylvania farmer's grey   925
With hocks as puffy as toy balloons,
A graceless horse, without gaits or speed,
But all he had for his time of need.
"I'd as soon be riding a Jersey cow."
But the Black Horse Troop was piebald ° now   930
And the Black Horse Troop was worn to the blade
With the dull fatigue of this last, long raid.°
Huger Shepley rode in a tense
Gloom of the spirit that found offence
In all things under the summer skies   935
And the recklessness in Bristol's eyes
Had lost its color of merriment.
Horses and men, they were well-nigh spent.
Wingate grinned as he heard the "Mount,"
"Reckon we look sort of no-account,   940
But we're here at last for somebody's fight."
They rode toward the curve of the Union right.°

At one o'clock the first signal-gun was fired
And the solid ground began to be sick anew.
For two hours then that sickness, the unhushed roar   945
Of two hundred and fifty cannon firing like one.
By Philadelphia, eighty-odd miles away,
An old man stooped and put his ear to the ground
And heard that roar, it is said, like the vague sea-clash

919–920 *"The enemy is there . . ."*: "The enemy is there, and I am going to attack him there," Lee as quoted by Longstreet, *Battles and Leaders*, III, 339.
930 *piebald*: spotted. See note, Book II, line 47.   932 *last, long raid*: See line 115,
above.   942 *curve of the Union right*: The major cavalry action took place on the
third day, about three miles east of Gettysburg.

In a hollow conch-shell, there, in his flowerbeds.   9
He had planted trumpet-flowers for fifteen years
But now the flowers were blowing an iron noise
Through earth itself. He wiped his face on his sleeve
And tottered back to his house with fear in his eyes.

The caissons began to blow up in the Union batteries. . . .°   9

———————

The cannonade fell still. All along the fish-hook line,
The tired men stared at the smoke and waited for it to clear;
The men in the centre waited, their rifles gripped in their hands,
By the trees of the riding fate, and the low stone wall, and the guns.

These were Hancock's men, the men of the Second Corps,   9
Eleven States were mixed there, where Minnesota stood
In battle-order with Maine, and Rhode Island beside New York.°
The metals of all the North, cooled into an axe of war.

The strong sticks of the North, bound into a fasces°-shape,
The hard winters of snow, the wind with the cutting edge,   9
And against them came that summer that does not die with the year,
Magnolia and honeysuckle and the blue Virginia flag.

Tall Pickett went up to Longstreet—his handsome face was drawn.
George Pickett, old friend of Lincoln's° in days gone by with the blast,
When he was a courteous youth and Lincoln the strange shawled man   9
Who would talk in a Springfield street with a boy who dreamt of a
    sword.

943–955 *At one o'clock the first signal-gun . . . The caissons began to blow
up . . . :* "At 1 P.M., a signal gun was fired and one hundred and fifteen guns
opened against Hancock's command, . . . both sides suffered severely in the two
hours' cannonade. Not less than eleven caissons were blown up," Doubleday, p. 189.
961–962 *Eleven States . . . :* in addition to those named: Pennsylvania, Connecticut, Delaware, Massachusetts, Indiana, Ohio, and West Virginia.   964 *fasces:* a
bundle of rods bound about the handle of an ax; in ancient Rome, the symbol of
authority.   969 *Pickett, old friend of Lincoln's:* "Pickett's uncle, Andrew Johnston,
of Richmond, in 1841 had legal business with Abraham Lincoln at Springfield,
Illinois. . . . Mr. Lincoln learned that the lad, whom he met and liked, desired to
be a soldier. . . . [His] law partner John T. Stuart, had been elected to Congress
[and] at Mr. Lincoln's request, Young Pickett was nominated as a cadet, and the
friendship thus begun lasted until the death of President Lincoln," Jesse B. Young,
The Battle of Gettysburg, pp. 313–314.

Dreamt of a martial sword, as swords are martial in dreams,
And the courtesy to use it, in the old bright way of the tales.
Those days are gone with the blast. He has his sword in his hand.
And he will use it today, and remember that using long.   975

He came to Longstreet for orders, but Longstreet would not speak.
He saw Old Peter's° mouth and the thought in Old Peter's mind.
He knew the task that was set and the men that he had to lead
And a pride came into his face while Longstreet stood there dumb.

"I shall go forward, sir," ° he said and turned to his men.   980
The commands went down the line. The grey ranks started to move.
Slowly at first, then faster, in order, stepping like deer,
The Virginians, the fifteen thousand, the seventh wave of the tide.

There was a death-torn mile of broken ground to cross,
And a low stone wall at the end, and behind it the Second Corps,   985
And behind that force another, fresh men who had not yet fought.
They started to cross that ground. The guns began to tear them.

From the hill they say that it seemed more like a sea than a wave,
A sea continually torn by stones flung out of the sky,
And yet, as it came, still closing, closing and rolling on,   990
As the moving sea closes over the flaws and rips of the tide.

You could mark the path that they took by the dead that they left be-
    hind,
Spilled from that deadly march as a cart spills meal on a road,
And yet they came on unceasing, the fifteen thousand no more,
And the blue Virginia flag did not fall, did not fall, did not fall.   995

They halted but once to fire as they came. Then the smoke closed down
And you could not see them, and then, as it cleared again for a breath,
They were coming still but divided, gnawed at by blue attacks,
One flank half-severed and halted, but the centre still like a tide.

977 *Old Peter's*: Longstreet's nickname among his troops was "Old Pete."   979–
980 *Longstreet stood there dumb.*/"*I shall go forward, sir,*": Longstreet "had no
voice to give the final command . . . [Pickett] saluted Longstreet and said, 'I shall
move forward, sir.' The corps commander, unable to speak, nodded his head, and
Pickett gallantly rode away," Young, p. 320.

Cushing ran down the last of his guns to the battle-line.   10

The rest had been smashed to scrap by Lee's artillery fire.

He held his guts in his hand as the charge came up the wall

And his gun spoke out for him once before he fell to the ground.

Armistead leapt the wall and laid his hand on the gun,

The last of the three brigadiers who ordered Pickett's brigades,   10

He waved his hat on his sword and "Give 'em the steel!" he cried,

A few men followed him over. The rest were beaten or dead.

A few men followed him over.° There had been fifteen thousand

When that sea began its march toward the fish-hook ridge and the wall.

So they came on in strength, light-footed, stepping like deer,   10

So they died or were taken. So the iron entered their flesh.

Lee, a mile away, in the shade of a little wood,

Stared, with his mouth shut down, and saw them go and be slain,

And then saw for a single moment, the blue Virginia flag

Planted beyond the wall, by that other flag that he knew.   1

The two flags planted together, one instant, like hostile flowers.

Then the smoke wrapped both in a mantle—and when it had blown
     away,

Armistead lay in his blood, and the rest were dead or down,

And the valley grey with the fallen and the wreck of the broken wave.

Pickett gazed around him, the boy who had dreamt of a sword   1

And talked with a man named Lincoln. The sword was still in his hand.

He had gone out with fifteen thousand. He came back to his lines with
     five.

He fought well till the war was over, but a thing was cracked in his
     heart.

1000–1008 *Cushing . . . Armistead . . .* : Lieutenant Alonzo H. Cushing, 4th
U.S. Artillery; Brigadier General Lewis A. Armistead. "Cushing, mortally wounded,
holding on to his intestines with one hand, ran his only gun down to the fence with
the other, and said: '*Webb, I will give them one more shot!*' . . . Armistead pressed
forward, leaped the fence, waving his sword with his hat on it. . . . He shouted,
'Give them the cold steel boys!' and laid his hands upon one of the guns," Doubleday, pp. 194–195. Compare Carter's account: "Cushing was not shot in the bowels,
nor did he . . . pull any lanyard while his bowels were protruding," *Four Brothers
in Blue*, p. 315.

Wingate, waiting the sultry sound
That would pour the troop over hostile ground,   1025
Petted his grey like a loving son
And wondered whether the brute would run
When it came to fighting, or merely shy.
There was a look in the rolling eye
That he knew too well to criticize   1030
Having seen it sometimes in other eyes.
"Poor old Fatty," ° he said, "Don't fret,
It's tough, but it hasn't happened yet
And we may get through it if you behave,
Though it looks just now like a right close shave.   1035
There's something funny about this fight—"

He thought of Lucy in candlelight,
White and gold as the evening star,
Giving bright ribbons to men at war.
But the face grew dimmer and ever dimmer,   1040
The gold was there but the gold was fainter,
And a slow brush streaked it with something grimmer
Than the proper tint of a lady's painter
Till the shadow she cast was a ruddy shadow.
He rubbed his eyes and stared at the meadow. . . .   1045

"There was a girl I used to go with,
    Long ago, when the skies were cooler,
There was a tree we used to grow with
    Marking our heights with a stolen ruler.

There was a cave where we hid and fought once.   1050
    There was a pool where the wind kept writing.
There was a possum-child we caught once.
    Caged it awhile, for all its biting.

There was a gap in a fence to see there,
    Down where the sparrows were always wrangling.   1055
There was a girl who used to be there,
    Dark and thin, with her long braids dangling.

1032 *"Poor old Fatty,"*: See lines 925–927, above.

Dark and thin in her scuffed brown slippers
  With a boy's sling stuck in her apron-pocket,
With a sting in her tongue like a gallinipper's°
  And the eyes of a ghost in a silver locket.

White and gold, white and gold,
You cannot be cold as she was cold,
Cold of the air and the running stream
And cold of the ice-tempered dream.

Gold and white, gold and white,
You burn with the heat of candlelight.
But what if I set you down alone
Beside the burning meteor-stone?

Blow North, blow South, blow hot, blow cold,
My body is pledged to white and gold,
My honor given to kith and kin,
And my doom-clothes ready to wrap me in
For the shut heart and the open hand
As long as Wingate Hall shall stand
And the fire burn and the water cool
And a fool beget another fool—°

But now, in the hour before this fight,
I have forgotten gold and white.
I will remember lost delight.
She has the Appleton mouth, it seems,
And the Appleton way of riding,
But if she quarrels or when she gleams,
Something comes out from hiding.

She can sew all day on an Appleton hem
And look like a saint in plaster,
But when the fiddles begin to play,
And her feet beat fast but her heart beats faster,
An alien grace is alive in them

1060 *gallinipper's*: mosquito's.   1077 *beget another fool*: Compare Book I, lines 259–272.

And she looks like her father, the dancing-master,   1090
The scapegrace elegant, 'French Dupré.' "

Then the word came and the bugle sang
And he was part of the running clang,
The rush and the shock and the sabres licking
And the fallen horses screaming and kicking.   1095
His grey was tired and his arm unsteady
And he whirled like a leaf in a shrieking eddy
Where every man was fighting his neighbor
And there was no room for the tricks of sabre
But only a wild and nightmare sickling.°   1100
His head felt burnt—there was something trickling
Into his eyes—then the new charge broke
The eddy apart like scattered smoke;
The cut on his head half made him blind.
If he had a mind, he had lost that mind.   1105

He came to himself in a battered place,
Staring at Wainscott Bristol's face,
The dried blood made it a ferret's mask.

"What happened?" he croaked.
                        "Well, you can ask,"
Said Bristol, drawling, "But don't ask me,   1110
For any facts of the jamboree.
I reckon we've been to an Irish wake
Or maybe cuttin' a johnny-cake
With most of the Union cavalry-corps.
I don't know yet, but it was a war.   1115
Are you crazy still? You were for a piece.
You yelled you were Destiny's long-lost niece
And wanted to charge the whole Yank line
Because they'd stolen your valentine.
You fought like a fool but you talked right wild.   1120
You got a bad bump, too."
                        Wingate smiled
"I reckon I did, but I don't know when.
Did we win or what?"
                        "And I say again,"

1100 *sickling:* unprofessional swordsmanship; slashing, as with a sickle.

Said Bristol, heavily, "don't ask me.
Inquire of General Robert Lee.
I know we're in for a long night ride°
And they say we got whipped on the other side.
What's left of the Troop are down by the road.
We lost John Leicester and Harry Spode
And the Lawley boys and Ballantyne.
The Major's all right—but there's Jim Divine
And Francis Carroll and Judson White—
I wish I had some liquor tonight."

Wingate touched the cut on his head.
It burned, but it no longer bled.
"I wish I could sleep ten years," he said.

———————

The night of the third day falls. The battle is done.
Lee entrenches that night upon Seminary Ridge.
All next day the battered armies still face each other
Like enchanted beasts.
                              Lee thinks he may be attacked,
Hopes for it, perhaps, is not, and prepares his retreat.

Vicksburg has fallen, hollow Vicksburg has fallen,
The cavedwellers creep from their caves and blink at the sun.
The pan of the Southern balance goes down and down.
The cotton is withering.

Army of Northern Virginia, haggard and tattered,
Tramping back on the pikes, through the dust-white summer,
With your wounds still fresh, your burden of prisoners,
Your burden of sick and wounded,
"One long groan of human anguish six miles long."
You reach the swollen Potomac at long last,
A foe behind, a risen river in front,
And fording that swollen river, in the dim starlight,
In the yellow and early dawn,
Still have heart enough for the tall, long-striding soldiers
To mock the short, half swept away by the stream.

1126 *a long night ride:* to join Lee's forces for the withdrawal that began on the
night of July 4.

"Better change our name to Lee's Waders, boys!"
"Come on you shorty—get a ride on my back."
"Aw, it's just we ain't had a bath in seven years
And General Lee, he knows we need a good bath."   1160

So you splash and slip through the water and come at last
Safe, to the Southern side, while Meade does not strike;
Safe to take other roads, safe to march upon roads you know
For two long years. And yet—each road that you take,
Each dusty road leads to Appomattox now.°   1165

1146–1165 *Army of Northern Virginia . . . Tramping back on the pikes . . . :*
For details of Lee's withdrawal, see Imboden, *Battles and Leaders*, III, 420–429.

❧ BOOK EIGHT ❧

It is over now, but they will not let it be over.

It was over with John Brown when the sun rose up
To show him the town in arms and he did not flee,°
Yet men were killed after that, before it was over,
And he did not die until November was cool °   5
—Yellow leaves falling through a blue-grey dusk,
The first winds of November whirl and scatter them—
So now, the Confederacy,
Sick with its mortal sickness, yet lives on
For twenty-one falling months° of pride and despair,   10
Half-hopes blown out in the lighting, heroic strokes
That come to nothing, and death piled hard upon death.

Follow that agony if you must and can
By the brushwood names, by the bloody prints in the woods,
Cold Harbor and Spottsylvania and Yellow Tavern°   15
And all the lost court-houses and country stores
In the Wilderness, where the bitter fighting passed,
(No fighting bitterer)—follow the rabbit-runs
Through the tangled wilds where the hair of the wounded men
Caught fire from the burning trees, where they lay in the swamps 20
Like half-charred logs°—find the place they called "Hell's Half Acre."
Follow the Indian names in the Indian West,
Chickamauga and Chattanooga° and all the words
That are sewn on flags or cut in an armory wall.
My cyclorama is not the shape of the world   25
Nor even the shape of this war from first to last,
But like a totem carved, like a totem stained
With certain beasts and skies and faces of men
That would not let me be too quiet at night
Till they were figured.
        Therefore now, through the storm,   30

---

3 *the town in arms and he did not flee*: Harper's Ferry, October 18, 1859. See
Book I, lines 561–563. 5 *did not die until . . .* : December 2, 1859. 10 *twenty-one falling months*: from the defeats of Vicksburg and Gettysburg in July 1863 to
the surrender at Appomattox in April 1865. 15 *Cold Harbor and Spottsylvania*
[*sic*] *and Yellow Tavern*: battles in Grant's advance through the Wilderness of Virginia, May–June 1864. 19–21 *wounded men/Caught fire . . .*: at Spotsylvania,
during the night of May 7–8, when some 200 died from burns or suffocation. 22–23 *Chickamauga and Chattanooga*: campaigns in Tennessee in the autumn of 1863.

The war, the rumor, the grinding of the machine,
Let certain sounds, let certain voices be heard.

A Richmond lady sits in a Richmond square
Beside a working-girl. They talk of the war,
They talk of the food and the prices in low-pitched voices
With hunger fretting them both. Then they go their ways.
But, before she departs, the lady has asked a question—
The working-girl pulls up the sleeve of her dress
And shows the lady the sorry bone of her arm.°

Grant has come East to take up his last command °
And the grand command of the armies.
                    It is five years
Since he sat, with a glass, by the stove in a country store,
A stumpy, mute man in a faded Army overcoat,
The eldest-born of the Grants but the family-failure,
Now, for a week, he shines in the full array
Of gold cord and black-feathered hat and superb blue coat,
As he talks with the trim, well-tailored Eastern men.
It is his only moment of such parade.
When the fighting starts, he is chewing a dead cigar
With only the battered stars to show the rank
On the shoulderstraps of the private's uniform.

It is sullen Cold Harbor. The Union attack has failed,
Repulsed with a ghastly slaughter.° The twilight falls.
The word goes round the attack will be made again
Though all know now that it cannot be made and win.
An anxious officer walks through his lines that night.
There has been no mutiny yet, throughout all these years,
But he wonders now. What are the men doing now?
He sees them there. They are silently writing their names
On bits of rag and sewing the scraps of cloth

33–39 *A Richmond lady . . . asks a question . . .* : A Confederate colonel's wife wrote from Richmond, April 4, 1863, "In the Capital Square . . . I sat on a bench near . . . a pale, emaciated girl, . . . her loose calico sleeve slipped up, and revealed the mere skeleton of an arm. . . . I was encouraged to ask: 'What is [the crowd]? Is there some celebration?' 'There *is*,' said the girl, solemnly; 'we celebrate our right to live.' . . . [The crowd] grew until it reached the dignity of a mob— a bread riot." See Pryor, *Reminiscences of Peace and War*, pp. 237–239.   40 *take up his last command*: on March 12, 1864.   53 *ghastly slaughter*: See note, Book IV, line 980.

To their jackets while they can, before the attack.
When they die, next morning, somebody may read the names.°

Pickett's son is born on a night of mid-July
While the two armies face each other, and Pickett's men
Light bonfires of celebration along his lines.   65
The fire is seen from the tents of the other camp.
The news goes back to Grant and his chief of staff.
"Haven't we any wood for the little Pickett?" says Grant,
And the Union bonfires are lighted for Pickett's son.
—All night those two lines of brush-fire, facing each other—   70
Next day they send the baby a silver service.°
Next week or so they move upon Pickett's works.

On a muddy river, little toy boats go out.
The soldiers are swapping coffee for rank tobacco,
A Northern badge for a Southern souvenir,   75
A piece of white-flour bread for a hunk of corn-pone.
A Northern lieutenant swims the river at night
To go to a Southern dance at a backwoods store,
Joke with the girls, swim back, and fight the next day
With his hosts of the night before.
                              On disputed ground,   80
A grey-clad private worms his way like a snake,
The Union sentries see him and start to fire.
"Aw, shut up, Yank," he calls in a weary voice,
"I just skun out to salvage the chaplain's hat,
It's the only one he's got and it just blew off."   85
The firing stops.
                "All right, Johnny," the sentries call,
"Get your hat, but be quick about it. We won't hurt you

56–62 *An anxious officer . . . sees them . . . sewing the scraps of cloth . . . :*
"I noticed that many . . . seemed to be engaged in sewing up rents . . . , but
upon closer examination it was found that the men were calmly writing their
names . . . and pinning them on the backs of their coats, so that their dead
bodies might be recognized," Porter, *Campaigning with Grant*, pp. 174–175.   63–71
Pickett's son is born . . . : July 17, 1864. "At the time our first baby was born
the two armies were encamped facing each other and . . . bonfires were lighted
in celebration all along Pickett's line. Grant . . . said to General Ingalls: 'Haven't
we some kindling on this side of the line? Why don't we strike a light for the young
Pickett?' . . . Later there was taken through the lines a baby's silver service, en-
graved: 'To George E. Pickett, Jr., from his father's friends, U. S. Grant, Rufus
Ingalls, George Suckley,' " LaSalle Corbell Pickett in *The Heart of a Soldier*, pp.
18–19.

But you better be back by the time our relief gets here."°
A Southern sharpshooter crouched in a blue-gum tree
Drills a tiny blue-coated figure between the eyes
With a pea-ball fired from a smooth-bore squirrel-rifle.
The dead man's brother waits three days for his shot,
Then the sharpshooter crashes down through the breaking boughs
Like a lumpy bird, spread-eagled out of his nest.
The desolate siege of Petersburg begins.
The grain goes first, then the cats and the squeaking mice,
The thin cats stagger starving about the streets,
Die or are eaten.° There are no more cats
In Petersburg—and in Charleston the creeping grass
Grows over the wharves where the ships of the world came in,
The grass and the moss grow over the stones of the wharves.
A Georgia belle eats sherbet near Andersonville
Where the Union prisoners rot.° Another is weeping
The death of her brother, killed in a Union raid.
In the North, the factory chimneys smoke and fume;
The minstrels have raised their prices, but every night
Bones and Tambo° play to a crowded house.
The hotels are full. The German Opera is here.
The ladies at Newport drive in their four-in-hands.
The old woman sells her papers about the war
The country widows stitch on a rusty black.°

74–88 *swapping coffee for rank tobacco* . . . : Such recollections by "Rebs"
and "Yanks" are widely recorded. For example, during the siege of Petersburg
(lines 95–98) "there was much . . . bartering. A rebel . . . comes about mid-
way to a stump . . . after depositing his treasure, which is generally tobacco . . . ,
he returns. 'Yank' advances with stores, generally soap, coffee or salt, picks up
Johnny's bundle, leaves his own," *Four Brothers in Blue*, p. 459.   95–98 *siege
of Petersburg . . . cats stagger starving* . . . : In mid-June 1864 Grant shifted
his main objective from Richmond to Peterburg, and the city remained under
attack until May 1865. "[That winter] rats and mice disappeared. The poor cats
staggered about the streets, and began to die of hunger," Pryor, p. 267.   102–
103 *eats sherbet near Andersonville* . . . : On January 11, 1865, at Pine Bluff,
about thirty miles from Andersonville, Eliza Frances Andrews wrote in her diary, "I
would rather face [the Yankees] anywhere than here in South-West Georgia, for the
horrors of the stockade have . . . enraged them. . . . It is horrible . . . but what
can we poor Confederates do?" And on February 2, "We spent the evening at Major
Edwin Bacon's. . . . We had no end of fun, and a splendid supper, with ice cream
and sherbet." See *The War-Time Journal of a Georgia Girl*, pp. 64, 83.   107
Bones and Tambo: traditional names of blackface end men of the minstrel shows,
who told jokes and played the "bones" (bone or wooden clappers) and tamborine.
111 *stitch on a rusty black*: sew mourning clothes using faded black cloth.

In the Shenandoah Valley, the millwheels rot.
(Sheridan has been there.) Where the houses stood,
Strong houses, built for weather, lasting it out,
The chimneys stand alone. The chimneys are blackened.   115
(Sheridan has been there.) This Valley has been
The granary of Lee's army for years and years.
Sheridan makes his report on his finished work.
"If a crow intends to fly over the Valley now
He'll have to carry his own provisions," says Sheridan.°   120

The lonely man with the chin like John Calhoun's
Knows it is over, will not know it is over.
Many hands are turning against him in these last years.
He makes mistakes. He is stubborn and sick at heart.
He is inflexible with fate and men.   125
It is over. It cannot be. He fights to the end,
Clinging to one last dream—of somehow, somewhere,
A last, miraculous battle where he can lead
One wing of the Southern army and Lee the other
And so wrench victory out of the failing odds.   130
Why is it a dream? He has studied grand strategy,
He was thought a competent soldier in Mexico,
He was Secretary of War once—
                        He is the rigid
Scholar we know and have seen in another place,°
Lacking that scholar's largeness, but with the same   135
Tight mouth, the same intentness on one concept,
The same ideal that must bend all life to its will
Or break to pieces—and that is the best of him.
The pettiness is the pettiness of a girl
More than a man's—a brilliant and shrewish girl,   140
Never too well in body yet living long.
He has that unforgiveness of women in him
And women will always know him better than men
Except for a few, in spite of Mexican wars,

112–120 *In the Shenandoah . . . Sheridan*: Following Early's raid on Washington
(see note, Book IV, line 896), Grant wrote Halleck, July 19, 1864, "The enemy . . .
should have on his heels veterans . . . to eat out Virginia clear and clean . . . so
that crows flying over it for the balance of this season will have to carry their provender with them," *Official Records*, Series I, Vol. XXXVII, Part 2, 300–301.
Between August 1864 and the following May, the newly formed Army of the
Shenandoah under Sheridan (see note, Book IV, line 752) carried out those instructions.   134 *Scholar we know . . . :* Consider Woodrow Wilson.

In spite of this last, most desolate, warlike dream.
Give him the tasks that other scholar assumed,
He would not have borne them as greatly or with such skill
And yet—one can find a likeness.
                So now he dreams
Hopelessly of a fight he will never fight
And if worst comes to worst, perhaps, of a last
Plutarch-death on a shield.°
               It is not to be.
He will snatch up a cloak of his wife's by accident
In the moment before his capture, and so be seen,
The proud man turned into farce, into sorry farce
Before the ignorant gapers.°
              He shades his eyes
To rest them a moment, turns to his work again.

The gaunt man, Abraham Lincoln, lives his days.
For a while the sky above him is very dark.
There are fifty thousand dead in these last, bleak months
And Richmond is still untaken.
              The papers rail,
Grant is a butcher, the war will never be done.
The gaunt man's term of office draws to an end,
His best friends muse and are doubtful. He thinks himself
For a while that when the time of election comes
He will not be re-elected. He does not flinch.
He draws up a paper and seals it with his own hand.
His cabinet signs it, unread.
              Such writing might be
A long historic excuse for defeated strength.
This is very short and strict with its commonsense.
"It seems we may not rule this nation again.
If so, we must do our best, while we still have time,
To plan with the new rulers who are to come
How best to save the Union before they come,
For they will have been elected upon such grounds
That they cannot possibly save it, once in our place." °

151 *Plutarch-death* . . . : See note, Book II, line 1303.   152–155 *a cloak of his wife's* . . . : Although witnesses later attested that Davis was otherwise in military clothing, the story that he was disguised as a woman was commonplace. Cartoons pictured him running away in a hoopskirt carrying bags of gold.   166–175 *He draws up a paper and seals it* . . . : Written August 23, 1864, it remained sealed until November 11 when Lincoln opened it before the Cabinet. "It

The cloud lifts, after all. They bring him the news.
He is sure of being President four years more.
He thinks about it. He says, "Well, I guess they thought
They'd better not swap horses, crossing a stream." °
The deserters begin to leave the Confederate armies. . . .   180

Luke Breckinridge woke up one sunshiny morning
Alone, in a roadside ditch, to be hungry again,
Though he was used to being hungry by now.
He looked at his rifle and thought, "Well, I ought to clean it."
He looked at his feet and he thought, "Well, I ought to get   185
Another bunch of rags if we-uns is goin'
To march much more—these rags is down to my hide."
He looked at his ribs through the tears in his dirty shirt
And he thought, "Well, I sure am thin as a razorback.
Well, that's the way it is. Well, I ought to do somethin'.   190
I ought to catch up with the boys. I wish I remembered
When I had to quit marchin' last night. Well, if I start now,
I reckon I'm bound to catch 'em."
                                       But when he rose
He looked at the road and saw where the march had passed
—Feet going on through the dust and the sallow mud,   195
Feet going on forever—
                            He saw that track.
He was suddenly very tired.
He had been tired after fighting often enough
But this was another weariness.

He rubbed his head in his hands for a minute or so,   200
As if to rub some slow thought out of his mind
But it would not be rubbed away.
                            "I'm near it," he thought,
"The hotel ain't a mile from here if Sophy's still there.
Well, they wouldn't give me a furlough when I ast.

seems exceedingly probable that this Administration will not be reëlected. Then it
will be my duty to so coöperate with the President-elect as to save the Union between
the election and the inauguration; as he will have secured his election on such
grounds that he cannot possibly save it afterward." See *Abraham Lincoln, A History*, IX, 251–252. 179 *better not swap horses . . .*: June 9, 1864, after his
nomination (but before the election) Lincoln commented, "The convention . . .
concluded . . . that it was not best to swap horses when crossing a stream."
Abraham Lincoln, Complete Works, II, 531–532.

Well, it's been a long time."

On the way to the plank hotel
He still kept mumbling, "I can catch up to the boys."
But another thought too vague to be called a thought
Washed over the mumble, drowning it, forcing it down.

The grey front door was open. No one was there.
He stood for a moment silent, watching the sun
Fall through the open door and pool in the dust.

"Sophy!" he called. He waited. Then he went in.
The flies were buzzing over the dirty plates
In the dining room and nobody there at all.
It made him feel tired. He started to climb the stairs.
"Hey, Sophy!" he called and listened. There was a creak
From somewhere, a little noise like a dusty rat
Running across a dusty, sun-splattered board.
His hands felt stronger.

He was on the second floor
Slamming the doors of empty room after room
And calling "Sophy!" At last he found the locked door.
He broke it down with his shoulder in a loud noise.
She was lying in bed with the covers up to her chin
And her thin hands clutching the covers.

"Well, Soph," he said.
"Well, it's you," she said.

They stared at each other awhile.

"The rest of 'em's gone," she said. "They went off last night.
We haven't had no business. The nigger said
The Yanks were coming. They didn't have room in the cart.
They said I could stay for a while and take care of things
Or walk if I wanted. I guess Mr. Pollet's crazy.
He was talking things to himself all the time they went.
I never slept in a bed like this before.
I didn't know you could sleep so soft in a bed."

"Did they leave any shoes?" said Luke.

She shook her head.
"I reckon you could maybe tear up a quilt.
I reckon they wouldn't mind."

Luke grinned like a wolf.
"I reckon they hadn't better," he said. "Not much.
Got anything to eat? I'm hungry as hell."

They ate what food she could find and she washed his feet
And bound them up in fresh rags.
                    He looked at the rags.   240
"Do for a while," he said. "Well, come along, Soph.
We got a long way to go."
                    Her eyes were big at him.
"The Yanks were comin'," she said. "You mean the war's over?"

He said, "I ain't had shoes for God knows how long."
He said, "If it was all Kelceys, you wouldn't mind.   245
Now I'm goin' to get me some shoes and raise me a crop,
And when we get back home, we'll butcher a hog.
There's allus hogs in the mountains."
                    "Well," she said.
"Well, you get your duds," he said.
                    She didn't have much.
They went along two days without being stopped.   250
She walked pretty well for a thin sort of girl like that.
He told her she'd get fatter when they were home.

The third day, they were tramping along toward dusk,
On a lonely stretch of road, when she heard the horse-hoofs.
Luke had heard them before and shifted his rifle then.   255

The officer came in sight. He was young and drawn.
His eyes were old in their sockets. He reined his horse.
"You're goin' the wrong way, soldier. What's your regiment?"

Luke's eyes grew little. "—th Virginia," he drawled,
"But I'm on furlough."
                    "H'm," said the officer,   260
"Where are your furlough-papers?"
                    Luke's hand slid down
By his trigger guard. "This here's my furlough," he said,
Resting the piece in the palm of the other hand.
The officer seemed to debate a thing in his mind
For a long instant. Then he rode on, in silence.   265
Luke watched him out of sight. When he was quite gone,
The hand slid back, the rifle was shouldered again.

The night had fallen on the narrow tent.
—Deep night of Virginia summer when the stars
Are burning wax in the near, languid sky
And the soft flowers hardly close all night
But bathe in darkness, as a woman bathes
In a warm, fragrant water and distill
Their perfume still, without the fire of the sun.

The army was asleep as armies sleep.
War lying on a casual sheaf of peace
For a brief moment, and yet with armor on,
And yet in the child's deep sleep, and yet so still.
Even the sentries seemed to walk their posts
With a ghost-footfall that could match that night.

The aide-de-camp knew certain lines of Greek
And other such unnecessary things
As birds and music, that are good for peace
But are not deemed so serviceable for war.
He was a youth with an inquisitive mind
And doubtless had a failing for romance,
But then he was not twenty, and such faults
May sometimes be excused in younger men
Even when such creatures die, as they have done
At one time or another, for some cause
Which we are careful to point out to them
Much later, was no cause worth dying for,
But cannot reach them with our arguments
Because they are uneconomic dust.

So, when the aide-de-camp came toward the tent,
He knew that he was sleepy as a dog,
And yet the starlight and the gathered scents
Moved in his heart—like the unnecessary
Themes of a music fallen from a cloud
In light, upon a dark water.
                              And though he had
Some bitterness of mind to chew upon,
As well as messages that he must give
Before he slept, he halted in his tracks.

He saw, imprinted on the yellow light
That made the tent a hollow jack-o'-lantern,   305
The sharp, black shadow of a seated man,
The profile like the profile on a bust.
Lee in his tent, alone.
He had some shadow-papers in his hand,
But you could see he was not reading them,   310
And, if he thought, you could not read his thoughts,
Even as shadows, by any light that shines.

"You'd know that face among a million faces,"
Thought the still watcher, "and yet, his hair and beard
Have quite turned white, white as the dogwood-bloom   315
That blossomed on the way to Chancellorsville
When Jackson was alive and we were young
And we were winning and the end was near.
And now, I guess, the end is near enough
In spite of everything that we can do,   320
And he's alone tonight and Jackson's dead.

I saw him in the Wilderness that day
When he began to lead the charge himself
And the men wouldn't let him.
                    Gordon spoke
And then the men themselves began to yell   325
"Lee to the rear—General Lee to the rear!"
I'll hear that all my life. I'll see those paws
Grabbing at Traveller and the bridle-rein
And forcing the calm image back from death.°

Reckon that's what we think of you, Marse Robert,   330
Reckon that's what we think, what's left of us,
The poor old devils that are left of us.
I wonder what he thinks about it all.
He isn't staring, he's just sitting there.

322–329 *that day* . . . *Lee to the rear* . . . : May 2, 1864, at Spotsylvania with
Major General John B. Gordon's Georgia Brigade. There are several versions of this
episode; the one here closely follows E. M. Law's in *Battles and Leaders*, IV, 132,
and Gordon's account, *Reminiscences of the Civil War*, pp. 278–279.

I never knew a man could look so still
And yet look so alive in his repose.

It doesn't seem as if a cause could lose
When it's believed in by a man like that.
And yet we're losing.
                              And he knows it all.
No, he won't ever say it. But he knows.

I'd feel more comfortable if he'd move.

We had a chance at Spottsylvania,
We had some chances in the Wilderness.
We always hurt them more than we were hurt
And yet we're here—and they keep coming on.

What keeps us going on? I wish I knew.
Perhaps you see a man like that go on
And then you have to follow.
                              There can't be
So many men that men have followed so.

And yet, what is it for? What is it for?
What does he think?
                              His hands are lying there
Quiet as stones or shadows in his lap.
His beard is whiter than the dogwood bloom,
But there is nothing ruined in his face,
And nothing beaten in those steady eyes.
If he's grown old, it isn't like a man,
It's more the way a river might grow old.

My mother knew him at old dances once.
She said he liked to joke and he was dark then,
Dark and as straight as he can stand today.
If he would only move, I could go forward.

You see the faces of spear-handling kings
In the old books they taught us from at school;
Big Agamemnon with his curly beard,
Achilles in the cruelty of his youth,
And Œdipus before he tore his eyes.

I'd like to see him in that chariot-rank,
With Traveller pulling at the leader-pole.
I don't think when the winged claws come down
They'll get a groan from him.°
                  So we go on.   370
Under the claws. And he goes on ahead.

The sharp-cut profile moved a fraction now,
The aide-de-camp went forward on his errand.

The years ride out from the world like couriers gone to a throne
That is too far for treaty, or, as it may be, too proud;   375
The years marked with a star, the years that are skin and bone.
The years ride into the night like envoys sent to a cloud.

Perhaps they dismount at last, by some iron ring in the skies,
Dismount and tie their stallions and walk with an armored tread
Where an outlaw queen of the air receives strange embassies   380
Under a tree of wisdom, between the quick and the dead.

Perhaps they are merely gone, as the white foam flies from the bit,
But the sparkling noise of their riding is ever in our ears—
The men who came to the maze without foreknowledge of it,
The losers and the finders, under the riding years.   385

They pass, and the finders lose, the losers find for a space.
There are love and hate and delusion and all the tricks of the maze.
There are always losers and finders. There is no abiding-place
And the years are unreturning. But, here and there, there were days.

Days when the sun so shone that the statue gave its cry   390
And a bird shook wings or a woman walked with a certain mirth,
When the staff struck out a spring from the stones that had long been
    dry,
And the plough moved on from the hilltop, but its share had opened the
    earth.

So the bird is caught for an instant, and so the bird escapes.
The years are not halted by it. The losers and finders wait.   395

364–370 *Big Agamemnon . . . Achilles . . . Œdipus . . .* : figures of epic tragedy: Agamemnon who led the Greeks against Troy; Achilles, the sulky Greek hero;
Œdipus, who unwittingly slew his own father.

The years move on toward the sunset, the tall, far-trafficking shapes,
Each with a bag of news to lay at a ghostly gate.

Riders shaking the heart with the hoofs that will not cease,
Will you never lie stretched in marble, the hands crossed over the breast,
Some with hounds at your feet to show that you passed in peace,   4
And some with your feet on lions?
                            It is time that you were at rest.°

John Vilas clucked to the scurvy rack of bones
Between the shafts. The rickety cart moved on
Like a tired insect, creaking through the dust.
There was another day behind them now   4
And any number of such days ahead
Unrolling like a long block-printed cloth
Patterned with field and stream and snake-rail fence,
And now and then, a flash of cavalry
Fording a backwoods creek; a big, slow star   4
Mounting in silver over lonely woods
While the fire smelled of pine and a cougar cried;
A warm barn, full of the sweet milky breath
Of cows; a lank-haired preacher on a mule;
A red-cheeked woman who rushed after them   4
Armed with a hot and smoking apple-pie
And would not take a penny from the old man
Who held the mended reins as if they were
The vast, slow-sweeping scythe of Time himself
—Old Time and the last children of his age,   4
Drawn in a rattling cart, too poor to thieve,
By a gaunt horse, too ancient to die,
Over a rutted road, day after day,
Returning to the East from whence he came.

It was a portent in the little towns.
The time had bred odd voyagers enough;
Disbanded soldiers, tramping toward the West
In faded army blouses, singing strange songs,

378–401 *Perhaps . . . some iron ring . . . stallions . . . outlaw queen . . . tree of wisdom . . . :* The kaleidoscopic image here reflects a variety of Western mythological material: iron, a charm against evil; horses, carriers of gods; outlaw queens, ruling heaven or purgatory; oracular trees, and so on.

Heroes and chickenthieves, true men and liars,
Some with old wounds that galled them in the rains   430
And some who sold the wounds they never had
Seven times over in each new saloon;
Queer, rootless families, plucked up by war
To blow along the roads like tumbleweed,
Who fed their wild-haired children God knows how   435
But always kept a fierce and cringing cur,
Famished for scraps, to run below the cart;
Horsedealers, draft-evaders, gipsymen;
Crooked creatures of a thousand dubious trades
That breed like gnats from the débris of war;   440
Half-cracked herb-doctor, patent-medicine man
With his accordeon and his inked silk hat;
Sellers of snake-oil balm and lucky rings
And the old, crazy hatless wanderer
Who painted "God is Love" upon the barns   445
And on the rocks, "Prepare to Meet Thy God,"
Lost tribes and maverick nations of the road—
The shiftless people, who are never still
But blow before the wind unquietly
And will so blow, until the last starved cur   450
Yaps at the last fat farmer, and lies down
With buckshot tearing at his ravening heart,
For the slow years to pick his carcass clean
And turn the little chapel of his bones
Into a dust so sifted by the wind   455
No winds that blow can sift it any more.

There were unquiet people on the road,
There were outlandish strays and travellers,
Drifting the little towns from day to day,
Stopping to mend a wheel or patch a shoe,   460
Beg, steal or sleep or write God's judgments out
And then pass on.
         And yet, when these three came,
John Vilas and his daughter and her child,
Like snail-drawn Time, along the dusty track,
The story had gone on ahead of them.   465
And there was something in the rickety cart
Or the gaunt horse or in his driver's eyes
That made a fable of their journeying,

Until you heard John Vilas was that same
Lost Jew that wanders after every war
But cannot die in any, being curst.°
He was the skipper, who first brought the slaves.
He was John Brown, arisen from his stone.
He was the drummer who had lost his way
At Valley Forge and frozen in the snow,
To rove forevermore, a dread old man
Beating a phantom drum across the wind.
He was a dozen such uncanny fetches,°
And, while one must not talk with him too long,
There was no luck at all in crossing him,
Because, and in the end, the man was Time;
White-headed Time, stoop-shouldered on his scythe,
Driving a daughter and a daughter's son
Beyond the war, to some wrought-iron gate
Where they would drop their heavy load at last
—Load of all war and all misfortune's load—
On the green grass of a New England grave
Set on the sea-cliffs, looking toward the sea.

While, for the other tale, the woman's tale,
The heart-faced girl with the enormous eyes,
Roving from little town to little town
Still looking for her soldier—it became
Mixed with each story of such fortune told
Behind drawn blinds, by women, in the dusk,
Until she too grew fabulous as a song
Sung to a beechwood fiddle, and all the old
Barely-recorded chants that are the land
And no one poet's or musician's
—"Old Dan Tucker," "The Belle of Albany,"
The girl who died for love in the high woods
And cruel Barbara Allen in her pride.

So she became a concertina tune
Played in plank taverns by a blind, old man,
A jew's-harp strain, a comb-and-banjo song,

469–471 *that same/Lost Jew* . . . : the legendary Jew condemned to wander the
world until the Second Coming because he chided Christ as He bore the cross to
Calvary.   478 *fetches*: apparitions.

The music of a soapbox violin 505
Shrilled out against the tree-toads and the crickets
Through the hot nights of June. So, though she passed
Unknowing, yet she left the legend-touch
Bright as a splash of sumach still behind
Wherever the gaunt horse pulled on his load. 510
Till, later, those who knew no more of her
Living, than they might know of such removed
And singable creations as "Lord Randall,"
"Colombo," "Little Musgrave," or "Jay Gould's Daughter"
Yet knew enough of her to sing about 515
And fit her name, Melora, to the same
Slow-dropping minor of the water, and earth—
The minor of the country barber-shops
That keens above the grave of Jesse James
And the lone prairie where the cowboy died, 520
The desolate minor of the jail-bird's song,°
Luscious with sorrow, and the minor notes
That tell about the tragic end of such
As loved too well to have such cruel fathers
But were so loving, even in the dust, 525
A red-rose brier grew out of their dead hearts
And twined together in a lover's knot
For all the county people to admire,°
And every lost, waif ballad we have made
And, making, scorned because it smelt of the earth, 530
And now would seek, but cannot make again
So she became a legend and a name.

John Vilas, moving always toward the East,
Upon his last adventure, felt the sun
Strike at his bones and warm them like the last 535
Heat of the wood so long within the fire
That long ago the brightness ate its heart
And yet it lies and burns upon the iron
Unready still to crumble and be cool,

499–521 *Old Dan Tucker . . . the jail-bird's song:* The popular ballads named or alluded to here can be found in various collections; for a general index, see Charles Haywood, *Bibliography of North American Folklore and Folksongs*, New York, 1961.
526–528 *A red-rose brier . . . :* as in American versions of "Barbara Allen."

The white, transmuted log of purest ash   5
Still glowing with a late and borrowed flame.

"This is the sun of age," he thought, "and so
We enter our last journeys with that sun
Which we have watched sink down ten thousand times
Knowing he would arise like Dedalus   5
On the first wings of morning,° and exult
Like our own youth, fresh-risen from its bed
And inexhaustible of space and light.
But now the vessel which could not be filled
By violence or desire or the great storm,   .
Runs over with its weight of little days
And when this sun sinks now, we'll sink with him
And not get up again.
                              I find it fit
That I, who spent the years of my desire
In the lost forest, seeking the lost stone,
With little care for Harriet or the rest,
With little trust in safety or the world,
Should now retrace at last, and in my age,
The exact highway of my youth's escape
From everything that galled it and take on,
Like an old snake resuming his cast skins,
The East I fled, the little towns I mocked,
The dust I thought was shaken from my shoes,
The sleepiness from which I ran away.

Harriet's right and Harriet is just
And Harriet's back in that chintz-curtained room
From which I took her, twenty years ago,
With all the children who were always hers
Because I gave them nothing but my seed
And hardly heard their laughter or their tears
And hardly knew their faces or their names,
Because I listened for the wind in the bough,
Because my daughters were the shooting-stars,
Because my sons were the forgotten streams
And the wild silvers of the wilderness.

545–546 *like Dedalus* [*sic*]/*On the first wings* . . . : Daedalus escaped the Cretan
Labyrinth using wings of wax and feathers.

Men who go looking for the wilderness-stone
And find it, should not marry or beget,
For, if they do so, they may work a wrong
Deeper than any mere intent of pain.
And yet, what I have sought that I have sought   580
And cannot disavouch, although it is
The double knife that cuts the giver's hand
And the unwilling taker's.
                         So I took
My wife, long since, from that chintz-curtained room
And so she has gone back to it again   585
After these years, with children of those years,
And, being kind, she will not teach them there
To curse me, as I think, though if she did
She could find reason in her neighbor's eyes,
And, being Harriet, she will bring them up   590
As all such children should and must be reared
In all such houses, till the end of time,
As if she had not been away at all.
And so, at last, she'll get the peace she should.
And yet, some time, a child may run away.   595

We have had sons and daughters, she and I,
And, of them all, one daughter and one son
In whom our strange bloods married with the true
Marriage that is not merely sheath and sword.
The rest are hers. Those two were partly mine.   600

I taught my son to wander in the woods
Till he could step the hidden paths with me
Light as a whisper, indolent as Spring.
I would not tame his sister when I might,
I let her follow patterans° of leaves,   605
Looking for stones rejected by the wise.
I kept them by me jealously and long.

And yet, the day they took him,° when he sat
There on his horse, before they all rode off,

605 *patterans:* patrins, gypsy trails marked by piles of grass or leaves.   608 *took him:*
took Bent Vilas. See Book VII, line 801.

It was his mother who looked out of him
And it was to his mother that he looked.

That is my punishment and my offence
And that is how it was. And he is dead.
Dead of a fever, buried in the South,
Dead in this war I thought a whirligig°
For iron fools to play with and to kill
Other men's sons, not mine. He's buried deep.
I kept him by me jealously and long.
Well, he walked well, alive. He was my son.
I'll not make tags of him.
                                    We got the news.
She could not stay beside me after that.
I see so clearly why she could not stay.

So I retrace the hard steps of my youth
Now with this daughter, in a rattling cart
Drawn by a horse as lean as famine's self,
And am an omen in the little towns—
Because this daughter has too much of me
To be content with bread made out of wheat.
To be in love and give it up for rest,
To live serene without a knife at heart.

Such is the manner and the bound escape
Of those a disproportion drives unfed
From the world's table, without meat or grace,
Though both are wholesome, but who seek instead
Their solitary victual like the fox.°
And who at last return as I return
In the ironic wagon of the years,
Back to the pasture that they found too green,
Broken of every knowledge but the last
Knowledge of how escape is not a door
But a slow-winding road whose hundred coils
Return upon each other, soon or late

---

615 *whirligig:* a merry-go-round, or any child's toy that spins or whirls. 632–635
those a disproportion drives . . . who seek . . . solitary victual . . . : Compare
Lee (Book IV, line 1499) and Thoreau (Book III, line 978).

—And how and when and under what cold stars
The old wound bleeds beneath the armored mind.

And yet, this journey is not desolate   645
Nor am I desolate in it, as we crawl
Slowly from little town to little town
Always against the sun, and the horse nods,
And there's my daughter talking, and her child
Sleeping or waking, and we stop awhile   650
And then go on awhile, and I can feel
The slow sun creeping through me summerlong.
Until, at times, I fall into a doze
Awake, a daydream without apparitions
And, falling so, inhabit for a space   655
A second childhood, calmer than the first,
But wise in the same fashion, and so touch
For a long, drowsy hour of afternoon,
The ripened thing, the autumn at the heart,
The one full star of evening that is age.   660

Yes, I must be a second child sometimes,
For as we pass and as they watch us pass,
It seems to me their eyes make stories of us
And I can hear those stories murmuring
Like pigeons in a loft when I'm asleep,   665
Till sometimes I must wonder for a while
If I've not changed myself for someone else
Or grown a story without knowing it,
And, with no intermediary death,
Stepped out of flesh and taken on a ghost.   670

For at such times, it almost seems to me
As if I were no longer what I am
But the deluded shade of Peter Rugg
Still looking for his Boston through the storm,°
Or the strange spook of Johnny Appleseed,°   675
Crept out of heaven on a windless night

673–674 *shade of Peter Rugg* . . . : William Austin's story, "Peter Rugg, the Missing Man" (1824), tells of the unending search of a man who swore he could get home to Boston with or without God's will.   675 *Johnny Appleseed*: John Chapman (1775–1843), an orchardist of fact and legend, who roamed the Ohio Valley frontier planting fruit trees.

To see if his wild orchards prosper still
And leave a heap of Baldwins and sweet russets
—Moonglittered, scrubbed with rags of silver cloud
And Indian magic—by the lucky doors   6
Of such good people as take care of them—
While for my daughter, though I know she's real,
She and her story, yet, in the waking dream
She mixes with that song I used to know
About the Spanish lady of old days   6
Who loved the Englishman and sought for him
All through green England in her scarlet shoes,
Knowing no word of English but his name.°

I hear her voice, where the guitar is mixed
With the sweet, jangling mule-bells of Castile,   6
I see her face under its high shell-comb
—And then it is my daughter's—and I wake—
And yet know, even in waking, that we are
Somewhere between a story and a dream.
And so, you see, I find a kind of peace   6
In this last foray, will not rail at the sun,
Eat, drink and sleep, in spite of what is past,
Talk with my daughter, watch the turning skies.
The Spanish lady found her Englishman.
Well, we may find this boy I've half-forgot,   7
Although our story is another story.

So life works in us for a little while
And then the ferment's quiet.
                              So we do
Wrongs much beyond intent, and suffer them.
So we go looking for the wilderness-stone.

I shall smell lilac in Connecticut
No doubt, before I die, and see the clean
White, reticent, small churches of my youth,

684–688 *that song . . . about a Spanish lady . . . :* probably a variant of "Young
Beichan" (Child No. 53C), in which Burd Isbel, opulently clad in scarlet, comes
to England, seeks, finds and marries Young Bekie, an English knight whom she met
in her father's court. Legend connected with this ballad has Isbel, a Saracen prin-
cess, arrive in England knowing only the word "London" and the name of the noble
Christian pilgrim who, seven years before, had promised to marry her. The Bekie of
the legend was Gilbert Beket, father of St. Thomas á Becket.

The gardens full of phlox and mignonette,
The pasture-bars I broke to run away.   710

It was my thought to lie in an uncropped
And savage field no plough had ever scored,
Between a bee-tree and a cast deer-horn.
It was my thought to lie beside a stream
Too secret for the very deer to find,   715
Too solitary for remembrance.
It was a dream. It does not matter now.

Bury me where the soldiers of retreat
Are buried, underneath the faded star,
Bury me where the courtiers of escape   720
Fall down, confronted with their earth again.
Bury me where the fences hold the land
And the sun sinks beyond the pasture-bars
Never to fall upon the wilderness-stone.

And yet I have escaped, in spite of all."   725

Lucy Weatherby smoothed out clothes in a trunk
With a stab at her heart.
                    The trunk was packed to the lid.
There wasn't an empty corner anywhere,
Pack as she would— but the blue dress wouldn't go in.

Of course she'd be getting a lot of new dresses soon   730
And the blue was old—but she couldn't leave it behind.
If only Henry wasn't so selfish, at times!
But Henry was like all brothers and like all men,
Expecting a lady to travel to Canada
With just one trunk and the boxes!
                    It was too bad.   735
He had a trunk of his own for razors and shirts,
And yet she couldn't take two—and there were the hoops;
He kept on fussing because she wouldn't leave them
When she knew he was hoping to take all those silly books,
As if you couldn't buy books wherever you went!   740

She pinched her cheek and stared at the trunk again.
The green could come out, of course, and the blue go in,
But she couldn't bear the idea of leaving the green.

The war, of course, and one thinks so much of the war,
And those terrible Yankees actually at our gates,
In spite of our fine, brave boys and poor Mr. Davis,
In spite of wearing old dresses for two whole years
And sending the servants out to work at the forts,
In spite of the cheers and the songs and the cause and the right.
Only, one must not be selfish. One must be brave.
One must think about Henry's health and be sensible,
And Henry actually thinks we can get away. . . .

The blue or the green? She couldn't decide it yet,
And there were all those letters to write tonight.
She'd simply have to write to Clay and Huger
About Henry's health—and how it just breaks my heart,
But one cannot leave one's sick brother—and afterwards,
One can always send one's address—and I'm sure if they do
We'll give them a real, old-fashioned Richmond welcome,
Though they say that the British leftenants are simply sweet
And every Southern girl is an absolute belle.
They play the "Bonnie Blue Flag" at the dances there,
And Sara Kenefick is engaged to an earl.
She saw herself, for an instant, walking the safe
Street of a calm and British-looking town.
She had on a new dress. Her shoes and her hat were new.
A white-haired, dim-faced man in a British coat
Walked beside her and looked and was listening,
While she told him all about it, and hearing the guns,
And how they'd actually lived without butcher's meat
For weeks and weeks—and the wounded—and General Lee—
And only Henry's health had forced them at last
To leave the dear South. She choked. He patted her hand.
He hoped they would stay in Canada for a while.

The blue or the green? It was dreadfully hard to choose,
And with all the letters to write—and Jim Merrihew
And that nice Alabama Major—
                              She heard the bells
Ring for a wedding, but this was a different groom,
This was a white-haired man with stars on his coat,
This was an Order° wrapped in an English voice.

780 *an Order:* a title.

Honey, sugar-lump honey I love so dearly,
You have eluded the long pursuit that sought you,
You have eluded the hands that would so enclose you
And with strange passion force you.
                              What was this passion?
We do not know, you and I, but we would not bear it   785
And are gone free.
                    So at last, if fair girls must marry,
As young girls should, it is after another fashion
And not with youth but wisely.
                              So we are ransomed,
And I am yours forever and you are mine,
Honey, sugar-lump honey.
                              So we attain   790
The white-haired bridegrooms with the stars on their coats
And yet have the beaus to dance with, for we like dancing,
So all the world finds our wifely devotion charming,
So we play all day in the heat of the sun.

She held the blue dress under her chin once more   795
And smoothed it with one white hand. Then she put it down
Smiling a little. No, it couldn't go in,
But she would see if she couldn't help Henry pack,
And if she did, the blue could go with his shirts.
It hardly mattered, leaving some shirts behind.   800

    Sherman's buzzin' along to de sea,
    Jubili, Jubilo!
    Sherman's buzzin' along to de sea,
    Like Moses ridin' on a bumblebee,
    Settin' de prisoned and de humble free!   805
    Hit's de year of Jubilo! °

    Massa was de whale wid de big inside,
    Jubili, Jubilo!
    Massa was de lion and de lion's hide.

806 *year of Jubilo!*: the year of jubilee, established by Hebrew law as an exalted
sabbatical to be observed every fiftieth year and marked, among other ways, by
emancipation of slaves. See Leviticus 25:8–17.

But de Lord God smacked him in his hardheart pride,
And de whale unswallered, and de lion died!
Hit's de year of Jubilo!

Oh, hit don't matter if you's black or tan,
Jubili, Jubilo!
Hit don't matter if you's black or tan,
When you hear de noise of de freedom-ban'
You's snatched baldheaded to de Promise Lan',
Hit's de year of Jubilo!

Oh, hit don't matter if you pine or ail,
Jubili, Jubilo!
Hit don't matter if you pine or ail,
Hit don't matter if you's been in jail,
De Lord's got mercy for your mumblin' tale!
Hit's de year of Jubilo!

Every nigger's gwine to own a mule,
Jubili, Jubilo!
Every nigger's gwine to own a mule,
An' live like Adam in de Golden Rule,
An' send his chillun to de white-folks' school!
In de year of Jubilo!

Fall down on your knees and bless de Lord,
Jubili, Jubilo!
Fall down on your knees and bless de Lord,
Dat chased old Pharaoh wid a lightnin'-sword,
And rose up Izzul fum de withered gourd,
Hit's de year of Jubilo!

Shout thanksgivin' and shout it loud!
Jubili, Jubilo!
Shout thanksgivin' and shout it loud,
We was dead and buried in de Lazrus-shroud,
But de Lord came down in a glory-cloud,
An' He gave us Jubilo!

———

So Sherman goes from Atlanta to the sea
Through the red-earth heart of the land, through the pine-smoke haze

Of the warm, last months of the year.

                             In the evenings   845
The skies are green as the thin, clear ice on the pools
That melts to water again in the heat of noon.
A few black trees are solemn against those skies.
The soldiers feel the winter touching the air
With a little ice.

                 But when the sun has come up,   850
When they halt at noonday, mopping their sweaty brows,
The skies are blue and soft and without a cloud.

Strange march, half-war, half trooping picnic-parade,
Cutting a ruinous swathe through the red-earth land;
March of the hardy bummers and coffee-coolers   855
Who, having been told to forage, loot as they can
And leave a wound that rankles for sixty years.
March of the honest, who did not loot when they could
And so are not remembered in Southern legend.
Rough-bearded Sherman riding the red-earth roads,   860
Writing home that his rascals are fat and happy,
Saying or else not saying that war is hell,°
Saying he almost trembles himself to think
Of what will happen when Charleston falls in the hands
Of those same rascals—and yet, when we read that march   865
Hardly the smoking dragon he has been called,
But the mere rough-handed man who rode with a hard
Bit through the land, unanxious to spare his foe
Nor grimly anxious to torture for torture's sake,
Smashing this and that,—and yet, in the end,   870
Giving such terms to the foe struck down at last
That the men in Washington disavow them and him
For over-kindness.°

               So now, through the pine-smoke Fall,

---

862 *Saying . . . war is hell:* There is no record of his using this particular expression publicly until long after the war. He did, however, on several occasions, call war terrible and barbaric; and on September 12, 1864, he wrote the mayor of Atlanta, "War is a cruelty and you cannot refine it." See W. T. Sherman, *Memoirs,* II, 126. 872–873 *disavow them and him/For over-kindness:* Nine days after Appomattox, Sherman offered J. E. Johnston terms designed to encourage surrender of his entire army. Coming a few days after Lincoln's assassination, the terms were disapproved in Washington and Sherman bitterly denounced. On April 26, Johnston surrendered under the same terms given Lee.

The ATLANTA CAMPAIGN and SHERMAN'S MARCH TO THE SEA

The long worm of his army creeps toward Savannah
Leaving its swathe behind.
                In the ruined gardens   87
The buried silver lies well hid in the ground.
A looter pocks bullet-marks in an old oil-portrait.
A woman wails and rages against the thieves
Who carry her dead child's clothes on their drunken bayonets.
A looter swings from a pine tree for thefts too crude.   880
A fresh-faced boy gets scars he will carry long
Hauling a crippled girl from a burning house,
But gets no thanks but hate from the thing he saved,
And everywhere,
A black earth stirs, a wind blows over black earth,   885
A wind blows into black faces, into old hands
Knotted with long rheumatics, cramped on the hoe,
Into old backs bent double over the cotton,
The wind of freedom, the wind of jubilo.

They stray from the lost plantations like children strayed.   890
Grinning and singing, following the blue soldiers,
They steal from the lonesome cabins like runaways
Laden with sticks and bundles and conjur-charms;
A huge black mother carries her sucking child
Wrapped in a quilt, a slim brown girl and her lover   895
Wander November woods like Adam and Eve,
Living on roots and rabbits and liberty,
An old grey field hand dimly plods through the mud,
Looking for some vague place he has heard about
Where Linkum sits at a desk in his gold silk hat   900
With a bag of silver dollars in either hand
For every old grey field hand that comes to him,
All God's chillun got shoes there and fine new clothes,
All God's chillun got peace there and roastin'-ears,
Hills of barbecue, rivers of pot-licker,   905
Nobody's got to work there, never no more.

His feet are sore with the road but he stumbles on
A hundred, a thousand others stumble as he,
Chanting, dizzied, drunken with a strange fever,
A child's delight, a brightness too huge to grasp,   910
The hidden nation, untaught, unrecognized,
Free at last, but not yet free with the free,

Ignorant, joyful, wronged, child-minded and searching,
Searching the army's road for this new wild thing
That means so much but can't be held in the hand,   91
That must be there, that yet is so hard to find,
This dream, this pentecost° changing, this liberty.

Some wander away to strange death or stranger life,
Some wander awhile and starve and come back at last,
Some stay by the old plantation but will not work   92
To the great disgust of masters and mistresses,
Sing idly, gamble, sleep through the lazy hours,
Waiting for friendly heaven to rain them down
The mule and the forty acres of their desire.
Some, faithful beyond the bond that they never signed,   92
Hold to that bond in ruin as in the sun,
Steal food for a hungry mistress, keep her alive,
Keep the house alive, try to pick the weeds from the path,
Gather the wood and chop it and make the fire,
With pitying scorn for the runaway sheep of freedom,   93
Freedom's a ghost and freedom's a foolish talk,
What counts is making the fire as it should be made. . . .
Oh, blackskinned epic, epic with the black spear,
I cannot sing you, having too white a heart,
And yet, some day, a poet will rise to sing you   93
And sing you with such truth and mellowness,
—Deep mellow of the husky, golden voice
Crying dark heaven through the spirituals,
Soft mellow of the levee roustabouts,
Singing at night against the banjo-moon—   94
That you will be a match for any song
Sung by old, populous nations in the past,
And stand like hills against the American sky,
And lay your black spear down by Roland's horn.°

Meanwhile, in Georgia, the scythe of the march mows on,   94
The Southern papers discount it as best they can.
Lincoln is anxious, Davis more anxious still.
The war is in its last winter of strife and pain.

---

917 *pentecost:* divinely bestowed. 944 *Roland's horn:* an allusion to the French
Chanson de Roland, suggesting the epic quality of the experience of the American
Negro.

Cudjo buried the silverware
On a graveyard night of sultry air   950
While the turned sods smelled of the winter damp
And Mary Lou Wingate held the lamp.
They worked with a will. They did not speak.
The light was yellow. The light was weak.
A tomb-light casting a last, brief flame   955
Over the grave of Wingate fame.
The silver bowl of the Wingate toasts,
The spoons worn hollow by Wingate ghosts,
Sconce and ladle and bead-rimmed plate
With the English mark° and the English weight,   960
The round old porringer, dented so
By the first milk-teeth of the long ago,
And the candlesticks of Elspeth Mackay
That she brought with her youth on her wedding-day
To light the living of Wingate Hall   965
While the mornings break and twilights fall
And the night and the river have memories. . . .

There was a spook in Cudjo's eyes
As he lowered the chests where they must lie
And patted the earth back cunningly.   970
He knew each chest and its diverse freight
As a blind man knows his own front gate
And, decade by decade and piece by piece,
With paste and shammy and elbow-grease,
He had made them his, by the pursed-up lips   975
And the tireless, polishing fingertips,
Till now as he buried them, each and all,
What he buried was Wingate Hall,
Himself and the moon and the toddy-sippers,
The river mist and the dancing-slippers,   980
Old Marse Billy and Mary Lou
And every bit of the world he knew,
Master and lady and house and slave,
All smoothed down in a single grave.
He was finished at length. He shook his head.   985
"Mistis, reckon we's done," he said.

960 *English mark:* hallmark identifying the maker and purity of the silver.

They looked at each other, black and white,
For a slow-paced moment across the light.

Then he took the lamp and she smoothed her shawl
And he lit her back to the plundered Hall,
To pray, with her old serene observance
For the mercy of God upon faithful servants
And a justice striking all Yankees dead
On her cold, worn knees by the great carved bed,
Where she had lain by a gentleman's side,
Wife and mother and new-come bride,
Sick with the carrying, torn with the borning,
Waked by the laughter on Christmas morning,
Through love and temper and joy and grief,
And the years gone by like the blowing leaf.

She finished her prayer with Louisa's child,
And, when she had risen, she almost smiled.
She struck her hand on the bedstead head,
"They won't drive me from my house," she said,
As the wood rang under her wedding-ring.
Then she stood for a moment, listening,
As if for a step, or a gentleman's name,
But only the gnats and the echoes came.

Cudjo, being less fortified,
Covered his ears with his hands and tried
To shut the noise of the risen wind
Out of the trouble of his mind.
He thought, "Ain't right for dat wind to blow.
She wasn't blowing awhile ago.
Jus' riz up fum de earth somewhere
When we buried dat orphan silver dere.
Got to hide it, and so we tried,
But silver like dat don't like to hide,
Silver's ust to be passed aroun'
Don't like lyin' in lonesome groun',
Wants to come back to de Hall, all right.
Silver, I always shone you bright,
You could see yo'self in de shine—
Silver, it wasn't no fix of mine!
Don't you come projeckin' after me!"

His eyes were shut but he still could see
The slow chests rising out of the ground
With an ominous clatter of silver sound,
The locks undoing, the bags unfastening,
And every knife and platter and spoon   1030
Clinking out of the grave and hastening
Back to the Hall, in the witches' moon;
And the wind in the chimney played such tricks
That it was no wind, be it soft or loud,
But Elspeth seeking her candlesticks   1035
All night long in her ruffled shroud,
The deep voice haunting the ocean-shell
To give her judgment and weave her spell,
"Thrift and love for the house and the chief
And a scone on the hob for the son of grief,   1040
But a knife in the ribs for the pleasant thief." °

Cudjo heard it, and Cudjo shook,
And Cudjo felt for the Holy Book,
And the wind blew on without peace or rest,
Blowing the straws from the dried-up nest.   1045

Bailey, tramping along with Sherman's bummers,
Grumbled and found life pleasant and hummed his tune.
He was well, the blood ran in him, he ate for ten,
He and the gang had salvaged a wall-eyed nig
To fix their victuals—and if the captain was on,   1050
The captain had a blind eye.
                          Last night it was turkey,
The night before it was duck—well, you couldn't expect
Such things to keep on forever, but while they did
It was pretty soft—it was war like it ought to be.
The Old Man marched 'em hard, but that was all right,   1055
The Old Man knew his job and the nig was a buster
And the gang was as good a gang as you'd hope to find,
None of your coffee-coolers and straggle-tails
But a regular gang that ran like an eight-day clock.
Oh it was gravy, it was the real duck soup,   1060
Marchin' into Atlanta after the fight

1039–1041 *Thrift and love* . . . : Compare Book I, lines 252–254.

And then this marchin'—well, they were due for it,
And he was a sergeant now.
                              And up in his pack
Were souvenirs for the red-haired widow in Cairo,
Some of 'em bought and some just sort of picked up
But not a damn one stolen, to call it stealin'.
He wasn't a coffee-cooler or a slick Susio.°
Poor little kid—she'd had a pretty tough time—
Cry like a fool when she gets a squint at that brooch—
They said you couldn't tell about widows much,
But what the hell—he wasn't a barnyard virgin—
He liked a woman who'd been over the bumps
And kept her get-up-and-git and her sassiness.
Spitfire-sweetie, you're my valentine now,
Bet the kids have red hair—well you can't help that—
But they'll all look like Poppa or he'll know why.

He mused a moment, thinking of Ellyat now.
There was another kid and a crazy kid,
Sort of missed him, hope he's gettin' it soft,
Must have got a banger at Gettysburg,
Wrote me a letter a couple of months ago,
Maybe six, I dunno, I sort of forget.
Ought to give him his old spread-eagle° now,
Darn good kid, but done enough for his pay.
Hope he finds that girl he was talkin' about,
Sounds like a pretty good piece for a storm-and-strife,°
Skinny, though—we like 'em more of a weight,
Don't we, Carrots?
                    Well, it's all in a life.
Ought to write him sometime if we get a chance,
Wish we was West—we'd have him out to the weddin',
Me and Bessie, show him the Cairo girls,
Hand him the fireman's grip and give him a time.

1046–1067 bummers . . . coffee-coolers . . . slick Susio: During the march from
Atlanta to Savannah and Charleston, organized teams of foragers (bummers) supplied
food for the Union army by carrying out Sherman's order to "forage freely." Those
who took advantage of the situation, to shirk duties, pillage, or steal were known
variously as "coffee-coolers," "slickers," and so on. See, for example, Daniel Oakey in
Battles and Leaders, IV, 671–679.   1083 spread-eagle: The army discharge certifi-
cate bore the eagle emblem.   1086 storm-and-strife: wife.

His heart was overflowing with charity,
But his throat was dry as the bottom of his canteen.
There was a big, white house, some way from the road. . . .   1095

He found his captain, saluted and put his question.
The captain's eyes were satiric but not displeased.
"All right, Sergeant, take your detail and forage,
We're running low on bacon, it seems to me,
And if you happen to find a pigeon or two   1100
Remember the Colonel's penchant for pigeon-pie.
But don't waste time and don't put your hopes too high,
The Nth Corps must have gone by there hours ago
And they're the biggest thieves in this whole, wide army.
"You'll be back, in ranks, all sober, in just two hours   1105
Or you won't have stripes. And if I find one more man
Trying to take a pet with him on this march,
I don't care if it's only a treetoad, I'll skin him alive."

So Bailey came to the door of Wingate Hall,
With the high wind blowing against him and gave his orders   1110
"Make it quick now, boys—don't cut any monkeyshines,
But be sure and get the pigeons if they're around.
Clark, you and Ellis stay with me by the door,
I'm going to talk to the house if there's anyone left."

He knocked and called. There was a long, heavy silence.   1115
"Hey you, the house!" The silence made him feel queer.
He cursed impatiently and pushed at the door.
It swung wide open. He turned to Ellis and Clark.
"I'm goin' in," he said. "If you hear me yell
Come in bilin'."
                    They watched him with mocking eyes.   1120
"Wish to hell they'd make me a sergeant, Clark,"
"A three-stripe souvenir sergeant."
                              "Aw, hell," said Clark,
"Bailey's all right. He'll let us in on the juice
If there's any lawful juice that a man could get."
"Sure he's all right. Who says that he ain't all right!"   1125
"But all the same, he's a sergeant."
                              Bailey, meanwhile
Was roving like a lost soul through great, empty rooms

And staring at various objects that caught his eye.
Funny old boy with a wig, hung up on the wall,
Queer sort of chairs, made your hands feel dirty to touch 'em
Though they were faded.

                    Everything faded and old
And quiet—and the wind blowin'—he moved as on tiptoe
Though he couldn't say why he did.

                        Old workbasket there.
He opened it idly—most of the things were gone
But there was a pair of little, gold-mounted scissors
Made like a bird, with the blades the beak of the bird.
He picked it up and opened and shut the blades.
Hadn't rusted—sort of handsome and queer—
Bessie would certainly like it—

                    He held it a minute.
Wouldn't take up any room. Then he frowned at the thing.
"Aw hell," he said, "I got enough souvenirs.
I ain't no damn coffee-cooler."

He started to put the scissors back in the case
And turned to face a slight grey-headed old woman
Dressed in black, with eyes that burned through his skin
And a voice that cut at his mind like a rawhide whip,
Calling him fifty different kinds of a thief
And Yankee devil and liar and God knows what,
Tearing the throat of her dress with her thin old hands
And telling him he could shoot her down like a dog
But he'd steal her children's things over her dead body.
My God, as if you went around shootin' old women
For fun, my God!

               He couldn't even explain.
She was like all of 'em, made him sick in his lunch.
"Oh hell," he yelled. "Shut up about your damn scissors,
This a war, old lady!"

                  "That's right," she said,
"Curse a helpless female, you big, brave soldier."
Well, what was a man to do?

                  He got out of the house,
Sore and angry, mean as a man could feel,
But her voice still followed, reviling, making him burn.
Now, where in hell was that detail?

                  He saw them now,

All except Clark and Ellis, gathered around
A white-polled° nigger wringing his hands and weeping.
One man had a neck-wrung pigeon stuffed in his blouse.
Well, that was something.
                              He laid his hand on the nigger.   1165
"Hey, Uncle, where's the well? You folks got a well?"
But the nigger just kept on crying like an old fool.
"He thinks we're goin' to scalp him," said one of the men,
"I told him twict that he's free but the shine won't listen.
I give him some money, too, but he let it drop.   1170
The rest of 'em run away when the army came."

"Well, tell him he's safe and make him rustle some water,
I'm dry as a preacher's tongue. Where's Ellis and Clark?"

He found Clark solemnly prodding the hard dirt floor
Of a negro cabin, while Ellis lighted the task   1175
With a splinter of burning pine.
                              His rage exploded
In boiling lava. They listened respectfully.
"And next time, I give you an order," he ended up,
"Why you——— ——— ———"
                              Clark wiped his face with his sleeve.
"Sorry, Sergeant," he said in an awed, low voice.   1180
"Well you better be! What the hell do you think you're at,
Playin' tit-tat-toe or buryin' somebody's dog?"
"Well, Sergeant," said Ellis, humbly, "I allus heard
They buried stuff, sometimes, under these here cabins.
Well, I thought we could take a look—well—"
                              "Huh?" said Bailey.   1185
He seized the torch and looked at the trodden floor
For an instant. Then his pride and his rage returned.
"Hell's fire!" he said, and threw the splinter aside,
"That's just about what you would think, you and Clark!
Come out of there on the double! Yes, I said you!"   1190

They were halfway down the driveway when Ellis spoke.
"Sergeant," he said. "There's somethin' on fire back there."
Bailey stopped—looked back—a smoke-puff climbed in the sky
And the wind was high.
                    He hesitated a moment.

163 *white-polled:* white-haired.

The cabin must have caught from the burning splinter.
Then he set his jaw. Well, suppose the cabin had caught?
—Damned old woman in black who called him a thief.
Serve her right if all her cabins burnt up.
The house wouldn't catch—and here they were, losing time—

"Oh well," he said. "That nigger'll put it out.
It ain't our detail—mosey along with it there—
The Cap won't mind if we run it on him a little,
Now we got the Colonel's squab, but we better step."

They hurried along. The smoke rose higher behind them.
The wind blew the burning flakes on Wingate Hall.

Sally Dupré stared out of her bedroom window
As she had stared many times at that clump of trees.
And saw the smoke rise out of it, thick and dark.

They hadn't had much trouble at Appleton.
It was too far off the main road—and, as for the slaves,
Those who straggled after the troops were better away.
The aunts complained, of course—well, the aunts complained.
They were old, and, at least, they had a man in the house,
Even if the man were but crippled old Uncle Paul.
It was the end of the world for him and the aunts.
It wasn't for her.
                    The years had worn on her youth,
Much had worn, but not the crook from her smile
Nor the hidden lightness of her narrow feet.

She looked at the smoke again, and her eyes were grey
And then they were black as that smoke. She felt the fire
Run on her flesh. "It's Wingate Hall and it's burning?
House that married my lover before he saw me,
You are burning, burning away in a little smoke,
Burning the wall between us with your fierce burning,
Burning the strife between us in your black flame,
Burning down."
                    She trod for an instant there
A light glass floor of omen, brighter than sleet
Over a hurtless fire.
                    Then she caught her breath.

The flesh was cool, the blackness died from her eyes.
"We'll have to get the slaves if the slaves will go.   1230
I know Ned will. I'm not sure about Bob or Jim.
Uncle Paul must give me his pistol. I'll have to start them.
They won't go without me. The aunts won't be any use.
Why wouldn't she come over here when we all first heard?
I know why she wouldn't. I never liked her so much.   1235
Hurry, Sally!"
              She ran downstairs like the wind.

They worked at the Hall that night till the dawn came up,
Two smoke-stained women, Cudjo and Bob and Ned,
But when the dawn had risen, the Hall was gone
And Elspeth's candles would not light it again.   1240

Wingate wearily tried to goad
A bag of bones° on a muddy road
Under the grey and April sky°
While Bristol hummed in his irony
"If you want a good time, jine the cavalry! °   1245
Well, we jined it, and here we go,
The last event in the circus-show,
The bareback boys in the burnin' hoop
Mounted on cases of chicken-croup,
The rovin' remains of the Black Horse Troop!   1250
Though the only horse you could call real black
Is the horsefly sittin' on Shepley's back,
But, women and children, do not fear,
They'll feed the lions and us, next year.
And, women and children, dry your eyes,   1255
The Southern gentleman never dies.
He just lives on by his strength of will
Like a damn ole rooster too tough to kill
Or a brand-new government dollar-bill
That you can use for a trousers-patch   1260
Or lightin' a fire, if you've got a match,

---

42 A *bag of bones:* See note, Book II, line 47.   1243 *April sky:* between April
nd 9, 1865. Petersburg has fallen, Richmond has been abandoned, and Lee's army
in its final retreat toward Appomattox.   1245 "*If you want a good time, jine
cavalry!*": the marching song of Jeb Stuart's cavalry. See Book II, line 1206.

Or makin' a bunny a paper collar,
Or anythin' else—except a dollar.

Old folks, young folks, never you care,
The Yanks are here and the Yanks are there,
But no Southern gentleman knows despair.
He just goes on in his usual way,
Eatin' a meal every fifteenth day
And showin' such skill in his change of base
That he never gets time to wash his face
While he fights with a fury you'd seldom find
Except in a Home for the Crippled Blind,
And can whip five Yanks with a palmleaf hat,
Only the Yanks won't fight like that.

Ladies and gentlemen, here we go!
The last event in the minstrel show!
Georgia's genuine gamboliers,°
(Ladies and gentlemen, dry those tears!)
See the sergeant, eatin' the hay
Of his faithful horse, in a lifelike way!
See the general, out for blood,
And try to tell the man from the mud!
See the platoon in its savage lair,
A half-grown boy on a wheezy mare.
Ladies and gentlemen, pass the hat!
We've got one trick that you won't forget,
'The Vanishin' Commissariat' °
And nobody's found the answer yet!
Here we go, here we go,
The last parade of the circus-show,
Longstreet's orphans, Lee's everlastin's
Half cast-iron and half corn-pone,
And if gettin' to heaven means prayer and fastin's
We ought to get there on the fasts alone.

Here we go with our weddin' bells,
Mr. Davis's immortelles,°
Mr. Lincoln's Thanksgivin' turkey,

1277 *gamboliers:* dancers.   1287 *Commissariat:* supply system.   1296 *immortelles:*
flowers which retain their color and shape when dried.

Run right ragged but actin' perky,
Chased right handsome, but still not carved,
—We had fleas, but the fleas all starved.   1300
We had rations and new recruits,
Uniforms and cavalry-boots,
Must have mislaid, for we can't find 'em.
They all went home with their tails behind 'em.
Here we are, like the old man's mutton,   1305
Pretty well sheared, but not past buttin',
Lee's last invalids, heart and hand,
All wropped up in a woolen band,
Oh, Dixie land. . . . oh, Dixie land! . . ."
He tossed his hat and caught it again   1310
And Wingate recalled, without grief or pain
Or any quietus but memory
Lucy, under another sky,
White and gold as a lily bed,
Giving toy ribbons to all her dead.   1315
She had been pretty and she was gone,
But the dead were here—and the dead rode on,
Over a road of mud and stones,
Each one horsed on a bag of bones.

Lucy, you carried a golden head,   1320
But I am free of you, being dead.
Father's back in that cluttered hall
Where the beds are solid from wall to wall
And the scrubbed old floor has a rusty stain.
He'll never ride with the dogs again,   1325
Call Bathsheba or Planter's Child
In the old, high quaver that drives them wild
—Rocketing hounds on a red-hot scent—
After such wounds, men do not ride.
I think that his heart was innocent.   1330
I know he rode by the riverside,
Calling Blue Ruin or Georgia Lad
With the huntsman's crotchet° that sets them mad.
His face was ruddy—his face is white—
I wonder if Father died last night?   1335

1333 *crotchet:* musical note; here, the huntsman's call.

That cloud in the sky is a thunderhead.
The world I knew is a long time dead.

Shepley looks like a knife on guard,
Reckon he's taking it mighty hard,
Reckon he loved her and no mistake,
Glad it isn't my wedding cake,
Wainscott oughtn't to plague him so,
Means all right but he doesn't know.
"Here we go, here we go,
The last events of the minstrel-show!"

Shepley suddenly turned his head.
"Mr. Bristol's funny," he said.
The voice was flat with an injury.
Bristol stared at him, puzzledly.
"What's the matter with you, Huger?
Lost your dog or your rosy cheeks?
Haven't been human for weeks and weeks.
I'll sing you a hymn, if you're so inclined,
But the rest of the boys don't seem to mind.
Are you feelin' poorly or just unkind?"

Shepley looked at him with the blind
Eyes of a man too long at war
And too long nursing a secret sore.
"Mr. Bristol's funny," said he,
In a level voice of enmity.
Bristol laughed, but his face grew red.
"Well, if you take it like that—" he said.

"Here we go, here we go,
The old Confederate minstrel-show!"
His mouth was merry, he tossed his hat,
"Belles skedaddled and left us flat—"

Shepley leaned from his swaying hips
And flicked him over the singing lips.
"Will you take it?" he said, "or let it go?
You never could sing for shucks, you know."
The color drained out of Bristol's face.
He bowed with an odd, old-fashioned grace.

"Name your people and choose your land,
I don't take a slap from God's own hand.
Mr. Shepley, your servant, sir."   1375

They stared at each other across a blur.
The troop stared with them, halted and still.

A rider lunged from the top of the hill,
Dusty man with a bandaged hand
Spilling his orders.
            "Who's in command?   1380
Well, it doesn't signify, more or less.
You can hold the Yanks for a while, I guess.
Make 'em think you're the whole rear guard
If you can do it—they're pressin' hard
And somebody's got to lose some hair.   1385
Keep 'em away from that bend down there
As long as a horse or a man can stand.
You might give 'em a charge, if you think you can,
And we'll meet sometime in the Promised Land,
For I can't spare you another man."   1390

Bristol whistled, a shrill, sweet slur.
"Beg to acknowledge the orders, sir.
Boys, we're booked for the shivaree.°
Give our regards to the infantry
And tell Marse Robert, with fortitude,   1395
We stacked up pretty as hickory-wood.
While might I ask, while bein' polite,
How many Yank armies we aim to fight?"

"Well," said the other, "about a corps.°
Roughly speakin'—there may be more."   1400

"Thank you," said Bristol, "that's mighty sweet,
You will not remain at the mourner's seat?
No sir? Well, I imagined not,
For from this time hence it will be right hot."
He turned to Shepley with his punctilious   1405

393 *shivaree:* a raucous mock serenade.   1399 *about a corps:* probably the II or
I Union Corps, which together cut off the Confederate rearguard on April 6.

Air of the devil turned supercilious
When the damned display a vulgar nettlement.
"Sir, I regret that our little settlement
Must be postponed for a fitter season,
But war and necessity know no reason,
And should we survive in this comin' fracas
I'll do you the honors—you damned old jackass!"

Shepley grinned at his sometime friend.
They took the cover they must defend.

Wingate, fighting from tree to tree,
Felt a red-hot skewer surgeon his knee
And felt his shoulder hitting the ground.
He rolled on his side and made a sound,
Dimly seeing through failing sight
The last brief passion of his last fight.
One Cotter dying, the other dead
With the brains run out of his shattered head.
Stuart Cazenove trying to squirm
His way to the road like a scythe-cut worm,
Weakly humming "Cadet Rousselle",°
Shot through the belly and half in hell,
While Shepley croaked through a bloody spray,
"Come on, you bastards, and get your pay.
We've fought you mounted and fought you standin'
And I got a hole I could put my hand in—
And they're comin', Wayne—and it hurts my head—"
Bristol looked at him, lying dead.
"Got the start of me, Shep," he said.
"Dirty welchers, killin' Huger
Before we could settle up properly."
He stooped to the body and took its pistol
And Wingate saw, through a rising mist,
The last, cold madness of Wainscott Bristol,
Walking out like a duellist
With his torn coat buttoned up at the throat
As if it were still the broadcloth coat
Duellists button to show no fleck
Of telltale white at the wrists or neck.

1425 *"Cadet Rousselle"*: a ballad popular in France in the late eighteenth century
but never widely known in the United States.

He stepped from his cover and dropped his hat.
"Yanks, come get it!" he said and spat   1445
While his pistols cracked with a single crack,
"Here we go on the red dog's back!
High, low, jack and the goddam game." °
And then the answering volley came.

Wingate waked from a bloodshot dream.   1450
They were touching his leg and he heard his scream.
A blue-chinned man said a word or two.
"Well now, Johnny, you ought to do
Till the sawbones comes with his movin'-van,
And you're lucky you're livin', little man.   1455
But why the hell did you act so strict,
Fightin' like that when you know you're licked,
And where's the rest of your damn brigade?"
The voice died out as the ripples fade
Into the flow of the running stream,   1460
And Wingate sank to the bloodshot dream.

—————

Richmond is fallen—Lincoln walks in its streets,
Alone, unguarded, stops at George Pickett's house,
Knocks at George Pickett's door. George Pickett has gone
But the strange, gaunt figure talks to George Pickett's wife   1465
A moment—she thinks she is dreaming, seeing him there—
"Just one of George Pickett's old friends, m'am."
                                                    He turns away.
She watches him down the street with wondering eyes.°
The red light falls upon him from the red sky.
Houses are burning, strange shadows flee through the streets.   1470
A gang of loafers is broaching a liquor-barrel

<hr>

1447-1448: *red dog's back!/High, low, jack . . .* : allusions to red dog poker and
casino, card games popular with gamblers.   1463-1468 *Pickett's house . . .* : Compare Mrs. Pickett's account: Lincoln "came to the old Pickett home to hunt up
his friend and former partner, the General's uncle . . . [see note, Book VII, line
969] 'Is this George Pickett's place?' 'Yes, sir,' I answered, 'but he is not here.' 'I
know that, ma'am,' he replied, 'but I just wanted to see the place. I am Abraham
Lincoln.' 'The President!' I gasped. . . . 'No, ma'am; . . . just Abraham Lincoln;
George's old friend,' " *The Heart of a Soldier*, p. 15.

In a red-lit square. The liquor spills on the cobbles.
They try to scoop it up in their dirty hands.°

A long, blue column tramps by, shouting "John Brown's Body."
The loafers scatter like wasps from a half-sucked pear,
Come back when the column is gone.

           A half-crazy slave
Mounts on a stoop and starts to preach to the sky.
A white-haired woman shoos him away with a broom.
He mumbles and reels to the shadows.

           A general passes,
His escort armed with drawn sabres. The sabres shine
In the red, low light.

           Two doors away, down the street,
A woman is sobbing the same long sob all night
Beside a corpse with crossed hands.

           Lincoln passes on.

On the way to Appomattox, the ghost of an army
Staggers a muddy road for a week or so
Through fights and weather, dwindling away each day.
For a brief while Davis is with them° and then he goes
To be tracked by his private furies into the last
Sad farce of his capture, and, later, to wear his chains.°
Benjamin is with them for some few days,
Still sleek, still lively, still impeccably dressed,
Taking adversity as he took success
With the silk-ribbed fan of his slight, unchangeable smile.
Behind that fan, his mind weighs war and defeat
In an old balance.

           One day he is there and smiling.
The next he is gone as if he had taken fernseed °

1472–1473 *a red-lit square. The liquor spills* . . . : Compare, "The Fall of Richmond," Clement Sulivane, *Battles and Leaders*, IV, 725–726: "Richmond [was] like a blaze of day. . . . The gutters ran whisky, and it was lapped as it flowed down the streets. . . ."   1487 *Davis is with them*: not on the way to Appomattox. On April 2, Davis, accompanied by miscellaneous military forces, removed the Confederate government and treasury to Danville, Virginia. Upon Lee's surrender (April 9), he again moved southward.   1489 *capture, and* . . . *chains*: Finally persuaded that the war was lost, Davis attempted to escape with a party of twenty. He was captured in Georgia on May 10, imprisoned at Fortress Monroe (see note Book IV, line 853), and, over his violent objections, put in fetters.   1490–1496 *Benjamin . . . taken fernseed*: In legend, fernseed makes one invisible; Benjamin disappeared from Davis' group one morning and made good his escape, first to the Bahamas by open boat, then to England.

And walked invisible so through the Union lines.
You will not find that smile in a Northern prison
Though you seek from now till Doomsday. It is too wise.
You will find the chief with the chin like John Calhoun's,   1500
Gadfly-stung, tormented by hostile fate,
You will find many gallant blockheads and tragic nobles
But not the black-eyed man with life in his eyes.

So this week, this death-march, these final, desperate strokes,
These last blood-spots on the harvest—until, at length,   1505
The battered grey advance guard, hoping to break
A last, miraculous hole through the closing net,
Sees Ord's whole corps° as if risen out of the ground
Before them, blocking all hope.
                          The letters are written,
The orders given, while stray fighting goes on   1510
And grey men and blue men die in odd clumps of ground
Before the orders can reach them.
                          An aide-de-camp°
Seeks a suitable house for the council from a chance farmer.°
The first one found is too dirty to please his mind,
He picks another.
                          The chiefs and the captains meet,°   1515
Lee erect in his best dress uniform,
His dress-sword hung at his side and his eyes unaltered.
Chunky Grant in his mudsplashed private's gear
With the battered stars on his shoulders.
                          They talk a while
Of Mexico and old days.
                          Then the terms are stated.   1520
Lee finds them generous, says so, makes a request.
His men will need their horses for the spring-ploughing.
Grant assents at once.
                          There is no parade of bright swords
Given or taken. Grant saw that there should not be.

1508 *Ord's whole corps:* the Union XXIV Corps, at one time commanded by Major
General Edward O. C. Ord, now included in Ord's Army of the James.   1512
aide-de-camp: Colonel Charles Marshall.   1513 *chance farmer:* Wilmer McLean,
who had owned a farm fought over during First Bull Run. See map, p. 92. He
had moved to Appomattox to avoid the Washington-Richmond battle arena.   1515–
1547 *The chiefs and captains meet . . . :* The details of the surrender scene have
been reported by various observers. Benét's account is close to that of Brigadier General Horace Porter in *Battles and Leaders,* IV, 729–746.

It is over, then. . . .
                    Lee walks from the little room.   15
His face is unchanged. It will not change when he dies.
But as he steps on the porch and looks toward his lines
He strikes his hands together once with a sound. . . . .

In the room he has left, the blue men stare at each other
For a space of heartbeats, silent. The grey ride off.   15
They are gone—it is over. . . .

The room explodes like a bomb, they are laughing and shouting,
Yelling strange words, dragging chairs and tables outdoors,
Bearded generals waltzing with one another
For a brief, wild moment, punching each others' ribs,   1
Everyone talking at once and nobody listening,
"It's over—it's done—it's finished!"
                       Then, order again.
The grey ghost-army falls in for the last time,
Marching to stack its arms.
                 As the ranks move forward
The blue guns go to "Present." Gordon sees the gesture.   1
He sweeps his sabre down in the full salute.
There are no cheers or words from blue lines or grey.°
Only the sound of feet. . . .
It is over, now. . . .
               The arms are stacked from the war.
A few bronzed, tattered grey men, weeping or silent,   1
Tear some riddled bits of cloth from the color-staffs
And try to hide them under their uniforms.

Jake Diefer, ploughing, a day of the early Spring.
Smelt April steam from the ground as he turned it up
And wondered how the new forty would do this year.

The stump of his left arm ached in the living wind.
It was not a new pain.
               When he got back to the house
The woman would ease it some with her liniments

1540–1542 *Gordon . . . sweeps his sabre down . . .* : Compare Gordon's account, *Reminiscences of the Civil War*, pp. 444–445.

But there wasn't much you could do.
The boy had been smart.
The boy had fixed the jigger so he could plough.   1555
It wasn't an arm you could show to company
With a regular-looking hand, but it did the work.
The woman still hankered after the varnished one
They'd seen that day in the Philadelphia store
—Well, he'd tried it on, and it was a handsome arm,   1560
And, if the new forty did well—
Meanwhile, the huge
Muscles of his right shoulder bulged with the strain
As the plough sheared on.
Sometimes, the blade of the plough
Still turned up such odd harvest as bullets leave,
A spoilt canteen, the brass of a cartridge-pouch,   1565
An eyeless skull, too white for the grin it wore.
But these were rarer now.
They had cleaned the well.
They could drink from the well again.
The earth was in plough.

He turned his team and started the backward furrow.
He was clumsy still, in some matters, but he could manage.   1570
This year he'd see his own wheat.
He thought to himself:
"You ain't the feller you was but the ground looks good.
It smells like good plantin' weather. We cleaned the well.
Maybe some time we'll get you that varnished arm,
For Sundays, maybe. It'd look good on Sundays."   1575
He gazed ahead.
By the end of the farther fence
A ragamuffin-something leaned on the rail,
Regarding him and his team.
"Tramp feller," he thought,
"Colored man, too—well, he can't hang around this farm,
Him or no other tramps. I wish I could get   1580
An honest to God cheap hired man."
The team drew near.
The negro did not move.
Jake halted the team.

They stared at each other. One saw a crippled ox,
The other a scar-faced spectre with haunted eyes

Still dressed in the rags of a shoddy uniform.
"Well, feller?" said Jake.
                    The negro said " 'Scuse me, Sarjun."
He scratched his head with the wreck of a forage-cap.
His eyes remembered a darkness.
                         "Huh!" said Jake,
Sharply, "Where did you get it?"
                    The negro shrank.
"I was in de Crater,° boss," he said with a dull
Stain in his voice. "You mebbe heard about us.
You mebbe heard of de Crater at Petersburg.
I doan' like thinkin' about it. You need a fiel'-han'?"

Jake thought for a moment. "Crater," he said at last.
"Yuh, I heard about that Crater."
                    The wind blew on
Hurting his arm. "I wasn't to there," he said.
"I knew some boys that was there."
                    The negro said,
"I'd work for my keep, boss, honest. I knows a team.
I knows how to work. I got hurt bad in de Crater
But I knows how to work a farm."
                    He coughed and was dumb.
Jake looked at him as he might have looked at a horse,
Measuringly.
          "I ain't runnin' a hospital,"
He said, in an aggrieved voice. "You was to the Crater.
I seen the way you colored folks farm down South.
It ain't no way to farm. You ought to be et.
We'll eat you up to the house when it's mealin'-time.
I don't know where we'll sleep you. How do I know
You can work your keep?"
                    The negro said nothing at all.
His eyes had resumed their darkness.
                    "Huddup!" said Jake,

1590 *Crater*: At Petersburg, on July 30, 1864, the Union army detonated an underground demolition that blasted an enormous hole (30-feet deep, 60-feet wide, and
170-feet long) in the Southern fortifications; in the Union follow-up attack, quick-
reacting Confederate forces slaughtered Union troops caught in the crater, including
portions of the Negro Fourth Division. See *Battles and Leaders*, IV, 545–567.

As the team swung round.
                    "Dat's ploughin'!" the negro said.   1610

Jake spat. "The woman'll fix you a snack to eat
If you holler the house."
                    The negro shook his head.
"I'll wait till you's done furrowin', boss," he said.
"Mebbe I kin help you unhitch when it's time for dat."

"Well," said Jake, "I ain't payin' a hired man much."   1615

"Dey call me Spade," said the negro.
                    The plough went on.
The negro watched it, cutting the furrow clean.

———————

Jack Ellyat, an old cudgel in his fist,
Walked from the town, one day of melting ice,
Past fields still patched with old snow but warm in the sun,   1620
His heart and mind being something like those fields. . . .
Behind him, in the town, the spangled flags
Still fluttered or hung limp for fallen Richmond,
And here or there, in corners, you could see
The burst firecracker-cases, rotten with rain, ·   1625
The guttered stumps of torches flung away
And other odds and ends of celebration
Not yet swept up.
                    The old cannon in the Square
Still had a blackened mouth from its salutes,
The little boys would not be good all week   1630
And everything wore airs of Monday morning. . . .

Jack Ellyat, remembering it all,
Was glad enough when he got past the houses
And could see nothing but the road ahead
Going up hills and down.
                    "It's over now.   1635
Finished for good. Well, I was part of it.
Well, it is over."
                    When he reached the crest
Of the Long Hill, he paused and felt the wind
Blow on his face, and leaned upon his stick,

Gazing at troubled Spring.
                  He carried still   16
Wounds of a sort, some healed into the scars
And some that hardly would be healed awhile,
Being in stuff few surgeries can reach,
But he was well enough, although the wind
Felt colder than it had in other Springs.   16

"Oh, yes," he thought, "I guess that I'm all right.
I guess I'm lucky. I remember once
Coming along this road with poor old Ned
Before they fired on Sumter.° Well, it's over.
I was a part of it."
                He flipped a stone   1
Down toward the hill and watched it strike and strike
And then lie quiet, while his mind recalled
The long, white, bloodless months of getting well
And the strange feel of first civilian clothes.
Well, that was over, too, and he was back,   1
And everybody knew he'd settled down,
Only he couldn't stand it any more.

He had a picture of Melora's face,
Dim with long looking-at, a carried image,
He tried to see it now, but it was faint.
He'd tried to find her but he couldn't find her.
Couldn't get any news while he was sick,
And then, at last, the news that they were gone—
That and no more—and nobody knew where.

He saw the clock upon the mantelpiece   1
Back in the house, ticking its fettered time
To fettered Phaëton.
                "I'll settle down.
I will forget. I'll wear my riddled coat
Fourth of Julys and have boys gape at me.
I'll drink and eat and sleep, marry a girl;   1
Be a good lawyer, wear the hunger out.
I hardly knew her. It was years ago.
Why should the hunger stay? A dozen men

1647–1649 *I remember once* . . . : See Book I, lines 1–5.

Might find a dozen girls and lose them so
And never once think of it, but perhaps 1675
As a dim fragrance, lost with their first youth,
A seashell in a box of cedarwood,
A silver mist that vanished with the day.

It was such years ago. She must have changed.
I know that I have changed.
      We find such things 1680
And lose them, and must live in spite of it.
Only a fool goes looking for the wind
That blew across his heartstrings yesterday,
Or breaks his hands in the obscure attempt
To dig the knotted roots of Time apart, 1685
Hoping to resurrect the golden mask
Of the lost year inviolate from the ground.
Only a fool drives horses in the sky."

And here he was, out walking on this road
For no more reason than a crazy yarn 1690
Just heard, about some gipsy travellers
Going through towns and looking for a soldier.
And even and supposing it were she . . .

He saw Melora walking down from the wood
With the sun behind her, low in the western cloud. 1695
He saw the long shadow that her slight body made.

The fetters fell like straws from the clock of time.
The horses moved from the gate.
      This life, this burning,
This fictive war that is over, this toy death,
These were the pictures of Phaëton.
      This is Phaëton.° 1700
He cast a final look down at the town,
Another at the fields still patched with snow.
The wind blew on his face. He moved away
Out toward the crossroads, where the wagons pass,
And when he got there, waited patiently 1705
Under a windbreak of three twisted elms
Half-hidden from the road.

1697–1700 *the clock of time . . . This is Phaëton:* See Book I, lines 1058–1065.

"Find her," he said.
"I guess we'll go back West then. Well, that's that."
The wind burned at his flesh. He let it burn,
Staring at a lost year.
          So he perceived   17
A slow cart creaking up a slope of hill,
Drawn by a horse as gaunt as poverty
And driven by a woman with great eyes.

Edmund Ruffin, old Secessionist,
Firer of the first gun that rang against Sumter,   17
Walks in his garden now, in the evening-cool,
With a red, barred flag slung stiffly over one arm
And a silver-butted pistol in his right hand.
He has just heard of Lee's surrender and Richmond's fall
And his face is marble over his high black stock.   17
For a moment he walks there, smelling the scents of Spring,
A gentleman taking his ease, while the sun sinks down.
Now it is well-nigh sunken. He smiles with the close,
Dry smile of age. It is time. He unfolds the flag,
Cloaks it around his shoulders with neat, swift hands,   17
Cocks the pistol and points it straight at his heart.
The hammer falls, the dead man slumps to the ground.
The blood spurts out in the last light of the sun
Staining the red of the flag with more transient red.°

The gaunt man, Abraham Lincoln, woke one morning   17
From a new dream that yet was an old dream
For he had known it many times before
And, usually, its coming prophesied
Important news of some sort, good or bad,
Though mostly good as he remembered it.   1

He had been standing on the shadowy deck
Of a black formless boat that moved away
From a dim bank, into wide, gushing waters—

1714–1729 *Edmund Ruffin, old Secessionist* . . . : After making a final declaration of "unmitigated hatred to Yankee rule," Ruffin killed himself, April 12, in Amelia County, Virginia. In less romantic accounts, he used a shotgun and there is no mention of the Confederate flag.

River or sea, but huge—and as he stood,
The boat rushed into darkness like an arrow,   1740
Gathering speed—and as it rushed, he woke.°

He found it odd enough to tell about
That day to various people, half in jest
And half in earnest—well, it passed the time
And nearly everyone had some pet quirk,   1745
Knocking on wood or never spilling salt,
Ladders or broken mirrors or a Friday,
And so he thought he might be left his boat,
Especially now, when he could breathe awhile
With Lee surrendered and the war stamped out   1750
And the long work of binding up the wounds
Not yet begun—although he had his plans
For that long healing, and would work them out
In spite of all the bitter-hearted fools
Who only thought of punishing the South   1755
Now she was beaten.
                    But this boat of his.
He thought he had it.
                    "Johnston has surrendered.
It must be that, I guess—for that's about
The only news we're waiting still to hear." °
He smiled a little, spoke of other things.   1760
That afternoon he drove beside his wife
And talked with her about the days to come
With curious simplicity and peace.
Well, they were getting on, and when the end
Came to his term, he would not be distressed.   1765
They would go back to Springfield, find a house,
Live peaceably and simply, see old friends,
Take a few cases every now and then.
Old Billy Herndon's kept the practice up,°
I guess he'll sort of like to have me back.   1770
We won't be skimped, we'll have enough to spend,

1731–1741 *an old dream . . . prophesied . . .* : On the day he was assassinated,
Lincoln told Grant, "I had a dream last night; and ever since this war began I have
had the same dream just before every event of great national importance," quoted by
Ward Hill Lamon, *Recollections of Abraham Lincoln, 1847–1865,* pp. 115–116.
1769 *Billy Herndon's kept the practice up:* Herndon had been Lincoln's law partner
in Springfield; see Book V, lines 143–145. 1757–1759 *Johnston has surrendered . . .* : See note, line 872, above.

Enough to do—we'll have a quiet time,
A sort of Indian summer of our age.

He looked beyond the carriage, seeing it so,
Peace at the last, and rest.

They drove back to the White House, dressed and ate,
Went to the theatre in their flag-draped box.
The play was a good play,° he liked the play,
Laughed at the jokes, laughed at the funny man
With the long, weeping whiskers.
                                    The time passed.
The shot rang out. The crazy murderer
Leaped from the box, mouthed out his Latin phrase,°
Brandished his foolish pistol and was gone.

Lincoln lay stricken in the flag-draped box.
Living but speechless. Now they lifted him
And bore him off. He lay some hours so.
Then the heart failed. The breath beat in the throat.
The black, formless vessel carried him away.

Sally, waiting at Appleton
On an autumn day of clear, bright sun,
Felt her heart and body begin to burn
As she hummed the lesson she had to learn.
"Yellow cornmeal and a jackass colt
And a door that swings on a broken bolt.
Comfort the old and pity the wise
And see your lover with open eyes.
Mend the broken and patch the frayed
And carry the sorrow undismayed
When your lover limps° in the falling rain,
Never quite to be whole again.
Clear the nettle and plant the corn
And keep your body a hunting-horn.
Succor your love at fire and frost
When your lover remembers the blood he lost,

1778 *a good play: Our American Cousin* (1858), a comedy of Yankee life, by English dramatist Tom Taylor.   1782 *Latin phrase:* "Sic semper tyrannis," the Virginia state motto.   1799 *your lover limps:* See line 426, above.

And break your hands on the hard-moved wheel   1805
Till they are tougher than hands of steel,
Till the new grass grows on the barren plain
And the house is built from the dust again,
With thrift and love for the house and the chief,
A scone on the hob for the son of grief,   1810
A knife in the ribs for the pleasant thief,°
While the night and the river have memories . . ."
She stared at the future with equal eyes.
And yet, in her glance, there was something still
Not to be ground by Wingate will   1815
Or under the honor of Elspeth's name,
A dancing flicker that went and came
But did not falter for joy or grief
Or the years gone by with the blowing leaf.
—French Dupré with his alien grace   1820
Always turning the buried ace.
French Dupré in his dancer's pride,
Leading a reel with his stolen bride—

She smiled a little and turned to see
A weed-grown path and a scarlet tree   1825
And Wingate coming there, painfully.

———————

John Brown's body lies a-mouldering in the grave.
Spread over it the bloodstained flag of his song,
For the sun to bleach, the wind and the birds to tear,
The snow to cover over with a pure fleece   1830
And the New England cloud to work upon
With the grey absolution of its slow, most lilac-smelling rain,
Until there is nothing there
That ever knew a master or a slave
Or, brooding on the symbol of a wrong,   1835
Threw down the irons in the field of peace.
John Brown is dead, he will not come again,
A stray ghost-walker with a ghostly gun.
Let the strong metal rust
In the enclosing dust   1840
And the consuming coal
That was the furious soul

1809–1811 *thrift and love* . . . : Compare Book I, lines 252–254.

And still like iron groans,
Anointed with the earth,
Grow colder than the stones
While the white roots of grass and little weeds
Suck the last hollow wildfire from the singing bones.

Bury the South together with this man,
Bury the bygone South.
Bury the minstrel with the honey-mouth,
Bury the broadsword virtues of the clan,
Bury the unmachined, the planters' pride,
The courtesy and the bitter arrogance,
The pistol-hearted horsemen who could ride
Like jolly centaurs under the hot stars.
Bury the whip, bury the branding-bars,
Bury the unjust thing
That some tamed into mercy, being wise,
But could not starve the tiger from its eyes
Or make it feed where beasts of mercy feed.
Bury the fiddle-music and the dance,
The sick magnolias of the false romance
And all the chivalry that went to seed
Before its ripening.

And with these things, bury the purple dream
Of the America we have not been,
The tropic empire, seeking the warm sea,
The last foray of aristocracy
Based not on dollars or initiative
Or any blood for what that blood was worth
But on a certain code, a manner of birth,
A certain manner of knowing how to live,
The pastoral rebellion of the earth
Against machines, against the Age of Steam,
The Hamiltonian extremes against the Franklin mean,
The genius of the land
Against the metal hand,
The great, slave-driven bark,
Full-oared upon the dark,
With gilded figurehead,
With fetters for the crew
And spices for the few,

The passion that is dead,
The pomp we never knew,
Bury this, too.   1885

Bury this destiny unmanifest,
This system broken underneath the test,
Beside John Brown and though he knows his enemy is there
He is too full of sleep at last to care.

He was a stone, this man who lies so still,   1890
A stone flung from a sling against a wall,
A sacrificial instrument of kill,
A cold prayer hardened to a musket-ball:
And yet, he knew the uses of a hill,
And he must have his justice, after all.   1895

He was a lover of certain pastoral things,
He had the shepherd's gift.
When he walked at peace, when he drank from the watersprings,
His eyes would lift

To see God, robed in a glory, but sometimes, too,   1900
Merely the sky,
Untroubled by wrath or angels, vacant and blue,
Vacant and high.

He knew not only doom but the shape of the land,
Reaping and sowing.   1905
He could take a lump of any earth in his hand
And feel the growing.

He was a farmer, he didn't think much of towns,
The wheels, the vastness.
He liked the wide fields, the yellows, the lonely browns,   1910
The black ewe's fastness.

Out of his body grows revolving steel,
Out of his body grows the spinning wheel
Made up of wheels, the new, mechanic birth,   1915
No longer bound by toil
To the unsparing soil
Or the old furrow-line,

The great, metallic beast
Expanding West and East,
His heart a spinning coil,
His juices burning oil,
His body serpentine.
Out of John Brown's strong sinews the tall skyscrapers grow,
Out of his heart the chanting buildings rise,
Rivet and girder, motor and dynamo,
Pillar of smoke by day and fire by night,°
The steel-faced cities reaching at the skies,
The whole enormous and rotating cage
Hung with hard jewels of electric light,
Smoky with sorrow, black with splendor, dyed
Whiter than damask for a crystal bride
With metal suns, the engine-handed Age,
The genie we have raised to rule the earth,
Obsequious to our will
But servant-master still,
The tireless serf already half a god—

Touch the familiar sod
Once, then gaze at the air
And see the portent there,
With eyes for once washed clear
Of worship and of fear:
There is its hunger, there its living thirst,
There is the beating of the tremendous heart
You cannot read for omens.
                              Stand apart
From the loud crowd and look upon the flame
Alone and steadfast, without praise or blame.
This is the monster and the sleeping queen
And both have roots struck deep in your own mind,
This is reality that you have seen,
This is reality that made you blind.

So, when the crowd gives tongue
And prophets, old or young,

1926 *Pillar of smoke . . . and fire . . .* : Compare Exodus 13–21. In the wilderness, the Lord went before Moses and the Israelites "by day in a pillar of cloud . . . and by night in a pillar of fire."

Bawl out their strange despair
Or fall in worship there,
Let them applaud the image or condemn   1955
But keep your distance and your soul from them.
And, if the heart within your breast must burst
Like a cracked crucible and pour its steel
White-hot before the white heat of the wheel,
Strive to recast once more   1960
That attar° of the ore
In the strong mold of pain
Till it is whole again,
And while the prophets shudder or adore
Before the flame, hoping it will give ear,   1965
If you at last must have a word to say,
Say neither, in their way,
"It is a deadly magic and accursed,"
Nor "It is blest," but only "It is here."

1961 *attar*: essence.

BIOGRAPHICAL AND BIBLIOGRAPHICAL REFERENCES

STEPHEN VINCENT BENÉT
Chronology

1898 — Born July 22, Bethlehem, Pennsylvania, third child of Frances Neill Rose Benét and James Walker Benét, Captain of Ordnance, United States Army. All three Benét children, William Rose, Laura, and Stephen are eventually to establish themselves as poets.

1899–1905 — Moves with the family to Watervliet (New York) Arsenal (1899), to Rock Island (Illinois) Arsenal (1904), and to Benicia (California) Arsenal (1905).

1910–1911 — Attends Hitchcock Military Academy, San Rafael, California.

1911 — Moves to Augusta Arsenal; enters Summerville Academy, Augusta, Georgia.

1915 — Publishes *Five Men and Pompey*, his first book of verse; in September, enters Yale.

1918 — Elected Chairman of *Yale Literary Magazine*; passes Army enlistment physical by memorizing the eye chart, but is discharged after three days' service; employed by State Department in Washington, August through December.

1919 — Graduates from Yale and is admitted to graduate study.

1920 — Receives Master of Arts Degree; attends the Sorbonne on traveling fellowship from Yale.

1921 — Publishes first novel, *The Beginning of Wisdom*; marries Rosemary Carr, November 26.

1922 — Publishes second novel, *Young People's Pride*.

1923 — Publishes "The Ballad of William Sycamore."

1924 — Daughter, Stephanie Jane, is born April 6.

1926 — Publishes *Spanish Bayonet*; receives a Guggenheim Fellowship and returns to France to begin work on a long narrative poem (*John Brown's Body*); son, Thomas Carr, is born in Paris, September 28.

1928 — Publishes *John Brown's Body*.

1929 — Wins Pulitzer Prize for Poetry; is elected to the National Academy of Arts and Letters.

1931 — Daughter, Rachel Carr, is born October 22.

1932 — Wins O. Henry Award (best short story of the year) for "An End of Dreams."

1933 — Receives the Shelley Memorial Award for poetry and a Theodore Roosevelt Medal for literary accomplishment;

in collaboration with his wife, publishes *A Book of Americans;* is named editor of the Yale Series of Younger Poets.

1937 — Wins second O. Henry Award, for "The Devil and Daniel Webster"; is awarded an honorary degree by Yale.

1940 — Wins third O. Henry Award, for "Freedom's a Hard-Bought Thing."

1943 — Dies March 13, having weakened his health writing for the American war effort; is posthumously awarded the Gold Medal for Literature by the National Institute of Arts and Letters.

1944 — *Western Star,* an unfinished epic poem of the western migration, published in July 1943, wins the Pulitzer Prize for Poetry.

JOHN BROWN'S BODY

First edition. Garden City: Doubleday, Doran and Company [1928].

Limited deluxe edition of 201 copies, signed by the author. Garden City: Doubleday, Doran and Company, 1928.

Second edition. Garden City: Doubleday, Doran and Company, 1929. Also, New York: Farrar & Rinehart, 1929.

Educational edition. With an introduction by Henry Seidel Canby. New York: Doubleday, Doran and Company, 1929. Reissued, New York: Farrar & Rinehart, 1937; Rinehart & Company, 1955.

With drawings by James Daugherty. Garden City: Doubleday, Doran and Company, 1930.

School edition. Edited and annotated by Mabel A. Bessey, with an introductory essay by Bert James Loewenberg. New York: Farrar & Rinehart [1941].

With an introduction by Leonard Bacon. London: Oxford University Press, 1944.

New York: Editions for the Armed Services, Inc. [1946].

With an introduction by Douglas Southall Freeman; illustrations by John Steuart Curry. New York: Limited Editions Club, 1948. Reissued, New York: The Heritage Press [1948].

With illustrations by Fritz Kredel and Warren Chappell. New York: Rinehart & Company [1954].

As staged at the Yale Drama School and Off-Broadway, under the direction of Curtis Canfield; music by Fenno Heath. [New York]: Dramatists' Play Service [1961].

WORKS CITED IN NOTES

The following works, cited in the footnotes, were available to Benét at the time of authorship (1927–1928) and suggest themselves as direct sources. Those which he credited by title in his prefatory "Note," p. xiii, are marked here and in first-entry notes with an asterisk (*).

Andrews, Eliza Frances. *The War-Time Journal of a Georgia Girl, 1864–1865*. New York: D. Appleton and Company, 1908.

*Battles and Leaders of the Civil War. 4 vols. New York: The Century Company, 1884–1887.

*Carter, Captain Robert Goldthwaite. *Four Brothers in Blue*. Washington: Press of Gibson Bros., Inc., 1913.

*Channing, Edward. *A History of the United States*, Vol. VI: *The War for Southern Independence*. New York: The Macmillan Company, 1926.

*Charnwood, Lord Godfrey Rathbone. *Abraham Lincoln*. New York: Henry Holt and Company, 1916.

Church, William Conant. *Ulysses S. Grant and the Period of National Preservation and Reconstruction*. New York: G. P. Putnam's Sons, 1897.

Davis, Jefferson. *The Rise and Fall of the Confederate Government*. 2 vols. New York: D. Appleton and Company, 1881.

Doubleday, Abner. *Chancellorsville and Gettysburg*. New York: Charles Scribner's Sons, 1882.

Gordon, John B. *Reminiscences of the Civil War*. New York: Charles Scribner's Sons, 1903.

Jackson, Mary Anna. *Memoirs of Stonewall Jackson*. Louisville: The Prentice Press, 1895.

Lamon, Ward Hill. *Recollections of Abraham Lincoln, 1847–1865*. Washington: Dorothy Lamon Taillard, 1911.

Lee, Captain Robert E. *Recollections and Letters of General Robert E. Lee*. New York: Doubleday, Page and Company, 1909.

Lee, Fitzhugh. *General Lee*. New York: D. Appleton and Company, 1897.

Letters of Ulysses S. Grant to his Father and his Youngest Sister, 1857–78. Edited by Jesse Grant Cramer. New York: G. P. Putnam's Sons, 1912.

*McMaster, John Bach. *A History of the People of the United States During Lincoln's Administration*. New York: D. Appleton-Century Company, 1927. Reprinted as *Our House Divided*. Greenwich, Conn.: Fawcett Publications, Inc., 1961.

*Nicolay, John G., and John Hay, eds. *Abraham Lincoln, Complete Works*. 2 vols. New York: The Century Company, 1907.

*Nicolay, John G., and John Hay. *Abraham Lincoln, A History*. 10 vols. New York: The Century Company, 1890.

Official Records. The War of the Rebellion: A Compilation of the Official Records of the Union and Confederate Armies. 70 vols. Washington: The Government Printing Office, 1901.

[Pickett, LaSalle Corbell, ed.] *The Heart of a Soldier: As Revealed in the Intimate Letters of Gen'l. George E. Pickett, CSA*. New York: Seth Moyle, Inc., 1913.

Porter, Horace. *Campaigning with Grant*. New York: The Century Company, 1906.

Pryor, Mrs. Roger A. *Reminiscences of Peace and War*. New York: The Macmillan Company, 1904.

*Sandburg, Carl. *Abraham Lincoln, The Prairie Years*. 2 vols. New York: Harcourt, Brace and Company, 1926.

Sherman, William T. *Memoirs of General William T. Sherman*. 2 vols. New York: D. Appleton and Company, 1904.

*Stephenson, Nathaniel W. *Lincoln*. Indianapolis: The Bobbs-Merrill Company, 1922.

*Tarbell, Ida M. *The Life of Abraham Lincoln*. 2 vols. New York: The Macmillan Company, 1917.

Taylor, Richard. *Destruction and Reconstruction: Personal Experiences of the Late War*. New York: Longmans, Green and Company, Inc., 1879. Edited by Richard B. Harwell and reprinted, 1955.

*Villard, Oswald Garrison. *John Brown (1800–1859): A Biography Fifty Years After*. Boston: Houghton Mifflin Company, 1910.

Young, Jesse Bowman. *The Battle of Gettysburg*. New York: Harper & Brothers, 1913.

Young, John Russell. *Around the World with General Grant*. 2 vols. New York: The American News Company, 1879.

RELATED BIOGRAPHICAL
AND CRITICAL WORKS

Allen, Hervey. "John Brown's Body," *Yale Review*, XVII (Winter, 1929), 391.

Arvin, Newton. [Review of *John Brown's Body*], "Books," *New York Herald Tribune*, August 12, 1928, p. 1.

Bacon, Leonard. "Stephen Vincent Benét," *Saturday Review of Literature*, X (April 7, 1934), 609.

Becker, Carl. "Benét's Sympathetic Understanding," *Mark Twain Quarterly*, VI (Winter–Spring, 1943–1944), 13.

Benét, William Rose. "My Brother Steve," *Saturday Review of Literature*, XXIV (November 15, 1941), 3 ff.

————. "Round About Parnassus," *Saturday Review of Literature*, VII (December 27, 1930), 491.

Benét, Stephen V. "Epic on an American Theme," *New Colophon*, II (January, 1949), 1–12.

Boyd, James. [Review of *John Brown's Body*], *Outlook*, CXL (September 5, 1928), 752.

Brenner, Rica. *Poets of Our Time*. New York: Harcourt, Brace and Company, 1941.

Butcher, Fannie. [Review of *John Brown's Body*], *Chicago Daily Tribune*, August 11, 1928, p. 11.

Canby, Henry Seidel. "Stephen Vincent Benét," *Saturday Review of Literature*, XXVI (March 27, 1943), 14.

Chubb, T. C. "Recollections of Steve Benét," *Mark Twain Quarterly*, VI (Winter–Spring, 1943–1944), 10–12.

Clemens, Cyril. "A Chat with Stephen Benét," *Mark Twain Quarterly*, VI (Winter–Spring, 1943–1944), 7–9.

Commager, Henry Steele. "America's Heroic Tragedy," *Scholastic Magazine*, XLIII (September 20, 1943), 22–23.

Cousins, Norman. *Present Tense: An American Editor's Odyssey*. New York: McGraw-Hill, Inc., 1967.

Daniels, Sidney R. "A Saga of the American Civil War," *Contemporary Review*, CXLVI (October, 1934), 466–471.

Fadiman, Clifton P. [Review of *John Brown's Body*], *New York Evening Post*, August 11, 1928, p. 5.

Fenton, Charles A. *Stephen Vincent Benét: The Life and Times of an American Man of Letters, 1898–1943*. New Haven: Yale University Press, 1958.

Flanagan, John T. "Folk Elements in *John Brown's Body*," *New York Folklore Quarterly*, XX (December, 1964), 243–256.

Gregory, Horace, and Mary Zaturenska. "The National Spirit of Stephen Vincent and William Rose Benét . . . ," *A History of American Poetry*, pp. 431–447. New York: Harcourt, Brace and Company, 1946.

Jackson, Frederick H. "Stephen Vincent Benét and American History," *The Historian*, XVIII (Autumn, 1954), 67–75.

Johnson, Merle. "American First Editions, Stephen Vincent Benét," *Publishers' Weekly*, CXXI (January 16, 1932), 290–291.

La Farge, Christopher. "The Narrative Poetry of Stephen Vincent Benét," *Saturday Review of Literature*, XXVII (August 5, 1944), 106–108.

Lovett, R. M. "The American Conflict," *New Republic*, LVI (August 29, 1928), 51–52.

MacLeish, Archibald, Christopher Morley, *et al.* "As We Remember Him," *Saturday Review of Literature*, XXVI (March 27, 1943), 7–11.

Maddocks, Gladys L. "Stephen V. Benét: A Bibliography," *Bulletin of Bibliography and Dramatic Index*, XX (1951), 142–146.

Melcher, F. G. "Poet and Gallant Fighter," *Publishers' Weekly*, CXLIII (March 20, 1943), 1257.

Moffett, Judith. "Some Corrections of [Parry Stroud's] *Stephen Vincent Benét*," *Notes and Queries*, XIII (November, 1966), 420–421.

Monroe, Harriet. "A Cinema Epic," *Poetry*, XXXIII (November, 1928), 91–96.

Nathan, Robert. "Stephen Vincent Benét and His America," *Mark Twain Quarterly*, VI (Winter–Spring, 1943–1944), 4–5.

O'Neill, Eugene, Jr. "S. V. Benét: 'John Brown's Body'," *Saturday Review of Literature*, XXXII (August 6, 1949), 34.

Richardson, Mary Lynn. "The Historical Authenticity of John Brown's Raid in Stephen Vincent Benét's *John Brown's Body*," *West Virginia History*, XXIV, 168–175.

Sickles, Eleanor M. "Stephen Vincent Benét," *College English*, XIV (May, 1953), 440–446.

Stroud, Parry Edmund. *Stephen Vincent Benét*. New York: Twayne Publishers, 1962.

Times Literary Supplement [Review of *John Brown's Body*], December 6, 1928, p. 960.

Wells, Henry W. "Stephen Vincent Benét," *College English*, V (October, 1943), 8–13.

Wiley, Paul L. "The Phaeton Symbol in *John Brown's Body*," *American Literature*, XVII (November, 1945), 231–242.

Winwar, Frances. "Two Poets, Stephen Vincent and William Rose Benét," *College English*, II (February, 1941), 415–427.

Zabel, Morton D. "The American Grain," *Poetry*, XLVIII (August, 1936), 276–282.

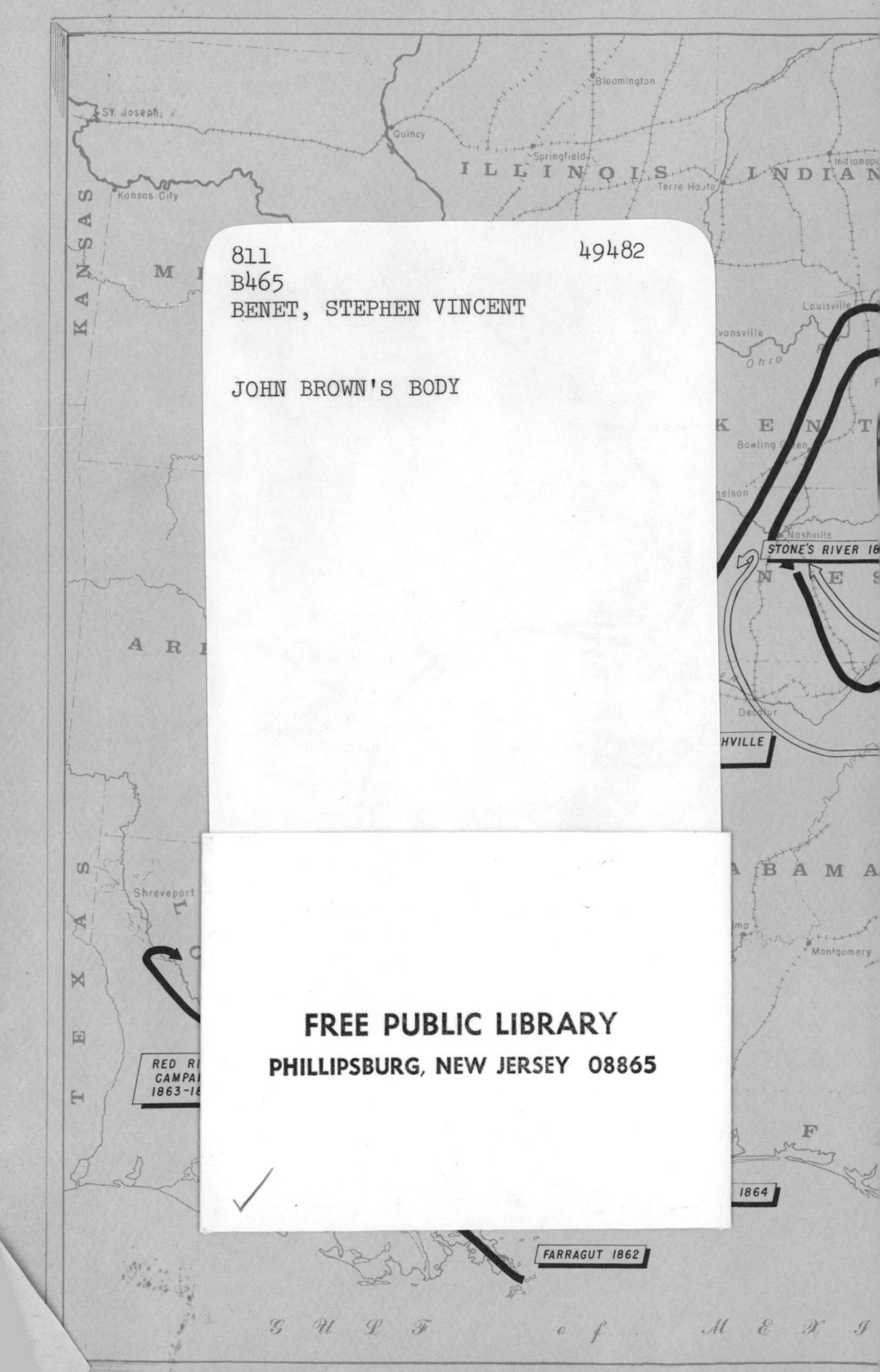